·

·· POSEIDON PRESS ··

New York

London

Toronto

Sydney

Tokyo

Singapore

BATTLEGROUND

One Mother's Crusade,
the Religious Right,
and the Struggle for
Control of Our Classrooms

STEPHEN BATES

POSEIDON PRESS

Simon & Schuster Building
Rockefeller Center
1230 Avenue of the Americas
New York, New York 10020

POSEIDON PRESS is a registered trademark
of Simon & Schuster Inc.

POSEIDON PRESS colophon is a trademark
of Simon & Schuster Inc.

Designed by Liney Li
Manufactured in the United States of America

10   9   8   7   6   5   4   3   2   1

Library of Congress Cataloging-in-Publication Data
Bates, Stephen, 1958—
Battleground : one mother's crusade, the religious right, and the struggle for
control of our classrooms / Stephen Bates.
p.   cm.
Includes index.
1. Religion in the public schools—Law and legislation—Tennessee—
History.   2. Textbooks—Censorship—Tennessee—Hawkins County—
History.   3. Trials—Tennessee—Hawkins County.   4. Religion in the public
schools—Tennessee—Hawkins County—History.   I. Title.
KFT392.7.B38   1993
344.768′0796—dc20
[347.6804796]   93-23832
CIP
ISBN: 0-671-79358-6

To Polly and Charlotte

·· CONTENTS ··

·· INTRODUCTION ··

In fundamentalist Hawkins County, Tennessee, Vicki Frost and a handful of other parents detected "secular humanism" in the classroom. They charged that the county's new textbooks promoted witchcraft, rebellion, pacifism, and Hinduism; reading them might even invite demonic possession. Unable to sway the school board, the protesters filed suit in federal court. Then, with the entry of powerful interest groups, what had begun as a ragtag schoolbook protest in Southern Appalachia mushroomed into a national spectacle—a spectacle with effects that are still being felt.

The story unfolded across the nation's front pages in the summer of 1986. Sixty-one years after the *Scopes* "monkey trial," the media reported, East Tennessee fundamentalists were once again trying to ram their faith into the classroom. According to news accounts, the parents detected sacrilege in *Macbeth*, *The Diary of Anne Frank*, *The Wizard of Oz*, and even "Goldilocks."

"Scopes II," as journalists dubbed the case, transfigured the public's understanding of school censorship. In the words of the president of People for the American Way, the liberal organization that came in on the side of the Hawkins County schools, the trial "became the lens through which people saw these issues. People had a different view after this case."

Religious-right activists developed a different view too. During the trial, the conservative organization that funded the lawsuit, Concerned Women for America, struggled to attract and shape news coverage. Now the head of CWA says, referring to the press: "Leave us alone. Let us get the job done." Applying the lessons of "Scopes II" and other high-profile conflicts of the 1980s, the religious right has adopted a "stealth strategy" for the 1990s.

Though it touched the rest of the nation, the case saved its severest repercussions for Hawkins County. It divided families, distracted public officials, and distressed schoolteachers. And it caused Vicki Frost and her allies to be denounced by George Will, chided by George Bush, mocked by Lewis Grizzard, lauded by the Ku Klux Klan—and understood by almost nobody.

Then and now, the beliefs of fundamentalists are alien to most Americans, myself included. During interviews for this book, I found the Tennessee parents' offhanded God-talk faintly disquieting. (I'm a lapsed Episcopalian who, upon first reading it, thought the "Humanist Manifesto"—the credo of secular humanism—made a lot of sense.) Many of their Bible-based political beliefs and conspiracy theories strike me as, to put it charitably, unpersuasive. Their notion of the proper education holds no appeal; I hope my young daughter will develop an abiding skepticism and an uncurbed imagination, traits they consider ungodly.

Nevertheless, I believe that the Hawkins County fundamentalists raised profound and difficult questions—questions that were lost amid the "Scopes II" hoopla. How should a secular, tolerant state cope with devout but intolerant citizens, in both the public school and the public square? How much control should parents wield over their children's education? How should the public schools handle religious topics and religious students?

We have been grappling with these questions since the birth of public education. Our answers will tell us much about our politics, our society, and our times.

Relating this story entailed choices that merit brief explanation. In most instances I use the present tense for recollections stated after the fact. Not all these statements were made to me; some came from depositions and news coverage. In the chapters that recount trials, I present testimony topically rather than chronologically in a few instances, and I don't recount the testimony of every witness. I often identify people by the positions they held in the fall of 1983, when the controversy began, even though they have since moved on.

Much of my information comes from interviews conducted up to ten years after the fact. Recollections, not surprisingly, differ. I note significant disputes in the text; with minor disputes, I present the most plausible (generally the most contemporaneous) version.

To avoid *sic*-pocked pages, I have altered some quotations. In those from written material, I have corrected spelling and, where errors might impede understanding, punctuation and grammar. In quotations from interviews and court transcripts, I have omitted "you knows," false starts, and repetitions.

Finally, the term *fundamentalism* perturbs some people. Though it arose some eighty years ago to describe American Protestants, it now applies to other religions in other nations as well. Once it denoted peaceable, if eccentric, Christians; now, to many people, it connotes hostages and car bombs. Unfortunately, however, no fully equivalent alternative has yet arisen. *Evangelicals* includes religious conservatives who are politically liberal; *conservative Christians* and *new Christian right* include Catholics. So I use *fundamentalists*, intending no offense.

CHAPTER ONE

SECULAR HUMANISM IN HAWKINS COUNTY

A ugust is the haziest month in Hawkins County, Tennessee. Curling off the north fork of the Holston River, the evening fog gradually drains the landscape of precision and detail. Soon the trees on Bays Mountains look flat and gunmetal gray, like Hollywood false fronts dotting the hillside. The mist closes around the boulder by Highway 11-W where a born-again vandal has spray-painted "HOLY GHOST." Farther down the road, near the Church Hill city limits, a pitted, rickety billboard slouches against a tree. "WHAT ELSE CAN GOD DO TO SAVE YOU?" the sign says. "HE—" The rest is indecipherable beneath wild honeysuckle and decay.

In late August 1983, Rogersville, the Hawkins County seat, was readying for the fifth annual Heritage Days street fair, featuring crafts and square dancing. Pop singer Richard Carpenter would be coming to Church Hill in a few weeks to dedicate a Strolee baby-stroller factory to his late sister Karen, who, before her death from anorexia, had been a major Strolee stockholder. On the banks of the Holston at Laurel Run, workers were completing a rustic farmhouse for *The River*, a film that would bring Mel Gibson and Sissy Spacek to Hawkins County over the next few months. And, less than a mile from the film site, a shy eleven-year-old girl with long blond hair was struggling over her homework. Though no one would have suspected it at the time, it was

Rebecca Frost's bewilderment, more than Heritage Days or the Strolee factory or *The River,* that would jostle Hawkins County and hurtle it into the national consciousness.

Rebecca's sixth-grade reading teacher had assigned "A Visit to Mars," a story about astronauts who, while exploring the Martian landscape, bump into strangers. "They were Martians!" reports Steve, the narrator. As they exchange pleasantries, Steve realizes that the Martians have no mouths and make no sounds: "It was as if their questions were forming by themselves in my brain!" One astronaut asks the Martians who they are. The response sounds like one phrase to some astronauts and a different phrase to others. "Steve, it's magnificent!" exclaims Mac. "Who would ever have thought it! It's so simple, man—don't you understand? It's *thought transference!*"

Rebecca, for one, didn't understand. The third comprehension question after the story asked why "Mac and Steve interpreted the name of the Martian tribe as 'the Beautiful People,' but Jacky, Paul, and Mike interpreted it as 'the Lovely Ones.' " How could that be? Puzzled, Rebecca paged back and forth in the sixth-grade reading textbook. Finally she took the story to her mother.

Thirty-one-year-old Vicki Frost regularly helped her children with their homework. She was born Vicki Kay Leslie in nearby Johnson City, and raised in Kingsport, across the county line from Church Hill. She attended public schools and then enrolled at the local branch of East Tennessee State University, but left to work at Krispy Kreme Doughnuts, "picking the holes out of doughnuts—literally." Seven months later she quit her job and married Roger Frost, a Vietnam veteran and fellow ETSU dropout who worked at Mead Paper's Kingsport mill. The Frosts lived in Kingsport until 1978, and then moved to Church Hill. With Roger's $24,000 salary, Vicki never had to work outside the home after marriage. Instead she spent her days cooking, cleaning, sewing, canning, tending to the family's four horses, and rearing four children: Marty, Rebecca, Sarah, and Lesha.

"I was just a homebody homemaker," Frost says in her high-pitched Tennessee accent. A short, stout woman with shoulder-length auburn hair, large brown eyes, and a pretty face, she speaks rapidly and gestures flamboyantly ("I wouldn't be me without talking with my hands"). When trying to concentrate or remember, she sometimes closes her eyes, bows her head, and cups her hands at her temples.

Saved at age fourteen by a Billy Graham film, Frost believes that any adult who doesn't accept Jesus will go to hell, that God created the earth in six days, that a giant fish swallowed Jonah, and that the Bible is absolutely, literally, wholly true. Asked how much of her life is controlled by this faith, she replies unhesitatingly, "*All* my life."

Over the years, God has gradually enabled Frost to recognize things that are antithetical to his ways. As an example she cites her early flirtation with the occult. "When I was a teenager, we'd have slumber parties," she says, "and we would light a candle and pretend we were calling people back from the dead. Or someone might try to hypnotize someone. We'd laugh and joke and have fun. . . . When I was nineteen or twenty, I discerned that this was evil, and I repented of it."

Frost also repented of something more momentous, something that still gnaws at her and, she says, "influences everything I do." It happened in 1970, when she was eighteen years old and less than two months into marriage. She missed her period and, at the same time, developed a rash. She had contracted rubella, her doctor told her, "at the worst possible time."

Frost said she would simply place her trust in God, but, she recalls, the doctor worked to change her mind. Showing her photos of children born without limbs, he maintained that "it would be morally wrong to cause another human being to suffer a lifetime like that." He also said that "this is just about an inch and a half of tissue, not a baby."

So she had a therapeutic abortion. "I didn't even think about it," she says, starting to weep. "I was in the church, but I did not know truth from error. There were no indicators out there that it was wrong." Only much later, after the birth of her third child, she says, did she realize what she had done. "I was walking in deception. Deception destroys people—it destroyed the life of my child!"

Resolving never to drop her guard again, she worked tirelessly to insulate her family from everything contrary to Scripture. She told her children that Santa Claus and the Easter Bunny don't exist, because "Jesus should be the center of our attention." The children could listen to gospel and easy listening, but never rock. They could see movies only at the Christian Cinema in Kingsport. They could watch sports, *Little House on the Prairie,* and *The Price Is Right,* but not cartoons or sitcoms. Even *Sesame Street* was off-limits after Bert recklessly called Ernie a fool. "The Scriptures say that if you call a man a fool without cause," Frost explains, "you're in danger." By contradicting Scripture, such programs would confuse her children. "Confusion is never acceptable," she stresses. "You teach the child *truth*."

She also tended to her troubled husband. "I guess I was her biggest anxiety," says Roger, a thickset man with a brown beard. Since serving as a Marine Corps cook and rifleman in Vietnam, where he had been wounded, burned, and exposed to Agent Orange, he had suffered from nightmares, paranoia, and incapacitating bouts of depression. Several times he had moved out of the house for a few weeks, staying at their fifty-five-acre farm in Sneedville or with his parents in Church Hill until he could pull himself together. At Mead Paper, he had transferred from cutter operator to janitor, at a lower salary, " 'cause I couldn't cope."

To Vicki, Roger's troubles were partly spiritual. "At first I encouraged him to be a Mason," she says. "I thought it was a high honor, and even helped buy his ring. Later the Lord convicted my heart and showed me the error." She pored over a Kingsport library copy of Albert Pike's 1871 book *Morals and Dogma of the Ancient and Accepted Scottish Rite of Freemasonry,* and grew convinced that Masonry is contrary to Scripture, perhaps even satanic. "I told Roger that part of his psychological problems could be stemming from some kind of entanglement with the occult. . . . He got aggravated and said if it came between the Masonic Lodge or our marriage, it would be the Masonic Lodge that would rule. I said, Would you do one thing? Will you just be honest enough to ask God if it's not of him, that he would reveal that to you? He said he would." Roger ultimately capitulated and left the Masons.

During the months before Rebecca stumbled over her reading assignment, Vicki and her friend Jennie Wilson had been talking about the Masons, secular humanists, and other threats to Christian truth. A prim fifty-three-year-old grandmother who wore her graying hair in a tight bun, Wilson avidly studied the literature of the religious right. From Tim LaHaye's *The Battle for the Mind,* she learned that "we are being controlled by a small but very influential cadre of committed humanists, who are determined to turn traditionally moral-minded America into an amoral, humanist country." Constance Cumbey's *The Hidden Dangers of the Rainbow* revealed that the New Age movement, beneath its channeling and crystals, "meets all the scriptural requirements for the antichrist and the political movement that will bring him on the world scene." Wilson says she passed "juicy tidbits" from her reading on to Frost, "the same as I shared recipes with her for enchiladas."

During the summer of 1983, Wilson and Frost picked up more

tidbits from religious radio programs. Cumbey, the New Age un-
masker, gave an eight-part lecture about secular humanism, telepathy,
and one-world government. "She is the one that brought these things
to my heart and mind," says Frost. Both women were also riveted by
the radio preaching of Charles Stanley, pastor of Atlanta's First Baptist
Church and a Moral Majority board member. In Stanley's view, the
United States was headed "down the road to socialism—I mean *extreme*
socialism—unless God intervenes dramatically and supernaturally."

Intense as it was, the women's interest in these threats was at first
merely academic. Whatever evils might befall New York City and
Washington, D.C., Hawkins County was safe. "Isn't it wonderful to
live back in these mountains of Tennessee," Wilson remembers thinking, "so that all this stuff is just going to pass us by?"

But now, as Frost examined her daughter's reading book, she realized that the evils weren't passing harmlessly by. The story's ebullient
depiction of telepathy was deeply alarming, because, according to Constance Cumbey, the Antichrist will be telepathic. Based on what Frost
had learned from Wilson, Cumbey, and the broadcast preachers, this
new textbook, *Riders on the Earth*, seemed to be proselytizing ungodli-
ness.

After instructing Rebecca to stop working on the questions, Frost
hurriedly phoned Wilson. "It's here, Jennie," she reported. "Humanism in Hawkins County."

Vicki Frost and Jennie Wilson had met five years earlier at Mount
Pleasant Missionary Baptist Church. Although neither of them stayed
long with that church—every Sunday, according to Wilson, the
preacher tediously retold the tale of his own salvation experience—the
women became best friends, meeting or chatting by phone nearly every
day. "Should have kept an open line, I guess," says Roger Frost.
"They talked a lot."

In some respects, they were an incongruous pair. Frost was rearing
four young children; Wilson, more than twenty years older, had two
grown children, three grandchildren, and a retired husband. Frost had
spent her life in East Tennessee; Wilson, born and reared in Mississippi, had lived in Washington State, Texas, Georgia, and Germany
while her husband was a military policeman and radar repairman in
the Army. Frost had held only the Krispy Kreme job; Wilson says she
had "a top-secret cryptographic clearance" as a civilian employee of

the Army. Frost had spent less than a semester in college; Wilson had credits (though no degree) from the Universities of Heidelberg, Maryland, and Texas, and she had audited classes at nearby Graham Bible College. Frost had little time to read anything but the Bible; Wilson read voraciously, especially "good conservative material."

The differences persist today as the two women look back on the textbook controversy. Frost deferentially refers to those who opposed her as "Mr. Snodgrass" and "Mrs. Price," though they refer to her as "Vicki." She often told those adversaries that she loved them, and, she remembers dolefully, one man responded that he didn't want her love; he only wanted to be left alone. She speaks at length of how her adversaries mistreated her, but she almost never criticizes them personally. When Roger chortles that someone is "the town drunk," she reproaches him. "But he *is!*" says Roger. "Well," says Vicki, "don't *say* it."

Wilson has no such compunctions. Though she smiles and laughs sunnily as she talks, her remarks can be scathing. She catalogues the misfortunes—illnesses, marital troubles, and business failures—that have afflicted some of her opponents, and then declares that a particular adversary, who died a few months earlier, is burning in hell.

Both women believe in supernatural anti-Christian conspiracies, but Frost is reluctant to elaborate. "Satan's kingdom is the enemy that comes against us, but as far as putting people's names with that, I just couldn't," she says. "I can't judge the hearts of men. . . . God is the judge."

Wilson, in contrast, readily fingers the conspirators, including the Masons, Illuminati, Rockefellers, Rothschilds, Bilderbergers, Trilateral Commission, and Council on Foreign Relations. The textbook controversy went to trial, she asserts, because the National Education Association "demanded" it. The organizations that opposed the protesters are led by "New Agers" who are "helping bring about the one-world government." Former Tennessee Governor (and U.S. Education Secretary) Lamar Alexander picked up his education reform program in Moscow. "He didn't bother to change the positions of them—each of the points were the very same points that are in the Russian schools." Soon the government will take children at infancy, she predicts with an air of resignation, and "from the cradle to the grave they will be the slaves of the state."

"Jennie is a very bold witness in the faithfulness of God," says Frost. "She has helped form a lot of my opinions and beliefs. Truly, she has influenced me in the things of the Lord more than any person in this life."

Indeed, some observers view Wilson as the messianic mastermind behind the textbook protest and Frost as her mouthpiece. On the witness stand in federal court in 1986, Frost had to ask for help pronouncing *pacifism, nuance,* and other words that cropped up in her testimony. She was "like a little robot that you wound up," says Phyllis Gibson, assistant principal of Hawkins County's Volunteer High. "Totally scripted," says someone else who watched Frost testify.

Frost's supporters disagree. "You've got to understand that Vicki Frost is a smart lady but not well read," says Mark Troobnick, who worked on the protesters' lawsuit. "I have known many college-educated people that were not able to pronounce S-L-O-U-G-H or any number of other words properly, although they have been reading them for years."

Frost concedes that she learned a great deal as the textbook protest went on. At first, she didn't know much about secular humanism. "But I *had* read the Bible," she says, "and I knew that the philosophy systematically being taught in the books was contrary to it. That's the key—the Bible."

A few days after reading "A Visit to Mars," Vicki Frost phoned school superintendent Bill Snodgrass. The telepathy in the story was "contrary to our religious beliefs," she told him, and exposure to the concept would harm Rebecca.

Snodgrass had never talked to Frost before, and, he says, "I was surprised—but then, you hear everything as superintendent. I didn't lose my seat or anything." He jovially told her, "Maybe we can take the scissors and cut that story out."

That wouldn't be necessary, said Frost, unsure whether he was being facetious. She just hoped there wouldn't be any more such stories.

But there were more, as Frost discovered by reading through *Riders on the Earth* over the next few days. The selection after "A Visit to Mars" described "the amazing ways honeybees communicate in their dark hives"; that was unobjectionable. Like the Martian adventure, however, two subsequent stories dealt with telepathy. In the textbook, as in the Masonic *Morals and Dogma,* the more Frost read, the more she found that contradicted God's word.

At Frost's urging, meanwhile, other parents were also perusing volumes in the school district's new reading textbook series. "As I got to looking through it," recalls one mother, "I got to seeing other things. Maybe not as much as Vicki saw, but I saw enough."

Seeking a larger audience for their views, Frost and Wilson decided to hold a public meeting. They took announcements to the radio station and area newspapers, and asked the schools to send notes home with students. These notes urged parents to attend an "emergency meeting," but didn't indicate the topic. Frost refused to be more specific. "I know a lot of parents who are upset about this, but I wouldn't care to talk about it right now," she told an inquiring reporter. "It will all be brought out at the meeting."

Wilson also started lobbying elected officials. She phoned Doug Cloud, a school board member whom she knew in passing from church, and told him that the new reading textbooks were filled with satanism, witchcraft, and secular humanism. "I wasn't expecting this kind of phone call," Cloud remembers. At Wilson's request he skimmed *Riders on the Earth*, but "I didn't see the viewpoints that they were portraying"; instead he was "quite taken with some of the stories." One he found "fascinating": "A Visit to Mars."

The morning before the "emergency meeting," Roger and Vicki Frost and Jennie Wilson separately denounced the book on a local radio call-in show. "This Book is part of the Antichrist system," Roger Frost wrote in the notes he spoke from. "It calls God our Father a liar. . . . The Book relates to the worship of the Zodiac, Astrology, Greek gods, Hinduism, evolution. . . . It teaches children to be Rebellious. . . . Children can learn about satan's powers here on planet Earth through the reading of this book."

That same morning, coincidentally, the *Kingsport Times-News* published a column by Marjorie Pike, the new president of the Tennessee Education Association. "No one knows better than the parents in Tennessee what they want for their children," Pike wrote, and added: "I urge every citizen of this state to become involved." In Hawkins County, citizens were becoming involved.

On Thursday, September 1, 1983, more than a hundred parents, students, teachers, and school administrators assembled in the Church Hill Middle School cafeteria. After a prayer, moderator Roger Frost introduced Jennie Wilson.

The schools' new reading textbooks, Wilson announced, promoted the Hindu faith. She pointed to wall charts she had posted, which connected telepathy, evolution, and other themes in the books to Hinduism. Hinduism was an arbitrary choice, Wilson recalls: "I could have picked any religion in the world—Zoroastrianism, Hinduism, Islam. Christianity is not a religion; Christianity is salvation by Jesus Christ. These others are all religions—somehow or other, by your own efforts, making it to your utopia."

After discussing the books' Hindu themes, Wilson said that the stories about telepathy were paving the way for the Antichrist. This was no accident, she explained: Holt, Rinehart & Winston, the publisher of the textbooks, was part of the Antichrist-linked New Age movement. Wilson also charged that the international symbols illustrated in the books promoted universal language and one-world government, that other illustrations contained a hidden swastika and an upside-down cross, that the communistic word *comrade* appeared twice, and that some pages had suspiciously few words for so-called reading textbooks. The readers were "saturated" with secular humanism, she declared. "The whole series is objectionable."

When Wilson was finished, Vicki Frost nervously stood up—"I'm a bit of a shy person," she says, "and I had never done anything like that in my life"—and outlined the ungodly themes she had detected in *Riders on the Earth*. "There are 130 pages in that basic reader devoted to mental telepathy," she reported. "I feel this book teaches mind control and how to do telepathy." She asked if anyone in the audience could read minds. No one responded. "I don't associate with people who do that," she said. With its relationship to Hinduism and the Antichrist, telepathy didn't belong in the public schools; after all, a textbook that "mentioned just one Christian principle" would be thrown out in an instant.

Frost noted other objections too. One story promoted dishonesty by depicting parents who reward a lying child. Other stories endorsed evolution, "women's liberation," and gun control; still others disparaged free enterprise, the military, Christianity, and the government. She was also troubled by a sinister retelling of "Jack and Jill," which included the stanza: "The stealthy shadows crept closer; / They clutched at the hem of Jill's gown; / And there at the very top she stumbled, / And Jack came shuddering down." To Frost, this "sordid type of devilish tale" implied that Jack and Jill's fall was to hell. "You can take every page of this book and there's something objectionable in it," she declared.

On top of everything else, Frost related, some teachers wouldn't let the new textbooks out of the classroom, which was preventing parents from examining them. "I don't say it's deliberate," she said. "But the force behind it is the work of Satan."

A preacher named Billy Christian spoke briefly. Christian had led seminars on the satanic messages hidden in rock music; in the readers he detected the same kinds of potent but well-camouflaged forces. By endorsing telepathy and witchcraft, he said, the books were "encouraging our children to indulge in the satanic realm." Reading the Holt books might even invite demonic possession.

Although most audience members listened politely to the presentations, some of the teachers and school administrators acted up. They giggled, passed notes, and behaved like "twelve-year-old schoolboys," Roger Frost remembers. "They thought we were a big joke," says Vicki ruefully, "which I guess we were, a big joke."

After Christian had finished, a few members of the audience spoke up. Perhaps, one man suggested, Vicki had read too much into the "Jack and Jill" ghost story. A teacher remarked that a universal language might have kept the Soviets from shooting down the Korean Air Lines plane the day before.

The speakers had made "a good case," declared Archie McMillan, the principal of Carter's Valley Elementary, but they were wrong. "I can remember sitting in the church pew on Sunday morning and misbehaving," he added. "My mother would give me that certain look and, if that's not thought transference, I don't know what is!" More seriously, McMillan reported that he had read the Holt stories, and "I see no evil in them."

Church Hill Middle School principal James Salley said that the county schools would never teach evolution. As for telepathy, he said, "I'd just like for you to find someone who can actually read another person's mind all the time."

Vicki Frost announced that she would take her complaints to the school board one week later, and she urged everyone to attend. The meeting adjourned.

Afterward, a few members of the audience came up front. One of them was Joe Drinnon, the county's supervisor of instruction. He had gone to the meeting expecting to learn that the new readers contained a four-letter word. "I thought I'd mark through it, which would be censorship," he recalls. "But I wouldn't be above just a little bit of censorship, for expedience." Upon hearing the actual complaints about the readers, "I was totally dumbfounded."

Drinnon says he assured Frost that the Bible-believing teachers of Hawkins County weren't about to teach Hinduism or witchcraft. "We are going to use these books as a vehicle to teach reading skills," he recalls saying. In his recollection, Frost agreed. "She seemed to feel she could trust our teachers."

Frost remembers the exchange differently. In her recollection, Drinnon said that the schools would gladly let children use different reading textbooks on request. "You should have an alternative by law," she remembers his saying.

Church Hill Elementary vice principal Delmar Gillenwater came up and told Frost and Wilson a joke that he considered pertinent. A psychiatrist holds up an inkblot card and asks what the patient sees. "Sex," the patient replies. Every subsequent image elicits the same response. Finally the doctor observes that the patient seems to have an obsession. "*I* don't have any problem," the patient says indignantly. "*You're* the one with all the dirty pictures." Frost and Wilson were unamused, Gillenwater remembers: "If looks could kill, I'd be dead."

The following Sunday, Frost borrowed more Holt readers from James Salley at the middle school. Students, she told him, shouldn't have to read these dreadful books. Salley said he couldn't understand why she felt that way; after all, the readers were "on the Gablers' list of approved books." Frost asked who the Gablers were. Textbook reviewers in Texas, Salley said.

They are much more than that. According to Jerry Falwell, Mel and Norma Gabler (pronounced *Gay*-bler) are dedicated Christians working "to improve the textbooks of America's schools." According to the anticensorship organization People for the American Way, they are "professional censors" with "a plan to control the minds of the nation's youth." And according to *Encyclopaedia Britannica*, they are among "the most influential voices in U.S. education."

The Gablers got their start in 1961 by glancing at their children's schoolbooks. They were appalled to find that the books endorsed one-world government, played down American accomplishments, and disregarded Christianity. The Gablers began talking about these flaws in speeches, radio programs, and testimony before the state textbook committee. Norma did most of the traveling and speaking, while Mel conducted the research and continued to work as a clerk for Humble Oil (until he retired in 1973). "I am convinced," their son once said to Norma, "that God gave you the mouth and Dad the brains."

The Gablers have little formal training. Mel spent less than a year in college; Norma is a high school graduate. Once, Norma recalls, the vice chairman of the state board of education—"a hard-nosed lawyer from Houston, the toughest man I have ever been pitted against"—asked what qualified her to analyze textbooks. "I thought of a thousand things I should *not* have said—Mel can tell you, I'm fast on my feet," she continues. "I said, 'I am so glad you asked that question. I've got three good reasons.' I had none! I prayed silently, 'Please God, give me three good reasons.' I said, 'Number one, my sons belong to my husband and I. They do not belong to you and the state—yet. Number two, as a taxpayer in this state, I'm buying the textbooks. *My money* is purchasing the books. And number three, we elect you to office. Do you have three better ones?' And he said, 'Case dismissed. I'll never ask you again.' "

For years, the Gablers worked out of their cluttered four-bedroom house in Longview. They had converted the spare bedrooms to office space for themselves and their half-dozen employees. Crates of textbooks, their own publications, and correspondence were piled everywhere, along with fifty file cabinets, two photocopiers, and three computers. They talked of erecting an educational research center to house the reviewing operation, but the "prayer partners" on their mailing list contributed only a few thousand dollars toward the $200,000 they estimated they would need. Finally in 1990 they were able to move to a spacious office suite over a local warehouse. The rent, they told their prayer partners, was "graciously provided by a godly businessman."

The Gablers owe their influence to the fact that Texas, like twenty-two other states, selects schoolbooks statewide rather than district by district. For each subject at each grade level, the state adopts several books from which local districts may choose. If a district wants different books, it must buy them without using state funds. Consequently, the state textbook committee operates as, in essence, the single portal to the Texas market. The second largest market in the nation (after California), Texas accounts for about 9 percent of textbook sales nationwide. A book adopted in Texas can sometimes show a profit even if no other district in the nation adopts it.

The Gablers have positioned themselves at the Texas portal. Especially at first, they sometimes persuaded the state textbook committee to reject proposed books or to demand extensive revisions in them.

After a while, books reaching the committee already reflected the Gablers' well-known views. In a few instances, eager-to-please publishers have produced special Texas editions of major books, edited with Gabler-type objections in mind, as well as regular versions for the rest of the country. ("The publishers are friends," says Norma. "They go out of their way to be nice to us.") When the state does adopt a book that the Gablers oppose, their critiques often dissuade local school boards from choosing it. And even when a book reaches the classroom, some teachers use the Gabler reviews to decide which material to skip.

The Gablers' influence reaches beyond Texas. They mail scores of their textbook reviews and other publications to concerned parents every week, in exchange for "suggested donations." As a consequence, conservative protesters across the country raise identical arguments against schoolbooks.

A principal objection is secular humanism. "Humanists," the Gablers write, "believe that man (individually or collectively), not God, determines values." Humanism enters the classroom through evolution, situational ethics, satanism, and dozens of other themes, all of which can have devastating consequences: "It is very unfortunate that many parents feel that the de-education isn't really hurting their child because they see no behavioral changes. . . . CONDITIONING TAKES TIME. IT IS A PROCESS!!! You often cannot notice his change from your value system until the process has been completed and THE DAMAGE IS ALREADY DONE."

Fundamentalist Christians, the Gablers cite Scripture in some of their publications, but not in the reviews they file with the Texas schoolbook committee. "Where we're trying to convince secular-minded people and trying to argue on their level," concedes Mel, "it makes it a lot harder on us." Indeed, some of the Gablers' assertions seem absurd to people who don't share their religious and philosophical views. The new math, they once contended, could "destroy the student's belief in absolutes" and thereby undermine his religious faith; "the next thing you know, the student turns to crime and drugs."

But other objections are more accessible to outsiders. The Gablers criticized a fifth-grade history book that lavished extensive attention on Marilyn Monroe (asking such questions as "What problems did Marilyn have in her marriage to Arthur Miller?") but gave only passing mention to George Washington. They uncovered hundreds of wrong dates and other clear-cut factual errors in supposedly classroom-ready textbooks. And they opposed a New Jersey sex-education curriculum that instructed students to "draw the world's largest penis" and "make up a wild story about this."

Dozens of reporters have journeyed to Longview to interview the Gablers. Much of the resulting coverage has labeled them censors, book-burners, and fascists. "I've quit reading all those kinds of articles," says Mel. But there have been positive encounters too. Phil Donahue called them "media-wise," Mel recalls, and Mike Wallace "sat on that counter over there and threw questions for three hours straight."

Mel speaks proudly of meeting Paul Vitz, a New York University professor whose empirical research found that textbooks of the 1980s largely ignored Christianity. When Mel thanked Vitz for conducting the study, Vitz replied that he should be thanking the Gablers, "the pioneers" in the field. Remembering the conversation, Mel says, his voice cracking, "I didn't even know he knew us."

"Very few people have had as much interesting things happen to them," says Norma. "And we only did it because we were unhappy about what our children were being taught."

The middle school principal had assured Vicki Frost that the readers carried the Gablers' seal of approval. This information had originated with Harry Hall, the regional Holt representative who had sold the books to Hawkins County. "I think the Gablers *had* to approve them, or they wouldn't have been listed in Texas," says Hall.

Frost vaguely remembered having seen the Gablers mentioned in a newsletter she had received from Southwest Radio Church, the radio program that had presented Constance Cumbey's exposé of New Age. On September 6, she phoned the radio church's Oklahoma City offices, got the Gablers' number, and then called Longview.

She asked Mel Gabler if the Holt readers were safe. He put her on hold while he checked his files. No, he said when he returned; in fact, they were among the worst. He sent Frost a review of the 1980 edition of the series (the Gablers hadn't yet reviewed the 1983 edition that Hawkins County had purchased), along with a brochure called *Humanism in Textbooks,* a page of instructions on "How Should Objections Be Made to Textbooks?" and a sheaf of other papers. Just five days after their "emergency meeting" to alert the public, Frost and her allies had made contact with supportive outsiders.

. . .

At the September 1 public meeting, Frost had announced her intention to take the complaints to the county school board. Now, as the board's meeting date approached, the protesters worked to stir up more opposition to the books. A father who had attended the antitextbook meeting drafted a petition charging that the Holt readers taught "the Wicca religion," and calling on Congress and the school board "to stop innocent children from being indoctrinated." Frost signed and circulated the petition, though she was less concerned about Wicca—witchcraft —than about "one-world government, the militant feminism, evolution as fact, and all those types of things." In the Holt books, she notes, "people saw different things that more strongly affected them."

Frost also urged Bob Mozert (pronounced *Moe*-zert), a father whom she knew slightly, to take a look at his children's reading books. Frost's statement reminded Mozert of a warning a few months earlier. "One of our son's teachers had made a comment to my wife at the supermarket in Church Hill," he remembers. "This teacher—she was on the textbook selection committee—told my wife: I'm afraid there's going to be trouble over these new reading textbooks that have just been selected. That's all she said." After talking with Frost, Mozert inspected a Holt reader. "What I saw in it did not look good."

Jennie Wilson also alerted two more members of the school board, Conley Bailey and Larry Elkins. She spent more than an hour telling Bailey about the sacrilege in the readers. "I guess I had a course," Bailey says.

The night before the board meeting, the Frosts met with several other parents opposed to the books. Sitting at a backyard picnic table, they decided that they needed a well-spoken representative to voice their concerns to the board. Believing that a preacher might have more influence with the board members, they settled on John Pendleton, the pastor of Calvary Lighthouse Baptist Church and a part-time volunteer deputy in the sheriff's department. Roger Frost and a couple of other fathers drove to the church to recruit him. Arriving just before Wednesday evening services, they told Pendleton about the "anti-God" themes and lent him a copy of one book. Pendleton agreed to act as spokesman.

The next evening, shortly before the seven o'clock board meeting, some of the board members met as usual for dinner at the Orange Bowl in Rogersville. These get-togethers gave the men a chance to discuss business privately, away from reporters, teachers, voters, and other

distractions. The existence of the pre-meeting dinners was common
knowledge. So was the fact that they violated Tennessee's open-meet-
ings law.

According to the agenda for tonight's meeting, the board would
accept teacher resignations, approve the new design for report cards,
request bids on a carpet cleaner, and hear complaints about the new
reading books. The board members had no reason to suspect it as
they ate dinner, but those complaints were destined to ignite a bitter,
neighbor-against-neighbor struggle for power in Hawkins County.

Hawkins County was born amid a power struggle. Originally the region was part of the Tennessee territory, which was governed by the
state of North Carolina. In 1784, settlers asked North Carolina for help
against Indian raiders, but instead of sending aid, North Carolina
ceded the territory to the federal government. Settlers in the eastern
part of the territory announced the creation of the state of Franklin, in
honor of Benjamin Franklin. "Here," gushed one Franklin supporter,
"the genuine Republican! here the real whig will find a safe asylum, a
comfortable retreat among those modern Franks, the hardy mountain
men!" By then, however, North Carolina wanted the territory back.
Too late, replied the new government of Franklin; "North Carolina
deserted us." North Carolina legislators threatened to retake "the re-
volted territory or render it not worth possessing."

In the ensuing impasse, Franklin stood alone. Congress never responded to Franklin's petition for statehood, and the Philadelphia constitutional convention in 1787 disregarded a subsequent petition.
Benjamin Franklin, while saying that he appreciated the "very great
honor," offered no support. The Franklin government tottered and
finally collapsed in 1788, and the Tennessee territory reverted to North
Carolina. (Tennessee became a federal territory in 1790 and a state in
1796.) The county west of the Holston River, which Franklin had
named Spencer County, was known thereafter by North Carolina's
name: Hawkins County.

Seventy-three years after the demise of Franklin, East Tennessee
again charted its own course. When Tennessee seceded from the Union
in 1861, the people of the northeastern counties refused to go along.
Instead they torched bridges, evaded conscription, harassed Confederate soldiers, and continued to send representatives to Congress—
prompting President Lincoln to order Union generals not to bother
"our friends in East Tennessee."

Hawkins County has remained loyal to the party of Lincoln. Though Democrats have won local offices, the county has voted Republican in presidential elections since the party's founding, with only one exception (1912, when Theodore Roosevelt's independent candidacy split the Republican vote). Hawkins County rejected FDR, Lyndon Johnson, and even the all-Southern Clinton-Gore ticket. James H. Quillen, the Republican congressman who represents the county, has earned a perfect 100 rating from the U.S. Chamber of Commerce for his efforts to "enhance free enterprise."

Governmental intrusions, trivial by urban standards, still cause a ruckus in rural East Tennessee. Church Hill incorporated as a town in 1957; a decade later, residents were so galled by town taxes that they nearly voted through an initiative to disincorporate. At a public meeting to discuss a proposed zoning ordinance in 1990, one opponent observed: "The first definition of communism in the dictionary is state control over private property." When the commissioners in neighboring Sullivan County contemplated having county workers remove broken-down cars from private property, a man threatened to come after anybody fool enough to lay a finger on one of his twenty cars. Glowering at the mustachioed county attorney, another man declared that he'd rather look at old cars than at facial hair. "There's a *strong* independent streak here," says Jim Fields, a fundamentalist pastor who lives in Church Hill.

Setting aside their independent streaks for eight hours, many Hawkins County residents work in the area's factories. Kingsport, a city of 36,000 in Sullivan County, has the massive Kodak chemical plant called Tennessee Eastman, the Arcata Graphics printing plant, and the Mead Paper plant (where Roger Frost works), among others. Hawkins County's own factories produce reclining chairs, pinion steering mechanisms, paper labels, and explosives. In a 1990 list of Tennessee's major polluters, Tennessee Eastman ranked first and Holliston Mills in Church Hill ranked fifth, but local people, grateful for the jobs, rarely complain. A few Hawkins County residents farm full-time, and many others dabble, growing small harvests of hay, corn, and burley tobacco.

On Sunday mornings, the roads of Hawkins County are clogged with churchgoers. The county's 44,565 people are served by more than a hundred places of worship. Some have steeples and stained glass; others operate out of garages and trailers. All are Christian, almost all are Protestant, and most are fundamentalist. "I don't know if you'd find many native-born people who would deny any of the doctrines of fundamentalism," says Pastor Fields, though he adds that "only a small percentage fully understand them."

As with the "HOLY GHOST" roadside graffiti, religious references are casual and ubiquitous in the region. In Kingsport in 1989, the Holiday Inn discounted its Sunday buffet 10 percent for anyone who brought in a church bulletin. Richard Watterson, Kingsport's vice mayor, used official stationery with the slogan "Now is the time to insert Christianity in leadership" for eight years, until the American Civil Liberties Union threatened a lawsuit. A billboard advertising Church Hill's Mountaineer Restaurant says, alongside an illustration of a bedraggled mountaineer clutching his musket, "WE THANK YOU GOD BLESS YOU *COME BACK*." A classified ad in the *Rogersville Review* seeks a "FRIENDLY, VIBRANT, CHRISTIAN person to write bail bonds."

Religion also enters the classroom. Vicki Frost, who finished high school in Kingsport in 1969, says that "to the very day that I graduated, we had Bible reading and prayer before every school day." As the textbook controversy began in 1983, Hawkins County school assemblies sometimes had a religious theme; a black belt in karate would demonstrate his skills, for example, and then urge the children to invite Jesus into their hearts. Teachers in some schools also had daily prayer and Bible reading, notwithstanding the Supreme Court's 1963 ruling that the exercises are unconstitutional.

And, as was common in East Tennessee, ministers and their assistants regularly visited elementary schools to teach Bible stories, a practice that the Supreme Court had struck down in 1948. "Those Bible ladies, as we called them, taught some moral and ethical stuff too," says supervisor of instruction Joe Drinnon. "Probably the impact was not any kind of establishment of religion. We were what religion we were, and nothing was changed." "They did a tremendous job of being totally nondenominational," says Carter's Valley Elementary principal Archie McMillan. "Well, not *totally* nondenominational. But at the time, here in Appalachia, we were pretty much Methodist, Baptist, Protestant. The world hadn't caught up with us."

The world still hasn't caught up in some respects. "Maybe the pace of life is a little slower here," says David Brand, an attorney who practices in the small Hawkins County town of Mount Carmel. "Perhaps we don't have access to more of the cultural things that y'all would have in a big city. My son couldn't take something at the little high school he went to, and it didn't serve him well in college. Advanced Chemistry or one of those things. But I'm not sure that we would swap our lifestyle for where you have to have bolts on your doors and guard dogs and stuff."

Outsiders, Brand says, often misperceive Hawkins County. He tells of an Atlanta lawyer phoning to ask if Brand might possibly have access to a fax machine. "Hell, man," Brand replied, "we even got a stoplight!"

"The mountain man very strongly resents the idea of being looked down on," says Pastor Fields. "He can detect that at a moment's notice. So he is very sensitive to outsiders. He's fought outsiders all his life, with their different way of thinking."

Outsiders, in turn, sometimes have trouble gaining the trust and respect of people in Hawkins County. "The people are clannish and closed-minded," says Pam Cox, a former reporter who covered the area. "Unless you was born and raised and went to school with these guys, you just don't fit in," says Junior Marshall, a manager at Arcata Graphics. Thirty years after moving to Hawkins County, Marshall adds, "I'm still an outsider." In 1992, the *Rogersville Review* reported that the new owner of a Hawkins County pinball arcade was trying to squelch a hurtful rumor. "I'm not a drug user," the exasperated man insisted. "Just because my family and I are from Florida, we're not drug users."

Vicki Frost had been raised in Kingsport, just a dozen miles away, and she had lived in Church Hill for five years. She had no reason to suspect it when she first began lobbying against the Holt readers, but, she says now, "I was an outsider."

It was the first school board meeting Vicki Frost had ever attended. Wearing a short-sleeved blue jacket over a white blouse, she sat in the audience with about twenty of her allies, facing the five board members (all men) in the dark-paneled room. After dealing with other business, chairman Harold Silvers, Jr., called on her delegation.

Jennie Wilson, wearing a dark dress, stood and outlined several broad principles that she had copied from a *Moral Majority Report*. She said she favored academic freedom and "viable multiple alternatives," and opposed censorship. Using the Holt books in a public school, she asserted, violated the Constitution: "Secular humanism is a religion, according to the U.S. Supreme Court. . . . Since we believe in separation of church and state we cannot allow this series of books to teach religion contrary to the laws of our land."

The parents' designated representative, John Pendleton, spoke next. The Holt books were teaching things contrary to the beliefs of the parents: satanism, evolution, telepathy, disobedience, and other ideas that conflict with Scripture. Hidden in one illustration, he said, was a satanic ram's head. The books were academically inferior too, with deliberate misspellings and improper English.

A few minutes into Pendleton's remarks, one board member interrupted: "We've heard from this so-called preacher. Now, who's next?"

Bob Mozert rose. Though he felt "very inadequately prepared," he says, he also felt compelled to voice his concerns. Wearing a short-sleeved white shirt and holding *Riders on the Earth*, he asserted that the reader had less than 20 percent educational value, because over 80 percent of its pages were devoted to stories and poems as opposed to nonfiction. In illustrations, the symbols for lightning bolts subliminally promoted sorcery. Observing that a poem had come from the *Christian Science Monitor*, he said that the schools shouldn't be promoting Christian Science.

Jennie Wilson stood again. Displaying her poster, she explained as she had at the "emergency meeting" a week earlier that the Holt books promoted Hinduism in violation of church-state separation. The Holt books spoke of brotherhood, but she was "not the brother of Buddha." The books also featured a number of stories about cats, which are associated with witches, as well as stories involving astral projection, Indian religions, animal rights, and other ungodly concepts. She observed that her remarks might not be comprehensible to people who knew less about religion than she did.

After Wilson had finished, Frost rose. She hadn't planned to speak, she says, but Pendleton had been able to say so little that she felt she must. Noting the telepathy in the readers, she observed that the schools would be liable to a lawsuit if a child were to learn mind control from the books and use it on his parents. One story mentioned a daiquiri, and thereby endorsed alcohol. Another story included the offensive phrase "as hot as hell." Still other materials featured animals helping people, conveying the message that hunting is immoral. In addition, one story suggested that Jesus was illiterate by saying that he needed the scribes to write down his teachings. Parents, Frost declared, were demanding books that didn't teach false religion. She presented the anti-Wicca petition, with 225 signatures.

Nearly an hour after the textbook discussion had begun, Frost showed no sign of finishing it. The meeting "looked like it was going to run way over," says board member Larry Elkins. "Instead of ending at eleven, it was going to be midnight or one o'clock."

No Hawkins County parents had ever complained about school books before, and the board men had never expected to hear complaints like these. Ninety percent of Hawkins County residents, Bob McKee thought, wouldn't know Hinduism from voodoo.

Certainly there was nothing unusual about these new books. They had been selected by a committee of reading teachers. Some teachers on the committee had preferred a series published by the Economy Co., which emphasized phonics. But others had strongly favored Holt. For one thing, the content of Holt's stories and poems seemed likelier to engage local students. "We're a rural county," says teacher Gay Grabeel, a member of the selection committee, "and it's hard for our kids to identify with a lot of stories which deal with New York subways."

In addition, Holt was generous: "They had a kit that had all the tests in it," says Grabeel. "I think they supplied the teachers' edition. They were very open to giving to the school system." In contrast, "Economy was cheap. They didn't want to give us any freebies."

Indeed, for the $73,000 price of the Holt readers, Hawkins County got far more than just books. According to supervisor of instruction Joe Drinnon, the Holt salesman threw in more than a dozen sets of skills management software, which carried a retail price of $20,000 per set. "Anybody that gets a sale from us has to throw in all they can," Drinnon boasts. "We nail it to the wall." (Permissible at the time, this practice of heaping on inducements now is prohibited by state regulation, though Drinnon says that Hawkins County still manages to extract premiums. Pointing at a box on the floor, he says, "I've got right down there somebody else's stuff, and I told them we won't even *look* at their book until they give us access to that.")

The Holt books had been adopted, and, in a financially strapped school system like Hawkins County's, there was no looking back. However flawed the readers might be, "we didn't have the money to replace those books," says Doug Cloud. To him and the other board members, the discussion was a waste of time.

Their impatience sometimes showed, Frost recalls. After she said that an upside-down cross in an illustration represented "Satan's victory over Christ," Silvers held up the cross he was wearing, turned it upside down, and asked if *that* offended her beliefs. When Frost talked about a story in which a character tells a lie, Bob McKee said, "Well, *I* would sure tell a lie if I got in trouble."

Recognizing that she hadn't persuaded the board members, Frost tried another tack. "If the children don't want to read these books, they don't have to," she announced. She had in mind her understanding of remarks by Joe Drinnon after the September 1 "emergency meeting." Drinnon, Frost thought, had said that the county would provide alternative reading textbooks. "Right, Mr. Drinnon?" she asked.

"Run that by me again," Drinnon said. "I was daydreaming."

Conley Bailey opened the general discussion. The books had been chosen by a committee of Hawkins County teachers, some of the most dedicated and professional ones in the school system, he said, and controversy would only bring shame on the county. He said he had no disrespect for the parents; he merely disagreed with them.

The Frosts' seventh-grade son Marty stood—unprompted, he remembers—and said he didn't want to read the Holt books.

"Who told you to say that?" demanded a board member. Marty sat down again.

His mother had another idea. What if the parents kept their children out of reading class?

"They will probably get an F," Bailey replied.

That was all right with Frost. "I would rather my children have an F than be taught demonology," she declared.

A teacher, Margaret Ashby, spoke up in defense of the Holt books. She said she had looked through the books and considered them excellent. "A lot of these stories are related to child problems, and I feel the stories will give children a good feeling about themselves."

Midway through Ashby's remarks, the Frosts got up and left. "Roger got agitated at the meeting because of the way they were mocking, making fun, being rather disrespectful," says Vicki. "He didn't want to be put in a position where he'd become angry."

With the Frosts gone, Silvers summarized the board's position. The issue, he said, was simply one of procedure. The board had chosen the teachers on the textbook committee, and that committee had selected the Holt series. That meant, he reasoned, that the Hawkins

County schools were going to use the Holt books until the state education department or a judge ordered otherwise, or until a board-selected
committee chose different books.

The meeting moved on to other matters. But, says Larry Elkins, "I
didn't feel like that would be the last time that we would hear from
them."

Looking back on that school board meeting, the protesters are adamant
that they weren't trying to ban the Holt books. "Jennie Wilson and I
purposefully talked about what we would do at the meeting," Vicki
Frost recalls. They considered trying to get rid of the books, but decided against it because "censorship brings a negative response a lot of
times." She is, she says, "absolutely sure" about this. "I never remember asking that anything be censored," says Jennie Wilson, who adds
that "censorship is contrary to the American way." "I never, ever
asked that the books be banned," says Bob Mozert. "All I ever asked
for was alternate readers."

Frost, Wilson, and Mozert are all misremembering. In a letter to
the Gablers, sent about two weeks after the board meeting, Frost
wrote: "As concerned parents, we took our case before the school
board to ask for removal of the Holt Basic Readers." Having failed in
their first effort, she added, the protesters planned to mobilize public
opinion so that the board would "take these books out." Further undermining the protesters' recollections, a December 1983 *Kingsport
Times-News* article quotes Mozert as saying that "it had not occurred to
me that an alternate reader was possible" at the time of the September 8
board meeting.

Although the protesters did call for "viable alternatives" and state
their opposition to censorship at the meeting, they also contended that
the Holt books violated the law by teaching religion. The protesters
thus denounced censorship and at the same time called for removal of
the books. They may have believed, as Wilson suggests, that removing
illegal books isn't censorship, and that the real censors were the Holt
editors who had omitted Christian values from the readers.

Two months later, in mid-November, the protesters no longer decried "illegal books"; instead they pushed only for "viable alternatives" for their own children. With time, Frost and her allies came to
believe that this had been their position from the outset. In an interview, Mozert first asserts that he asked for an alternative reader at the

September board meeting. Then, after reading the *Kingsport Times-News* article quoting him to the contrary, he speaks more hesitantly: "Apparently from what I said—if that's true, and I'm going to have to assume it is—we didn't consider having an alternate reader at that time because we didn't know that was a viable option." In those early days, he adds, "We didn't know a whole lot. We were green behind the ears."

Perhaps owing to that naiveté, Frost and her allies had failed to anticipate the school board's attitude. In Hawkins County, membership in a particular denomination—Baptist, Methodist, and Presbyterian have always been the major ones—matters little. The Frosts had at times attended churches of all three denominations. Instead, what counts is a belief in the inerrancy of the Bible and adherence to the other fundamentals of the conservative Christian faith.

"We were one of their own," says Frost, referring to the school board members. "If you sat down and asked them, Do you believe in creation? They'd say, Yes, sir, I believe the Bible's the word of God." Since the textbook protest has ended, in fact, several candidates for school board and superintendent have pledged that if elected they will purchase biology textbooks that omit the theory of evolution.

The protesters thought this spiritual overlap would be enough. When Jennie Wilson phoned board member Larry Elkins, she asked if he was a churchgoing Christian. Yes, he replied. "Well," she said, "I'm sure you won't have any problem seeing what we see in these books."

Though the officials shared the protesters' conservative Christian faith, however, they didn't share their eagerness to deconstruct texts in search of hidden sacrilege. The school people had never heard of secular humanism—"human secularism," board member Doug Cloud calls it. They had read the Bible, but not *The Battle for the Mind* and *The Hidden Dangers of the Rainbow*. They might agree with the protesters about scriptural inerrancy and the virgin birth, but not about secular humanism and the New Age.

So far as the school officials were concerned, the Holt readers were benignly neutral. "I read the textbooks and I couldn't see anything that would be offensive to anybody," says Harold Silvers, who also notes that "anything that I would classify as being offensive would never be there to start with." Asked if the parents' objections were unreasonable, Bill Snodgrass says, "Yes, because I saw nothing wrong with the books." The Hawkins County officials intended to impose their vision of neutrality on the classroom, as, indeed, school administrators had been doing since colonial times.

CHAPTER TWO

GOD IN PUBLIC SCHOOLS

AND PUBLIC SQUARES

I n the beginning, Americans considered education an intrinsically religious undertaking. When Massachusetts required its larger communities to hire teachers in 1647, the statute explained why: It is a "chief project of the old deluder, Satan, to keep men from the knowledge of the Scriptures." Some colonies let ministers veto schoolbooks and teachers, or required that teachers hold a particular religious faith.

Religion dominated the curriculum. Early colonial teachers used the Bible, a catechism, and the Psalter as their texts. The first widely used textbook, the *New England Primer*, instructed students to memorize the Lord's Prayer, the Ten Commandments, the Westminster Catechism, and the books of the Bible. Christianity imbued even the alphabet in the *Primer:*

> A   In Adams Fall
>   We Sinned all.
> B   Heaven to find,
>   The Bible Mind.
> C   Christ Crucify'd,
>   For Sinners dy'd.

Later textbooks commended their topics on religious grounds: Spelling was essential to understand the Bible; arithmetic, to find particular

Bible verses; geography, to facilitate missionary work; and astronomy, to "arrive at so clear a conception of many things delivered in the Scripture." Noah Webster's 1798 spelling book included a Moral Catechism. To the question "What rules have we to direct us?" students were to answer: "God's word contained in the Bible has furnished all necessary rules to direct our conduct."

With time, however, different churches propounded different interpretations of God's word, and each church vied to get its version taught in the schools. In the 1840s, Horace Mann of Massachusetts suggested a solution to this intensifying struggle: presenting in the classroom only the "common core" of American religion, "the religion of the Bible." Students should read Scripture but not discuss or comment on it, Mann advised, and thereby allow the Bible "to do what it is allowed to do in no other system,—*to speak for itself.*"

Mann's approach soon won out. While continuing to believe that religion was a vital element of education, educators came to agree that sectarianism must be avoided. A proper "secular education," said a New York school board attorney, should include "those common sanctions of religion which are acknowledged by everybody."

The trouble was, not quite everybody acknowledged those sanctions. Then as now, Catholics used the Douay Bible, and they believed that Scripture must be interpreted and explained by a religious authority. The King James Bible readings, presented with no interpretation, violated the Catholic faith. Catholics also complained that schoolbooks were seeking to "bring contempt upon our Church and its members." An 1818 geography text, for instance, reported: "The monks and ecclesiastics themselves, who today will pardon your sins for a groat, tonight will become defiled with your bosom-companion in her marriage-bed. And the daughter on whom you dote, while saying her mass, will become debauched by a pretending saint!"

Some schools tried to appease Catholic objectors. A few communities removed the Bible from the classroom, though administrators were accused of trying to "hand the public schools over to Pope, Pagan, and Satan." A few other communities excused Catholics from Bible-reading. New York City's Public School Society tried to expunge anti-Catholic sentiments from books in 1840, and some publishers began sending textbook manuscripts to Catholic as well as Protestant clergy for prepublication approval.

In most places, however, Catholic pleas were rebuffed. To complaints about anti-Catholic schoolbooks in New York, a member of the

Public School Society responded that if everybody were permitted to veto schoolbooks he didn't care for, the schools would have no books whatsoever. Some administrators declared that they would sooner close down the public schools than remove the King James Bible. The American and Foreign Christian Union thundered that the Bible would remain in the classroom "so long as a piece of Plymouth Rock remained big enough to make a gun flint out of."

The disputes soon kindled violence. In 1842, the bishop of Philadelphia asked that Catholic students be excused from classroom prayers, hymns, and King James Bible readings. A rumor spread that Catholics were trying to ban the religious practices outright. Riots ensued, killing a dozen people and destroying two Catholic churches and a convent. When Catholics petitioned New York City to remove the "Protestant Bible" from the public schools and to allot school funds to parochial schools, a mob rioted and attacked the bishop's house behind St. Patrick's Cathedral. In Maine, Protestants tarred and feathered a priest who had instructed Catholic children to refuse to read the King James Bible.

A Boston conflict of 1859 illustrates the era's warped conception of religious neutrality. An eleven-year-old Catholic boy refused to recite the Ten Commandments. His teacher whipped the boy's hands with a long rattan stick until, after half an hour, the boy capitulated. His father filed assault charges against the teacher, but the police court dismissed them on the ground that "the punishment inflicted, when compared with the offence committed . . . was neither excessive, nor inflicted through malice." The teacher, the court added, had quite rightly refused to excuse the boy from the recitation. "May not the innocent pleading of a little child for its religion in school, if granted, be used like a silken thread, to first pass that heretofore impassable gulf which lies between Church and State, and when . . . secured, may not stronger cords be passed over it, until cables, which human hands cannot sever, shall have bound *Church and State together forever?*" The Protestant Bible exercises seemed so altogether secular that, in the judge's eyes, exempting dissenters would violate the state's obligation of religious neutrality.

Finally Catholics shifted their focus away from public schools and concentrated instead on establishing parochial ones. It was only fair, they reasoned, for tax money to go to these Catholic schools as well as to the nominally public "Protestant schools." (Promoting educational vouchers in the 1980s and 1990s, fundamentalists similarly spoke of nominally public "secular humanist" schools.) A handful of communities did provide equal funding to parochial schools. A larger number offered tax-supported bus transportation, textbooks, medical care, and the like, though such subsidies covered only a small portion of the cost of parochial education. But even these minor subsidies enraged some Protestants. In 1876, Congress came within two votes of passing a constitutional amendment, endorsed by President Ulysses S. Grant, that would have barred states from aiding religious schools. The amendment included a disclaimer reflecting the era's understanding of neutrality: "This article shall not be construed to prohibit the reading of the Bible in any school or institution."

Catholics were not alone in dissenting from the religion of the public school. In Brooklyn in 1906, Jewish parents complained about the December festivities at their children's schools. One principal gave an annual Christmas speech exhorting students to try to be "more like Christ," which rankled parents in the predominantly Jewish neighborhood. Their pleas unanswered, many parents took their children out of school for most of December. The boycott generated press attention and public sympathy, and the school board agreed to excise the more divisive elements from the Christmas program.

A Los Angeles conflict in 1907 had a different outcome. To help Jewish students feel comfortable in the public schools, the school superintendent told teachers that they could talk in the classroom about Santa Claus but not about Jesus. Some teachers burst into tears upon hearing the decree. "Christianity is the religion of the civilized world," a minister inveighed. "Christ is not sectarian. He is the representative of the human race." The beleaguered superintendent withdrew the directive and, a short time later, resigned.

Along with Catholics and Jews, a third group was soon sparring over the nature of religion in the public schools. Like Catholics and Jews, these new dissenters contended that seemingly neutral classroom practices were antithetical to their faith. They were conservative Christians, who called themselves fundamentalists.

Fundamentalism was born largely as a protest movement. As the twentieth century began, liberal Christians modified their beliefs to accord with Darwin's theory of evolution, newly unearthed manuscripts, and other recent discoveries. One of the most prominent modernists, the

University of Chicago's Shailer Matthews, wrote that "scientists know more about nature and man than did the theologians who drew up the Creeds and Confessions."

To religious conservatives, anything that conflicted with Scripture was, perforce, wrong. As liberals loosened their doctrinal tenets, conservatives tightened theirs. In 1895, the Niagara Bible Conference listed the five essential principles of Christianity. One, scriptural inerrancy, applied to the Bible. The others all concerned Jesus: the virgin birth and divinity; "substitutionary atonement," by which the crucifixion atoned for the sins of others; the bodily resurrection; and the future return to earth. To conservatives, this list and similar ones separated the true believers from the heretics.

To bolster the conservative cause, two prosperous brothers, Lyman and Milton Stewart, bankrolled the publication and distribution of a series of tracts by conservative theologians called *The Fundamentals: A Testimony to the Truth*. "It is not enough for a man just to believe in God," one *Fundamentals* author warned; "the consequences of accepting or rejecting Christ are final and eternal." More pointedly, tracts in the series called Christian Science a "farrago of irreligion and nonsense," Mormonism "depraved and cunning," and Roman Catholicism "the essential and deadly foe of civil and religious liberty, the hoary-headed antagonist of both Church and State." *The Fundamentals* was so popular—more than three million copies were printed between 1910 and 1915—that conservative Protestants were soon known as fundamentalists.

Although *The Fundamentals* concentrated on theology, fundamentalists soon turned to politics. First they added their efforts to the temperance movement. With the passage of Prohibition in 1919, political and religious liberals started to fret. One predicted that full-scale "Protestant political supremacy" was on the horizon. If fundamentalists managed to capture the government, another liberal said, "we shall be headed backwards toward the pall of a new Dark Age."

Fundamentalists next set their sights on evolution in the public schools. If the Bible couldn't be trusted on creation, in their view, it couldn't be trusted on salvation or anything else. "If evolution wins," William Jennings Bryan declaimed, "Christianity goes—not suddenly, of course, but gradually, for the two cannot stand together." Parents, he argued, "have a right to say that no teacher paid by their money shall rob their children of faith in God."

The fundamentalists' battle started auspiciously, with several state legislatures banning Darwin's theory from the classroom. In the 1925 *Scopes* trial in Dayton, Tennessee, Bryan and the fundamentalists won in the courtroom: John T. Scopes was found guilty of violating the law against teaching evolution (though the conviction was later overturned). Outside, however, thanks to the biting reportage of H. L. Mencken—who, behind the scenes, was giving Clarence Darrow tips on defending Scopes—the fundamentalists suffered a devastating defeat. In the public eye, their faith seemed ludicrously, obstinately anachronistic.

More setbacks followed. Prohibition was repealed in 1933, and, in the process, the notion of legislating morality was discredited for a time. More and more Protestant leaders adjusted to Darwinism, leaving fundamentalists increasingly isolated.

Wounded, fundamentalists abandoned public life. They came to believe that a minister's primary place is leading his flock, not leading a political charge. Individual fundamentalists continued to involve themselves in politics, and they sometimes formed groups—mostly local, ad-hoc, and single-issue, addressing such matters as temperance, pornography, and communism. William Dudley Pelley, Gerald B. Winrod, and a few other ministers spoke out. But they were exceptions; they rarely assembled significant political organizations; and their extremist rantings (often anti-Semitic) further lowered fundamentalism's public standing. For more than fifty years, fundamentalists remained largely detached from politics.

During the fundamentalists' wilderness years, classroom religion continued to evolve. Educators of the 1960s, like those of the 1860s, embraced two principles: that the schools should inculcate religion, and that they should do so in a nonsectarian fashion. The scope of the second principle had changed with time. Material that might legitimately offend Catholics or Jews now was forbidden, though the legitimacy of the offense was judged by Protestants, who often accused objectors of hypersensitivity. Any objection raised by an atheist was, ipso facto, illegitimate.

Classroom religion still centered on the Bible. The day opened with Bible reading in fewer than half of American schools, down from about three-fourths at the turn of the century. Students recited a prayer—most frequently the Lord's Prayer, which some courts had adjudged nonsectarian—in about one-third of schools. Most schools would excuse a child from these religious exercises at the parents' request. The exercises were nearly universal in the South, common in the East, and relatively rare elsewhere.

This Bible-centered religion, which had been supported by Protestants since Mann's era, now had the backing of Catholics as well. Recognizing that parochial schools weren't likely to derive much public money, and that most Catholic children would continue to be educated in the public schools, Catholics came to support religious exercises in the public schools. In a 1962 statement, Catholic bishops declared that the public schools could not hope to inculcate morality without religion, even though the religion was almost sure to be Protestant. Protestantism, they believed, was better than no religion at all—the converse of their nineteenth-century position.

Over the course of more than a century of protests, petitions, threats, and bloodshed, the classroom had grown increasingly secular. From the 1830s to the early 1960s, this process had been gradual, erratic, and decentralized. The only serious effort to impose a national standard, the proposed constitutional amendment barring states from aiding parochial and other religious schools, had failed. Then the Supreme Court stepped in.

In 1951 the governing body of New York State public schools, the Board of Regents, composed what law professor Paul Freund once termed a "to-whom-it-may-concern prayer": "Almighty God, we acknowledge our dependence upon Thee, and we beg Thy blessings upon us, our parents, our teachers, and our country." Hoping to placate Jews who objected to use of the Lord's Prayer, the Regents commended the prayer as an "act of reverence" that "might well" be recited in classrooms before or after the Pledge of Allegiance. The vast majority of New York schools declined, as they had the right to do, and continued to use the Lord's Prayer or Bible readings.

The public schools in a Long Island suburb, New Hyde Park, did use the Regents' Prayer, which prompted five local families to file suit in 1959. Two of the plaintiffs in *Engel v. Vitale* were Jewish, one was Unitarian, one was in the Society for Ethical Culture, and one was agnostic. They contended that the prayer violated the First Amendment's prohibition against religious establishments ("Congress shall make no law respecting an establishment of religion . . ."), the provision that the Supreme Court interprets to mandate separation of church and state. Letting dissenters leave the room, as the Regents required, didn't help; in fact the plaintiffs' children had all stayed in class because they hadn't wanted to become "pariahs."

After losing at all three levels of the New York state judiciary, the plaintiffs won before the Supreme Court in 1962. Writing for the majority, Justice Hugo Black concluded that "it is no part of the business of government to compose official prayers." The only constitutional issue was whether the government was acting to endorse a particular religious viewpoint, he said. Allowing students to leave the room made no difference; regardless, "indirect coercive pressure" probably dissuaded many students, like those in the plaintiff families, from walking out.

The Court's ruling was endorsed by Jewish organizations; some liberal Protestant leaders, including Martin Luther King, Jr., and the dean of Harvard Divinity School; and a few newspapers, including the *New York Times* and *Washington Post*. And, up to a point, by President Kennedy, who said guardedly: "The Supreme Court has made its judgment, and a good many people obviously will disagree with it. Others will agree with it. But I think it is important for us, if we're going to maintain our constitutional principle, [to] support Supreme Court decisions even when we may not agree with them." Kennedy added that "we have in this case a very easy remedy and that is to pray ourselves . . . at home and attend our churches with a good deal more fidelity."

Supporters, though, were a distinct minority. Far more common was the response of Cardinal Francis Spellman of New York, who pronounced himself "shocked and frightened" by the Court's action. Cardinal Richard Cushing of Boston declared that "the Communists are enjoying this day." Reinhold Niebuhr said the decision "practically suppresses all religion, especially in the public school." Senator Robert Byrd of West Virginia castigated the justices for "tampering with America's soul," and asked whether we must now "embrace the foul concept of atheism." Congressman George Andrews of Alabama linked *Engel* to another decision detested by Southerners: "They put the Negroes in the schools and now they're driving God out."

Albeit in gentler tones, some academics also disapproved. "Of course, the rights of all, especially those of minorities, must be protected and preserved," wrote Erwin Griswold, the dean of Harvard

Law School. "But does that require that the majority, where there is such a majority, must give up its cultural heritage and tradition?" In his view, a student who left the room during school prayer learned two valuable lessons: that his beliefs differed from those of other students and that other students and the school itself tolerated the divergent beliefs.

In two editorials, the liberal *New Republic* came down against *Engel*, though not necessarily on the side of school prayer. The Regents' Prayer was "relatively innocuous," and the embarrassment felt by students who left the room was not "a grave invasion" of their rights—certainly not when compared to such invasions as schools' "indoctrinating them about the dangers of godless Communism." Furthermore, eliminating all religious ceremonies from the public schools "would be an undertaking of the magnitude and duration of the racial integration endeavor," an undertaking that, even if it succeeded, might not be worth the price. Finally, the editors worried that the ruling would strengthen those who wanted federal aid for private schools, give middle-class parents one more reason to take their children out of urban public schools, and, as Congressman Andrews had demonstrated, further intensify Southern fury at the Supreme Court.

In 1963, a year after *Engel*, the Court faced two more cases about religious exercises in the classroom. *School District of Abington Township v. Schempp* challenged the daily recital, without comment or interpretation, of the Lord's Prayer and ten verses from the Bible in the Abington, Pennsylvania, schools. At trial, Edward Schempp testified that various Biblical doctrines conflicted with his family's Unitarian beliefs. Like the *Engel* families, the Schempps had not taken advantage of the available excusal provision, lest their children be set apart as "oddballs."

The second case, *Murray v. Curlett*, marked the first appearance of someone who would later call herself the "most hated woman in America," Madalyn Murray O'Hair. Madalyn Murray, as she was then known, says that her militant atheism dates back to childhood. One weekend when she was twelve or thirteen, she read the Bible from cover to cover. "I'll never forget the shock of it," she recalls. "The improbability of it was just too much, and the miracles would stop anybody."

By her account, her fourteen-year-old son Bill experienced his own antireligious awakening in 1960. He too was an atheist, he told his mother, and he wasn't going to participate in the daily school prayers and Bible readings anymore. (According to Bill Murray—who, to his mother's consternation, announced his conversion to Christianity on Mother's Day 1980, and went on to become an evangelist—the no-prayers stance was actually his mother's idea.) After administrative skirmishes, the Maryland attorney general ordered the Baltimore schools to let Bill leave the room during the devotionals. Madalyn Murray filed suit anyway. She argued that, like the Regents' Prayer, the classroom devotionals were unconstitutional even if participation was optional.

The plaintiffs in *Engel* and *Schempp* didn't want to be seen as "pariahs" or "oddballs." Mad Murray, as she sometimes called herself, had no such worries. "We find the Bible to be nauseating, historically inaccurate, replete with the ravings of madmen," she proclaimed. "We find God to be sadistic, brutal, and a representation of hatred, vengeance. We find the Lord's Prayer to be that muttered by worms groveling for meager existence in a traumatic, paranoid world."

In her 1970 book about the lawsuit, O'Hair railed against those who didn't adequately appreciate her. The American Civil Liberties Union earned her "great hostility" because it "*never, in any way, assisted us.*" Atheists, "extraordinarily niggardly with funds," didn't keep their pledges to her. Humanist and free-thought organizations never "gave us any real assistance"; instead they pressed her to identify herself as a "rationalist" or "humanist" instead of atheist. The Schempps earned her fury by refusing to reveal publicly what they confessed to her privately: that they were atheists, not Unitarians. (Schempp doesn't contest O'Hair's account. "I am very confused as to atheist, agnostic, nonbeliever," he says. "These terms vary. I may have said that to her.") Another enemy was the clerk of the U.S. Supreme Court, who, O'Hair wrote, merged the two cases under the Schempp case name instead of the Murray one in order to avoid having "the name of Atheists be reported out in any official United States legal reports!!"

When the consolidated cases reached the Supreme Court, the issue was whether the school day could constitutionally include Bible reading and the Lord's Prayer. Though these were religious words, they weren't written by any branch of government, the factor that the Court had emphasized in *Engel*. Accordingly, the lawyers representing the school districts argued that *Engel* was inapplicable.

The lawyers also argued that these were not religious words at all.

One lawyer said that, although the Bible is a "religious document, in a sense," the exercises were actually moral and ethical instruction. Another lawyer maintained that reciting the Lord's Prayer helped rambunctious students calm down and prepare for their studies.

Such arguments had swayed judges in the late nineteenth and early twentieth centuries, but not anymore. If the religious materials had such positive effects, Justice Black said, why not devote the whole day to them? And why weren't schools using other texts, such as the Koran, for moral guidance? Justice Byron White said he was surprised that schools would excuse dissenting students from such salutary secular exercises. And Justice Potter Stewart suggested that teachers might more effectively soothe rowdy students with tranquilizers.

The questions at oral argument augured the ultimate ruling: The Court struck down the prayers and Bible readings. Any religious exercise, the justices held, is unconstitutional as part of the official school day. "It is no defense to urge that the religious practices here may be relatively minor encroachments on the First Amendment," the Court said, for "the breach of neutrality that is today a trickling stream may all too soon become a raging torrent."

Although this ruling had a much larger impact than *Engel*—thousands of schools used the Lord's Prayer and Bible readings; only a few dozen used government-written prayers—the response to it was much milder. Nearly every Protestant denomination endorsed *Schempp*. Relatively few politicians spoke as heatedly as they had a year earlier. This time, broadcast evangelists and Roman Catholic cardinals were virtually the only ardent opponents, and with time some of the Catholic leaders conceded that the decision was proper.

Several factors helped tamp down the public reaction. The Court's only Jewish justice (Arthur Goldberg) and only Roman Catholic justice (William Brennan) signed on to the decision; Felix Frankfurter, the only Jewish justice at the time of *Engel*, had not participated in that decision. The majority opinion's author, Tom Clark, was known to be a churchgoing Presbyterian. The opinion heartily endorsed the role of religion in the curriculum through courses on comparative religion, religious history, or the Bible as literature; *Engel* had included only a terse footnote about the secular study of religion. These aspects suggested, *Time* magazine said, that since *Engel* the Court had "learned a bit about public relations."

People may not have complained much about *Schempp*, but they didn't rush to comply with it either. The National Education Association advised teachers: "Keep on with what you have been doing. But don't make it anything official." In New York and Massachusetts, state authorities told schools to comply with the ruling, but many disobeyed. Officials of some other states, especially in the South, ordered schools to disregard the Court. Any Alabama school that dropped its religious exercises, Governor George Wallace announced, could kiss its state aid goodbye—and if a judge enjoined the Bible readings, "I'm going to that school and read it myself." In Texas, scarcely any school districts had taken an official position on religious exercises when *Schempp* came down; four years later, nearly 90 percent of Texas districts *required* daily prayers.

Although the federal government could have moved to force compliance, no president was eager to dispatch National Guard troops into classrooms to unclasp students' hands. Enforcement, consequently, lay with individual plaintiffs supported by groups like the ACLU. Where no one sued, school prayer continued—and, indeed, continues today. A 1985 survey found devotional Bible reading in 5 percent of school districts nationwide, and spoken prayer in 15 percent. The South continued to lead: More than two decades after the Supreme Court had outlawed the practices, 20 percent of Southern schools still had Bible reading and 43 percent had spoken prayer.

The potential political firepower of the prayer issue had distressed the *New Republic* in 1962. Banning classroom prayer, the magazine predicted, was likely to "provide a rallying cry for the Radical Right with great evocative power among religious-minded people and, in particular, among those fundamentalist groups already attracted to the gospel according to John Birch." The prediction was on the mark. Though it would take more than a decade, the Supreme Court's prayer decisions would help propel fundamentalists back into public life.

In the 1960s, Jerry Falwell, like other fundamentalist preachers, steered clear of politics. "Believing the Bible as I do," he said in a 1965 sermon, "I would find it impossible to stop preaching the pure saving gospel of Jesus Christ, and begin doing anything else—including fighting communism, or participating in civil rights reforms. As a God-called preacher, I find that there is no time left after I give the proper time and attention to winning people to Christ." Even then, though, Falwell was reconsidering. The school prayer decisions, he says, had demonstrated what calamities were possible if godly Christians avoided politics.

Soon there were other provocations: raucous student protests, widely tolerated drug use, "forced busing," uncloseted homosexuality, constitutionalized abortion rights, criminal acts in the White House, the "God is dead" movement. By 1980 the "secularist, socialist emphasis" had grown so powerful, says fundamentalist author Tim LaHaye, that "another four years would have been deadly" for the nation. Patriotism mandated activism.

So did self-interest, for government's tentacles were reaching deeper and deeper into religious enclaves. The state was telling churches whom to hire, what to teach in church schools, and how to use church-owned land. The Internal Revenue Service was trying to withhold tax exemptions from church schools that, as a matter of religious faith, refused to admit blacks. While some of the new interventions, like zoning regulations, affected all churches equally, others, like regulation of home schooling and of religious schools, fell particularly hard on fundamentalist Christians. To remain apart from politics in the face of such threats seemed suicidal.

In these respects, the rise of the religious right was largely reactive. "It is significant that virtually every item in the New Right's social agenda is a protest against a liberal initiative," political analyst William Schneider said in 1985. "They weren't anti-ERA until there was an ERA. They were anti-gay only after a pro-gay ordinance passed in Florida. They were for creationism after laws passed mandating the teaching of evolution. Others see them as an aggressive right-wing movement attempting to impose their values, but the right sees it exactly the opposite."

In the mid-1970s, Falwell eased into politics by leading "I Love America" rallies on state capitol steps, protesting the Supreme Court's *Roe v. Wade* abortion ruling, and joining Anita Bryant's crusade against homosexuals. "The idea that religion and politics don't mix," he declared, "was invented by the Devil to keep Christians from running their own country." He pronounced his 1965 sermon, about the preacher's duty to steer clear of politics, "false prophecy."

Then Falwell met with several leaders of the new right in 1979: Howard Phillips and Ed McAteer of the Conservative Caucus; Paul Weyrich, founder of the Heritage Foundation and the Committee for the Survival of a Free Congress; Robert Billings, a Christian school activist; and Richard Viguerie, the inventor of the new right's direct-mail fundraising machinery. The men first proposed a religious newspaper, but decided that a national organization would be more fruitful. Someone—Phillips and Weyrich both claim credit—came up with "Moral Majority," a name that captivated Falwell.

Fifty years earlier, the best known of the politically active fundamentalists was William Jennings Bryan. In the view of a sympathetic journalist, Bryan "stood for as much of the idea of socialism as the American mind will confess to." Bryan's three campaigns for the presidency, writes Garry Wills, were "the most leftist mounted by a major party's candidate in our entire history."

The fundamentalist standard-bearer this time was no leftist. Communists, Jerry Falwell said in 1977, should not only be required to register; "we should stamp it on their foreheads and send them back to Russia." "If you would like to know where I am politically," he wrote later, "I am to the right of wherever you are." Satan, he joked, was "the first liberal."

To the newly politicized fundamentalists, liberalism also had a dire and unfunny side: It was an aspect of secular humanism. "There isn't a nickel's worth of difference between a secular humanist and a liberal," said Tim LaHaye, the religious right's leading analyst of secular humanism.

Humanism, according to LaHaye, poses "the greatest danger facing our nation today." It is responsible for "the dreadful increase in venereal disease in our country, the rise of sexual perversion, the aborting of millions of babies, the escalating crime rate, and practically every social evil facing our society today." Indeed, "behind each social problem in America, we will find a secular humanist thinker or theorist."

Although critics contend that "trying to define secular humanism is like trying to nail Jell-O to a tree," its basic elements are in truth relatively predictable. They grow out of the natural desire to see one's deepest beliefs reflected in the community and the nation. Fundamentalists, as Harvard theologian Harvey Cox observes, "want not only to 'keep the faith,' but to change the world so the faith can be kept more easily." In this regard, fundamentalists don't insist that everyone adopt their religious beliefs, though that would no doubt gratify them. Instead, they seek to impose social norms, or if necessary legal ones, that will make everyone behave like a fundamentalist. "We can't compel people to be Christians," a Maryland antiabortion activist explains, but "we can say we are under Christian law." American society used to impose such norms, fundamentalists believe, but progress and modernity have diverted the nation from its rightful course. *Secular humanism* comprises the changes that they lament: the new rules concerning sex (premarital sex, homosexuality, abortion, pornography) and gender (feminism), signs of laxity toward communism, the decline of Biblical morality, the acceptance of the theory of evolution, and the diminution of religion in public life.

Opposition to an overbearing secularism dates back a century. In his 1886 book *Our Country,* Congregational minister Josiah Strong decried the "perils of secularism" and argued that the "individual rights" of atheists must give way to "the necessities of the State." In 1948 the National Catholic Welfare Conference warned of "the impending danger of a judicial 'establishment of secularism' that would ban God from public life." Ten years later, Jesuit theologian John Courtney Murray wrote that "secularists" were seeking to "banish from the political order . . . all the 'divisive forces' of religion." In its 1962 editorial on *Engel v. Vitale,* the *New Republic* spoke of "the relatively recent phenomenon of a widespread secular humanism in the country which constitutes, as it were, a new religion of its own."

Starting in the 1970s, secular humanism became a target of schoolbook protests. In 1972, parents in Montgomery County, Maryland, charged that the schools were promoting secular humanism. After conducting a two-year investigation, the state board of education concluded that "secularity" in the classroom did not amount to a religion. In 1974, fundamentalist protesters in Kanawha County, West Virginia, claimed that local textbooks were spreading secular humanism. The schools agreed to let the protesters' children use different books. In 1976, the Heritage Foundation published an influential booklet called *Secular Humanism and the Schools: An Issue Whose Time Has Come,* which accused the schools of concentrating on students' values and attitudes to the neglect of skills and factual knowledge.

A major breakthrough came in 1980 with the publication of Tim LaHaye's *Battle for the Mind,* a book "dedicated to explaining humanism in simple terms, so that the man on the street can both understand its danger and be motivated to oppose it at the place it can be defeated —the ballot box." The book became a huge best-seller in Christian bookstores, and LaHaye sent 85,000 free copies to fundamentalist preachers. He later observed that his book just might have played a part in the Reagan landslide: "Only God himself knows what impact the book had on potentially millions of people as those principles were taught during August, September and October of the crucial election year of 1980."

According to LaHaye, secular humanism isn't merely a collection of disparate, unscriptural views; it is also a "militant religious system" engaged in a relentless battle against Christianity. "Humanists will never be content to let us exist," he writes. "They are going to destroy us and wipe the Christian church from the earth, if possible." The humanists, LaHaye contends, have a bible, the 1933 "Humanist Manifesto"; two supplementary scriptures, the 1973 "Humanist Manifesto II" and the 1980 "Secular Humanist Declaration"; and an official church, the American Humanist Association.

If LaHaye's conclusions are fanciful, his evidence is indisputable. In 1933, John Dewey and thirty-three others signed the "Humanist Manifesto," which refers to humanism as a religion. Forty years later, Isaac Asimov, Sidney Hook, B. F. Skinner, Betty Friedan, Gunnar Myrdal, and Andrei Sakharov, among others, signed "Humanist Manifesto II," partly because the first manifesto "did not go far enough." Asimov, Hook, Skinner, and others also signed the "Declaration" in 1980. These three statements embrace evolution, endorse euthanasia and the right to commit suicide, object to the "proreligious bias" in the media, advocate a "socialized and cooperative economic order," and "deplore the division of humankind on nationalistic grounds."

Created in 1941, the American Humanist Association has about 4,300 members. Its "Humanist of the Year" award has honored, among others, Carl Sagan, Kurt Vonnegut, R. Buckminster Fuller, Benjamin Spock, and Ted Turner. In his acceptance speech in 1990, Turner likened the concept that Jesus died for mankind's sins to the sacrifice of virgins. "Weird, man, I'm telling you," he said.

AHA also has a strident in-house magazine with a circulation of about 15,000. *The Humanist* features reviews (the critique of campus political correctness, *Illiberal Education,* is "reprehensible," and its author, Dinesh D'Souza, is "lizardly"), political commentary (in questioning Anita Hill, Senators Alan Simpson and Arlen Specter "behaved like the penis-wielding thugs they really are"), and first-person narratives ("I Was an Atheist in a Foxhole"). In a 1983 article, which fundamentalists excitedly quote as proof of humanism's true plans, John Dunphy declared that humanism must triumph over "the rotting corpse of Christianity" if "the family of humankind is to survive."

As LaHaye and others charge, secular humanism does resemble a religion in some respects. Like adherents of other faiths, humanists hold a comprehensive worldview that answers life's ultimate questions. They also claim that their answers are universally valid and superior to other views. True, humanists' answers lack any reference to the supernatural, a mainstay of more traditional faiths. Nevertheless, sociologist James Davison Hunter believes that secular humanism qualifies as a religion of sorts.

Even so, however, secular humanism doesn't amount to an especially influential religion. The Manifestos never reached a sizable audience. AHA's membership is minuscule, less than half the size of the American Latvian Association. The humanists are getting on in years too: The median age of "Humanist Manifesto II" signers was seventy-seven, and the humanist publisher Prometheus prominently features such "Golden Age Books" as *Eldercare, After the Stroke,* and *Understanding "Senility."*

In depicting humanism as a religion, fundamentalists have an ulterior motive. When they try to weave their ultimate values into law, they often are accused of breaching the First Amendment's wall between church and state. Courts sometimes nullify their legislative successes on that ground. But when secular humanists try to weave *their* ultimate values into law, they succeed. No one charges them with breaching the church-state wall.

Depicting secular humanism as a religion evens the score. "If it is illegal to teach Christianity in the public schools of our 'pluralistic' nation," argues LaHaye, "it should also be illegal to teach the doctrines of the religion of secular humanism." Just as creationism is barred from the classroom as a tenet of Christianity, evolution should be barred as a tenet of secular humanism. Jennie Wilson raised this argument before the Hawkins County school board when she asserted that "we cannot allow this series of books to teach religion contrary to the laws of our land."

While the Church Hill controversy was growing, fundamentalists in Alabama were claiming that public schoolbooks unconstitutionally established the religion of secular humanism. Chief Judge W. Brevard

Hand of the federal district court in Mobile concluded that secular humanism is indeed a religion and that the books at issue systematically promoted it; he prohibited the schools from using them.

In 1987, however, the federal appeals court in Atlanta overturned the Hand ruling. The appellate judges said that "we need not attempt" to decide whether secular humanism is a religion, because even if it is, the parents had not proved that the schoolbooks unconstitutionally established it. While noting that "the textbooks contain ideas that are consistent with secular humanism," the judges stressed that "mere consistency with religious tenets is insufficient to constitute unconstitutional advancement of religion." The First Amendment bars a state from erecting a Secular Humanism Cathedral but not from teaching evolution in the public schools—just as it bars a state from erecting a Christian Cathedral but not from enforcing "Thou shalt not kill" through the criminal laws.

In the 1980s, fundamentalists unearthed a second adversary: the New Age movement. While secular publishers were tapping the booming New Age market with books on reincarnation, crystals, channeling, and pyramids, religious publishers started turning out such titles as *Unholy Sacrifices of the New Age, Unmasking the New Age,* and *Secrets of the New Age: Satan's Plan for a One World Religion.* Pat Robertson warned that "New Age thought has successfully penetrated nearly every facet of our society" and that it offers "the same deception Adam and Eve succumbed to in the garden of Eden!"

New Age practices, fundamentalists charged, were infiltrating the classroom. Some schools were teaching meditation, "progressive relaxation," and hypnosis. To show the enormity of the peril, the Gablers published side-by-side excerpts of "Book X" and "Book Y." In similar terms, both books described an exercise in which the subject relaxes, breathes slowly and deeply, and pictures himself attaining his goals. Book X turns out to be a drug-education textbook for fifth-graders called *Discover Skills for Life.* Book Y is *The Complete Book of Witchcraft.*

From the fundamentalist perspective, New Age shares substantial ground with secular humanism. Both favor policies that the religious right despises, including environmentalism, feminism, abortion, disarmament, animal rights, and socialism. Both teach that there are no absolutes, that sin is illusory, and that mankind is the proper measure

of everything. Both deny God, at least the God of the fundamentalists.
To fundamentalists it is blasphemy to declare, as Shirley Maclaine did,
"I am God."

The enmity is mutual. Like humanists, New Agers view the religious right as an enemy—indeed, as a barrier to utopia. The religious
right "converts, manipulates or holds its followers with fear," the New
Age journal *Self-Help Update* cautions, and the "New Age of peace
and harmony cannot begin while people are controlled through fear."

Antipathy toward the religious right, however, is about all that
secular humanists and New Agers have in common. Whereas humanists believe that reason and science can answer everything, New Agers
believe that only faith and spirituality can render life fully meaningful.
Consequently, the two movements regularly take potshots at each
other. Critiques of New Age concepts appear in a journal called *Skeptical Inquirer*, whose parent organization was founded by the most prominent secular humanist, Paul Kurtz. (*Skeptical Inquirer* also runs
articles deriding fundamentalist "creation science," which tries to muster scientific evidence for creationism.) For their part, New Agers
denounce secular humanists as "professional skeptics and debunkers"
who are "prosaic rather than lyrical."

To New Agers, God is everywhere, and fundamentalists and hu-
manists are shackled to outmoded ways of thinking. To humanists,
God is nowhere, and New Agers and fundamentalists are irrational.
To fundamentalists, God is precisely where the Bible places him, and
New Agers and humanists are bound for hell.

Many fundamentalists believe that secular humanism and the New Age
movement are more than worldviews contrary to Christianity, and
more than religious faiths competing with Christianity for public support. They are conspiracies.

According to Tim LaHaye, whose books Jennie Wilson read, secular humanists control Hollywood, the television networks (network
executives "hate the Gospel of Jesus Christ"), most public schools
(public education is "exactly as [the humanists] planned it"), the news
media, and nearly all colleges and universities. In addition, some
275,000 "committed humanists" hold high positions in the federal
government. These secular humanists, collaborating with the Council
on Foreign Relations, the Trilateral Commission, the Rothschilds, and
the Illuminati—all longtime favorites of conspiracy theorists—are plot-

ting to merge the United States with "all other countries" and, in the process, "wipe the Christian church from the earth."

Constance Cumbey, whose radio talks impressed Wilson and Vicki Frost, contends that the New Age movement is paving the way for the Antichrist. Her certitude rests partly on a remark that a New Ager blurted out to her in an unguarded moment: "The antichrist is *not* the negative thing the Bible's made him out to be!" In Cumbey's view, the conspirators include the animal rights movement, the Guardian Angels, Montessori schools, and vegetarian restaurants.

Cumbey's Antichrist apprehensions rest on the Book of Revelation, which is a fertile ground for conspiracy theories. As interpreted by some fundamentalist authors, Revelation discloses that the final days are at hand. "For all those who trust in Jesus Christ," writes Hal Lindsey, "it is a time of electrifying excitement."

In his book *The Late Great Planet Earth,* which by some estimates was the number-one nonfiction best-seller of the 1970s, Lindsey construes Scripture to predict that all "true believers in Jesus Christ" will soon disappear from the earth, lifted to "a glorious place more beautiful, more awesome, than we can possibly comprehend." On earth, meanwhile, war-weary peoples will rally around an attractive, charismatic man who has miraculously survived a mortal-seeming head wound. This fellow—who is actually the Antichrist—will become world dictator, declare himself to be the one true god, and denounce Christianity. Midway into his seven-year reign, an Arab-African confederacy led by Egypt will invade Israel, igniting World War III. After horrific nuclear exchanges, the Antichrist's forces will face the Chinese. Then, on the eve of the final battle, Jesus will return to earth with the true Christians and, writes Lindsey, "prevent the annihilation of all mankind."

The Book of Revelation says that during the Antichrist's reign, no one will be allowed to buy or sell anything unless he bears the "beast's mark," which is identified as 666. In Lindsey's interpretation, the beast is the Antichrist; other writers believe the beast is the Antichrist's deputy, also known as the "false prophet." Whoever the beast is, the meaning of his "mark" fascinates fundamentalist authors. According to Pat Robertson, the mark is all around us: Social Security numbers, computers, and electronic fund transfers. As for 666, Robertson writes that six is the number of man, so 666 "may refer to the quintessential humanist." Another theorist assigned each letter of the alphabet to a sequential multiple of six ($A = 6$, $B = 12$), and discovered that "Kissinger" totals 666.

When an upside-down 666 was discovered in Procter & Gamble's logo in 1980, word spread that the company was fronting for the Church of Satan—that, indeed, the company's president had recently divulged the Satan connection on *Donahue, 60 Minutes,* or another program. By 1982, the company's toll-free consumer hotline was fielding 15,000 calls a month about the rumor. P&G removed the logo from some products, circulated a Jerry Falwell letter absolving it of any satanic connection, and hired former Attorney General Griffin Bell to sue people who were spreading the tale. Finally the corporation, while denying that the rumor had anything to do with it, redesigned its 140-year-old logo to eliminate the 666.

Although not all fundamentalists embrace the secular humanism and New Age plots—skeptics have included textbook critic Mel Gabler, writer Cal Thomas, and theologian Francis Schaeffer—many do seem to feel that, in Walter Lippmann's phrase, their lives are being "misshapen by the plucking of invisible hands." This attitude partly reflects what historian Richard Hofstadter termed "the paranoid style" of American politics: a worldview, often held by those at the extremes of the political spectrum, that postulates "a vast and sinister conspiracy, a gigantic and yet subtle machinery of influence set in motion to undermine and destroy a way of life." According to Hofstadter, political paranoia often arises when "fundamental fears and hatreds, rather than negotiable interests," enter the political sphere; such fears pulled fundamentalists back to politics in the late 1970s.

More important than the paranoid style, though, is fundamentalist theology. Fundamentalists believe in an omnipotent God. Everything results from God's plan, much of which is revealed in the Bible; there are no accidents. They also believe that evil exists, that they can recognize it, and that they see it all around them. To them, as historian George M. Marsden observes, "the world is divided between the forces of God and of Satan." Beverly LaHaye, the president of Concerned Women for America (and Tim LaHaye's wife), demonstrates this dualistic outlook: "The battle lines are becoming more clearly defined. The forces of darkness are becoming darker. There is no neutral ground in the battle to come."

The utterances about secular humanism and the New Age movement, with or without the conspiratorial overlays, didn't help the religious right achieve mainstream acceptance and support. Political writer Charles Krauthammer called the notions about humanism "paranoia" and "lunacy." A front-page *Los Angeles Times* article opened sarcastically: "Watch out, moral-minded, patriotic Americans. The humanists are out to get you!" In the 1980s as in the 1920s, fundamentalists' unorthodox beliefs invited ridicule.

What ultimately turned public opinion against the religious right, however, was not the humanism and New Age demonologies. It was fundamentalists' intolerance.

When fundamentalists had last taken the national stage, claims of absolute, monopolistic religious truth were commonplace. In Muncie, Indiana, in 1924, sociologists Robert and Helen Lynd asked high school students whether "Christianity is the one true religion and all peoples should be converted to it." Yes, said 94 percent. Such claims subsequently fell into disrepute. When the Lynds' question was asked again fifty years later, support for the statement had dropped to 38 percent. Two-thirds of respondents in a 1991 nationwide survey said that Christians, Jews, Muslims, and Buddhists "pray to the same God."

Instead of exclusive, fiercely denominational religious beliefs, many Americans now hold what sociologist Will Herberg termed "faith in faith." To them, religion, whatever its content, is redemptive—and intolerance, especially religious intolerance, is altogether intolerable.

This shift reflects elemental changes in the role of religion in the United States. Although 94 percent of Americans believe in God, and 84 percent think Jesus was the son of God, only four in ten know who delivered the Sermon on the Mount, or can name the first four Gospels or five of the Ten Commandments. When respondents are asked to rank various elements of their lives, religion falls low on the roster, after health, family, love, and friends. Trying to convey to American Christians how deeply Salman Rushdie's *Satanic Verses* had affronted the Islamic world, a Muslim professor compared the book to a sexually perverted portrayal of, not Jesus or Moses, but Martin Luther King.

Americans don't want preachers or anyone else telling them what to do. They want their faith to provide, in Herberg's words, "sanctification and dynamic for goals and values otherwise established"—a sort of freely given, all-purpose seal of approval. Theirs is a God of love, not of judgment; as historian Martin E. Marty notes, "Hell disappeared." Moral codes have come unmoored from religious absolutes. "Traditional concepts of right and wrong," pollster Daniel Yankelo-

vich writes, "have been replaced by norms of 'harmful' or 'harmless.' " Pastor Jim Fields of Hawkins County laments that people are
no longer willing to fight for their deepest beliefs. "Live and let live,"
he says ruefully. "You see that a great deal now."

Religion has also lost its prominence in public discourse. Having
caught a televised glimpse of professional football players praying after
a game, a *Sports Illustrated* columnist was aghast: "Sure, athletes are
entitled to freedom of religion like anybody else. But let them exercise
it on their own time." The *Washington Post* sometimes lists the contents
of its Saturday sports section as "HOCKEY / RACING / RELI-
GION."

With American religion substantially privatized, compartmental-
ized, and declawed, people stopped publicly proclaiming that their
faith was superior to others. In what sociologist John Murray Cuddihy
calls America's "religion of civility," a believer may embrace his own
god but not, explicitly or implicitly, deny the reality of anyone else's.
"The rule is," syndicated columnist "Miss Manners" writes, "that one
does not denigrate others' faith by declaring that what they believe is
not true."

As they re-entered politics, fundamentalists did try to adapt to the
changed environment. The Moral Majority attracted a number of Catholics, with its antiabortion stance; Jews, with its support for Israel; and
nonfundamentalist right-wingers, with its cultural conservatism. The
key, writes Beverly LaHaye, was to "agree to disagree on theology and
then work side-by-side for a common goal." This ecumenism was
something new for fundamentalists, and it incensed a few die-hards.
Bob Jones, Jr., the chancellor of Bob Jones University, condemned
Jerry Falwell as "the most dangerous man in America today as far as
Biblical Christianity is concerned."

Similarly, the religious right tried to cover its spiritual certitude
with a veneer of political humility. Gary Jarmin of the Christian Voice
said his organization wasn't "*the* Christian Voice," but merely one of
many (though "we certainly believe ours is the correct one"). In his
1988 presidential campaign, Pat Robertson insisted that he wasn't running as "God's candidate"; doing so would be "arrogant and unfair."
The high-profile preachers often framed their goals in moral rather
than religious terms. They were not, Tim LaHaye maintained, trying
"to make the American government Christian"; they were striving

only "to make it moral." Even on morality, Falwell tried to avoid giving offense. Although he thought the Moral Majority represented the beliefs of most Americans, he said he intended no reflection on "the morality of those who disagree with us."

All these were significant concessions, as sociologist Steve Bruce points out—but they didn't go far enough. Especially at first, the religious right repeatedly violated the new rules of religious civility. They injected exclusionary religion into politics by making such assertions as "send another Christian to Congress" and "the Christians have won." They implied, and sometimes stated outright, that they would apply a religious test to candidates for public office. And they hinted that no true Christian could differ with their political agenda.

The most damaging breach came in August 1980. At the Religious Roundtable's "National Affairs Briefing" in Dallas, the featured speakers included Jesse Helms, John Connally, and the Republican presidential nominee, Ronald Reagan—whose presence ensured that dozens of reporters would be on hand—as well as Robertson, Falwell, and Bailey Smith, an Oklahoma preacher who was the new president of the Southern Baptist Convention. In his speech, Smith noted that a political rally typically includes prayers by a Protestant, a Catholic, and a Jew. "With all due respect to those dear people," he continued, "my friends, God Almighty does not hear the prayer of a Jew. For how in the world can God hear the prayer of a man who says that Jesus Christ is not the true Messiah? It is blasphemy."

In the furor that followed, scarcely anyone noticed that Smith had accurately stated fundamentalist theology. Fundamentalists believe that Christianity is the one true faith and the only road to heaven. Using only slightly more delicate wording, Smith later said of Jews, "unless they repent and get born again, they are in trouble." TV evangelist James Robison unblushingly defended Smith's original remark. While it may seem "unkind, unfair, unloving, not even scriptural to say that those who reject Christ will spend eternity in Hell," Robison declared, "it's still God's truth."

Such statements doomed the religious right's political crusade. The problem wasn't theological; according to theologian John Hick, every major faith teaches that it holds the true answers to life's fundamental questions, and that the answers provided by other faiths are, to the degree that they differ, false. Rather, the problem was voicing the intolerant aspects of the theology. In the 1980s, no one could publicly say what Bailey Smith had said. Public life had no place for such uncivil religion.

With People for the American Way and other liberal groups energetically publicizing this intolerance, opinion solidified against the religious right. As early as the fall of 1980, a survey found that Americans had warmer feelings toward "people on welfare" than toward the Moral Majority; of the twenty-two groups listed, only "radical students" and "black militants" scored lower. This hostility soon extended to conservative Christians broadly. Voters of 1980 said they would be more likely to vote for a candidate if he identified himself as an evangelical; in 1987, they said they would be less likely to do so. A 1989 Gallup survey found that 3 percent of Americans wouldn't want to live next door to a Catholic; 5 percent wouldn't want to live beside a Jew; and 30 percent—nearly one in three—wouldn't want to live next to a fundamentalist. The only people less popular than fundamentalists were members of religious cults.

These attitudes took their toll. From a peak of $11.1 million in 1984, the Moral Majority's annual revenue fell to $3 million in 1988. Activists and donors had shifted to single-issue groups, such as the antiabortion Operation Rescue, or to local politics. In 1989, Falwell disbanded the organization.

The religious right stepped back from national politics, but not from politics overall. Activists concentrated on local and state issues, including school board elections, gay-rights referenda, and the like. They tried to avoid Falwell's missteps. "Jerry *was* the Moral Majority for the most part," says Beverly LaHaye of Concerned Women for America. "He spoke and that was it. CWA is very different from that. We have state leaders, state chapters, steering committees, almost a thousand prayer action chapters—an army of people out there working on local issues and state issues." Falwell's example offered another lesson too. "He took a lot of flak," says LaHaye. CWA may not get much press attention, she notes, "but I'm not sure I miss it. Leave us alone. Let us get the job done."

CHAPTER THREE

CITIZENS ORGANIZED

"Attacks on school systems often follow a specific pattern," Mary Anne Raywid wrote in her 1962 book *The Ax-Grinders: Critics of Our Public Schools*. First someone voices a complaint. Others, often spurred by unrelated grievances against the schools, join the protest. Together they demand action from the school board, or bombard newspapers with letters, or both. Then the protesters form an organization to probe the condition of local education. By this point the objections have mushroomed, Raywid wrote, "to include vague criticisms of 'progressive' education, warnings of subversion in schools, and protests against specific educational methods."

The Hawkins County protest of 1983 followed this pattern. Vicki Frost complained about *Riders on the Earth*, the sixth-grade Holt reader. She got support from other parents, some of whom nursed private grievances (one mother was angry because she believed a teacher had given her son an undeserved paddling). They petitioned the school board and started writing letters to the editor. Then, having failed to dislodge the Holt books, the parents expanded their mission. "We decided that we were going to become involved in public education," says Frost. "It was like we had just awakened."

The protesters depict the September school board meeting as the catalyst. As parents, taxpayers, and voters, they felt entitled to a respectful hearing. "They're supposed to sit there in service of the public, not to look down on me," says Frost. "They laughed and sneered and made fun of us," says Bob Mozert.

But the board members' arrogance wasn't the only stimulus. After the board's position had become clear at that meeting, Frost gravely told the members that "there will probably be other action on this, I hope you know." A few minutes later, a *Kingsport Times-News* reporter asked what she'd had in mind; she refused to elaborate. Issuing veiled threats to officials and flinging "no comments" to reporters—these were heady experiences for a self-described "homebody homemaker."

"We are 'dug in' by our faith, and we won't be rooted out," Frost told the Gablers. She added: "We can be just as stubborn as a mule when we know we are right and have the word of God to stand on."

Even so, Vicki Frost recognized her limitations. "A woman is not supposed to be seen or heard in public, hardly, in this area," she says. After the September board meeting, she and Jennie Wilson prayed, Wilson remembers, "that a man would come along to assume this responsibility." John Pendleton, the preacher who had acted as spokesman at the board meeting, had been a disappointment.

Then Bob Mozert, an insurance adjuster who had attended the meeting only as a concerned parent, volunteered to lead the group. A Florida native, Mozert had moved to Church Hill when his employer transferred him to Kingsport in the mid-1970s. Like Frost and Wilson, he had never taken a prominent role in public affairs.

Also like them, he was a born-again Christian. He had been saved at age twenty-four, newly returned from Army service in Vietnam. "I had been brought up in the Methodist church, sprinkled when I was about twelve years old—which the Methodists call baptism—but I did not have a heart knowledge of Jesus Christ. I had not personally met him," says Mozert, a compact man with silvery hair. "And that occurred at about eleven-thirty at night on June the thirteenth of 1971. Alice, my wife, was a Baptist. She was born in Speedwell, Tennessee —born dead, but they revived her—and she was saved when she was eleven years old. This particular night she asked me if I had been saved. I knew that I had not, and I said no. I always had a heart of stone, and I would never cry, because tears were a sign of weakness to a man. But when I finally realized I was not saved, I cried. I said, God, I need help! And as soon as I did, it was just like a ball of fire descended

from heaven, and I was completely engulfed and bathing in the love of
Jesus Christ. I never knew what it was before. And I felt the weight of
my sins, like a ton of bricks, fly right up off my chest." He pauses for
a moment, and then adds: "And I *know* that it wasn't post-combat
syndrome."

Mozert's faith differs from Frost's and Wilson's in one respect.
"Six months later, and I remember the exact date then also," he says,
"I received what the Bible calls a baptism in the holy spirit, with the
evidence of speaking in tongues. I received that in a restaurant. So I
was saved in my bedroom and filled with the holy spirit in a restaurant.
I don't really know what that makes me, other than a Christian."

To some fundamentalists, the charismatic or Pentecostal practice
of speaking in tongues is satanic, or at least unchristian. Larry Anderson, a Baptist preacher whose church the Frosts sometimes attended,
refused to involve himself in the textbook controversy because charismatics "preach, teach, believe, and practice false doctrine." In a letter
to one protester, Anderson wrote: "Maybe we are a bit too careless
about the crowd with which we run."

Frost and Wilson, however, weren't bothered by Mozert's different
beliefs and practices. "Every one of us agreed on the fundamental
doctrines of the faith," says Wilson. "Jesus Christ is divine, he was
virgin born, he was crucified, dead and buried, he arose the third day,
he's coming again in power and glory."

Besides being male and fundamentalist, the thirty-seven-year-old
Mozert had other attractive qualifications. He held a master's degree in
business and economics from Appalachian State University in Boone,
North Carolina, and he had credits toward a doctorate in education
from East Tennessee State University in Johnson City. Moreover, he
had taught for three years at Steed Business College in Kingsport,
though he had left to return to insurance adjustment.

These credentials set him apart. Of the fathers in the seven families
that ultimately sued and went to trial over the Holt readers, all but
Mozert worked in factories. "I had more education than the school
board members and most of the teachers," he says. "Not that I'm
anybody, you know, but I was in a position where I did know a little
bit about what I was talking about."

With his education and experience, Mozert speaks the secular language of law and policy more fluently than Frost or Wilson. "I'm
wise to the ways of the world," he says. Nevertheless, he shares their

distinctive worldview. In Dover, Delaware, where he moved in 1989, his receptionist's desk was piled high with copies of a flier in late 1991. "The *President of Procter and Gamble* appeared on the Phil Donahue show on March 1, 1991," the flier says. "He announced that due to the openness of our society, he was coming out of the closet about his association with the church of satan." It goes on to urge Christians to boycott all Procter & Gamble products, which can be identified by the telltale 666 on the label.

With Mozert on board, the protesters formed an organization. Mozert came up with the name, Citizens Organized for Better Schools, and he titled himself director of the group. Notwithstanding Mozert's role, however, Frost, Wilson, and the other women remained active and vocal. Mozert held a full-time job, whereas none of the women worked outside the home; they had more time to analyze textbooks, plan meetings, and write letters to the editor.

Consequently, COBS struck many Hawkins County residents as a women's movement—which, just as Frost had feared, offended local sensibilities. In early 1984, Carter's Valley Elementary principal Archie McMillan declared, "Why are these men letting themselves be egged on by their crazy wives? Why don't they stand up for what's right?" Larry Anderson, the preacher who disapproved of charismatics, also disapproved of female political activists: "Why are the women the predominant ones in the activity of this group? . . . Where are the husbands of these ladies?" Another local observer says that, with the possible exception of the Mozerts, "the women dominated" in all the families of the protesters.

COBS, the women's group with the male figurehead, aimed to put the public back in public education. "The *Public* should actively participate in the operation and regulation of *public* schools, both economically and politically," the organization declared in a newspaper advertisement published in late September. The concerns were much broader than the Holt books. COBS wanted the schools to teach "love of God and country," but not evolution, secular humanism, or "nihilistic fantasy." Schools should have "daily prayer or a moment of silent meditation." Apparently with reference to the skills-tracking software that Holt had given Hawkins County, COBS also declared that a student "should not be treated as a computerized statistic."

COBS announced that its first official meeting would be September

29, four weeks after the "emergency meeting." Notices posted at the laundromat and elsewhere urged parents to "bring your child's reader and any interested taxpayers. You will be able to quickly determine objectionable matter in the textbooks."

Whatever had brought a hundred people to the "emergency meeting"—curiosity, most likely—had evaporated. Only a dozen parents attended this meeting. Huddled together in the Carter's Valley Elementary cafeteria, they compiled a list of the failings of the Hawkins County schools. "Our children were not saying the Pledge of Allegiance—they had not said it in years in some classes," Frost remembers. "We thought, well, let's bring that to the school board's attention as a suggestion for improvement. So we wrote that down." Someone said that students on field trips shouldn't eat at places that serve alcohol. Someone else suggested that the schools needed a dress code. Despite the small turnout, the protesters were buoyant. "I thought, Jesus started with twelve disciples too," Mozert says, then adds hastily: "I'm not Jesus. Don't think this guy's off the wall."

Frost sent the Gablers another progress report. Along with "continuing our efforts to make the public aware of these deadly books," she wrote, the parents were now addressing "many issues" in public education. COBS, she added proudly, "is growing and beginning to accomplish much through the faithful work of our Lord."

Identifying himself as the head of Citizens Organized for Better Schools and a "parent advocate," Bob Mozert stood to address the school board at its October 13 meeting. Chairman Harold Silvers, remembering the lengthy presentations the previous month, asked Mozert to keep his remarks under ten minutes.

Some schools weren't beginning the day with a moment of silence or the Pledge of Allegiance, Mozert said, and the moment of silence was required by state law. Some classrooms had no American flags; others had obsolete forty-eight-star flags. Students were wearing inappropriate attire to school: strapless tops, cutoffs, "distracting jewelry," and T-shirts advertising "left-wing punk rock groups who advocate rebellion, riots, revolution and satanic religions." Finally, buses on field trips were stopping at stores and restaurants that sell alcohol.

In Frost's recollection, mention of the Pledge of Allegiance prompted Silvers to relate an anecdote. At a ball game recently, the young man in front of him was wearing a cap during the national anthem. Silvers told him to take it off. The command had no effect. So Silvers knocked the cap off his head. "He turned around to do something," Silvers recalled, "but I pulled out my persuader, and he backed off."

"You mean your hammer?" another board member said.

"No, I mean my *persuader*." Silvers motioned as if aiming a pistol.

("I don't know where they get all this crap," Silvers says now. He denies saying he pointed a gun at anyone, though he adds, "If somebody wouldn't take his cap off for the national anthem, I probably *would* do that.")

On the topic at hand, one board member questioned the wisdom of mandating the Pledge of Allegiance. "If it's not a law to do so, maybe we'd better think twice." Another board member was concerned that a dress code would infringe on students' rights. "We cannot legislate morality," he said.

Mozert couldn't let that pass. "We legislate laws against murder," he said. "We legislate laws against nudity. Our law books are full of laws against the immoral."

In the end, Silvers directed the superintendent to remind principals of the moment-of-silence law, and appointed a committee of three board members to study the other suggestions.

The COBS leaders considered the meeting a triumph. "Mr. Silvers seemed respectful and right receptible to what Mr. Mozert had to say," says Vicki Frost. "We weren't demanding that they do anything. We just had suggestions for them to look into, and they immediately acted upon the moment of silence. So we thought we were off to a good start."

The COBS activists hadn't forgotten the Holt books. Having gotten nowhere with the school board, they were trying to work out individual accommodations with principals. They began with James Salley at Church Hill Middle School.

The fifty-five-year-old Salley had spent nearly twenty-five years working as a teacher, coach, and principal in Hawkins County. "You will not find anyone in this town that dislikes him," says Volunteer High assistant principal Phyllis Gibson. "He is probably the most beloved figure here." Administrator Joe Drinnon calls Salley "the last of the kinder, gentler people." Salley was also known to be a worrier. "He took *everything* very serious," remembers Salley's assistant, Delmar Gillenwater. Carter's Valley Elementary principal Archie McMillan says, "Coach Salley, if you gave him one job, and that was to stand here and make sure that that door didn't fall off the hinges, he would experience some anxiety that there might be an earthquake come and make that door fall off."

A few days after the board's September meeting, Vicki and Roger Frost appeared in Salley's office. They would, they announced, begin removing their children from reading class every day in order to teach them out of a different textbook. Where did the principal want them to conduct their tutoring: in the cafeteria, the gym, the library?

"You can't do that," Salley said. He asked the Frosts to leave his office for a moment, and then phoned superintendent Bill Snodgrass. The two of them developed a plan. Snodgrass called Harold Silvers, the board chairman, to run it past him. Silvers said he had no objection.

Salley ushered the Frosts back in and presented his offer: The children could go to the library during reading period, where they would study from an older reading textbook on their own, without the parents as tutors. The Frosts delightedly accepted.

A few days later the Frost children brought home the alternatives the school had provided. Vicki judged Marty's book acceptable, but she felt that Rebecca's alternative had "similar thought patterns" to the Holt books. At her request, the teacher found a different reader, which met with Frost's approval.

Over the next few weeks, more parents requested alternative readers. To one parent, Salley said he understood the objections; after all, he was a Christian too. "Well, I haven't read the book," he told another parent, "but if it's what you say it is, I can understand why you feel the way you do."

By mid-October, ten middle school children were using older readers—in some cases, twenty-five years old. Some of the students stayed in the room and read the alternative readers silently while their classmates discussed the Holt books. Several went to the library. Rebecca Frost and Gina Marshall used a small office beside the classroom. Travis Mozert studied in the cafeteria while, he says, the "cafeterians" prepared lunch.

Being set apart bothered some of the students. "Anytime you are embarrassed if you have to go up in front of the room and do something different from everybody else," says Gina Marshall.

But others were untroubled. "It really didn't matter to me," says Brad Eaton. Marty Frost recalls only one comment from a classmate: A boy said, "Do what you can to get rid of these readers—I don't want to read 'em, either." Steve Whitaker says that doing something different from most classmates didn't bother him, because he had been brought up to be different. "I can't say that none of the other students in the class were Christians," he remembers, "but most of them really didn't care about it. They were wanting to go party, using foul language—wild, you might say. I'm not saying we were perfect little angels, but we were different. We were trying to lead a Christian life."

In a note to Salley, Vicki Frost praised the reader that Marty was now using. As she compared the book to the Holt books, she wrote, "I could not help but cry. How could we have come so far from basic truths, and love for God, country, and fellow men, to such reading materials as we have today?" She could conceive of only one explanation: "We've all been asleep and let the forces of evil overtake us." Frost closed on a hopeful note. "Thank you, Mr. Salley. I know that there will be problems to overcome as we go along, but we can work together in a spirit of respect and concern for the children."

The issue seemed to be resolved, to Salley's relief. "I really wanted to avoid trouble," he remembers, "and I wanted to grant the parents' request."

"He was trying to make everybody happy," says Volunteer High's Phyllis Gibson. "And that was his downfall."

Having persuaded the middle school to accommodate Marty and Rebecca, Vicki Frost turned her attention to her daughter Sarah's school, Church Hill Elementary. In a note, Frost declared that the second-grade Holt reader was full of "Humanism, distorted realism, self authority, Sun Worship, Occult symbols," and she asked that Sarah be given an alternative. Principal Jean Price responded that only the school board could grant such a request. She believed that the board, by adopting the Holt readers, had implicitly barred the use of any others.

Two weeks later, Frost sat down with Price and pointed out some of the sacrilege in the Holt readers. She also lent Price a copy of the Gablers' review of the previous edition of the readers. Price seemed sympathetic and respectful during the hour-long conversation. "She was the only school official that I had found that . . . wanted to find out what I was really thinking and what I found offensive," says Frost. "I trusted her."

In truth, Price was flabbergasted. "Anything that had come up, usually we could resolve it in a fashion that was agreeable with the parent and the school," she says. "But when Vicki began complaining about those stories, it just hit me like a bolt of lightning: I was dealing with something I wasn't going to be able to resolve. . . . When she talked about that book, it was really—help! I need some help!"

That night, Price and other school officials got their first outside help. For nearly two months, the school people and the protesters had been disagreeing about the meaning of the materials in the books. It was time, superintendent Bill Snodgrass said, for someone from Holt to explain "how they chose the literature that went into their books." Supervisor of instruction Joe Drinnon phoned and asked for a meeting. Holt executives in New York dispatched the supervising editor of the reading series, Barbara Theobald.

In a conclave at the Kingsport Holiday Inn, Theobald said, in the recollection of school people who attended, that the series "had to meet needs of all people," which meant that "it couldn't have been all men stories or all stories about women." She also emphasized that the stories were "established, accepted literature"; the editors hadn't "hauled off and written a lot of fresh literature." And she stressed that Holt had gone to great lengths "to insure that nothing controversial or anti-religious was in their material, because it would interfere with sales."

"We of course were in the dark," remembers principal Archie McMillan. "This was the first time any such controversy had occurred. When enough people tell you that the boogieman's in the corner, you start to look in the corner." Theobald's remarks, he says, reinforced what he had already suspected, that the protesters were "people losing some touch with reality."

A few days later, Frost again implored Jean Price to let Sarah use an alternative book. This time Price gave in slightly. Sarah wouldn't have to read the Holt book aloud in class, she decreed, but she would have to fill out the reading comprehension sheets.

Frost said she appreciated the compromise. By the way, she added nonchalantly, had Price given a copy of the Gabler report to the Holt editor at their "secret meeting"?

Price replied that she had given it to Snodgrass, who had indeed made a copy for the editor.

Frost responded enigmatically: "The Lord works in mysterious ways."

Meanwhile, Jennie Wilson had marched into the center of the textbook fray. Early that fall, Wilson had told her twenty-seven-year-old daughter, Rachel Baker, about the growing textbook controversy. At Wilson's urging, Baker drove from her home in nearby Bristol for the September 1 "emergency meeting."

Baker then examined the books that her second-grade daughter Heather was using in the Bristol public schools. After discovering references to magic in one of them, Baker spoke to Bristol's assistant superintendent of schools. "He asked me what humanism was, and he assured me that he wouldn't allow anything of that sort to go on, and that he was a Sunday School teacher," says Baker. "He thought my concerns were something humorous." Baker also spoke to her daughter's teacher, who "told me she was a Christian woman and she would never teach my child something contrary to the Scriptures."

Then in early October, Rachel Baker, her husband James, and their two children moved to Church Hill. By some accounts, they relocated only because Jennie Wilson wanted them to take a role in the blossoming controversy, an allegation that the family members deny. Rachel Baker says they moved for "convenience." "I had a desire to move," says James Baker, "but at that time we did not know where."

"To be perfectly frank they were having difficulty with his mother," says Wilson. "They lived on her place and there were some in-law disagreements." She says she would have preferred to have the Baker children enroll in a Christian school, but James Baker was against the idea, so she let the matter drop. "If you don't have a mother-in-law," she says, "you don't understand how we have to tip-toe."

Whatever brought the Bakers to Church Hill, second-grader Heather and first-grader Vicky Baker enrolled at Carter's Valley Elementary in early October. Within a few days, the school began receiving requests for special treatment. An October 14 letter, written by Rachel Baker but signed by her husband, asked the principal to give Heather another reader. (Vicky hadn't yet been issued a reader at all.) "If you cannot provide acceptable reading material," Rachel added, "we can." She had in mind the original 1830s *McGuffey's Readers,* which had been reprinted by Bob Jones University Press; the Wilsons had purchased a set.

Then, before principal Archie McMillan had replied to that request, Jennie Wilson appeared at school. She wanted to ensure that her granddaughter Vicky was being taught to read with phonics, and not with the alternative method, whole-word sight-reading. The prolific Tim LaHaye once suggested that sight-reading is part of a plot to "lower the literacy level in the western countries, particularly America, and raise it in the Soviet Union," with the ultimate goal of merging the two nations into "a one-world socialist state." Along with her familiarity with LaHaye's writings, Wilson had firsthand experience with the two teaching methods. Trained with phonics, her daughter Rachel became "such a good reader," Wilson says; but her son—"he is not saved," she specifies, "but he does have a Judeo-Christian foundation" —learned to read via sight-reading, "and it's just a real good thing that he has a secretary, because he scarcely can spell his name."

So Wilson strode into her granddaughter's classroom. She was there, she told the startled teacher, to observe quietly, consistent with the school district's policy of welcoming family members. The teacher said she wasn't familiar with that policy, but she let Wilson stay.

The room was a "madhouse" with the children "going around there like bees," says Wilson. "I found out later that's the way humanism is. Everybody does what's right in their own sight. Everybody does what makes them feel good." The children, Vicky included, were brazenly ignoring the teacher. This too was a manifestation of humanism: "The secular humanists say, if you learn it, you learn it, and if you don't, you get your diploma anyway, whether you can read and write or not."

After the children went outside for recess, Wilson remained in the classroom and helped sort papers. The teacher left. A few minutes later, principal McMillan appeared and asked Wilson to follow him.

"You just don't know how embarrassing this is for a grandmother," Wilson says, "but I got expelled from school." The teachers viewed Wilson and COBS as a "threat," she says McMillan told her, so she would have to leave the campus and stay away. In Wilson's recollection, McMillan added: "Mrs. Wilson, these children belong to us." "I beg your pardon, Mr. McMillan," she said indignantly. "You don't own Heather and Vicky."

McMillan's recollection differs. He says the only problem was that Wilson didn't stop by the office before going into the classroom. "I just told Mrs. Wilson if she wanted to come by and do an observation, then she needed to stop by the office and let me make the teacher aware that she was going to come." Wilson's unannounced arrival in the classroom, he says, was "intimidating to the teacher."

At home, Wilson sat down at her typewriter and wrote to the school board. Declaring herself "appalled" by her expulsion from Carter's Valley Elementary, she asked the board to clarify its policy on classroom visitors. Focusing her ire on McMillan, she praised the teacher as "efficient" and the class as "well-disciplined."

A few days later, Rachel Baker sent another note asking the school to give Heather a different reader. She and her husband worked during the day, Baker wrote, so "if you have any questions, Mr. and Mrs. Wilson are capable of answering them in our stead."

After reading the letter, McMillan phoned Jennie Wilson. The school lacked the space and the personnel to provide special classes, he said. Heather would simply have to read the Holt books.

In her recollection, Wilson said she would provide a different reading book and tutor Heather at school every day.

That wouldn't be possible, McMillan said.

Well, she said, could she take Heather off campus and tutor her elsewhere during reading class?

No.

As a last resort, Wilson suggested that Heather skip reading class and take a failing grade in the subject. She had in mind the board member's remark that children who refused to read the Holt books would get an F in reading.

McMillan again refused. "She's got to read this book," he declared.

"No, she's not either," Wilson insisted.

Even as Wilson was laying out all these options, she and her daughter didn't expect McMillan to accept any of them. Rachel Baker says, "I figured either Mr. McMillan would make her read the book or would ask us to take her out."

In Wilson's account, that's what happened: "Come and pick her up," McMillan snapped, "and have her educated elsewhere."

Wilson dispatched her husband Marion to Carter's Valley Elementary ("I had already been expelled from school," she says, "so I couldn't go"). He found both Baker children waiting in the office with their school supplies: second-grader Heather, whose class was reading the Holt books, and first-grader Vicky, whose class hadn't yet been issued textbooks.

"I says, how come?" remembers Marion Wilson. "Vicky can't even read. He said, Yeah, but next year she'll have to read the same book, and we'll have the same hassle." Then, in Marion Wilson's recollection, McMillan uttered a threat: "You've got five days to have her registered in a school or I'll have the sheriff knock on your door."

McMillan disputes this account. "I said that if the materials are objectionable to you, there just is no alternatives. You need to take them somewhere where they've got textbook materials that are not objectionable to you. So they withdrew the kids. . . . I've never kicked anyone out of school in twenty-three years."

With financial help from the Wilsons, the Baker children enrolled in a Christian school. A few days later, the Bakers received a certified-mail letter from McMillan. "Until such time that the Hawkins County Board of Education directs us to use another reading series, all children attending Carter's Valley School will be taught reading from the Holt, Rinehart and Winston series," the principal wrote. "Because of this, Mr. and Mrs. Marion Wilson have elected to remove your children from our school. Since you have informed me in writing that they are your representatives, I hope this meets with your approval." He closed, "Have a Good Day."

A request for alternatives was also raised at one other school in Hawkins County. A woman named Sandra Couch worried that the Holt books would harm her third-grade son, and she conveyed her fears to Mount Carmel Elementary principal Quentin Dykes.

Dykes at first tried to brush her off. "Well, I wouldn't worry about it if I were you," he said. "You just teach them what's right at home and love them real good."

Couch pressed the matter. She wanted Sam to be excused from the room while several stories were being read and discussed.

Dykes reluctantly agreed. When the class reached each of those stories, Sam left the room and sat in the hallway.

So, by the end of October, Church Hill Middle School was letting ten students out of every reading class and providing an alternative textbook. Mount Carmel Elementary was letting one student out of a small number of classes, but not providing an alternative. And Church Hill Elementary and Carter's Valley Elementary had refused to budge.

As parents and grandparents tried to negotiate individual accommodations, COBS and its members continued to agitate publicly about the Holt books and other educational issues.

About fifty people attended a late October COBS meeting, quadruple the turnout of the previous one. Mozert told the audience about his appearance before the school board. Then he dimmed the lights and showed *Let Their Eyes Be Opened*, a half-hour Christian Broadcasting Network film that Mozert had gotten through a church friend. In the film, the avowed secular humanist Paul Kurtz declares that people should "pursue their sexual inclination as they see fit," that no evidence supports a belief in life after death, and that euthanasia simply means "a good death." To illustrate Kurtz's views, the film shows an unconscious boy with a syringe hanging from his arm, a leering Hugh Hefner, prostitutes, and fetuses in a trashcan.

When the film ended, COBS leaders addressed more immediate concerns. Mozert told the group that their taxes were being used to buy library books filled with profanity, including Erich Segal's *Oliver's Story*. A mother at the meeting told Mozert that her ninth-grade daughter had checked out of a school library Norma Fox Mazer's novel *Up in Seth's Room*, in which a fifteen-year-old girl reluctantly has sex with her boyfriend. Frost read aloud from the Gablers' review of the 1980 Holt series, and passed out copies of the Gabler instruction sheet "How Should Objections Be Made to Textbooks?"

As part of their campaign against the Holt readers, Frost and her allies were also trying to attract outside help. Frost informed the National Rifle Association that the Holt books promoted gun control. At the organization's request, she sent photocopies of the offending stories. Then, when an NRA staff member called and said the materials had never reached Washington, Frost sent a second set. The NRA never replied. Wounded, Frost wrote the organization again: "I did not ask for financial support or require any action that would cause the non-repliance of my letters. . . . Pro-gun control taught to America's children for one generation will help bring the fall of America's society as we know it." Once again, the NRA didn't reply.

Frost shared her concerns with Tennessee Governor Lamar Alexander too. "Our Basic readers," she wrote, "should be to 'lift up' the child in a positive direction—to encourage love of God, Country, and family. Instead, some of our children are becoming afraid—fear of being Alone—the things in these books scare them. . . . We will not let our children be indoctrinated in this satanic-Communistic theology —even if they never receive any basic reading skills from the state." Once again undermining her claim that COBS never set out to ban books, she urged that the Holt readers "must be taken off the State approved list."

Jennie Wilson also wrote to the governor and requested answers to three questions. Observing that the Alexander administration was trying to improve public education in Tennessee, she asked: "If they have pigs' ears like this material to teach, do you honestly think the most capable teacher in the nation can make a silk purse out of it?" Concerning some principals' unwillingness to excuse students from the Holt readers, she wondered: "Does the state of Tennessee now own our children as in the USSR?" And finally: "As a professing Christian will you please give me an answer I can give to Almighty God as I attempt to explain to Him why I allow my tax dollars to be spent on this kind of anti-christ propaganda?"

COBS had no officers other than "director" Bob Mozert, no structure, no dues, and no membership roster. Vicki Frost later said that the only people who were indisputably members were the founding families—the Mozerts, the Wilsons, and the Frosts. Other anti-Holt parents attended meetings without considering themselves part of the organization. "We weren't no members of COBS," says one father. "We were just parents."

Frost, Mozert, and Wilson agreed on the centerpiece of their anti-Holt strategy. "We intend to organize and inform the public about what's going on and let the public 'outcry' take these books out— through public pressure," as Frost had told the Gablers. In doing so, though, the three leaders of the unregimented COBS went their own ways.

In a *Kingsport Times-News* op-ed article, Mozert laid out the humanist plot in detail. "How did humanism get its widespread acceptance in the educational establishment? John Dewey, who is known as the father of progressive education, was a signatory of the Humanist Manifesto I in 1933. Mr. Dewey is quoted as saying, 'There is no God and there is no soul. Hence, there are no needs for the props of traditional religion.' " Next, "to eliminate the antithesis of coincidence," Mozert quoted John Dunphy's infamous *Humanist* article: "The battle for mankind's future must be waged and won in the public school classroom by teachers who correctly perceive their faith as the proselytizer of a new faith, a religion of humanity." After citing several examples of "humanistic dogma" in the Holt books, Mozert closed by inviting readers to send COBS one dollar for a copy of the Gablers' brochure *Humanism in Textbooks*.

In a series of published letters to the editor, Mozert critiqued individual volumes in the reading series. (Playing up his credentials, he usually included "M.A." after his name.) Not only did the eighth-grade reader, *Great Waves Breaking*, promote situational ethics, he charged in one letter; the plots were woefully implausible too. "How realistic is it that two presumably eighth graders would attempt a dangerous underwater venture without the aid of scuba gear and wearing heavy clothing, particularly when one of them could not even swim? And doesn't it strike you rather odd that all five characters in this story are depicted as being of the black ethnic group?"

Vicki Frost also wrote several letters to the editor. She faulted the Holt books for their "lessons in rebellion, self-authority, situational ethics, distorted realism, magic, occult symbols, and scary artwork." COBS leaders, she noted, had consulted "the nationally used *Gabler Textbook Evaluation*" of the Holt books. "Twenty years of objective reviewing have earned this textbook research center the admiration of the most critical publishers." The protesters weren't censors, she stressed: "COBS is against censorship! That's one reason we oppose these readers. Traditional values have been censored out, leaving the teachings of humanistic philosophies."

Jennie Wilson, who had begun carrying a zippered satchel full of literature about secular humanism, articulated more extravagant arguments. First she told a reporter that the Holt books were only the tip of the iceberg; the books represented, the reporter wrote, "a widespread secular humanist attitude that prevails in the teaching of all subjects in Hawkins County, ranging from art to mathematics." Neither Frost nor Mozert had publicly criticized any non-Holt textbook or the style of teaching in the schools. In a letter to the editor, Wilson suggested that the lack of moral absolutes in the schoolbooks had induced "the vast majority" of high school students to practice "fornication." The newspaper chastely edited out this passage.

Wilson also produced a seething, murky letter to the editor (signed with her husband's name). After suggesting that the Holt books were responsible for "the lack of rain this summer," she linked the "atheistic" doctrine of Darwinian evolution to "murder [of] the unborn in burning saline solutions to appease the god of lust and pleasure." The Equal Rights Amendment had been defeated, she continued, but "now antichrist fills our little ones' textbooks full of ERA propaganda." She closed by referring to the mark of the beast: "The antichrist system is here in Hawkins County. $60,000 was spent on these ungodly books and $60,000 was spent on the computer to speak to the children, teachers and parents. . . . That's too many sixes for me. We'd better wake up—our Redemption is near! Even so, come Lord Jesus!"

In their effort to foment public pressure against the books, the protesters inundated local newspapers with columns, news releases, and letters to the editor. The Rogersville and Kingsport papers published more than twenty-five COBS writings between late September and late November, an average of three a week.

The most consequential letter, signed by Mozert, objected to several stories in the reader *Rhymes and Tales*. In one story, a little boy cooks. Consequently, "the religion of John Dewey is planted . . . that there is no God-given roles for the different sexes." In Holt's version of the "Three Little Pigs," the wolf gets burned even though he didn't harm the pigs; "there is punishment meted out but no crime was perpetrated." In a version of "Goldilocks," authentic crimes go unpunished: After Goldilocks trespasses and uses the bears' property, the bears peaceably bid her farewell instead of frightening her. This tale will "frustrate and confuse the first grader, thereby 'preaching' secular humanism to impressionable minds."

A few weeks after the letter appeared, Mozert voiced second thoughts. He told a reporter that there was "much more material in the book that is obvious and blatant," and he was worried that the "very subtle" points in the letter might be "used to discredit" COBS.

Still later, Mozert denied having written the letter, and Jennie Wilson admitted that it was her handiwork. Some newspapers had a policy of publishing only one letter per month from a person, and one of hers had already appeared, so she had used Mozert's name. When she read the letter to him in advance, Mozert listened closely for attacks on local authorities. "There's a Scripture that says that we should not speak evil of the leaders of the people," he says, "and I made sure that we did not." Hearing nothing like that, he said the letter sounded fine, though he may not have realized that she planned to affix his name to it. Afterward he told Wilson not to sign his name to anything else.

Mozert's concerns were well placed. A short time after the "Goldilocks" letter appeared, the *Rogersville Review* published the first anti-COBS letter to the editor. "Secular humanism," wrote Archie McMillan, the Carter's Valley principal. "Nihilistic fantasy. Thought control. Distorted realism. Things That Go Bump In The Night. Ideas to strike fear in the hearts of parents. Ideas which 'COBS' can strangely connect with such Satan-oriented stories as 'The Three Little Pigs' and 'Goldilocks.' "

McMillan's sardonic letter was only the beginning. In the months and years to come, the allegations in the "Goldilocks" letter were to haunt the protesters. Increasingly over time, their opponents would ridicule rather than debate them, and the complaints about fairy tales would provide potent ammunition. To defuse such attacks, the protesters ultimately stopped mentioning the earliest volumes. The lawsuit they filed charged that the second- through eighth-grade readers violated their religious beliefs, but not the kindergarten or first-grade ones. Even so, the protesters never managed to live down the allegation that they had discerned sacrilege in "Goldilocks."

Having worked to create a respectable, influential organization, Mozert was dejected by Wilson's letter. Looking back on it, he says, choosing his words with care: "She is a zealous person, and I respect that zeal. I think sometimes our zeal can get before our wisdom. Things that we say or do have repercussions."

Wilson, while conceding that the letter was ill-advised public relations—"I'm the one that got 'em all in trouble"—continues to defend it on the merits. Holt's "secular humanist version" of "Goldilocks," in which the bears treat Goldilocks hospitably, is, she insists, "*completely* contrary to the traditional story."

As Archie McMillan's letter to the editor illustrates, school authorities were losing whatever patience they'd had. They had concluded that the complaints about the Holt books were groundless. Superintendent Bill Snodgrass—a "very religious" man, according to his colleague Joe Drinnon—asked his pastor to examine some of the readers. "He said he saw nothing wrong with the books," reports Snodgrass. Board members Conley Bailey and Doug Cloud also had pastors look at the books. Cloud recalls that his pastor "thought it was a fantastic book as far as kids using their mind to reason." Administrators were consulting other authorities too. "My mother was well studied and very religious, and she said you're doing the right thing," says Drinnon. "She'd examined through the newspapers what we were doing, and she was kind of watching over me."

Drinnon was also seeking a context for the complaints. He got the "Humanist Manifesto" and read it. He talked with administrators in Kanawha County, West Virginia, about a textbook conflict there in

1974. Later he heard that Jennie Wilson had checked out from the library *Poisoned Ivy*, Benjamin Hart's account of his years at Dartmouth College and his role in founding the conservative *Dartmouth Review*. "You know *God and Man at Yale?*" says Drinnon. "This was kind of an easier-reading version of that." So Drinnon checked it out and read it. "Many other things," he says. "Everything I could get my hands on. I was having to get a whole frame of mind, because they were making outlaws out of us. Evil, unmoral, causing the kids to be rebellious."

The ruckus was particularly hard on middle school principal James Salley. On November 10, Frost asked him if, as she had heard, he was refusing to grant alternatives to some parents. No, he said, that wasn't true. Poking her in the arm, he added, "You tell that jaybird I didn't say that." Later that day Salley phoned Frost to apologize for his rudeness. He explained, in Frost's recollection, "I've got so much pressure on me I'm doing well just to be here." A few hours after he spoke, the school board would take action to put pressure on the protesters, action that would also put more pressure on James Salley.

At the school board meeting that night, Bob Mozert gave the board members copies of letters from three concerned parents. The members put the letters aside, and nothing was said about them at the time.

Addressing the board, Mozert made several points. School libraries contained inappropriate novels, including such "pornography" as *Oliver's Story*. Volunteer High's sex education class "contradicts the traditional values and mores already established in our area"; at a minimum, the boys and girls ought to be separated. The parents didn't oppose sex education, he emphasized; they opposed sex *indoctrination*. In addition, he had done some legal research and determined that schools may impose reasonable dress codes without infringing on students' constitutional rights, a matter that had concerned some board members the last time. Finally, one elementary school had a plaque with the pre-1954 version of the Pledge of Allegiance, omitting the words "under God." He asked that it be replaced.

With Mozert's presentation complete, Vicki Frost stood up. She too was concerned about library books. The young adult novel *Up in Seth's Room*, she said, is nothing but pornography.

Harold Silvers asked her to repeat the name of the book; "I sure want to read it!"

When the laughter died down, Frost told the board that COBS, "a local citizens' group involved with the education in Hawkins County," was holding regular meetings, and she thought school board members ought to attend.

That was too much for Conley Bailey, who declared that COBS was "just four or five of you who are stirring up people" and "giving the county bad publicity." He told Frost not to invite him to any COBS meetings, "because I'm not interested." Bailey's face reddened as he spoke. As several teachers in the audience loudly applauded Bailey's remarks, Silvers announced a recess.

When the board reconvened a few minutes later, Jennie Wilson told of her granddaughters' expulsion from Carter's Valley Elementary. Was it official policy, she wondered, to expel children whose parents complained about books?

One school official replied that the principal had explained the Holt-only policy to Wilson in writing.

Yes, Wilson said, in a letter sent *after* the expulsion.

Rachel Baker, Wilson's daughter and the mother of the girls, spoke up. She complained about the expulsion, and added that, though she was not a COBS member, she disliked the Holt books. The books said that dinosaurs were extinct before man walked the earth, she noted, whereas scientists have actually discovered human and dinosaur bones mingled together.

Why, Frost asked, had Carter's Valley Elementary forced the Baker children to read the Holt books when Church Hill Middle School was letting children use alternative readers?

Because, administrator Joe Drinnon replied, the middle school accommodations hadn't done any good. Parents whose children were using alternative books had continued to "evangelize" against the Holt books.

This alternative program was news to one board member, and he didn't like the sound of it. Who, Bob McKee asked, had authorized the middle school to use different textbooks?

They were just supplemental texts, superintendent Bill Snodgrass replied, so board approval was unnecessary.

McKee let the matter drop, but he remained out of sorts. The requisite lines of authority had been disregarded.

A third-grade teacher, Martha Snelson, raved about the Holt books. "This series teaches some thinking skills that have been missing in other series. I think it's one of the best programs—and the children's grades are up."

Board chairman Silvers agreed. He had looked at one of the Holt books, he said, and "I couldn't find any of these alleged things in there. To me, it was a good book. . . . It would increase a child's mind."

The board moved to other matters: a Red Cross student program, typewriter bids, authorization to buy a cotton-candy machine. Frost, Baker, and the *Kingsport Times-News* reporter left. Mozert and Wilson remained.

In Wilson's recollection, McKee put his head down on the table and closed his eyes while other members talked. Then, abruptly, he sat up and blurted, "I don't like her kids using an alternate textbook." He seemed to be referring to Frost, who had left. Pointing at Snodgrass, he said, "You tell all the teachers tomorrow that the only textbooks that are going to be approved by the board are those adopted by the state, and they will be the usual textbooks used in Hawkins County."

Once again, chairman Silvers called a recess. The board members left the room, evidently to confer in private.

When they returned a few minutes later, McKee formally moved that Hawkins County schools use only the Holt readers, in order "to protect the teacher" from unnecessary "lesson plans and grading and teaching." Larry Elkins seconded the motion.

Without warning, the board was suppressing the accommodations. How, Mozert asked in consternation, could the board strike the alternative texts in the blink of an eye, and yet claim that his month-old Pledge of Allegiance request needed further study?

No one answered. Instead the men voted unanimously to instruct teachers to "use only textbooks adopted by the board of education as regular classroom textbooks," except in the case of "special educational needs." The protesters' children would have to read the Holt books, or else leave the school system.

The protesting parents "stepped in the manure right from the start and they never did get it off," says Jim Fields. A Church Hill resident who is pastor of a Kingsport church, Fields talked frequently with people on both sides of the textbook dispute. The protesters trusted him as a fundamentalist preacher who detested the Holt readers ("I don't know

if you could roast a weenie if you built a fire with 'em," he says),
though he never attended a COBS meeting or directly involved himself
in the controversy. School officials trusted him as a longtime resident
and a fellow educator (his church ran a private school). Fields recalls
that he and instruction supervisor Joe Drinnon "would sit around the
country store, sometimes three or four hours," and talk about the
schoolbook controversy.

To begin with, says Fields, the acronym COBS didn't exactly in-
spire respect. "That really was a point of ridicule. . . . Anybody that
ever got out of *Ned's Reader* would know better than that." Then, he
continues, the protesters didn't know the first thing about how to
approach elected officials. "They thought that people ought to do
things strictly on a right and wrong basis. Well, that ain't how the
game is played. . . . They should've gone down and met one of these
fellows at the country store, got acquainted, had a cup of coffee, talked
a while, and then said, Hey, Charlie, I think we got a problem. . . .
But when you come with a frontal assault, he's going to dig in his heels
—that's a mountain man's first reaction."

Had the protesters taken the country-store approach, they might
have learned about a treasured project of some school administrators.
In 1957, the county had operated fifty-five elementary schools, thirty-
eight of which had only one or two teachers. Some of the schools
couldn't be reached by car, recalls Guy Tilley, a pastor who taught
Bible classes in the schools. "You'd have to walk through a pasture to
get there." In a report issued in 1957, the Tennessee Department of
Education concluded that "schools with fewer than eight teachers are
inferior" to larger schools. Thereafter, Hawkins County (and the rest
of the state) shut down one-room schools and routed students to larger,
centralized facilities. The fifty-five elementary schools of 1957 dwin-
dled to eleven by 1983.

Having consolidated students, administrators now wanted to con-
solidate the curriculum. "We had every old textbook in the world,"
says Drinnon. "There wasn't anything consistent. You couldn't evaluate because you couldn't tell from one school to the other what was
going on. We didn't have a central curriculum that was elaborate
enough to measure against. So we met and agreed that we would be
patient and as a new textbook came through we would adopt uni-
formly. . . . It was a whole new era, with a very systematic approach to
teaching and monitoring and evaluating." Combined with the uniform

readers, the Holt software provided a way to track students' progress. Every six weeks, Drinnon would visit each school, examine the computer printouts, and look for problems.

"I wanted to improve these reading scores, and I wanted to have a systematic way of evaluating," Drinnon says. With the COBS attacks on the Holt readers, "I saw that all falling apart, or the potential for that to happen. And, looking back, maybe that was what made us want to be so aggressive. See, they were going to tear up something, not because they were mad at it, but because they were blundering into it."

In addition, COBS, with its ever-mutating agenda, seemed poised to become a long-term irritant to the school board. Two weeks after the protesters first appeared at a board meeting, Mozert sent a letter asking superintendent Snodgrass for the school's most recent fiscal report, an explanation of how tax monies were allocated among the county schools, and the school system's academic ranking among Tennessee counties. The following month he mailed more requests to Snodgrass and board chairman Silvers. In these letters Mozert employed an imperious tone, never saying please or explaining why he wanted the information.

From the viewpoint of Silvers and his fellow board members, a handful of disgruntled strangers had materialized and leveled obscure, sometimes absurd accusations against seemingly ordinary textbooks. Then they had demanded all sorts of internal information. Then they had griped about forty-eight-star flags, dress codes, and library books. "We had all kinds of problems at the time," board member Larry Elkins recalls. "Funding education, overcrowding at some of the schools, things of that nature. And they were worried that, out of nineteen schools, one classroom had an old flag."

School people concluded that the protesters were simply out to make trouble, and that the Holt books happened to be the primary vehicle. "Instead of defending Holt, if we could've all snapped our fingers and went to the Economy series, and that would've appeased it, we would have done it," says Carter's Valley Elementary principal Archie McMillan. "But that wasn't what the problem was. It wouldn't have made any difference." "Every time you'd do one thing, they'd want something else," remembers Silvers. "All they were looking for was publicity."

The board members had reason to expect positive consequences from their Holt-only resolution. "We had to do something to draw it to a head, and that served the function," says Silvers. If the protesters took their children out of the school system, the problems would disappear. If the protesters filed suit, the problems would shift into court. "There was no need of hashing and rehashing something that the court's going to have to settle anyway," Silvers adds.

Either way, the protesters would learn who was in charge. "You reach a point where it's not constructive criticism," says Silvers. "Next thing you're going to tell us how to run our bus routes, how to spend our money—so we just all of a sudden said, Well, this is it." Nat Coleman, an attorney who represented the school board, says that the board members felt they had to convey a message: *"We're* running this school board, not you, Vicki Frost."

If the protesters had stopped pestering the board, the middle school alternatives probably would have continued indefinitely. "After a while," says Coleman, "the kids would've said, We're lonely over here by ourselves, we want to be with the rest of the kids, we feel different. It would've been all over within a few months or less." "If a person has religious beliefs, and we've got an alternate book," says Silvers, "why, let them use it."

The protesters' maladroit tactics don't excuse the board's peremptory action. Dealing with pesky supplicants is part of the job for every elected official. But those tactics do help explain the board's action. It's an explanation, moreover, that has nothing to do with the merits of allowing alternative textbooks. The board members didn't know how children and teachers were coping with the alternative reading books at the middle school. In fact, they knew scarcely anything about the accommodation except that it was being undertaken to oblige COBS. The board members enacted the Holt-only policy, not because alternative readers were unreasonable—the argument they would later advance in court—but because the protesters were unreasonable.

The protesters perceived the board's action more ominously. "I believe this was a planned offensive against a minority of people who held different views," says Jennie Wilson. "Though we were taxpayers, we were not represented in the textbooks, and you know as well as I that taxation without representation is tyranny. I think this was the beginning of a tyrannical reign."

Looking back on the board's action, Frost and Wilson sound almost like Marxists discoursing on the class struggle. Hawkins County's rulers had no interest in the textbooks, says Frost; they cared only about "stopping this rebellion from the little people" who were "threatening the power structure and the corruption." "The people are intimidated by the powers that be," Wilson asserts. "They can't stand alone against the power structure. It's just depressing." Frost and Wilson, like their adversaries, believed that the textbook controversy wasn't about religion at all; it was about power.

From the protesters' perspective, meek petitions for redress had gotten them nowhere. It was time to try civil disobedience.

For the first time ever, Vicki Frost told her children to disobey their teachers: Marty and Rebecca were not to read the Holt books. So that the teachers would understand that the children weren't being "rebellious," but were merely minding their mother, Frost went to Church Hill Middle School to explain.

Vice principal Delmar Gillenwater (principal James Salley was out for the day) refused to call the teachers to the office. There was no point, in his view; every child was going to read the Holt books. "You'll have to take your kids out of school," he told Frost.

"No, I won't," she replied.

On her own, Frost tracked down Dee Smith, Marty's teacher. The children had "absolutely no will in the matter," Frost said, and their refusal to read the books was entirely her doing.

Smith said she appreciated the explanation.

If Marty got into "a situation that you feel like that he needs my help or my decisionmaking," Frost asked, would Smith let him phone home?

She'd be glad to, the teacher said.

Frost next located Carol Williams, Rebecca's teacher, and started to give her the same message. Before she could finish, Gillenwater walked up and interrupted.

"Mrs. Frost," he said, "you are going to have to leave the school."

Frost followed him down the hall, complaining all the way. Wasn't this a public school? Wasn't she the public?

Well, Gillenwater replied, the school couldn't handle visitors and keep educating students too.

"Maybe when parents come to the schools and get back into the education of their children," Frost said, "we could start having good schools again."

As it happened, Marty, Rebecca, and the other children didn't have to read the Holt books that day. In Salley's absence, no one told the teachers of the new policy. On Monday, though, Salley would be back.

That night, Sandra Couch, whose son Sam had been reading an alternative book at Mount Carmel Elementary, called Doug Cloud. She and Cloud had known each other long before he was elected to the school board. "Her family and ancestors have been friends of my family and ancestors for years and years and years," says Cloud. Was it true, she asked, that Cloud had voted to ban the alternatives?

Yes, he said. The previous month, the state ACLU had announced plans to sue an unidentified East Tennessee school system for holding Bible classes on campus, and Cloud thought Hawkins might be the target. The ACLU was eager "to take what little bit of Bible study was left in Hawkins County out," he told Couch, and the Holt controversy could provide "just the excuse they were looking for."

But safeguarding the classroom religion wasn't the only reason Cloud gave for withdrawing the alternatives, in Couch's recollection. COBS "could not be allowed to continue stirring up trouble." These "troublemakers," he said, must be "dealt with."

On Monday morning, James Salley apologetically informed parents that all children would have to read the Holt books. "If it was left up to me," he explained, "I would leave the children in the library and let them read the books they've been reading." But disobeying the board might cost him his job, and he was looking forward to retiring soon. One mother responded sternly that "it would be honorable if he would do what was right" instead of fretting about his pension.

A few hours later, Dee Smith sat down with Marty Frost and the other students in her class who had been using the alternative readers. Under the new policy, she said, they would have to read the Holt books like everybody else. She told them to go to the office, phone their parents, and explain the situation.

The five students trooped to the office. Before they could use the phone, vice principal Gillenwater ordered them to return to class.

While the other four resumed their seats, Smith took Marty aside. "You're not going to read those books," she said. Handing him a dime, she told him to use the pay phone in the hallway.

Marty phoned, but no one was home. As he was hanging up, Gillenwater spotted him again and angrily asked what was going on.

Marty explained. He didn't know what to do, he said.

Gillenwater led Marty to the office. Marty sat on the couch and fidgeted while Gillenwater and Salley discussed the situation in the next room. After about five minutes, Salley hollered out: How would Marty like a "three-day vacation"? "I said, Yeah, I believe I need one," Marty recalls with a laugh. "Then it dawned on me—Well, he's talking about suspending me."

When the final bell rang, Marty got his books and walked home. So far as he knew, he wasn't suspended.

About a dozen parents descended on the office after school. Salley and supervisor of instruction Joe Drinnon were waiting for them.

"You're asking us to do something that violates our conscience," said a mother, "and what choice are you going to give us?"

Drinnon shrugged.

A father said that his son wasn't going to read the Holt books.

"Well," Salley replied, "I guess you need to see an attorney then." If the boy didn't attend class, he would be expelled.

"Whatever you have to do, you have to do," the father said. "What I have to do, that's what I have to do."

That evening, the parents and school administrators talked with reporters. "We are totally, absolutely committed," said Bob Mozert. "We have made our decision; our children will not be reading in that reader."

If the students refused to read the Holt books, Salley said, "disciplinary action" would have to be taken; "that's the only thing I can do."

Early the next morning, Vicki Frost, Alice Mozert, and their children appeared at the middle school office. Frost outlined a new plan to Salley and Joe Drinnon: She would hire a tutor, who would teach reading to the dissenting parents' children. The school officials, however, weren't going out on any limbs. They said that only the board could authorize such an arrangement.

When the bell rang, Rebecca Frost proceeded to class. She carried a note for her reading teacher: "Thank you for all your kindness towards Rebecca during this textbook situation. You have portrayed the attributes of a real professional. Rebecca *will not* be allowed to read the Holt Basic Reader or sit in class and listen to others read it orally. Please excuse her to Mr. Salley's office." It was signed, "Thank you again, *love* in Christ the Lord, Vicki Frost."

Rebecca never had a chance to deliver the note. Before reading class started, her mother intercepted her in the hallway and told her to come to the office. There, Salley handed Rebecca a suspension slip. While he was at it, he wrote one for Marty too, even though his reading class wouldn't begin for several hours. Salley also suspended Travis Mozert and other children—ten in all.

Alice Mozert, with Frost and her children tagging along, went to the pay phone to tell her husband what had happened.

Gillenwater, once again patrolling the hall, spotted them and declared: "I am not having this—I will call the law!"

Ten minutes later, a policeman named Bucky Cooper entered the building. Explaining that he was there to "make sure that things go smooth," he asked Frost and other parents to leave.

The Frosts obligingly walked outside, but Marty realized he had left his books in the office. He and his mother walked back in. Inside, Frost paused to comfort a crying girl who had been suspended. Suddenly Cooper loomed over them.

"Didn't I ask you to leave the school grounds?" he said.

"Yes, but—"

Before she could finish he grabbed her arm in one hand and Marty's arm in the other, and marched them outside.

That afternoon, the participants again justified their actions to reporters. Salley's tone was anguished. "I really hate that it happened," he said, "but I had to do something because they refused to go to class."

The parents were resolute. They had a "constitutional right not to have this rammed down our throat," Mozert maintained. The children weren't going to read the Holt books—not now, and not after the three-day suspensions expired. "The children are obeying their parents," he said. "They are submitting to our authority." Unless the school system backed down, "a suit will be filed."

CHAPTER FOUR

CHRISTIANS IN JAIL

"Hawkins County as a whole has been looked down upon from people in Sullivan County," says school board member Doug Cloud. "We're always comparing to them. They're a step ahead. They have more money to spend. We've been looked at as a stepchild here, and I kind of resent that." Sullivan County has a sprawling mall, a symphony orchestra, a twenty-four-hour Wal-Mart; Hawkins County has nothing to compare.

In education too, Hawkins County falls behind its neighbor. With the Tennessee Eastman chemical plant and other large taxpayers, the Kingsport school system in Sullivan County could afford to pay first-time teachers, fresh out of college, $23,909 in the 1992–93 school year—more than Hawkins County paid teachers with twenty years' experience ($23,540). On pass rates for the state's ninth-grade proficiency exam, Kingsport ranks in the top third of Tennessee school systems; Hawkins County is in the bottom fifth. Because of the disparity, more than a hundred students who live in Hawkins County pay tuition to attend the Kingsport public schools.

Now the textbook controversy was giving Sullivan County another reason to scorn Hawkins County. In December, the *Kingsport Times-News* published a cartoon showing a middle-aged couple standing on the Hawkins County line holding a sign that reads "DOWN WITH

FREE THINKING." The woman is saying, "We don't want your kind around here! You practice levitation, advocate world unity and encourage the use of imagination." On the other side of the county line is Santa in his sleigh. The woman, her hair in a bun, resembles Jennie Wilson.

School officials were getting fed up. "Just when Hawkins County schools were coming up to par with Sullivan County schools," Conley Bailey told Vicki Frost at the November board meeting, "you people start causing trouble." In a long interview with the *Johnson City Press-Chronicle*, superintendent Bill Snodgrass said of COBS: "They don't want to find solutions to problems; they want to create them." The vast majority of Hawkins County residents, he added, "wish these people would hush."

The school people weren't alone in their indignation. Letters to the editor columns, at first dominated by the COBS book reviews, now were decidedly anti-COBS. Letters condemned the protesters as "fanatical troublemakers" and "dark-age religious fanatics." One likened the COBS crusade to "the historic witch hunts of Salem"; another observed that "the people of Nazi Germany and Russia let a small vocal minority seize these respective countries while the majority remained silent." In a regular column called "Speak Your Piece," which printed comments left anonymously on the newspaper's answering machine, the *Kingsport Daily News* published a two-word commentary on the textbook protest: "Shoot COBS."

"You all are going to have to have some legal advice," a friend urged Jennie Wilson. The COBS members had been looking.

In mid-November, they met with Les Bailey, a Kingsport attorney whom Mozert knew from church. According to Bailey, parents could be prosecuted for truancy if their children missed more than five days of school without good cause. The parents *might* be able to defend themselves under the First Amendment's guarantee of religious freedom, but he wasn't sure; he had never litigated a religious-freedom case before. He also offered some public relations advice, according to Wilson's notes: "Press people look for scoop. Brief as possible, loving as possible. . . . Don't get in a hurry. SATAN is the enemy." Bailey was willing to take the case, but the protesters weren't sure they could afford his fees.

Bailey and one of the protesters spoke with Sam Ericsson, director of the Christian Legal Society's Center for Law and Religious Freedom in Falls Church, Virginia. A Swedish-born lawyer who specializes in religious liberty, Ericsson is conservative in theology but middle-of-the-road in politics; he approvingly cites one author's description of him as a man "obsessed with moderation." Ericsson listened to the facts and then offered guidance. "Go for the jugular," he remembers saying. "Go for what really offends you. . . . It's basically a strategy of focusing on the really offensive parts, and not to dilute the case by adding on peripherals." He advised dropping most of the objections to the Holt readers, but the protesters weren't willing to do that.

The protesters made other efforts to attract legal help. In a flurry of activity, Jennie Wilson reported on the Holt books to the Moral Majority, the Rutherford Institute, Bob Jones University, the *700 Club*, and Paul Harvey, among others. In addition, she called the office of William Bentley Ball, a prominent religious freedom lawyer based in Pennsylvania. "The amount he was going to require," says Wilson, "we'd all have to mortgage our homes for that one."

As the protesters continued their search for help, they remembered that a conservative Washington organization had been involved in a lawsuit in nearby Bristol. The dispute began in early 1982, when the *Bristol Herald Courier* published an attack on Reagan administration policies by two National Education Association officials. A woman named Suzanne Clark wrote a rebuttal accusing the NEA of, among other things, favoring the use of narcotics to subdue unruly students. When the newspaper published the response, the NEA filed a $100,000 libel suit against Clark. Concerned Women for America came to her aid and filed a countersuit. Before trial, both sides agreed to drop their suits.

"That was a fairly high profile case in that part of the country," says Michael Farris, the CWA lawyer who was Clark's co-counsel. "People who had a philosophical orientation similar to Suzanne Clark tended to know each other." Clark, who had a master's in English from Johns Hopkins, taught at the small Graham Bible College in Bristol, and Marion Wilson had taken her English course. While the NEA libel suit was pending, the Wilsons had included Clark in their prayers.

Jennie Wilson had contacted CWA about the Holt books, but so far there had been no response. Maybe a word from Clark would make a difference. "We thought if anybody can help us, she would know something about it," says Wilson.

"Vicki came to my home with a few other people to bring some textbooks for my husband and I to see, because she had been told that we were interested in public education and textbooks," Clark recalls. After hearing about the Hawkins County situation, she spoke of her admiration for CWA and Beverly LaHaye, a name Frost had never heard before. Clark said she was going to be seeing some CWA people at a conference in Alabama that weekend, and she promised to tell them about the Hawkins County situation.

"She said, I'm quite sure they would be interested in what's going on," remembers Marion Wilson. "And that they was a good bunch."

For the past few weeks, Church Hill Elementary had been granting Sarah Frost a minor accommodation. She didn't get an alternative book, and she still had to answer comprehension questions, but she no longer had to read aloud in class.

Now, however, Vicki Frost had learned that Sarah was overhearing other second-graders reading the stories. That wouldn't do, Frost told principal Jean Price, first in a 9:30 P.M. call to her home and then in a meeting at the school. Overhearing the Holt material was making Sarah, "the meekest of my children," demanding, noisy, and rebellious, so she would have to be excused from the room during reading class. Price refused.

Frost next called Price at home on Saturday morning. Sarah was growing more disobedient by the day, Frost announced, and if Price wasn't going to remove her from class, Frost would do it herself. She added, in Price's recollection, that Price "might want to expel" Sarah.

Price replied that she would never dream of expelling a second-grader. Frost's plan to take Sarah out of class, Price continued, might not work. Schools must teach reading to all students, and students must attend classes for six and a half hours a day. A child who missed a class every day might be deemed truant under state law.

Furthermore, Price said, she was going to have to cancel the existing compromise. Sarah's teacher had reminded her that the school graded oral reading and reading comprehension separately. Unless Sarah resumed reading aloud from the Holt book, she would fail oral reading.

During the conversation, Price heard a child playing rambunctiously in the background. Frost had to tell Sarah to be quiet several times. It was, Frost said, Holt-inspired rebelliousness at work.

On Monday morning, Frost walked into Church Hill Elementary.

In the office, she found school board member Doug Cloud and Joe Drinnon, the supervisor of instruction. They had come to back Price, who recalls that she was feeling "in desperate need of some help from a higher up."

Frost announced that she would come to school every day and teach Sarah in a study hall, library, cafeteria, or wherever was convenient. They would work on the comprehension sheets if they were permitted outside the classroom, or on other materials if they weren't. If that wasn't acceptable, then she would hire a tutor to teach Sarah somewhere on campus during reading class.

Price explained once again that Sarah would have to read the Holt books. A parent, she added, could take a child out of class by signing a form in the office, but the parent and child would have to leave the campus. According to Frost, Price made a further point: "If you take Sarah out of the reading class, I will have to automatically fail her for the entire year."

In Frost's account, "I told them lovingly and straightforwardly that if Sarah would have to fail because of our religious conviction . . . then *I was resolved to accept that consequence* because Christ Jesus had commanded us to be *faithful unto death*. . . . They sat there speechless!"

Overcoming his speechlessness, Cloud asked why the Frosts didn't transfer their children to a Christian school.

"I told him," Frost remembers, "that if he would like to contribute four hundred dollars a month, I would be glad to do that, but I just did not have the money to put all four of our children in a private school." In Price's recollection, Frost added that she also wanted to keep her children enrolled "to protect the other children in our school."

Frost stood up. She would not sign the removal form, she declared, because the school might somehow use it against her. She walked to the classroom and removed Sarah. At the door, Sarah's teacher told Frost that she was praying for a peaceful resolution to the conflict.

Frost had to hurry. The three-day suspensions had expired, so Rebecca and Marty were back at Church Hill Middle School that day; it was almost time for Rebecca's second-period reading class to begin. With Sarah, Frost drove to the middle school and stood outside Rebecca's classroom.

Inside, the teacher began passing out the Holt readers. *All* the students would have to use the books, she explained quietly when she reached Rebecca; the principal had said so.

"I can't read it," Rebecca replied, and handed the book back. With that, her mother opened the door and motioned for Rebecca to come along.

At the office, Frost gave principal James Salley a note explaining that her children would not read the Holt books. Salley filled out suspension slips for Rebecca and Marty. This time they were suspended for ten days, effective the next day, for refusing to attend class. (By day's end, ten children had been newly suspended. Three were first-timers, with three-day suspensions for refusing to go to class. Seven of the original ten students were resuspended; the other three, while still objecting to the books, had returned to class.)

Salley passed Frost the suspension slips. Frost read them and protested the wording. The *children* hadn't refused to attend class, she insisted. They were being suspended "because *I* came to the school and took them out. They have exerted no will in the matter whatsoever."

Salley said it didn't matter.

It *did* matter, Frost replied, and unless Salley corrected the slips, she would bring the children back to school the next day.

Salley took Rebecca's suspension slip and, next to where he had written that she refused to attend class, wrote in, "Her mother refused." In the recollections of Frost and another mother standing beside her, Salley also muttered: "If you bring them back, I'll have you put in jail."

Before classes began the next morning, Frost appeared at the elementary school office and again announced her intention to tutor Sarah on campus.

Jean Price said that wouldn't be possible. She reiterated that any mother was free to take her child out of class, but that she must sign the child out and then leave the building.

Frost said she wouldn't sign Sarah out.

Then, Price says she replied, she might be violating Tennessee statute 49–818, "Persons Improperly on School Premises."

Frost was unfazed, according to Price and a teacher's aide who was in the room. "You will just have to call the police on me and Sarah," she declared, "and we will go and sit in jail. Won't we, Sarah?" She patted her daughter on the head.

"I was very shocked at the statement," recalls Price, "because I had never had a parent before—and I hope I never do again—even *imagine* that they could be arrested." In particular, she found it "beyond my belief that any mother would ever take a child to jail."

Frost denies making any remark about jail, and she says Price never said anything about a trespassing law. In her account, *she* was the distraught one. She believed she could avoid a truancy prosecution if her daughter stayed on campus all day, even though she skipped reading class. Yet Price was adamant that if Sarah was out of class she would have to leave the building. Frost also thought a truancy prosecution would be less likely if she refused to sign Sarah out, but Price was insisting that she do so. A miscalculation could be calamitous. "Truancy, to me, meant I could have Sarah taken away from me," Frost says.

Reading period was beginning; there was no time to reflect. Without saying anything to Price, Frost walked to the classroom, got Sarah, and headed for the cafeteria.

Price intercepted them in the hall and ordered them to leave the campus.

"I knew that I was about to be in a situation that was very threatening," Frost recalls. With Sarah at her side, she borrowed a phone and called Mozert's lawyer friend Les Bailey, but he wasn't available. Then she called Wilson. "Jennie," she said, "pray for me. I'm in trouble." She hung up.

(Distressed, Wilson phoned the police department and said, "Have you arrested Vicki Frost?" Asked why Frost's cryptic "I'm in trouble" led her to think immediately of an arrest, Wilson says: "That's very possible with the number of people getting arrested and their children taken away from them at that time in America.")

After leaving the school office, Vicki Frost and Sarah walked to the parking lot and sat in their Jeep Wagoneer. There, Frost hoped, they would be safe. They were out of the building, as Price had demanded, but they were still on school grounds, which might forestall a truancy prosecution. While Frost fretted, Sarah studied a Christian schoolbook.

Meanwhile, Price called superintendent Snodgrass and then the police. A few minutes later Joe Ashbrook, chief of the five-man Church Hill Police Department, drove up. A balding, square-jawed man with a deep voice, Ashbrook consulted with Price and then walked out to the Frosts' Jeep.

"What are you doing," he asked jovially, "having school in your car?"

Sarah was reading, Frost replied.

"Mrs. Price has asked you to leave," Ashbrook said. "Will you please leave?"

"Yes, sir," Frost said. "I will be glad to." She was indeed glad to leave, now that Ashbrook knew "that I wasn't committing truancy, that they were *making* me leave." Compulsion, she thought, might operate as a defense in court.

Before driving off, she handed Ashbrook a note for Price: "I will be here tomorrow by appointment (9:00 A.M.–9:15 A.M.) to take Sarah out of the Holt Reading class, without disturbing the classroom or entering it. It is against our Christian beliefs that a child should be 'forced' to read and participate in a reading class which teaches against our faith in God. We desire to practice our 1st amendment right guaranteeing our 'freedom of choice.' "

That afternoon Sarah Ekstrom, a Kingsport woman who had accompanied the protesters to Suzanne Clark's house, called Frost. Ekstrom had heard about the confrontation with Ashbrook. "Vicki, you have *got* to get some help. I am afraid for you," she said. "Call Suzanne Clark and get the number of Concerned Women for America."

Concerned Women for America claimed more members than the National Organization for Women and other feminist groups, yet it attracted only a fraction of their press coverage. The group was "God's best-kept secret," said its founder, Beverly LaHaye.

She was born Beverly Jean Ratcliffe in 1929 in Detroit. As a student at Bob Jones College, in Cleveland, Tennessee, she met Tim LaHaye, a twenty-one-year-old Baptist minister and World War II aerial gunner. They married when she was eighteen. After college they moved wherever his church assignments took them: Pumpkintown, South Carolina; Minnetonka, Minnesota; and finally El Cajon, California.

Tim LaHaye soon branched out beyond his Southern California pulpit. He wrote books about Bible prophecies, religion in American history, self-help psychology, homosexuality, and secular humanism, which sold millions of copies in Christian bookstores. When he discovered his children "espousing humanistic philosophy" that they'd picked up at school, he founded the San Diego Christian Unified

School System, which ultimately comprised four elementary and two high schools. He also helped found Christian Heritage College, and served as its president from 1970 to 1976. At the college he helped start an anti-evolution think tank, the Institute for Creation Research.

Like Jerry Falwell, LaHaye started speaking out politically during the 1970s. He became a leader of Californians for a Biblical Morality, which campaigned against abortion and homosexuality. He also helped Falwell start the Moral Majority, served on its six-man board, and headed the California chapter.

During their early years in California, Beverly LaHaye concentrated on raising the couple's children (Linda, Larry, Lee, and Lori), keeping house, and volunteering at church. "I was a very internal, shy person," she says. "My father died when I was two years old, and I was later raised by a stepfather. When I married Tim, and even when the children came along, I did not have a good self-image. I love my children, and I was a good mother, a good wife, but outside of my little home, I was not very comfortable." She pauses, and then adds: "Being a pastor's wife, you have to get involved in *something*. I chose Sunday school because I felt comfortable with children."

At a conference for Sunday school teachers, she listened to a speech by Christian psychologist Henry Brandt. Afterward she went up to Brandt and alluded to her melancholy state of mind. "I thought he would feel sorry for me, this poor pastor's wife with all that was expected of her," she remembers. "Instead he looked at me and said, Young lady, you sound like a very selfish woman. And he was right. It was *exactly* what I needed. I realized that I was focusing on me, and God really wants us to focus on other people, what we can do to help others. When you can do that, your own self-esteem comes right along with it. I've been a different person ever since."

Her husband agrees. In a foreword to one of her books, he writes: "I have witnessed a sweet, soft-spirited worry machine that was afraid of your own shadow become transformed into a gracious, outgoing, radiant woman. . . . Since you became a Spirit-filled woman, I find you much more exciting and easier to love."

With newfound verve, Beverly ventured into public life. She traveled around the country giving speeches, just as her husband was doing. "Then the day came when I was getting on a plane to speak someplace to a woman's group about the family, and he was going to another place. We thought, Hey, why don't we do this together? And so we did." They offered two-day Family Life Seminars, designed to show Christians how to have happy marriages. The seminars were so successful that the LaHayes started selling cassette tapes by mail, at one point earning a million dollars a year. In addition, they hosted a weekly half-hour program syndicated to Christian TV stations, *The LaHayes on Family Life,* and they collaborated on a sex guide for Christian couples, *The Act of Marriage.* Beverly also wrote several books on her own.

In the late 1970s, her "nausea" over feminism propelled Beverly into politics. "Betty Friedan was on Barbara Walters's show, and she said, 'I'm representing the women of America.' She was not representing *my* values at all, or any of the women that I knew in San Diego County. And then she closed the show by saying, 'Barbara, I'm going to spend the rest of my life seeing that America becomes a humanist nation.' And I knew she was a signer of the [second] 'Humanist Manifesto,' so I knew what she was referring to. My husband says I sat right up and said, 'Well, I'm going to spend the rest of *my* life seeing that America doesn't become a humanist nation!' Never dreaming at all what the future would hold."

At the time, conservative women weren't organized, weren't even aware of what was going on. "We were concentrating on raising our families and working in our churches," she says. "We didn't know what ERA stood for; we didn't know what NOW was doing." So she decided to organize a meeting for church women from the area. "We would have a speaker come in and talk about the Equal Rights Amendment, to educate them. One night, and it would be over," she says. "When I look back on it now, I just have to laugh. It was like the seed had been planted."

In January 1979, she founded Concerned Women for America, based in San Diego. "I can remember how thrilled we all were in March 1979," she writes, "to find that we had 24 members. By May we had 88. And by June it had grown to 229." According to CWA, its membership skyrocketed to nearly half a million in 1984, after the publication of her book *Who But a Woman?* Today CWA claims 600,000 members, making it the largest women's organization in the country. Although feminist organizations dispute the membership figures, there is no doubt that CWA has flourished. The success is, she writes, "a sovereign work of the Lord, to be sure."

• • •

A portion of CWA's success has stemmed from its ability to convey a mixed message. It offers women a way to be politically active—every woman, Beverly LaHaye says, "can lobby from the kitchen table"—while simultaneously commanding them to stay home and submit to their husbands' authority.

Submit is the operative word. "A woman is here by God's design," she explains, "and a woman plays a servant's role. I know I could be really stoned for that, but that is what God has called us to be." Picking up her husband's dirty socks is, she says, just another way of "serving the Lord Jesus."

In keeping with this belief about the woman's role, CWA's most important target in the early years was the Equal Rights Amendment. The ERA, Beverly said, would "invite total government control over our lives" and "*totally* destroy the traditional American family." She believes her organization contributed appreciably to its demise. She asked CWA members to pray for the amendment's defeat every Wednesday from January 1 to June 30, 1983. "And, do you know," she writes, "out of the seven states that were needed for ratification, five of them voted on Wednesdays. And, in every one of them, the ERA was defeated."

Along with opposing the ERA, Concerned Women for America takes fairly standard right and far-right positions on social, economic, and defense issues. It opposes abortion, comparable worth legislation, state lotteries, pornography, violence and vulgarity on television and in comic books, gay rights, and the nuclear freeze. It supports voluntary school prayer, teaching creationism in biology classes, educational vouchers, mandatory HIV testing for marriage licenses, and full funding for the Strategic Defense Initiative. CWA keeps members apprised of the latest anti-Christian plots too, such as the Satan worshipers who supposedly murder day-care children.

CWA also combats "the pernicious philosophy and effects of Secular Humanism." "Feminism and the sexual revolution are tentacles of the octopus Humanism," Beverly writes, "which is seeking to destroy Christianity and Christian principles in American life." As to whether secular humanism is a conspiracy, as some of her husband's books suggest, she presents herself as an agnostic. "I've heard the argument about a conspiracy," she says. "I'm not sure I believe in that. . . . If I could see some absolute documentation, I'd be willing to look at it, but I believe it's a mindset that is anti-God." A moment later, though, she indicates that she's amenable to at least some conspiracy theories. "They've had great influence on some of our leaders, the Trilateral Commission," she says. "When you look back, you can see almost every president down the line can be identified with it. And you do begin to wonder, Is there something back here in the unknown that is directing? This year [1992] the two leading candidates are both members of the Trilateral Commission. We don't have a choice."

CWA's issues sometimes don't quite mesh. It takes some imagination to see SDI funding and contra aid as "protecting the rights of the family," CWA's mandate. While it opposes mandatory parental leave —by many definitions a pro-family measure—as contrary to free enterprise principles, CWA doesn't hesitate to call for market regulation elsewhere: It supports a ban on beer and wine TV commercials, and it wants the FCC to eliminate indecent TV programming.

And notwithstanding their support for an assertive military, the LaHayes (like most parents) don't want *their* children near the front lines. "When our son was drafted into the Army," Beverly writes, "he was selected because of his excellent marksmanship to attend a specialized school for sniper training. His father pleaded with God not to allow this great specimen of a young man to come home with only half a body. Through very miraculous circumstances he was taken out of the sniper school and given an eight-hour-a-day desk job in Hawaii! The Lord delivered him!"

Such occasional inconsistencies haven't hindered CWA's rise, though. President Reagan delivered the keynote address at CWA's 1987 convention, and the Reagan White House named Beverly LaHaye to its Family Policy Advisory Board. She also testified before the Senate Judiciary Committee in favor of Supreme Court nominees Antonin Scalia, Robert Bork, and Clarence Thomas. (Bork—who Senator Howell Heflin suggested was an atheist—later addressed a gathering of CWA's devout Christians.) Conservative activist Paul Weyrich judged CWA the most effective organization on the religious right in the late 1980s.

"I really believe that my gift is to motivate people to action," Beverly LaHaye says. "That's basically what I've been doing over the past several years."

During his wife's ascent, Tim LaHaye's career had faltered. He stepped down as senior pastor of Scott Memorial Church in 1981 and started a television ministry, but he dropped it after three years. In

1983, he started the American Council for Traditional Values, which would try to mobilize Christians to register and vote. There was talk that the group could become his own Moral Majority, particularly after both LaHayes moved their operations to Washington, D.C., in 1985, but he disbanded ACTV after the 1986 elections.

Tim's hopes of becoming the new Falwell were fading, in part because of a series of public-relations mishaps. In 1980, the press discovered that Scott Memorial Church was funding the local Mission to Catholics, whose literature spoke of the Catholic church as "the old harlot church still sitting on the seven hills of Rome, drunk with the blood of martyrs and fornicating with the political leaders of the world." A local priest denounced LaHaye as "our American ayatollah." Under fire, LaHaye's church stopped funding the anti-Catholic group but refused to condemn it.

Then in 1985, a freelance reporter borrowed a CWA cassette to tape an interview with Beverly LaHaye. At the end of the tape the reporter discovered a letter dictated by Tim LaHaye to Colonel Bo Hi Pak, Sun Myung Moon's second in command at the Unification Church and the head of the Unification-affiliated *Washington Times*. In the letter, LaHaye thanked Pak for "your generous help to our work." The reporter publicized this indication of a LaHaye-Moon alliance. Although LaHaye insisted that the "generous help" had consisted only of introductions to important Washingtonians, the coverage was damaging, even among LaHaye's fundamentalist followers. It seemed imprudent for believers in the unique divinity of Jesus to be accepting favors from people who believe in the unique divinity of Sun Myung Moon.

And then in 1987, LaHaye resigned as co-chair of the Jack Kemp presidential campaign after newspapers, with what appears to be uncredited help from People for the American Way, unearthed and publicized divisive passages in LaHaye's writings: among others, his assertions that Catholicism is a "false religion" and that Jews have "all too frequently been devoted to philosophies that have proved harmful to mankind."

So, while Beverly was starting to challenge Phyllis Schlafly as the religious right's leading woman—CWA had far more members than Schlafly's Eagle Forum—Tim was continuing to toil in Falwell's shadow. "She has turned out," Paul Weyrich said, "to be at least as important—if not more important—than her husband."

. . .

Shaken by the recent turn of events, Vicki Frost phoned her CWA contact, Suzanne Clark. The policeman had ordered her to leave the elementary school parking lot, Frost recounted, and the principal had spoken of a truancy prosecution.

Clark was sympathetic. She said she had mentioned the Hawkins County controversy to attorney Michael Farris of CWA. Now, Frost should call him.

Reaching Farris at his Washington office, Frost described the situation during a ten-minute call. "She was worried," Farris remembers, "that if she went back the next day and took her daughter out of the class, she might be arrested for truancy." Frost wondered if he could help, both with this immediate problem at the elementary school and with the continuing suspensions at the middle school.

Farris said he couldn't unilaterally agree to represent the parents in a lawsuit against the school system—Beverly LaHaye would have to authorize that—but he would call the superintendent and try to avert an arrest.

In Farris's account, he phoned Snodgrass and told him that "our organization was interested to the point of checking out what was going on." He explained Frost's fears, and he asked for "some assurances that she would not be arrested if she went to the school property." Snodgrass "assured me that she would not be arrested and that he would talk to the principal in that regard."

Even after hearing about Snodgrass's assurances, Frost felt uneasy. At home that evening, Roger urged her to call the police and arrange for an officer to escort her to school the next day. The policeman could protect her and, if necessary, serve as a credible witness. "When I would have to come into truancy court before a judge," says Vicki, "the policeman would say Mrs. Price *asked* her to leave—it wasn't that I was committing truancy of my own free will." So she called the police, and the dispatcher said they would try to have someone accompany her.

After the call, the Frosts drove to a COBS meeting. An audience of about seventy-five watched *The Children's Story*. In Jennie Wilson's recollection, the film opens with a dowdy, dejected woman leaving a classroom of young children, and being replaced by a dapper young woman in a uniform. The new teacher asks the children if they like candy. Yes, they exclaim. She instructs them to shut their eyes and pray as hard as they can for candy. After a moment she tells them to open their eyes; there's no candy. Then, as they shut their eyes again, she places candy on their desks. As they chomp away happily, she explains that they must look to the state, not God, to supply all their needs. To Wilson, the message was that unless parents wake up, their children will become "slaves of the state."

Also at the meeting, Mozert gave a status report. COBS had been in touch with Concerned Women for America, he said, and the organization had promised free legal help. The CWA lawyer would come to Church Hill the following week to investigate, and a lawsuit would follow. The lawyer, Mozert added, had characterized the case as "foolproof." (According to Farris, this depiction of CWA's commitment was greatly exaggerated.)

Frost told friends at the meeting about her encounter with Chief Ashbrook that morning. She said she planned to return to school the following morning, this time with her own police escort.

Though she asked for their prayers, she maintains that she no longer felt she had anything to worry about. "As long as I was peaceable and law-abiding, and I had the police with me," she says, "I thought, What could happen to me?"

The next morning, the day before Thanksgiving, Frost wrote two notes to Jean Price. "Because of the dictates of conscience, I (Her Father & I) am taking Sarah out of the Holt Basic reader program," one note said. "I request to sit quietly in the lunchroom with her, acting as a 'parent volunteer' and aide to the teacher. Parents have the right to protect their children from ideas that molest their minds." Frost hoped that the "parent volunteer" angle would protect her from trespassing and truancy charges.

While Frost was getting ready to leave, something happened that gave her a momentary start. "The Holy Spirit sometimes, in this still, quiet, small voice, zaps a thought into your mind," she says. "The question came, Are you willing to go to jail for me today? And I thought, How ridiculous! Then I had to stop and think: Lord, I've said in my heart that I'm willing to even die for you if need be. So if that's where you lead today, I'm willing to accept it."

In the Frost household that morning, only Sarah caught the bus for school. Rebecca and Marty were suspended from the middle school, and Lesha had stopped attending kindergarten at Church Hill Elementary a few days earlier because of the dispute between her mother and the principal. As she was leaving the house to get Sarah out of class, Frost told her children that she would be back in twenty minutes.

She stopped first at Church Hill's City-County Building. Inside, she went to police headquarters to get her escort, but the small office was empty.

Then she went upstairs to photocopy her letters to Price. As she used the copier, she talked with the two women who worked in the office. She had grown friendly with them on previous visits to make copies; once, one of them had promised to pray for her. Now Frost told them about her encounter with Chief Ashbrook the day before. "Pray for me," she said as she left. "They might try to arrest me today."

Alone, without her police escort, Frost strode into Jean Price's office and asked breezily, "What are my orders for today?"

"Same as yesterday and the day before," Price replied. She explained yet again: Sarah would have to use the Holt book and remain in class; to take her out of class, Frost would have to sign a removal form; if she took Sarah out of the classroom, they would have to leave the school premises.

Frost asked Price to wait a moment, and then walked to the outer office and called the police. "Please send someone to Church Hill Elementary School," she whispered, and hung up without identifying herself. She felt that she "absolutely had to have a bona fide witness" that she was being forced to leave the building.

Price walked out of her office as Frost was hanging up the phone. Frost sat in silence.

Price asked: Were they waiting for someone?

Yes, Frost said.

A few minutes later, Frost went to get Sarah out of class, but she returned alone. As a Thanksgiving project, the children were making Indian headdresses to wear to the lunchroom that day; reading was postponed for twenty minutes. While Price photocopied papers, she and Frost chatted about Thanksgiving and the weather.

Then Price looked up and saw Chief Ashbrook entering. "Hello, Joe," Price said. "Are you visiting today? Or do you have some business here?"

Frost leaped up. "*I* called him to come," she announced.

As she handed Price the two letters, she told Ashbrook, "I want you to be a witness as I present these letters to Mrs. Price asking her for permission to stay on the school grounds."

Ashbrook said he didn't want to be a witness.

Ignoring his protestations, Frost read aloud part of one letter, and said that she was going to sit in the library or cafeteria and tutor Sarah.

"What are your qualifications?" Price asked.

"I am a parent and a taxpayer," Frost replied.

At this point, accounts diverge. According to Price, the two women argued heatedly with raised voices. According to Frost and Atha Simpson, the school secretary who was at her desk nearby, the discussion was calm, with no raised voices. According to Ashbrook, the women were "arguing, not real loud." Price, Simpson, and Ashbrook all contend that Frost said she wouldn't leave voluntarily; she would have to be arrested. Frost denies saying any such thing. Price and Ashbrook say that Price instructed Frost to leave. Frost says no one ever flatly instructed her to leave.

"I seen that a problem was getting out of hand," Ashbrook says. "I had to do something." So he asked for a copy of the school trespassing statute.

As Price was getting it, Frost said the law didn't apply to her because parents have an absolute right to be on school property.

Price replied that the right existed only while the parent had "lawful and valid business" at the school. Frost had no lawful business at the school. In Price's view, breaking school rules by trying to tutor Sarah on campus would be unlawful.

"I don't feel I have unlawful intent in my heart," Frost responded, "simply because I love my daughter and came over here to protect her."

Ashbrook read the statute aloud: "In order to maintain the conditions and atmosphere suitable for learning, no person shall enter onto the grounds or into the buildings of public schools during the hours of student instruction except students assigned to that school, the staff of the school, parents of students, and other persons with lawful and valid business on the school premises. Any person improperly on the premises shall depart on the request of the school principal or other authorized person."

"I don't believe I'm here unlawfully," Frost repeated.

"Mrs. Frost," Ashbrook said, "you are under arrest."

"If you want to arrest me, go ahead," Frost replied. "But I am getting my daughter. You can just take us both." She hurried toward the door. Her eagerness to get Sarah and take her to jail, Frost says now, was "a natural response." She had come to the school to remove her daughter from reading class, and she intended to do so.

"Is the *child* under arrest?" asked Price, feeling, she says, "just shocked and amazed—it was kind of like a disbelief type deal."

Ashbrook grabbed Frost's arm. "It's *you* going to jail, not your daughter." He led her away.

"I've talked to the Lord about this, and he told me that I would be arrested," Frost said as they walked down the hall. Outside the building, she threw up her hands and proclaimed, "Praise the Lord!" Then she asked Ashbrook if he was a Christian.

"I'm a preacher," he answered.

"Pray," she instructed.

As they drove the twenty miles to the county jail in Rogersville—passing the Mountaineer Restaurant's "GOD BLESS YOU" billboard, the Jolly Roger drive-in, rolling hills, barns, silos, pastures, and churches—Frost talked. "I told him that I believe I know how Joseph must have felt when he was taken captive into Egypt," she says. "And I told him that I had never been through anything like this, that I had never even gotten a speeding ticket before, that I had never been charged with any violation. And I told him to pray for me because I was about to cry. I did not want to cry to the extent that my eyes would be swollen and my mouth and nose would be swollen. My blood vessels in my eyes break easily when I cry. I did not want to be completely disfigured by the time I got to the Hawkins County Sheriff's Department." Shaken by his refusal to let her bring Sarah—"I had never had my motherhood threatened before"—Frost did weep quietly, while Ashbrook smoked cigarettes and drove in silence.

At the jail, Frost submitted to a mug shot and fingerprinting. After surrendering her handbag, which contained a bankbook, a checkbook, and $1.31 in change, she phoned Jennie Wilson. "Jennie," she said, "I'm in jail in Rogersville."

Wilson was flabbergasted—but less by Frost's arrest than by her whereabouts. What, Wilson asked, was she doing in the Rogersville jail instead of the Church Hill one, which was much closer to the elementary school?

Frost said she didn't know.

"You mean," Wilson said, "they took you out of the city limits of Church Hill, through Hawkins County, and into the city limits of Rogersville?"

That's right, Frost said.

"I thought, Well, they've kidnapped her," says Wilson. (According to Ashbrook, no holding cell was available in Church Hill.)

Wilson asked about the charges and the bail.

Frost said she didn't know, but she shouldn't have to post any bail because she hadn't done anything wrong; she should just spend Thanksgiving in jail. She asked Wilson to look after her children, call her husband, and try to reach Mike Farris in Washington. Before she could say more, the line went dead.

Frost was led to a cell that reeked of pesticide. A female jailer conducted a pat-down search and then left her alone.

"I didn't sit down too much," Frost remembers. "I walked back and forth. And I thought, What did Paul do when he was in prison? . . . And I scolded myself for being weak because I had cried on the way down. I guess I tried to encourage myself." Remembering the experience, she clears her throat, looks at the floor, apologizes, and begins weeping anew. In a moment she composes herself. "I *knew* God was in control and that he would take care of me," she says firmly. "I scolded myself for my faith not being as strong as it should've been."

Her husband Roger was at work at the Mead Paper Mill. At about 11:15 A.M. he got a phone call from Jennie Wilson: Vicki was in jail. "I was mortified," he remembers. "I couldn't believe it." During his eleven-thirty lunch break, he "went to a place where I could be alone with my thoughts to recompose myself. . . . I wondered how could they do this. All kinds of thoughts started flooding my head. I had plenty of thoughts." He finished his assigned tasks—"I hadn't fully recomposed myself, and I knew my temperament"—then withdrew $1,000 from the credit union to pay bail, and drove to the Wilsons'.

Meanwhile, Jennie Wilson was working the phones. She called other COBS members, told them what had happened, and instructed them to alert area reporters. She made media calls of her own, to "let them know a parent had been unlawfully arrested in Hawkins County." She reached, among others, Donald Wildmon, the high-profile Mississippi preacher who led boycotts of companies that sponsored off-color TV shows. Wilson contemplated calling Amnesty International and reporting Frost as a political prisoner, but decided not to bother; "I knew they were just so far left they nearly dropped over the side." And she called Concerned Women for America.

Michael Farris was home packing for a Thanksgiving trip to Pennsylvania when his secretary phoned. Somebody named Jennie Wilson had just reported that Vicki Frost was in jail.

Farris called Rogersville and reached Kindall Lawson, the judge who would preside over the case. What, Farris asked, was Frost charged with?

"I don't know, that's what we're trying to figure out now," Lawson replied. He added that she would be released shortly.

After about two hours in jail, Frost was brought before Lawson. He told her to return on Monday for a hearing and, in the meantime, to stay off school property. She was free to go.

Frost started to speak, but Lawson commanded, "Don't say anything."

Uncowed, Frost said, "I merely want to ask, how do I get home?"

"You walk out the door and find your own way home."

"Can I use a telephone in here, or do I have to go out and find my own telephone?"

"You walk out the door and you find your own telephone."

From a pay phone in a laundromat, Frost called Wilson again. After explaining what had happened, she asked Wilson to come pick her up.

"They took you down there," Wilson exclaimed. "Now let *them* bring you back." She quickly apologized for saying "such an awful thing" and dispatched her husband to Rogersville.

To reporters that evening, participants gave sharply conflicting versions of what had prompted the arrest. "She stated that she would not leave but would have to be arrested," said Ashbrook. Frost insisted that no one had ever directly instructed her to leave. "If they had asked me just one time to leave, I would have left. All I said was, I don't feel like I'm being unlawful, and then he arrested me." Price refused to comment.

Price spent Thanksgiving weekend writing an account of events for the district attorney. "It is very difficult to put into writing the many facets regarding the Vicki Frost case," she wrote in a cover letter. "We definitely need your expertise in trying to help Mrs. Frost get some realistic perspective in regard to her children. . . . At this point we have had no contact with the father and feel that he must be brought into the situation either by the school or the court for the sake of the four children. . . . We need to get things back to normal as soon as possible for our 480-plus students and staff." She says she hoped the prosecutor would persuade the Frosts that, if they didn't want their children to read the Holt books, "there was other possibilities, other schools."

Price found herself in a role she hadn't expected or desired. To begin with, she was no great fan of the Holt textbooks. She had favored the Economy series, because she felt that Holt slighted phonics.

Then, as the protest against the Holt readers got rolling, "a lot of us seemed to be blundering," says Joe Drinnon, the supervisor of instruction. The middle school was suspending children at the recommendation of the legal counsel to the state Department of Education. "His advice was that we had no other choice," Drinnon recalls. Pursuant to this advice, Drinnon instructed Price to suspend any elementary students who wouldn't read the Holt book, "but she wouldn't do it." ("I hope I *never* suspend an elementary child!" Price says now.)

In Drinnon's view, Price thought she could avoid divisive confrontations at her school. "Jean wanted to be above all that," he says, "and she finally ended up more in the thick of it than anybody."

"We use four criteria in deciding whether or not to get involved in a case," Michael Farris told the *Saturday Evening Post* in 1985. "First, is it a precedent-setting issue? Are we fighting for something larger than the individuals involved? Second, how close is it to our concerns? Does it deal with family rights? Religious freedom? Third, can the people afford to fight the case themselves? We're not likely to take it on if they're millionaires. Lastly, how busy are we? There are many cases that meet all our criteria, but we turn them down because we don't have an open slot. Sometimes we get ten requests a day, and we can only take on about ten cases a year."

In the Hawkins County case, an additional factor entered the equation. With Frost's arrest, the school system was behaving "in such a bizarre fashion," Farris says, that it "helped me decide in a flash who was right and who was wrong." Frost, clearly, was right. "For anybody to arrest a mother over a deal like this is just so far out in left field that any doubts about her evaporated."

A boyish-looking thirty-two-year-old when he got Frost's call, Michael Paul Farris was a Baptist who believed the Bible is literally true, a recently ordained minister, and a father who taught his children at home in order to safeguard them from the corruptions of the public schools. The son of a school principal, he grew up in Kennewick, Washington. He was drawn to debate in college, and his skills at oral argument won awards at Spokane's Gonzaga Law School. After graduation he practiced law in Spokane.

From the start, however, law was merely a means to another end. When Farris was leading "Fourth Graders for Goldwater," his father told him: "I know you're interested in politics. If you want to be involved in the political world, you need to become a lawyer."

As a lawyer, Farris soon branched out. In early 1980, he joined two Baptist ministers to found a Moral Majority chapter in the State of Washington. A short time later he left his law firm for solo practice and became the chapter's executive director. "I was absolutely committed to the causes Moral Majority espoused," he says, "and I felt that it was my responsibility as a Christian to act upon my beliefs, rather than just sit back and 'tut-tut' immorality from a comfortable distance." Soon Farris ran the largest Moral Majority chapter in the nation.

As the only Moral Majority chapter head who was an attorney, Farris pursued legal victories as well as political ones. He sued the Mead School District, near Spokane, to remove from the curriculum Gordon Parks's novel *The Learning Tree*. In the book, a drunken man says as he shoots wildly with a shotgun: "I'm gonna blow the ass off Jesus Christ, the long-legged white son-of-a-bitch!" By having students read such an anti-Christian book, Farris contended, the school was establishing the religion of secular humanism (the same reasoning that federal Chief Judge W. Brevard Hand would later use to ban textbooks in Alabama, until he was overruled on appeal). Two levels of federal judges rejected Farris's argument, in part because the teacher had allowed the objecting student plaintiff to read Twain's *Pudd'nhead Wilson* while others read *The Learning Tree*. Farris also sued the Washington State Library to get a list of any school districts or school employees that had borrowed the explicit film *Achieving Sexual Maturity*. This case too he dropped before trial, but not before it had generated a public outcry—an outcry that prompted several states to pass laws protecting the privacy of library borrowing records. In recognition of his ceaseless efforts on behalf of the Moral Majority, *Hustler* christened Farris "Asshole of the Month" for August 1981. Farris said he felt "honored that they find me that effective of an enemy to their cause."

Farris's association with Concerned Women for America began in 1980. CWA helped fund his appeal of the *Learning Tree* case, and supported his lawsuit to prevent Congress from extending the deadline for ratification of the ERA. In 1982, working part-time for CWA, Farris helped defend Suzanne Clark against the NEA's libel suit.

Then Farris had a fateful conversation with the LaHayes. "We have a little mountain cabin in California," says Beverly LaHaye. "Michael came up with my husband and me, and spent all day with us. He told how all these cases were coming in and it was demanding more of his time, so he couldn't do what he originally was going to do in Washington. And he says, Would you consider opening a legal division of CWA? Well, I really hadn't given it that much thought. He laid it all out for us. I said, Well, to do that, I think you'd have to live in D.C. That's where everything seems to spring from." A few months later she offered him the job of CWA's in-house legal counsel, in charge of a new office in Washington, D.C. Farris accepted.

From his new post, Farris filed suit over the so-called Nebraska Seven conflict. When seven fathers refused to answer state investigators' questions about the Christian school their children attended, the fathers were sent to jail, ultimately for ninety-three days. "I got the down payment for my house," Farris says. "I did a federal civil rights suit and was awarded $45,000 in attorney's fees."

Later, Farris argued a CWA case before the United States Supreme Court. Larry Witters, a blind man, had sought aid from a Washington State program to educate the handicapped. But because Witters wanted to study at a Bible college, the state denied his application on the ground that such aid would breach the separation of church and state. Farris argued that this was a misreading of the Constitution. By a unanimous vote, the justices agreed.

As his Supreme Court victory illustrates, Farris often comes across as a temperate proponent of mainstream views. Writing in the *New Republic,* Joseph Nocera called him "such a model of reasonableness that he stood the stereotype on its head," and lamented that "not all Moral Majoritarians display Michael Farris's comparative open-mindedness." In 1981, Farris surprised an interviewer by saying he had no position on gun control; he opposed capital punishment except in "very, very limited circumstances"; and, though he opposed gay-rights legislation, he didn't think gay schoolteachers should be fired. In his 1992 book *Where Do I Draw the Line?* Farris audaciously suggested that the religious right rethink one of its favorite issues: "We have to ask ourselves if a minute of [school] prayer—prayer that is likely to be so watered down as to be of questionable value—is worth the effort, especially in light of the energy that could be spent on issues that have a greater chance of success."

"Other sides have their right to their point of view," says Farris. "I simply want to beat them at the ballot box." His positions have been misunderstood, he maintains. He wanted *The Learning Tree* to remain in school libraries, just not in the required curriculum. The *Achieving Sexual Maturity* lawsuit was merely "our attempt to find the answer to legislative and press inquiries as to how often this film was being shown in our public schools," not an effort to intimidate anyone. He says he is utterly unconcerned about "what people do privately"; he cares only about "public morality." "I'm a nice person," he told the *Washington Post* in 1993. "I'm not a jerk."

Sometimes, however, Farris's moderate mien slips. Anyone who doubts the literal truth of the Bible, he once said, isn't a "thinking person." At CWA's 1987 convention, according to a transcript prepared by People for the American Way, he contended that public schools invariably transmit a religious worldview, so they are "per se unconstitutional." On another occasion, he charged the ACLU with undertaking a McCarthy-style witch hunt against fundamentalist Christians, and during a debate he accused an ACLU officer of "slander against the word of God." During a Baltimore panel discussion he grew "very angry, very upset," and threatened to leave, according to another member of the panel. "I tweaked him a lot—that was my way of defusing what would otherwise be raw anger," says Judith Lonnquist, a lawyer who opposed Farris in the *Learning Tree* case. "He seemed very repressed."

During and after the Church Hill litigation, Farris blasted Hawkins County as "one of the most bigoted school districts I've ever seen," and compared its officials to Soviets, Nazis, and the Mafia. "If we lose this case," he told reporters at one point, "we're talking about the most stringent, strident political upheaval that this country has known since the Civil War."

"I tend to be fast on my feet," Farris says now, "to my benefit and detriment sometimes." He remembers that a friend once compared him to a trained Doberman pinscher, but another friend said that wasn't quite right; he was more like an *untrained* Doberman.

Farris's outbursts didn't disturb his employer, though. "Sometimes you have to become quite forceful just to get your point across,"

Beverly LaHaye says. "It never was a problem for us. He was strong, but he had to be."

"He is a brilliant lawyer and a firmly committed believer in Jesus Christ," she wrote in her book *Who But a Woman?* "He is determined to see that Christianity is not stamped out in America. . . . I believe he has been divinely appointed to serve as a defender of the rights of Christians."

Feeling "persecuted for our religious beliefs," Bob Mozert wrote to CWA on Thanksgiving day. He described Frost's arrest the day before, and Michael Farris's role in getting her released from jail. "Our children," Mozert wrote, "are still being denied their right to a public education while currently undergoing their second suspension from school. . . . Fellow believers in Christ, we need your help!"

CWA was committed to aiding the Tennesseans even before Mozert's letter reached Washington. With Frost's court hearing only a few days away, there was no time to ponder the pros and cons. The arrest "did basically force us to accelerate our evaluation of the case," says Farris. After hearing about the situation and the time pressure, Beverly LaHaye agreed to put CWA behind Frost. The organization would defend her in the trespassing case, and it would file a federal civil-rights action against the school district for making children read the Holt books.

On Monday, Farris stood with Frost at the preliminary hearing in Rogersville. She pleaded not guilty and asked for a jury trial; another pretrial hearing was set for December 9.

Four days after the first hearing, Farris returned to Tennessee, this time accompanied by Tim and Beverly LaHaye, and filed suit on behalf of the anti-Holt parents. The lawsuit contended that the schools had infringed the students' First Amendment right to the free exercise of religion by forcing them to read books "in violation of their religious beliefs and convictions." It requested an injunction to protect students from having to read the books, and "damages in amounts as of yet uncertain." As the head of COBS, Bob Mozert was the first plaintiff listed, and so the case was called *Mozert v. Hawkins County Board of Education.*

Outside the courthouse, Farris explained the lawsuit to a crowd of reporters. Wearing a three-piece suit, hair falling across his forehead, he stood between Beverly LaHaye and Vicki Frost. "Our bone of contention is they kicked the children out of school, after forcing them to read books that are against their expressed religious conviction. It's a clear violation of their civil rights."

The two suspended Frost children also stood outside the courthouse. Questioned by reporters, they sounded careworn. "I miss my classmates," said twelve-year-old Marty. Eleven-year-old Rebecca, whose perplexity over "A Visit to Mars" three months earlier had sparked the conflict, said: "I hope we don't fail on our report cards."

That evening, the LaHayes spoke at Victory Baptist Church in Kingsport. "The local people were being told real distortions about it," says Beverly, "so we went in there to let them hear from us how the case really came about." Before an audience of about eighty-five people, Tim denounced secular humanism as "the devil's religion," and said that those who wanted to learn more about the humanist threat should "read my books." Beverly said: "Praise God for families who are resisting the evil day. . . . It is scriptural to be alert." As Beverly spoke, Jennie Wilson turned to the woman sitting next to her and whispered, "Isn't she a lovely lady?"

Within a few weeks, the conflict was a centerpiece of CWA fundraising appeals. "This is no ordinary fight! Children are being kicked out of school," one letter declared. Another said that Frost had been "jailed for objecting to her second grader's reader." Still another observed, "It seems like we should be talking about some country behind the Iron Curtain when we discuss Christians being in jail."

Frost was elated to have powerful Washington allies. "The school board, knowing our financial incapabilities, became tyrannical," she wrote in a note to Farris. "After all, I told them I had *no money*, and who would help this nobody, uneducated (that's what they think) mother down in the hills of Tennessee?" Now she had the answer: Concerned Women for America.

CWA's commitment was the protesters' greatest victory, but it wasn't the only one. Surprisingly, in light of the school officials' hostility toward COBS, the superintendent had canceled the county's voluntary sex-education program after hearing Mozert's complaints.

Since the arrest, the press had paid more attention to the controversy too. An area radio station broadcast a five-day series called "Fanatical Parents or Damaging Textbooks?" in which reporters read excerpts from the Holt books. The school system was running low on the books, in fact, with so many parents and reporters asking to borrow them. And Frost had become a minor celebrity, appearing on CBS's *Nightwatch* from Washington ("my first airplane ride," she says) and giving more than fifteen other interviews.

During one interview on a radio call-in show, Chief Ashbrook phoned and challenged her account of the arrest. Frost, he maintained, had been arguing with Jean Price and disrupting the school. Hawkins County had "some of the best-qualified teachers in the state of Tennessee . . . people that's been raised in Christian homes," and it was terrible for them to be "harassed by any parents."

"Now you can say what you say," Frost replied evenly, "but truth will always stand." There had been no disruption, no argument, just an out-of-the-blue arrest. "If there was any confusion going on that day," she scolded Ashbrook, "it was in your mind."

"You know what's going to happen there, don't you?" the interviewer said. "Because of the organizations around the country that are getting involved, this is going to turn into a *Scopes* trial before it's over. It'll end up in the national press, probably. What do you think about *that* for Hawkins County?"

Ashbrook replied, "I don't think it'll go that far, myself."

·· CHAPTER FIVE ··

THE SUPERPOWERS

A few weeks before her arrest, Vicki Frost crossed out one sentence in a letter she'd just written to the *Rogersville Review:* "Supt. Snodgrass has made no effort to learn of COBS complaints, so how could he represent our complaints to the Holt representatives?" At the bottom of the page, Frost told the newspaper editor: "Please disregard the above marked out sentence. I do not want to get too personal—even though it's the truth."

Later Frost sent copies of her published letters to her CWA attorneys, with a note saying: "I know probably the school system will try to portray me as a radical religious Bible thumping nut. I think these letters are an example of the attitude that I would not speak against the system or persons. . . . Christ has lived through me in these trying moments. . . . I did not attack the school system!"

Frost had reason to sound defensive on the point. Shortly after her arrest, newspapers reported that the protesters weren't just criticizing schoolbooks and dress codes; they were also denouncing Hawkins County teachers and students. With this revelation, public opinion swung, decisively and irreparably, against COBS.

At the November 10 meeting, Bob Mozert had given the school board three handwritten letters about Volunteer High School. He had presented the letters privately, saying nothing about their contents and anticipating that they would be treated confidentially. They weren't: From superintendent Bill Snodgrass, they went to Pat Lyons, the principal of Volunteer, and then to teachers at the school, and finally to students.

The breach of confidentiality still galls the Frosts. Vicki grumbles, "They took those, duplicated them, and handed them out to everybody! . . . Gave them out for the purpose of enraging the students, to entice them to commence acts against us!" "They tried to make it out like we were against the teachers and the educational system," says Roger. "That wasn't it at all. Me and Vicki were public school students."

The letters, two signed and one unsigned, advanced a hodgepodge of charges. In one letter, a Church Hill woman named Wanda Owens reported that her daughter's tenth-grade sex education class included "language that is not used in my house and I don't appreciate her hearing it from a teacher at school." At the bottom of the page, her daughter Sandra elaborated: "Such expressions as 'balls,' 'rubbers' etc. were used in our mixed class." Sandra added that the teacher had held up a diaphragm and started to pass it around until several students asked her not to.

In the second letter, another mother, Jan Whitaker, alleged that a coach "curses in front of his boys," a teacher "often uses finger language," and another teacher "is very critical of a decent student but permits a smart-aleck to get by with most anything." "KKK," she reported, was written on a wall of the vocational building. The curriculum was "trying to teach against everything we are trying to teach our children at home and church." In Whitaker's view, "If the teachers don't straighten up themselves I say replace them with teachers that still believes in having morals and teaching them as well. We need *God Fearing Teachers*."

Moreover, according to Whitaker, debauchery was rampant at the high school. "There are several things that go on at Volunteer that should be checked into such as: students mooning each other in the halls (showing their naked behind), girls exposing their breast to boys —and grabbing boys in their private parts. . . . Students congregate in the restrooms to take drugs. . . . Drugs are exchanged and sold in the halls at Volunteer. Heavy language is also used between students in halls and classrooms. . . . What are the future children going to be like—sexual perverts—pot heads—drug addicts—alcoholics—you name it."

The third letter, which was unsigned, also addressed sex. The library book *Up in Seth's Room*, which Frost had criticized at the school board meeting, "relates sexual encounters between two teenagers—very graphic." Echoing Whitaker's allegations, the letter went on to decry "Sexual Abuse & Sexual Permissiveness at Volunteer High." It reported that girls at Volunteer "make a game out of approaching boys from behind and grabbing their male parts"; that " 'mooning' or revealing the buttocks is not unusual"; and that "sexual seduction, manual sex, and exposure" had all occurred in the classroom. Frost now acknowledges that she wrote this third letter. The information, she says, came from a high school student she knew, Joni Lynn Deel.

Soon the frenzied allegations were common knowledge at Volunteer. While some students joked that "the COBS are out to get you," others took umbrage. More than five hundred students signed a petition saying they were "highly indignant and resentful of the untrue and unjustified criticisms," and calling on COBS to "reveal names, dates and acts." A school organization called "Students Against COBS" was formed. The group announced ambitious plans to "file such lawsuits as may be necessary" to restore Volunteer's reputation, though its only project in the end was to sell Students Against COBS T-shirts at school.

Recognizing that students, parents, and teachers were furious, Mozert tried to distance himself and COBS from the letters. He had delivered them to the board as a favor to the letter-writers, he told a reporter, without in any way endorsing the contents. He was a mere conduit. The authors were not members of COBS; in fact, he hadn't even known them previously.

Here Mozert misspoke. In reality, all three letter-writers were mothers of suspended children. All three were plaintiffs in the pending textbook suit (Wanda Owens later dropped out). Though COBS had no formal membership list, Frost had co-founded the organization, and Whitaker and Owens had each attended at least one meeting. According to Whitaker, Mozert had solicited her letter and then had picked it up at her house.

Furthermore, contrary to Mozert's line of argument, the COBS leaders didn't uncritically transmit every allegation that came their way. Mozert and Frost received anonymous letters charging that a particular county teacher was a lesbian. "This sinful woman should not work with our young children," the informant wrote. "Please drive these kinds of people out of teaching our children." COBS disregarded the tip. "That wasn't our business," says Frost.

Revelation of the COBS letters attacking Volunteer High was a "turning point," says elementary school principal Jean Price. "That was *the* fatal mistake, I can tell you," says Volunteer High assistant principal Phyllis Gibson.

The Holt readers engendered no particular loyalty, but people did feel a fierce loyalty to local teachers, local students, and local schools. The schools consume half of all governmental expenditures in Hawkins County. Not only is education the largest governmental activity; it is also the most visible one, with prominent buildings, buses, football games, and heavy coverage in the local newspaper. Moreover, in sprawling, sparsely populated Hawkins County, the schools serve an important unifying function. They give people at opposite ends of the county a stake in a common enterprise. And, for many parents in Hawkins County, education is the means by which their children can improve themselves—the "lights set on a hill," in the words of a nineteenth-century East Tennessee historian. "Let me tell you something about the Appalachian mountain people," says Phyllis Gibson. "It's been a long, hard struggle to build our schools, and they were not going to stand by and let a little group come in and destroy them."

Hawkins County's response to COBS owed more to this pro-schools reflex than to any issue of religion. In several counties near Hawkins in the mid-1980s, the Tennessee ACLU challenged the public schools' on-campus religion classes, which were taught by so-called Bible ladies. "It was just incredible," says Hedy Weinberg, executive director of the ACLU chapter. "These Bible ladies didn't know what hit them. They'd been doing it for twenty years. They never even *thought* that it could be illegal or unconstitutional." The public over-whelmingly sided with the Bible ladies. One Carter County resident who had sued to block the classes, according to Weinberg, became an outcast; he and his family finally moved out of state. As former *Kingsport Times-News* reporter Mike Dye points out, the Carter County plaintiffs, who wanted less religion in schools, and the Hawkins County plaintiffs, who wanted more religion in schools, met with similar hostility from their neighbors. In both cases, people backed the schools and the status quo.

By advancing the reckless criticisms of Volunteer High, COBS had assaulted the schools. What had begun as an attack on the faraway Holt textbook company had become, in the public mind, an attack on Hawkins County itself.

While the perceived nature of their target was shifting, so was the perceived nature of the protesters. Vicki Frost and Bob Mozert might live in Hawkins County, but they seemed curiously reliant on outside help: Concerned Women for America's lawyers, the Gablers' textbook reports, and who knew what else. By raising questions about these "outside agitators," school officials deftly shifted the debate in a second way, from Holt's hidden messages to COBS's hidden motives.

Elementary school principal Jean Price emphasized the outsider theme in a letter to the editor written shortly before Frost's arrest. "I feel this is not just an isolated incident happening here in Hawkins County," she wrote. "It's part of a national anti-public education movement that would like to indoctrinate students to its narrow religious and philosophical point of view."

If anything was worse than public disparagement of Hawkins County schoolchildren, here it was: public disparagement by outsiders. "*Outsider*," says local pastor Jim Fields, "is the most devastating accusation you can make in Hawkins County." "Hawkins Countians are quick to criticize each other," a local resident told a doctoral student in the late 1980s. "But when an outsider comes in who does it, they're quick to, maybe not support the one being criticized, but to attack."

"There are several points pertaining to nearly all attacks against the public schools that we should be repeating over and over again— especially to reporters," counsels the People for the American Way book *Protecting the Freedom to Learn*. Among the points is this one: "This is not just an isolated incident happening here on Main Street, U.S.A. It's part of a national anti-public education movement . . . that would like to indoctrinate students to their narrow religious and philosophical point of view."

Of her four-paragraph letter to the editor, Price had cribbed three paragraphs from the People for the American Way guide. The outsider theme, which would prove crushingly effective against COBS, was itself formulated by outsiders.

Ten years before creating People for the American Way, Norman Lear gave birth to Archie Bunker. *All in the Family,* wrote *Chicago Sun-*

Times critic Gary Deeb, "was the master stroke that forever changed the face of that living room tube—bringing an honest slice of modern big-city homelife to a situation comedy arena that had been dominated for years by the pleasant, but astonishingly phony, likes of Fred MacMurray and Ozzie Nelson."

For a time, Lear's instinct seemed unerring. Five of the twenty top-rated shows of 1975 were his: *All in the Family, Good Times, The Jeffersons, Sanford and Son,* and *Maude.* By the end of the decade Lear was one of the wealthiest people in Hollywood.

Along with introducing previously taboo topics (abortion, homosexuality) and language (*nigger, wop*), these shows brought a pronounced left-of-center ideology to traditionally centrist, timorous television. The *New York Times* referred to Lear as "the executive producer-as-public ideologue"; in truth, Lear delegated this political function. Exponents of liberal causes would visit his aide, Virginia Carter, and plead for sitcom exposure. She would pass meritorious causes on to the producers and writers, who would inject them into scripts. While other production companies tried to dodge advocacy groups, Lear's company welcomed them. Carter liked to call herself an "advocate"; *Esquire,* less charitably, termed her a "propagandist."

In 1978, Lear took "extended leave" from TV production to work on feature films. One project was to be a comedy called *Religion,* which would, he says, portray "people who become ministers in order to write off a chunk of their living expenses." As research, he watched Jerry Falwell, Pat Robertson, and other TV evangelists. Their manipulation of Scripture in pursuit of political ends "mesmerized and disturbed" him. He worried that "I could take three years to write and direct that one film and miss the target. And it was too serious to miss the target."

So Lear took aim with a commercial instead of a movie. The sixty-second ad featured a hard-hat steelworker ticked off about the religious right. "Here comes a whole bunch of ministers on the radio and TV and in the mail, trying to tell us on a whole bunch of political issues that if we don't agree with them, we're not good Christians—or we're bad Americans. . . . Now there's got to be something wrong when anyone, even if it's a preacher, tells you you're a good Christian or a bad Christian depending on your political point of view. That's *not* the American way."

This ad "was all I had in mind," Lear recalls, but several liberal religious leaders urged him to do more. After further research, he concluded that the religious right's "threat to our nation and to our pluralistic society" could be met only with a counterorganization. One such group was already at hand: the American Civil Liberties Union, which was running its own ads ("If the Moral Majority has its way, you'd better start praying"). But Lear, a former ACLU supporter, wanted an organization all his own. In 1980, Lear put up (according to various accounts) $100,000 or $200,000 to create People for the American Way.

John Buchanan, a former Republican congressman from Alabama and an ordained Baptist minister, headed the organization. Elected as part of Birmingham's "Goldwater landslide" of 1964, Buchanan began his political career as a staunch conservative, espying communists in and behind the civil-rights movement and earning zero ratings from Americans for Democratic Action. In the 1970s, his politics began to move leftward. He endorsed the Equal Rights Amendment, the Panama Canal treaty, and District of Columbia statehood, and he opposed school prayer. His ADA rating hit 40 in 1977, higher than that of most Alabama Democrats. In 1978, he managed to defeat a conservative challenger in the Republican primary, Albert Lee Smith, only by persuading Democrats to cross over. Smith went on to help organize Alabama's Moral Majority chapter, and in 1980 he ran again, now with Jerry Falwell's endorsement. This time Smith won by ten points. "I lost to the Moral Majority," Buchanan lamented. "They beat my brains out with Christian love." Dejected over losing his job (he called Congress "the truest home I ever had") and irritated that the new Reagan administration hadn't given him another one, Buchanan became chairman of PAW.

Buchanan is a forceful speaker and, according to former PAW employees, a courtly Southern gentleman. But from the PAW hierarchy's perspective, his most important attribute was his capsule biography, which helped PAW depict itself as nonpartisan. One ex-employee recalls: "Southern Baptist minister? Former Republican congressman from Alabama? Boy, can we use him!" "Totally a front man," says another PAW alum.

As befits an organization founded by Norman Lear, PAW made heavy use of television. In 1981, the organization released commercials directed by Jonathan Demme and starring, among others, Carol Burnett, Goldie Hawn, and Muhammad Ali. In the ads, the celebrities and several anonymous citizens declared their preferences in eggs, music, and sports. The ads closed: "Freedom of thought. The right to have and express your own opinions. That's the American way."

In 1982, PAW undertook a more ambitious TV project, a two-hour extravaganza called *I Love Liberty* that ABC financed and aired. It featured Robin Williams, Rod Steiger, Barbra Streisand, Christopher Reeve, Mary Tyler Moore, Jane Fonda, Martin Sheen, Big Bird, and a prominent conservative who was then at odds with the Moral Majority, Barry Goldwater. The response was mixed, and some critics questioned whether a network should turn over air time to an advocacy group.

From the outset, PAW also invested heavily in its library. The organization hired a clipping service to collect newspaper articles about, among other topics, school censorship; these articles in turn became the fodder for an annual report called "Attacks on the Freedom to Learn." To keep watch on the religious right, PAW sent donations to the Moral Majority and like-minded organizations, using the names and home addresses of PAW employees, and systematically filed the fundraising letters and publications. PAW employees and interns also attended these organizations' conferences and conventions, sometimes carrying hidden tape recorders, and wrote up reports for the library files. In addition, the library purchased hundreds of religious right books, subscribed to the leading right and far-right magazines, and videotaped the major TV evangelists.

PAW cannily used its archives and its contacts with journalists to embarrass the religious right. In a 1984 letter to the *Christian Science Monitor,* PAW's communications director wrote that "we monitor the television programming of the far right, and we came across something that we thought you might be interested in knowing about"—namely, Jerry Falwell's assertion that Christian Science is a cult based on false teachings. On another occasion, PAW publicized the fact that a Falwell fundraising letter had spoken of a particular rainy morning in Lynchburg, Virginia, whereas weather bureau records indicated that the morning was actually dry. On the day Pat Robertson announced his 1988 presidential candidacy, PAW leased satellite time to air politically awkward moments from Robertson's TV ministry, including his claim that his prayers had deflected Hurricane Gloria from his Virginia studios. Many TV news programs used part of the PAW footage in their coverage, undercutting Robertson's efforts to present himself as a mainstream candidate.

TV and PR skills alone, of course, can't account for People for the American Way's success in the 1980s. Plainly, the public was receptive to its messages. From history books and *Inherit the Wind*, most Americans knew a bit about the *Scopes* "monkey trial" but scarcely anything else about fundamentalists. Then, abruptly, Falwell appeared and claimed credit for the 1980 Republican landslide. Americans shared the religious right's positions on many issues but had reservations about aspects of the movement: its disdain for church-state separation, its shrillness, and especially its intolerance. By reinforcing these misgivings, PAW helped turn public opinion against the religious right.

"We honest to God didn't know that there was an organization that would help us," says Phyllis Gibson, assistant principal of Volunteer High. "Up until then, the biggest decision that we had to make as a community was whether to put one red light or two in town. And then this, like somebody hit you over the head with a skunk! . . . I thought, How do you fight people like this? *How* do you organize and fight?"

Gibson and her allies found some answers in *Protecting the Freedom to Learn*, People for the American Way's guide "to assist local communities where the freedom to learn is actively under assault." The 122-page book first revealed "the censors' strategies and tactics" and "their most recent, frightening victories," and then described "successful anti-censorship campaigns," including "practical advice on how to mobilize support for the freedom to learn in your community."

Published a few months earlier, *Protecting the Freedom to Learn* had reached Hawkins County by happenstance. A Knoxville teacher had torn a mention of the book out of a magazine and sent it to her brother-in-law, Hawkins County supervisor of instruction Joe Drinnon. "I was doing research about censorship, reading everything I could get my hands on," recalls Drinnon. "I called immediately and asked for this book. And it described just what I was seeing, to the point it'd make your hair stand up. I realized it was an orchestrated thing."

Drinnon in turn passed the book and photocopies of it to other school defenders. "I chose people who first of all felt strong about freedom to learn, moral and ethical people who were verbal, who had plenty of strength and will," says Drinnon. "I let them read that book. And I must've placed it well."

Superintendent Snodgrass read *Protecting the Freedom to Learn* "lid to lid" and found it "astounding, the problems that were mentioned in that book and how similar they were to the problems I was having. So I guess it was kind of a misery-loves-company type thing." On November 21, the day of the second suspensions at the middle school, he borrowed some of the book's motifs in talking to a TV reporter: "We are guaranteed a freedom to learn. We cannot permit a small minority of people, regardless of how loud they are, to prevent the freedom to learn for all of our students."

Jean Price also found the book enlightening. "I was priding myself that I could work out any situation with a parent," she says. "After I read that book I thought maybe this is *not* between me and a parent; it's something bigger than it looks."

Meanwhile, a man named Phil Junot had concluded that the school people needed outside help, if only in the form of information. Junot, the vice-president of the elementary school PTA and the husband of an elementary school teacher, was spending the week of Thanksgiving in Atlanta with his parents. He went to the local library, got addresses, and sent nearly twenty letters to anticensorship organizations. When he returned to Church Hill the following Sunday, he says, "my mailbox was bulging."

"I was working late one night going through the mail—we got tons of mail there," says Barbara Parker of People for the American Way, co-author of *Protecting the Freedom to Learn*. "This letter, just addressed to the office, was sent back to me because it seemed to have to do with censorship. It was from Phil Junot. . . . It said we seem to be having a problem with some people in our community who are using objections prepared by—he said the Gaithers, rather than the Gablers. Can you send any information? And that was it."

Parker phoned Junot's home. After missing him several times, she reached him late that week. "He explained it as an isolated incident that was occurring there in this little town, and why on earth would it happen," she remembers. "I began asking some questions and it all seemed to fit a very familiar pattern."

Parker was well acquainted with the Gablers, for they had been her introduction to schoolbook protests. As a writer for the *American School Board Journal* in 1978, she had spent two days interviewing them in Longview. The Gablers had trusted her, and, when her unfavorable article appeared, they "just couldn't believe I had turned against them." (After reams of hostile coverage, the Gablers still resent Parker's piece. "She hates us so bad, so much hatred in her," says Norma, "and I don't feel that way with her.") The article "wound up winning a couple of awards," Parker recalls, and "it was just a story I couldn't let go of—I was just fascinated by these people." For the *School Board Journal* and other publications, she continued to report on censorship, creationism, and other conflicts between the religious right and the public schools. In 1982, she joined People for the American Way as director of its Freedom to Learn Project. She was, she says, eager to "quit writing about all of this and try to do something."

"It is essential," counseled *Protecting the Freedom to Learn*, "to organize the broadest possible base of support for academic freedom and against censorship." As she was studying the PAW book, Jean Price was hearing similar advice from elsewhere. Dozens of reporters had come to Church Hill Elementary since Vicki Frost's arrest. At one point, says Price, "it wasn't unusual to look up and see somebody looking in your window." But Snodgrass had ordered her not to talk to the press, so Frost's account was dominating news coverage. Several people had come to Price, she recalls, and asked impatiently, "*When* are y'all going to present your side?"

To try to orchestrate a public response to COBS, Price met with several other principals, PTA officers, and a few spouses on a Sunday afternoon, four days after the arrest. They quickly agreed, Price remembers, to hold a community meeting "to present to the public the textbook selection process." ("Set up meetings with local groups to discuss education issues—and publicize them," the PAW book recommended.)

But a mere meeting wouldn't be enough, insisted Reece Gibson, the husband of Phyllis Gibson of Volunteer High. Echoing the analysis that had led Norman Lear to found People for the American Way, Gibson said that the Hawkins County schools were under organized attack; defending them was going to require a counterorganization. A pro-schools group would give "the man on the street, the average citizen, an opportunity to stand up and defend the school system," he said, and it would provide one spokesman to answer the charges ("More than one will confuse the press and the public," according to the PAW book, which Gibson had read).

Although Gibson was attending only as a spouse, the others listened attentively. A beefy forty-year-old man with short, curly hair, Gibson was among the county's leading citizens. After moving to Hawkins

County as a teenager, he had been a high school football star (his coach, James Salley, had gone on to become principal of Church Hill Middle School). Gibson had gotten a law degree from the University of Tennessee, then returned to Hawkins County in 1972 and opened a practice. Since 1979, he had also been the county's part-time juvenile judge, an elected position.

In his spare time he was an energetic supporter of Hawkins County's good causes. He gave time, money, organizational skills, and legal advice to scholarship drives, drug-abuse programs, and other nonprofit groups. "He probably chartered over three-quarters of the nonprofit organizations in this area, all for no charge," says Phil Junot. In the late 1970s, Gibson filed two lawsuits to force the county to build a new high school near Church Hill; the county capitulated and built Volunteer High. When children from troubled families came before him in juvenile court, he frequently took them home with him. "I've had, let's see, at least eight in the house at the same time," says Phyllis Gibson, a lean woman with piercing eyes. "I've had some that stayed three or four years."

Once, during a heavy winter storm, a Church Hill woman called Reece Gibson at home. They had never met, she explained, but she had heard about his kindness. Would he please go to the store and buy sanitary napkins for her retarded daughter? Gibson obliged. "That's just typical," says David Brand, Gibson's law partner. "That's nothing exceptional for Reece Gibson. That's just his nature."

Reece Gibson persuaded the others at the Sunday afternoon meeting; they would form an anti-COBS organization. But what to call it? After kicking around acronyms, someone—"I guess primarily myself and/or my wife," Gibson said later—came up with Citizens Advocating the Right to Education, CARE.

"I want to personally apologize for the adverse, undue, and often untrue publicity that Church Hill Elementary School is getting," Price wrote in a letter to parents a few days later. Touching again on the outsider issue, she asserted that "a few local people, controlled by outside sources," were seeking "to impose their beliefs on all." The meeting of her school's PTA the following Monday would "explain the democratic procedure that a textbook must go through before it can be used." She closed: "Your child's future is at stake—please come!"

On the rainy Monday, a short time before the meeting, the Gibsons prayed. They didn't want to do anything contrary to God's will, recalls

Phyllis. Then they drove to Church Hill Elementary, where they met with the other CARE activists in a classroom.

There, Reece passed out the bylaws he had drafted. CARE would "Defend the Public Education System of America," and in particular "promote every child's right to an education, free from . . . censorship by a fanatical minority." The organization's other founders read the bylaws and signed them.

Someone suggested that Gibson become the group's president, and others concurred. He agreed, because, he said later, he figured "nobody else would take it."

As Reece Gibson was accepting the CARE presidency, people were arriving for the PTA meeting. Soon cars clogged the Church Hill Elementary parking lot and lined the roads for a mile in every direction. Inside the gymnasium, beneath pep-rally posters, more than a hundred Volunteer High students sat in the bleachers, and hundreds of adults sat in folding chairs on the gym floor. Latecomers stood two and three deep along the walls and spilled into the hallways. Reporters estimated the crowd at more than eight hundred, perhaps a thousand. "I've never seen as many people in that school gym in my life," says Phyllis Gibson. "There were people out of these mountains—people that I never *dreamed* would be there."

No PTA meeting in the county had ever attracted more than a hundred people. No PTA meeting, for that matter, had ever attracted high school students—though, as Phyllis Gibson acknowledges, teachers may have given them a homework-free night in exchange for attending. But it soon became apparent that this was no ordinary PTA meeting.

Vicki Frost wasn't in the audience—she stayed home because her husband "feared for her life" in such hostile territory, and because Judge Lawson had ordered her to keep off school grounds—but about a dozen of her COBS allies were. "They saved us front-row seats, the opposition did," recalls Bob Mozert, a note of bitterness entering his voice. "Put us down there. I'm sure that was not by accident." As the speakers mocked and denounced them, Mozert and the others sat stonily and, at times, held hands and prayed.

Standing at the podium in front of a green curtain, Jean Price opened the meeting. "I want to point out to you that I am *not* an outsider," she said. She was a graduate of Hawkins County public schools, and so were her parents, her husband, and her daughter. "I come from within your ranks." She added that Hawkins County was facing a grave threat, and "it's not only from within; it's from without. It's the *without* that scares me." She asked people to listen to the program and "make up your own minds. Do we want the democratic process? Or do we want our books censored or to be told what to do by a small group and an outside force?"

After a member of the state textbook committee explained how that body operated, the local adoption procedures were described by Gay Grabeel, a seventh-grade teacher who had served on the reading textbook committee. "Our children are physically stronger, more intelligent, and better informed than any generation in the history of the world," she proclaimed, reading nervously from notes. "They are our future, and they *must* be led into the twenty-first century!"

The next speaker, school board chairman Harold Silvers, promised that he would "put some teeth into what Mrs. Grabeel said." In response to the "extremist groups" that were interfering with the schools, he had written a resolution to protect academic freedom, which he planned to introduce at the next school board meeting. In a halting voice, Silvers read the lengthy statement. Here were more echoes of *Protecting the Freedom to Learn:* Not only did the PAW book advocate a formal academic freedom policy, it also reproduced Connecticut's 1981 policy in an appendix—a policy that was virtually identical to the Silvers resolution.

After the Grabeel and Silvers speeches, the audience was growing restless in the stuffy gym. Although the topics might be important, the presentations had been, as the *Rogersville Review* noted, "dull at times." But the next speech was livelier. During it, the *Review* reporter observed, the mood in the gym "reminded me of a political rally, pep rally or even a sports event where the home team was winning." The speaker was Bill Snodgrass, the forty-three-year-old superintendent of schools, and he was fuming.

"It was suggested that I take a scholarly and low-key approach to what I say to you tonight," Snodgrass began. "But we've had pretty good scholarly speakers. And besides, it's pretty difficult to be scholarly, and *impossible* to be low-key, when you're being accused of being unpatriotic and anti-God!" The audience whooped and applauded. The cheering recurred every few seconds thereafter, sometimes drowning out the speaker.

"We are determined," Snodgrass thundered, "to have schools where teachers can practice their profession without being hampered by extremist groups. . . . We were getting along quite well before they appeared on the scene." Hawkins County people were justifiably proud of their schools, he added, and "we sure don't need some little group of outside agitators trying to tear down what we have with patience and hard work built over the last few years. A favorite saying of mine: Anyone can tear a house down, but it takes a carpenter to build one. Applied to the present situation, my message to extremist groups is become a carpenter and help us build a great school system!

"If you cannot do this," he continued, "and insist upon becoming a wrecking crew, take your unsound ideas to Washington, D.C.!" The applause swelled.

"Or Longview, Texas!" he said, referring to the Gablers. Applause and cheers echoed in the gym.

"Or if *they* don't like them either—" He paused artfully.

"Come on, Bill," a woman cried, "tell 'em where to go!"

A man shouted, "Say it! Say it!"

"I'm not going to say that," Snodgrass replied, and the crowd laughed. "Take them where they *will* be accepted."

"Russia!" yelled a man.

"Because," Snodgrass continued, "we in Hawkins County sure don't want them!"

After reading a poem about the difference between building and tearing down, Snodgrass addressed the "unfounded and untrue allegations" about "one of the finest high schools anywhere." In the bleachers, the Volunteer students cheered enthusiastically. "I not only think the behavior and discipline is good at Volunteer High School," he added; "I think it is exemplary in every respect!"

Snodgrass next turned to the Holt readers and their critics. "Our books *must* be challenging and interesting! The right to have challenging and interesting material must not be taken away by outside agitators with their fat wallets and attorneys from Washington, D.C.!" After boisterous applause, he continued, his hands on his hips: "We had a *local* group from *Hawkins County* pick out our textbooks, and we had a *local* school board from *Hawkins County* to adopt those textbooks. And that right must not be taken away by extremist groups!"

Citizens must, he urged in closing, "stand and march with us to make sure that the extremists and outside agitators don't use their wrecking ball on our fine Hawkins County school system!" Perspiring from his performance, Snodgrass left the stage to uproarious applause.

"I think most folks that know me would say I'm a quiet-type person," Snodgrass says now. "I don't believe in wasting words, but when you've got something to say, I also believe in saying it."

After a flat talk by a regional PTA official, Jean Price stood at the podium again and described "an experience as an educator that I never thought could happen": being served a summons in the textbook lawsuit. She asked the other named defendants—board members and principals—to stand and be recognized.

Another school principal, Robert Cooper, announced a petition drive. Trained teachers and administrators should have "sole authority over book selection," the petition declared, for "this process is the most democratic way, the basis on which this country was founded." It called on the school board "to take whatever action necessary to insure that our children are not deprived of educational privileges."

Two PTA officials spoke briefly, and then, in a formality lost on many people attending, the PTA meeting ended and the CARE meeting began.

"Hawkins County is going to fight!" proclaimed Reece Gibson. Like Snodgrass, he was repeatedly interrupted by applause. Gibson said he was "tired of attacks from outside groups, outside agitators, against our good Christian teachers and the moral character of the students." So, "because myself and other people believe that you care, we have organized CARE—that stands for Citizens Advocating the Right to Education." The organization would "defend the integrity of the Hawkins County school system against biased accusations, misleading statements, and outright lies and slander," as well as "solicit the support, both legal, moral, and financial, of citizens." In short, CARE would "tell them all where to get off."

Gibson introduced Charles Dyer of the Church Hill Ministerial Alliance, who expressed the pastors' "confidence in and our encouragement of" the school system, and called on the people of Hawkins County to conduct themselves with "patience, forbearance and love." Putting aside his text, Dyer said that the alliance members had found nothing harmful in the books. "Not a teacher in our system," he said reassuringly, "would do *anything* to destroy the mind of a child."

After a Volunteer High student described Students Against COBS, Reece Gibson closed the meeting: "We are going to get involved in this lawsuit! We're going on the offensive because we *care!*"

With the evening's program over, more than five hundred people came forward to sign the petition. Many of them handed contributions to Gibson, more than five hundred dollars in all.

For the CARE organizers, the meeting was a triumph. Jean Price says, "We had went for a long period of time—it felt like a long period of time, anyway—not knowing whether the community was in support of us, of me, of the school. . . . I didn't realize that that support was out there." Joe Drinnon had initially feared that the protesters might prevail. But with the CARE rally, he says, "I felt that it was going to be all right."

For their success in rallying Hawkins County against COBS, the CARE organizers owed a debt of gratitude to People for the American Way, Barbara Parker, and especially *Protecting the Freedom to Learn*. The book had provided the idea for a counterorganization, tips on generating favorable publicity, and the language in Price's letter to the editor and Harold Silvers's academic freedom policy. "What it says is what we did," says Drinnon. "Just think where we might be today if we had not read your book *Protecting the Freedom to Learn*," Price later wrote in a letter to Parker. "After reading it, I realized that we had better get busy and inform the general public what we're dealing with. Needless to say, it was very frightening, but with people like you . . . on our side from People for the American Way, there is hope against censorship groups like 'COBS.' " Parker recalls being delighted "that the book was actually being used the way it was supposed to be."

The COBS supporters, huddled together during the long program, were hardly delighted. "I really felt threatened," says Jan Whitaker, author of one of the letters about Volunteer High. "I got really angry," says Junior Marshall. "I knew I couldn't be violent, but I kind of wanted to be." Mozert likens the rally to Jesus's hearing before Pontius Pilate, though he hurriedly stipulates that "I wasn't at the incident, of course, where they crucified Jesus Christ." "We can only thank the good Lord that he gave grace to the people who felt as we did to keep our mouths shut," says Jennie Wilson. She was particularly offended that the ministerial alliance had asked God to bless CARE. "When you ask blessings on that group, you are asking curses on the other group that would oppose you," she observes, suddenly sensitive to the perils of injecting religion into political disputes.

More important than what was said at the CARE rally was the turnout. No longer could the COBS protesters maintain that they reflected majority opinion in Hawkins County. Their most successful meeting, on September 1, had attracted a hundred people; now nearly a thousand people had rallied against them.

Barely three months old, the anti-Holt crusade was spent as a political force. COBS would not hold another public meeting. Its leaders would send no more critiques of the Holt books to newspapers. Only in the courts would the dispute live on.

Emboldened by their success, school officials continued to lash out at the protesters and their backers. "I think that COBS is trying to dictate education regardless of textbooks or anything else," said Conley Bailey at a special school board meeting that week, which no COBS members attended. "If textbooks were not the issue, they'd bring up something else." Bailey added that "every tactic they've used so far has come out of Longview, Texas."

The purpose of the meeting was to deal with the protesters' two-month-old requests. Not surprisingly, the board decided not to comply. The existing dress code prohibited T-shirts with "obscene" messages, one board member said, and that was enough. Larry Elkins observed that patriotism can't be mandated, so there was no point in requiring a daily Pledge of Allegiance.

Two days later, the board held its regular monthly meeting. Harold Silvers handed out copies of his academic freedom resolution. He had decided to postpone voting on the policy until the following month, "because I want everybody that wants to, to get a copy of it." It was, he said, "a masterpiece."

"We're going through some trying times," Doug Cloud declared. "But we must go forward and do what we're supposed to do, and that is educate the children."

Silvers agreed. He said that he and the other board members were "truly proud" of the teachers and administrators, as well of the "people of Hawkins County who gave us a vote of confidence Monday night."

The same week, the second suspensions at the middle school ended. Rebecca and Marty Frost returned to school with notes saying they still weren't to read the Holt books. Principal James Salley and superintendent Snodgrass sat them down in the office. On the desk was a tape recorder, which Marty believes was taping the conversation (Snodgrass says it wasn't). "They sort of interrogated us," Marty recalls. "They kept saying, So you're refusing to go to class? They asked that five or six times. I said, No, I'm not refusing; Mom and Dad don't want me to go. Who am I supposed to obey, the school board or my mom and dad?" After forty-five minutes of questioning—Snodgrass later characterized it as a counseling session—the children were sent home.

"I don't know why in the world they ever suspended us," Marty says now. "We couldn't help it. It was out of our hands. It's like if I was doing something wrong, and Momma went and kicked my dog. The school board was objecting to Mom and Dad—why punish us? I still don't know why they did it."

To boost the suspended students' morale, CWA asked them to write essays on the topic "Religious Freedom: What It Means to Stand Alone." In their essays, the students concluded that they were doing the right thing, but they admitted that it wasn't easy.

"Standing alone on what we believe is right is hard," wrote seventh-grader Bill Couch. "Not many are taking a stand with us. It's hard for people to stand alone without much support."

"I am only one of the eleven children who is standing against this," wrote seventh-grader Travis Mozert, "but even if I was the only one, there is no doubt in my mind that I would stand against it. Standing alone means commitment and bravery. Some kids try to make wisecracks and laugh a little. Everyone likes to be part of the crowd and be popular. Sometimes it's hard to be different. When the Lord is on your side, you'll always have a friend and never be alone."

"I have been suspended, so far, thirteen days from school, and I am the only child out of my reading class," wrote Rebecca Frost, the sixth-grader whose bafflement over "A Visit to Mars" had sparked the textbook protest. "Standing alone has made me realize that God will bless those who obey him. Even though my teachers can't allow me to make up any work and I will not complete this six weeks, I'd rather get a zero on my report card and get an A with Jesus for obedience."

Four days after the CARE rally, Judge Kindall Lawson was scheduled to hear Vicki Frost's trespassing case. When Frost and her allies reached the Rogersville courtroom, however, they discovered that the one o'clock hearing would be delayed. "The rumor was," says Jennie Wilson, "that Judge Lawson had decided it would be a much better show if they postponed it till four o'clock, so that all the teachers could get out of school and come over."

While they waited, an older woman approached Frost and introduced herself. Her name was Floride Miller, she said, and she was a missionary to Hawkins County jail inmates. She had finished her business in the building and had been preparing to leave, but, she said, God told her to wait in the hallway. Now she knew why: to pray with Vicki Frost. Frost and some of her supporters followed Miller into an empty room in the back of the building. Frost recalls, "She prayed, Ye shall be delivered and you shall hold your peace and the Lord shall fight for you."

After school let out, teachers streamed into the courtroom. Once the room was full, the hearing began.

On the witness stand, Chief Joe Ashbrook described the arrest. Frost "kept stating" to Jean Price that she wasn't going to leave unless she was arrested. "There was a little bit of arguing started, not real loud, but enough to kind of disturb both parties." Price said Frost was there unlawfully. Ashbrook read the law aloud; Frost again refused to leave; and he arrested her. As he was leading her to the car, she shouted, "Praise the Lord!" and threw her hands up, seemingly pleased.

"A lot of what Joe Ashbrook said was false in his testimony," Frost remembers. "I wanted to say something! I wanted to say that's not true; I wanted to defend myself. But Mrs. Miller had prayed, Ye shall hold your peace and the Lord shall fight for you." Frost held her peace.

Meanwhile, Jennie Wilson was keeping tabs on Jean Price. Price might be called to testify, so she wasn't supposed to hear any other testimony. But, in Wilson's recollection, Price had stationed herself just outside the crowded courtroom, and teachers were strolling out and repeating Ashbrook's statements to her. Earlier a court officer had said that the courtroom doors should remain closed; Wilson decided to enforce the decree. She worked her way to the back of the room and pulled the doors shut.

A schoolteacher glowered at her and said, "Who made you doorkeeper?"

Wilson replied by paraphrasing Scripture: "I'd rather be a doorkeeper in the house of the Lord than abide in the tents of the wicked."

Wilson squeezed back to her seat, turned around, and saw the doors open again. "I thought, I'll *never* get back there again. Lord, please give me a way to get that door shut. And so—I wouldn't recommend this; the Lord died for this sin the same as he did all others, and the fact that he died for my sins doesn't give me a license to sin—but I said, 'I'm getting sick, it's so hot in here.' And of course no one wants to be regurgitated on. I *was* hot, but I lied when I said I was sick. 'Whew, it's hot in here.' Like the Dead Sea, it just parted and I went straight through. The moment I got there, I whirled around and closed that door."

As it happened, Wilson needn't have sinned; Price wasn't called to the stand. After Ashbrook stepped down, the lawyers argued the case to the judge.

Frost's attorney, Mozert's church friend Les Bailey, contended that the trespassing law Ashbrook had read aloud in the principal's office was inapplicable. He pointed out that the law, section 49–818 of the state code, expressly exempted "parents of students."

Frost was also charged with violating another state law, section 39-3-1204. The story behind the second charge later emerged. While Frost sat in the holding cell, Chief Ashbrook called Berkeley Bell, the thirty-six-year-old prosecutor for the four-county region, and told him about the arrest. Bell pointed out that section 49–818 seemed to exempt parents, which undercut the case against Frost. After hanging up, Ashbrook told Judge Lawson that they needed to find another statute. Lawson himself then called prosecutor Bell and, after a five-minute discussion, added the second statute to the charges. Judge Lawson, a forty-three-year-old engineer and part-time country singer, wasn't a lawyer—the elected judgeship didn't require a law degree—and he periodically asked Bell for legal help. Prosecutors and judges don't ordinarily collaborate on charging decisions, though such rules aren't always followed in low-level state courts.

Now Les Bailey turned to this second statute, which prohibited acts that interfere with the normal, orderly operations of a school. This "very vague" language, Bailey asserted, would require an expert witness to flesh out, and the prosecution had failed to call one.

Michael Farris, who had flown down from Washington for the hearing, called Bailey over for a quick consultation, after which Bailey offered a more cogent argument. "Your Honor, let me say one other thing, and I think this is important. Just called to my attention. In 1970, in the United States district court for one of the districts of Tennessee, in a case called *Baxter v. Ellington* . . . it says, 'Tennessee Code Annotated 39-1215 is vague and overbroad, and therefore, declared to be unconstitutional.' " The second statute used against Frost contained the language found unconstitutional in that case, as the official statute book noted. In adding the second charge against Frost, Lawson and Bell had evidently neglected to read the fine print.

When Bailey finished, prosecutor Skip Simmons (a deputy of Bell's) presented the government's argument to Judge Lawson. Bickering with the principal and refusing to leave, he said, "certainly constitute a breach from the normal and the orderly activities of the typical school day." Indeed, "the officer had no choice but to take her into custody," because she "was continually in violation of both of these statutes." About the parents' exception in the first law and the unconstitutionality of the second one, Simmons said nothing.

After Bailey responded briefly, Farris asked to be heard. Having gauged Judge Lawson, he remembers, "I thought a simple presentation was needed." "Because of the exception clause" in the first law, Farris argued, "it's just impossible for a parent to commit that crime. . . . She is not a person unlawfully on the school premises no matter how much she argues, no matter how much she's disruptive. Since the other statute's been declared unconstitutional, both of those are taken care of. They just can't charge her under those two laws." At Lawson's request, Farris pointed out precisely where in *Baxter v. Ellington* the court had struck down the trespassing statute.

"I need to take a few minutes to look at this," Lawson said. "Recess for about fifteen minutes."

During the recess, Farris left the courtroom. In the hallway outside, he passed a man who, he later learned, was William Price, the chairman of the county Republican Party and the husband of Jean Price. William Price, in Farris's telling, turned to him and said: "When this is all over we're having you lynched, boy."

Farris was stunned. "For the first time in my life," he says, "I really understood what it was like to be a civil rights advocate in Selma, Alabama."

Price later maintained that Farris had misheard a remark about how the Holt books were being used in Jerry Falwell's school in *Lynch*burg, Virginia (as indeed they were, though with some pages razored out). Jean Price insists that her "calm, very cool, soft-spoken" husband would never threaten to lynch anyone. But Pam Cox, a journalist friend of the Frosts', says she overheard Price talk about lynching someone, though she thinks it was Frost rather than Farris.

Several of Jean Price's allies also find Farris's account plausible. "I wouldn't put it past William," says Carter's Valley Elementary principal Archie McMillan. The statement was "in character" for Price, says Volunteer High assistant principal Phyllis Gibson, but he probably didn't mean it literally. "There's an old saying here when somebody's giving you trouble: 'Somebody ought to burn him out,' " Gibson explains. "It's sort of a cliché in this section of the country. They don't mean actually setting you afire; they're just telling you to shut up." Board member Conley Bailey says, "He might've said it out of bitterness, but he's not the type of person that would mean it."

While Farris was encountering William Price in the hallway, Reece Gibson was standing on the balcony over the parking lot. He had left the courtroom for some fresh air, and several reporters had followed. Gibson told them that he had decided to step aside as juvenile judge in any proceedings involving COBS children. As the president of CARE, "I certainly do not intend to embarrass the position of juvenile judge by giving the appearance of a kangaroo court." He was appointing another Hawkins County attorney, Tex Morelock, to act in his stead. Morelock would ask school officials to drop the middle school suspensions so that the children would be required to return to school.

What, the reporters asked, if the children didn't return?

"The parents have instructed these children to take this action," Gibson replied. "So what you have, then, is that the children are committing unruly acts. The parents are encouraging, or aiding and abetting, or contributing to the unruly acts. That, then, could make the parents guilty of a misdemeanor, which would carry up to a maximum of eleven months and twenty-nine days in the county jail." The reporters scribbled this information down.

A few minutes later the audience filed back into the courtroom. Judge Lawson began with a warning: "Let me say first, before I announce my decision, I know that there is considerable feeling about this issue here. . . . The court's required to make the decision, and we'll do so. And we ask that there be no reaction to the decision. Of course, if there is, there could be contempt of court."

Then, in a grudging tone, he referred to the two statutes. The first law "excluded parents," he said, so it "does not apply." The other one had been "declared unconstitutional by the district court in '70. Since it has been declared unconstitutional, the court must find that it is null and void. Therefore the court must dismiss the charges."

With Lawson's contempt warning in mind, Frost and her supporters left the courtroom quietly. Outside, they beamed, hugged, and said a prayer of thanks. Frost, remembering Miller's prayer before the hearing that the Lord would fight for her, proclaimed to reporters: "The Lord has fought for me today and won."

Frost also spoke to two of her adversaries, according to notes that she later prepared for her lawyers. She "gently and lovingly" laid her hands on Joe Drinnon and Archie McMillan "and told them *I loved them*," which seemed to perplex the men. "The Lord had performed so wondrously," she wrote, "that I was ready to forgive and be reconciled with those who had offended me. But because of the hardness of their hearts, they began to devise *new ways* to keep me from my child. . . . Their hearts were set to do more evil."

The next morning, newspaper articles quoted Reece Gibson as saying that the COBS parents might be criminally prosecuted unless their children read the Holt books. Gibson later insisted that reporters had quoted his remarks out of context. He hadn't meant "to intimidate or threaten" anyone.

To the Frosts, though, it sounded like a threat. Gibson's statements suggested that "the children might be made wards of the state," says Roger. "That's when we had to leave," says Vicki. "We thought if they're only going to suspend the children, we can teach them at home or make other accommodations. But when Reece Gibson issued that order, we *had* to put them in private schools. We just couldn't suffer any more arrests." The Frosts began pricing Christian schools in the area.

Meanwhile the two sides' attorneys tried to negotiate a truce. The parents offered to let their children overhear other students reading the Holt books, as long as they would be excused from doing so themselves. "Each infant Plaintiff," according to one draft agreement prepared by the plaintiffs' attorneys, "shall be permitted and given full freedom to sit quietly in a remote portion of the classroom and read the Holy Bible or other reading matter brought with them from home." Under this plan, the parents would tutor the children in reading at night, and the children would take basic skills tests to chart their progress.

School officials, under Reece Gibson's guidance, presented a counteroffer: The existing suspensions would be canceled and the children would return to school, where they would read the Holt books. This offer wasn't especially generous; as Gibson had told reporters on the courtroom balcony, he had decided to urge the schools to drop the suspensions anyway.

The two sides wouldn't budge. In the end, Gibson said, "nothing could be worked out."

On the following Tuesday, Church Hill Middle School did lift the suspensions. Principal James Salley told Vicki Frost to bring her children to school the next day and to have them ready to read the Holt books. Instead, the Frosts enrolled their four children at Cedar View Christian School in Kingsport.

Salley also called other families and told them that the suspensions were lifted. Over the next few days, several children returned to the county schools, but most transferred elsewhere. Some enrolled at Cedar View or other Christian schools. For $112 per month, the Mozerts began sending their two children to the Kingsport public schools, which didn't use the Holt readers.

Two of the children who returned to the Hawkins County schools received unpublicized accommodations. In his call to Jan Whitaker, the mother of a suspended student (and the author of one of the letters about depravity at the high school), principal Salley said, in her recollection: "Jan, I've enjoyed having Steve here. . . . If you'll just let him come back to school here, I promise you he won't be forced to read the book." She agreed.

Several weeks later, however, Salley backtracked. He told Whitaker that his superiors were coming down on him, and he couldn't continue to accommodate Steve. "We'll work something out, but please leave him here in this school system," Salley said. "Don't take him out." Whitaker reluctantly agreed. At Salley's suggestion, she noted which stories were particularly offensive, and the teacher passed over them quickly in class.

Brenda and Junior Marshall had talked of transferring their daughter Gina to a Christian school. But, Brenda Marshall says, Gina "got real upset about it"; in fact she "was crying because she wanted to come back" when Salley phoned to say that the suspensions were canceled. "I told him she couldn't read the book," Marshall recalls. "He said she doesn't have to read it."

Gina returned to school December 12. During reading class each day, she left the room and studied alone in a small anteroom. Her accommodation, unlike Steve Whitaker's, lasted all year.

The Whitakers and the Marshalls—the only families to be accommodated after the suit was filed—were longtime Hawkins County residents. "We had known Mr. Salley for years," says Jan Whitaker. "A lot of the other parents, he wasn't that close to." "They were part of the network," observes Roger Frost.

Junior Marshall, moreover, played golf with school board member Conley Bailey and principal Archie McMillan. On the course, the school men had pressed Marshall. The Holt books were harmless, they insisted; Gina should come back to school. The discussions grew "real heated," Marshall recalls. "Archie and I almost came to blows a couple times." McMillan and Bailey liked Gina, who sometimes played golf with them. "She was sort of the golf course pet," her father says. But, though he wasn't devout—"I'm not a churchgoing person"—Junior Marshall backed his wife's decision about the Holt books. She had done a fine job raising the children, he told Bailey and McMillan, and he wasn't going to second-guess her. A short time after this conversation, Salley offered to excuse Gina from the Holt assignments.

Did the golf games help explain why Gina Marshall was accommodated and Rebecca Frost wasn't? "That's exactly right," says Phyllis Gibson of Volunteer High. "Oh, yes. Pure and unadulterated!"

A few days after the CARE rally, Jean Price talked with Barbara Parker of PAW for the first time. Price sheepishly introduced herself as the "bad woman who got Vicki Frost arrested." "Jean was a real pillar in the community," Parker remembers. "She was real worried about how people were going to perceive her. Were they going to believe her, or were they going to believe Vicki?" Parker tried to reassure her by explaining that "you are a player" in a "much larger scenario than just Hawkins County." And, she added, Price shouldn't feel alone: "We'll help you."

Three weeks later, Parker provided a bit of help. She visited Hawkins County and met with about twenty of the CARE organizers.

At the meeting, she showed the PAW film *Life and Liberty . . . For All Who Believe*. In the film, narrator Burt Lancaster warned about "a powerful, wealthy movement" with "one dangerous goal: to mix religion with partisan politics so they can force—and I mean *force*—their narrow doctrine on all of us." After footage of burning books, Norma

Gabler testifying before the Texas textbook committee, and an assortment of immoderate remarks by TV evangelists, Lancaster likened the religious right to "witch hunts, slavery, McCarthyism." The traditional American obligation to "respect the rights of others" was "under attack today," he added, and "without your help, our freedoms could be lost." PAW's 800 number appeared on the screen, alongside the emblems of Visa and Mastercard.

Parker also told the Hawkins County people about the Gablers and their nationwide influence. "I had never met Vicki up to this point," Parker recalls, "but I had read enough of their stuff to say she's not preparing these objections; she's clearly getting them directly from Mel and Norma Gabler."

In contrast to the December 5 CARE rally, this gathering was surreptitious and small. Having blasted COBS for accepting outside aid, the school people didn't want to be "seen with somebody who the rest of the community might perceive as an agitator," says Parker. Phyllis Gibson recalls being apprehensive about having "a Yankee" coming to town; they were relieved to learn that Parker was originally "a Memphis girl."

Ten days after Parker's trip to Church Hill, a second PAW agent arrived. Roberta Hantgan was a freelance production manager and associate producer who had worked on training films, industrial films, and a PBS series. Her specialty was illuminating the human side of an issue. "Find a teenager with epilepsy—that's the kind of thing that I tend to do well," she says. With Washington filmmaker Daniel Bailes and his company, Motion Inc., she had spent several months working on a film about creationism for People for the American Way.

PAW executives had been looking for a censorship incident that could be the centerpiece of a film. The Hawkins County conflict looked like a possibility. So, in early January 1984, Bailes dispatched Hantgan to Church Hill.

"My mandate," Hantgan wrote in a memo about her trip, was in part to "gain access and make direct contact with the right-wing organizers of COBS." She met with the Mozerts and the Frosts in the Frosts' Church Hill living room. Bob Mozert, with occasional help from Vicki Frost, held forth on the Holt books, John Dewey, and the humanist infiltration of public schools for more than two hours. Mozert and Frost said they would be glad to be part of a film if it would "promote public education and expose humanism."

Hantgan also visited Jennie Wilson, whom she found "open, friendly, enthusiastic, and fanatical." At one point, Wilson asked about Hantgan's faith. After trying to evade the question, Hantgan said she was Jewish. Wilson, in Hantgan's recollection, said, "I knew it, I knew it, I knew it!" and told her husband that Hantgan "looks just like" a TV reporter named "Hedy Levine or something like that." Then Wilson asked her to read a word in Hebrew, which Hantgan couldn't do. Later Wilson offered her some fish, "because, after all, I was Jewish and she wouldn't assume I would eat anything else."

After they had discussed the textbook controversy, Wilson returned to the matter of Hantgan's faith. "Let me ask you something," she said. "Where will you spend eternity?" "You know," replied Hantgan, "I really haven't thought about it too much." She started to feel that "the most gold stars one can get is to convert a Jew, and she had gotten me in a place she could work on me." Hantgan managed to escape unconverted.

To the Wilsons and the others she interviewed, including school officials Bill Snodgrass and Archie McMillan, Hantgan said nothing about People for the American Way. "My story," she wrote in her memo, "was that 'I was working for a small documentary film company, Motion, Inc. We've heard about the controversy in Church Hill. This seems to be the kind of situation which is presenting itself, not only in Church Hill, but in communities all over the country. Many parents seem to have a number of complaints about the schools. We're interested in hearing what these people have to say, with the possibility of later using Church Hill as part of a larger future project.' " She noted that the COBS members might not agree to be filmed "if they knew who we were."

"I don't think I ever quite lied to them," Hantgan recalls, "because that would've been hard for me. But 'I'm doing research for People for the American Way'—I never said that. . . . I remember feeling that it was a difficult situation to be in, and I felt slightly compromised at times. I didn't feel I could do the job effectively by telling them absolutely everything."

Even so, the Hawkins County protesters didn't fully trust her. At the outset of the meeting, Bob Mozert asked to see her driver's license in order to confirm her identity. "It is apparent," she wrote in her memo, "that both Frost and Mozert, but particularly Mozert, have become suspicious of any outsiders seeking information." Hantgan, moreover, wasn't just any outsider. "We kind of always felt that she

had something to do with Norman Lear," says Vicki Frost. "You
know, she *is* Jewish."

(Hantgan herself is wary too. Midway through an interview, she
says, "I'm starting to feel a little bit—I mean, I'll share information,
but it occurs to me I don't really know who you are, or whether you
are really from where you say you are. You're not insulted or anything,
are you?")

After four days in Church Hill, Hantgan returned to Washington
and recorded her impressions. The COBS people "present their stories
in a careful, logical, and at times even heart-warming manner," she
wrote. "These people have learned the value of appearing guileless.
Mozert couches his demands with statements like 'We believe in public
education' and 'Our quarrel is not against the system.' And although
the Wilsons will occasionally get a gleam in their eyes when speaking
about humanism and the NEA, their presentation is neither diabolical,
shrill nor frightening."

After studying the memo, filmmaker Bailes advised People for the
American Way against pursuing the project. "The COBS group is only
asking for alternative textbooks for their kids," he noted. "On the face
of it, this appears to be a mild request, although one that would make
education difficult. Vicki Frost and Bob Mozert, the COBS leaders,
claim to support public education and the right of other children to
read the textbooks. . . . We need to look for opportunities that portray
the issues clearly. And the overriding issue is the attack on public
education and freedom to learn. The Church Hill situation does not
allow us to focus in sharply on this issue."

Though Bailes was arguing only against making a film, his points
also apply more broadly. PAW aimed to stop the religious right from
imposing its orthodoxy on the public schools. For the reasons Bailes
cited, it was debatable whether the Hawkins County situation fit that
pattern. But Hawkins County did fit another pattern: fundamentalist
Christians seeking political power. For PAW in the early 1980s, that
was enough.

People for the American Way dedicated its research, fundraising, and
public-relations skills to combating "what we believe to be the greatest
immediate threat to our pluralistic society: the growing power of the
Religious New Right." But, in contrast to the unabashedly conservative Concerned Women for America, PAW portrayed itself as nonpar-

tisan. "This is not a movement of people of one particular view—a battle, say, of liberals against conservatives," a 1980 PAW publication said. If "a highly vocal minority" were steering the country to the left, Norman Lear declared in 1981, "I would be concerned about it." Publicity materials identified the organization as a "nonpartisan constitutional liberties foundation," and played up chairman John Buchanan's Republican credentials.

In practice, though, the most reliable way to predict PAW's position on an issue was to invert the religious right's stance. PAW denounced conservatives for boycotting sponsors of off-color TV shows, but it urged TV stations to refuse to do business with religious broadcasters unless they abided by voluntary financial-reporting standards. It deplored the Moral Majority for exerting "a chilling, intimidating effect" on people who disagreed with it, but it boasted that its own monitoring of television evangelists had "substantially moderated" their rhetoric. It criticized Accuracy in Academia for planting "spies" in college classes to report on professors' biases, but it dispatched its own undercover employees to attend and sometimes tape-record meetings of religious right groups. It denounced conservatives as censors for opposing schoolbooks over the ideas in them, but it urged a California agency to reject a history text that said the Bible inspired the authors of the Constitution. It opposed conservatives' efforts to have textbooks identify the political affiliations of people quoted in them, but, in the California incident, it declared that the textbook author's "radical right-wing beliefs . . . alone should have been grounds for close scrutiny of the book by members of the commission." And it argued that the First Amendment protects symbolic speech of the fringe left, flag-burning, but not that of the fringe right, cross-burning.

More than anything else, this reflexive opposition drew PAW into the Hawkins County controversy. "Michael Farris was not unknown to us," PAW president Tony Podesta remembers. "Where he popped up, we tended to pop over." Asked whether PAW would have intervened had Amish students, rather than fundamentalist Christians, sought excusals from a public school reading class, Barbara Parker replies: "I think People for the American Way might have *defended* their right to do that."

Despite their mirror-image political convictions, People for the American Way and Concerned Women for America had much in common in the early 1980s. Each held a well-defined worldview, which it wanted law and culture to reflect. PAW considered homosexuality normal, for example, and CWA considered it a "life-controlling sin." Each claimed to represent the truest traditions of the United States (Concerned Women for *America*, People for the *American* Way). Each saw the other as part of a wealthy, well-disciplined cabal aiming to quash dissent: to outlaw Christianity, to outlaw pluralism; to force antireligious views on everyone, to force religious views on everyone.

In the process, each side was quick to detect plots and sinister motives. While Tim LaHaye saw the humanist conspiracy behind whole-word reading, Norman Lear detected anti-Semitism behind the fundamentalists' emphasis on salvation and damnation. "When a preacher week after week talks about some people going to heaven and those who do not believe going to hell, unworthy of redemption and therefore condemned," Lear wrote in 1984, "I can't think of a more profound indoctrination into anti-Semitism anywhere in American life. And that frightens me, deeply."

Each side often portrayed opponents' aberrant, extreme statements as representative. Just as LaHaye trumpeted that "some secular humanists" favored legalizing incest, Podesta proclaimed that a Moral Majority official—a low-level one, it turned out—favored capital punishment for homosexual acts. Reading the organizations' materials, one might conclude that only atheists oppose school prayer (LaHaye called PAW "People for the Atheists Way") and that only anti-Semites oppose schoolbooks.

Each side also selectively omitted or misstated facts, as their fundraising letters about the Hawkins County conflict illustrate. In the CWA version, Vicki Frost "was thrown in jail because she didn't want her children reading anti-Christian school textbooks." She and her fellow plaintiffs—Beverly LaHaye had "never met more humble and more appreciative people"—only wanted their religious freedom; they "*never* asked for objectionable books to be removed." On the other side was "ultra-liberal" People for the American Way, with its "150 high-powered lawyer staff." "This is the most important case CWA has been involved in and we need your help. Please send your gift in the enclosed envelope and make it as generous as possible. God Bless You."

In the PAW version, "history was repeating itself" sixty-one years after the *Scopes* trial. Not only did the plaintiffs oppose "diversity, discussion and just plain thinking"; they were also racist (they believed that "God doesn't want children to read a book or sit in a class that deals with different races") and anti-Semitic (the Liberty Lobby was "helping the local censors by running a feature article in their national publication"). "Deeply connected to national censorship groups," these protesters enjoyed the support of Jerry Falwell, Pat Robertson, Tim LaHaye—"the entire Religious Right," people who "operate in unity—almost as one." "We agreed to help defend the school board. . . . It's clear we need assistance. . . . Even $35 could help us out of this bind. *I wouldn't ask if it wasn't absolutely necessary.*"

PAW had originally portrayed itself as fundamentally different from the religious right. Its "Statement of Purpose" decried the "voices of stridency and division" and "the temptation to grasp at simplistic solutions for complex problems." Lear pledged that his organization would succeed by "appealing to the best instincts in our people—not to their fears and anxieties."

Yet its fundraising letters and some of its publications seemed indistinguishable from religious right materials in stridency and divisiveness. Consequently, PAW was criticized by the press—not only the *Indianapolis News* and far-right columnist John Lofton, but also *Commonweal* magazine and liberal columnist Richard Cohen. After the *Commonweal* critique appeared in 1982, Monsignor George Higgins resigned from the PAW advisory board, saying he was troubled by the "letter and spirit" of certain PAW publications. Some donors dropped the organization too.

PAW staff members raised questions internally. One complained that the fundraising letters were employing "the same kind of rhetoric from a different perspective as the Jerry Falwells and the Pat Robertsons," in which "if the fact didn't fit the right pattern, it didn't matter what the fact was." In retrospect, this staff member now considers those complaints naive. "The cold, hard reality is that you have to raise money if you're going to have a viable organization that's going to do wonderful things."

The two Washington-based "superpowers," as Reece Gibson called them, were reshaping the Hawkins County dispute. Soon Gibson was declaring that "we want to teach them how to think, not what to think," and that "censorship and a free society just don't match," both PAW mottos; and the protesters, parroting their CWA lawyers, were depicting themselves as America's last beleaguered minority.

The organizations' influence went beyond pithy phrases. Litigation always shifts some measure of control from the parties to the lawyers. As a personal or political struggle becomes a legal one, with the law's arcane and unforeseen twists, the parties are obliged to defer to their attorneys. Here, in addition, the nature of the issues changed. The political struggle, dominated by arguments about who held ultimate authority over the Hawkins County schools, became a constitutional struggle dominated by arguments about pedagogy, religious burdens, and the intricacies of running a public school.

But something more was involved. A heavily publicized constitutional case can become "the vehicle for a bigger crusade of warring perspectives," says Oliver S. Thomas, a church-state lawyer in Washington. Where advocacy groups are providing legal counsel, as in *Mozert*, "it's even worse."

Concerned Women for America and People for the American Way wanted to prevail in court, but they also wanted to raise money, to generate publicity, and to craft a legal precedent that would bind the nation. Even if the lawyers disregarded the national groups' goals and singlemindedly advocated their clients' cases, as professional ethics require, the clients were still going to be buffeted by the advocacy groups' publicity machines. "Most organizations that do these kinds of cases have an agenda," says Mark Troobnick of CWA. "That's why we would take a case like that."

In this regard, Vicki Frost's remark about her adversaries applied equally to herself and her fellow plaintiffs in the textbook suit: "What they had done, and this is not maybe correct to say, but they had sold their souls to a national organization. They accepted their financial help, and they were bound to them."

CHAPTER SIX

RELIGIOUS BURDENS

O n the morning of November 23, 1983, while Vicki Frost was pacing in a Rogersville jail cell, Thomas Gray Hull was being sworn in as a federal judge in Greeneville. "As many of you know, I have waited a long time for this day, and I do not take it lightly," the man who would preside over the textbook case told a crowd of supporters. It was "right appropriate that this ceremony be held on the eve of Thanksgiving," he said, for he was truly a "thankful man."

The son of a Greeneville blacksmith who had a third-grade education, fifty-six-year-old Hull was no utopian idealist. "I'd like to say that I went to law school to try to create a better world for people," he says, "but that's not right. . . . I guess I went for the money, to be quite honest. My parents were getting old, and I needed to help support them and support myself. We had come from modest circumstances. I went because I thought it would be a good profession in which I could achieve monetary success along with other success." Hull had indeed succeeded: A thriving law practice combined with astute investments had made him a millionaire.

Hull had succeeded politically too. A moderate Republican in the Howard Baker mold, he had won a seat in the state legislature while still in his twenties. He had gone on to become chief clerk of the legislature, a state trial judge, and legal counsel to Governor Lamar Alexander.

Upon learning that the federal judge in Greeneville intended to retire, Hull returned to his hometown in 1981. "I came back here, really, to work on this," Hull acknowledges. But the sitting judge wouldn't step down until he had sold his house, which ultimately took another year. In the meantime, Hull ran for a seat on Tennessee's elected supreme court. "We have a stale supreme court—it's all male, all white, all Democrat, and all big city," he told voters. Hull, a small-town white male Republican, lost.

For a time it looked as though he would lose out on the federal court seat as well. He didn't have extensive experience as a judge or as a federal court litigator, and there was talk that he wasn't brainy enough for the federal bench. "Not a legal scholar," said one attorney who had dealt with him as a state court judge, "but likable." Worse, one of Hull's associates—a woman who had spent some eighteen years as his secretary, gone to law school, and then practiced law with him for about a year—had been convicted of smuggling marijuana. Although no evidence implicated Hull, the scandal left its stain. "A lot of things have happened to people around me," Hull observed at the time.

His friendships, however, stood him in good stead. "It was Reagan's appointment," says Hull, "but Senator Baker was running the show. . . . A friend of mine, name of Johnny Waters, was the campaign chairman for Senator Baker when he first ran. He and I had gone to school together, been up at the same fraternity, and been real close. He was supporting me too. I guess we just ganged up on Senator Baker. But anyhow, when you get one of these jobs, these federal judgeships, it's just amazing how you're appointed. You couldn't try to work your way in here at all. It's just fate."

In October 1986, Hull got a call from President Reagan. Did Hull have any objections to being nominated for the district court? None that came to mind, Hull said.

The Senate approved the nomination, and Hull took the oath of office. The following week, on the day he returned to Greeneville from a course for new judges, a constitutional lawsuit was filed in his court: *Mozert v. Hawkins County Board of Education.*

At issue in *Mozert* was the First Amendment's free-exercise clause: "Congress shall make no law respecting an establishment of religion, or *prohibiting the free exercise thereof. . . ."* Initially, the Supreme Court construed this clause as protecting only a person's right to believe, and not any right to act. Mormons were free to believe in polygamy, for instance; they just couldn't practice it. Then, starting in 1940, the Court reinterpreted the free-exercise clause. Now the Court held that the clause confers an absolute right to believe, as well as—this was new—a limited right to live by one's religious beliefs. (The Court also ruled that the clause constrains state and local governments as well as Congress.)

One of the leading cases concerned unemployment compensation. In *Sherbert v. Verner,* a Seventh Day Adventist was fired for refusing to work on Saturday, her sabbath. She was denied unemployment compensation on the ground that she was to blame for her dismissal. Not so, the Supreme Court ruled in 1963. Denying the unemployment benefits "puts the same kind of burden upon the free exercise of religion as would a fine imposed against [Sherbert] for her Saturday worship." Because she was fired for acting in accordance with her religious beliefs, the state must give her the benefits. The Court has applied the *Sherbert* doctrine in several subsequent unemployment cases.

A second landmark case concerned public education. In *Wisconsin v. Yoder,* Amish parents refused to send their children to school after age fourteen, even though Wisconsin law required attendance to age sixteen. Convicted of violating the compulsory attendance statute, three Amish fathers appealed to the Supreme Court.

In 1972, the Court reversed the convictions and, for the first time, created a religious exemption to a criminal statute. In his opinion for the Court, Chief Justice Warren Burger emphasized the magnitude of the threat to the Amish faith. High school would expose Amish children to contrary values "during the crucial and formative adolescent period of life." Many children might be lured out of the faith, which would pose "a very real threat of undermining the Amish community and religious practice." The Court added: "There can be no assumption that today's majority is 'right' and the Amish and others like them are 'wrong.' A way of life that is odd or even erratic but interferes with no rights or interests of others is not to be condemned because it is different."

In *Sherbert, Yoder,* and other cases, the Court set forth a test for determining whether government has violated the free-exercise clause. Someone seeking special treatment from government must demonstrate that his beliefs are religious and sincere, matters so subjective that the government often concedes them in litigation, and that the government action "burdens" his beliefs. He need not demonstrate that his beliefs are true or even logical.

If the claimant has proved that the government has burdened his sincere religious beliefs, the government must prove that it has a strong reason for refusing to accommodate the claimant. It must show, first, that its policy pursues a particularly important goal; and, second, that accommodating the claimant would unduly interfere with the fulfillment of this goal. In legal jargon, the government must show that it is pursuing a "compelling state interest" through "the least restrictive means." If the government makes these showings, it wins; otherwise, the claimant wins. (This test applied to *Mozert,* though the Supreme Court has subsequently modified it.)

In the amended complaint he filed in December 1983, Michael Farris followed this framework. The parents had "sincere bona fide religious beliefs . . . based upon a literal interpretation of the Holy Bible," he wrote. The Bible commands Christians to be "wise about that which is good and innocent as to that which is evil," which the plaintiffs interpreted as an injunction to avoid "any story or selection which teaches or exposes to children values, beliefs, or concepts which the Bible teaches as being evil."

Having outlined their beliefs, the plaintiffs next had to show how the Holt books offended those beliefs. They didn't have to prove that there was anything wrong with the readers. The constitutional issue wasn't the books; it was how the plaintiffs perceived the books.

But Michael Farris the litigator was also Michael Farris the born-again Christian, a man who had sued a school district for establishing the religion of secular humanism in the classroom, a man who would later label an adversary's legal argument "heresy" in a *Mozert* court brief. "You could see the true believer in him," a member of the *Mozert* defense team recalls, "in tone, rhetoric, style of argumentation." Another source remembers being struck by Farris's "religious fervor—he thought the other side was sinful."

Rather than depicting the plaintiffs' conclusions about the Holt books as subjective faith, Farris depicted them as objective fact. The books, he wrote, "teach" witchcraft, evolution, disobedience, and "the religion of humanism." In a secular courtroom, this tactic was risky. If Judge Hull—a churchgoing Methodist who characterizes himself as a moderate Christian—concluded that a story depicting witchcraft didn't thereby "teach" witchcraft, with "teach" defined by secular experts, then the plaintiffs would lose.

Farris, the constitutional litigator from Washington, didn't initially impress the Greeneville lawyer who was representing the Hawkins County schools. "His pleadings were inept," says Nat Coleman. "I thought to begin with, when we first saw him, Who in the hell is this rube?"

The plaintiffs faced a more immediate problem than Farris's miscalculation. On February 24, 1984, Judge Hull dismissed eight of the nine counts in the suit, including the allegations that the books taught witchcraft, situational ethics, humanism, and disrespect to parents. Hull ruled that even if these charges were true, the free-exercise clause wouldn't be implicated, and so a trial would be pointless.

To Hull, the free-exercise clause would apply only if the Holt books cast doubt on the overall validity of Christianity, and not merely on particular tenets of it. He wrote: "Only if the plaintiffs can prove that the books at issue are teaching a particular religious faith as true (rather than as a cultural phenomenon), or teaching that the students must be saved through some religious pathway, or that no salvation is required, can it be said that the mere exposure to these books is a violation of free exercise rights." Just one count in the complaint met that standard: the fifth one, which claimed that the books "teach that one does not need to believe in God in a specific way but that any type of faith in the supernatural is an acceptable method of salvation." If the books did teach that all religious pathways lead to God, Hull ruled, "that is a kind of religion in and of itself, and would be a constitutional claim."

Here Judge Hull was applying the wrong constitutional benchmark. The First Amendment's establishment clause—"Congress shall make no law respecting an establishment of religion"—forbids government from substantially advancing one particular religion or religion in general, such as by sponsoring school prayer. If the Holt books violated the establishment clause, the judge would be compelled to ban them from the classroom. But the plaintiffs were citing the First Amendment's other religion provision, the free-exercise clause, and they were seeking only to have their own children excused from reading the books. Government may violate free exercise even though the policy—the unemployment law in *Sherbert,* the mandatory schooling law in *Yoder*—doesn't substantially advance one particular religion or religion in general. Judge Hull, a newcomer to religion-clause jurisprudence, had overlooked this distinction.

Farris professed to be unconcerned about the eight-count dismissal. The ruling was "not too bad," he told a reporter. "We can live with it; we can win with it."

To keep the one count alive, Farris had to show that the books promoted a particular conception of salvation. Hull was approaching the inquiry just as Farris had framed it, as an objective assessment of empirical evidence. "The books have either got that in there or they haven't," the judge said. He asked Farris to point out particular passages in the readers that dealt with the salvation issue; "if you can't do it, I will just go through the books myself." The plaintiffs' subjective, Scripture-based interpretations of the stories were immaterial.

In response to Judge Hull's request, Farris filed a seven-page "Memorandum Regarding Stories on Issue of Salvation." Much of this memorandum was devoted to analyzing an essay that few if any students would ever read: Thomas J. Murphy's "More Than Reading," which appeared in the teachers' edition of the Holt eighth-grade reader.

"The McGuffey readers," Murphy wrote, "emphasized a Judeo-Christian values system in a most direct way. . . . The nature of today's reading programs has evolved because we want today's children . . . to have a sense of themselves as participants in a national and world community; to understand and to be mindful of the richness of our diversity; to value life and living. It seems to me that this is a noble idea and a sign of growth in the idealism that is a part of our people."

"I always have taken an interest in historical things," explains Murphy, who was Holt's senior vice-president for marketing, "and it had occurred to me that we had three interesting examples of how reading books were not just instruction, but in a way represented their times. The *McGuffey Readers*, which were very Biblical; the Dick and Jane . . . which was very white, very nuclear, very traditional; and the Holt Reading, which was an attempt to represent many people." This observation led him to write a banquet speech for a 1976 Holt sales conference, which ultimately became "More Than Reading."

To Farris, this essay was the smoking gun. "Murphy has communicated several important concepts to those who listen closely," the lawyer wrote. "First, he has clearly communicated that the point of these books is not merely the teaching of reading skills. The books are designed to promote a 'noble idea.' Second, he clearly contrasts McGuffey's readers and their Judeo-Christian values with 'today's reading program' and its value system (which is not specifically labeled). He conveys the concept that the 'noble idea' constitutes 'growth' and is therefore superior to the 'old' Judeo-Christian values. We know two things about this 'noble' new value system. It is contrasted with Judeo-Christianity. It is also designed to make children willing participants in a 'world community.' " With regard to the "world community" notion, Farris included a nod to the conspiracy-mongers of the far right: "What is a 'noble idea' to one is a 'subversive plot' to another." After discussing examples from the Holt books, he closed: "Holt Readers are indeed different than McGuffey readers. Purposefully."

Farris was miscalculating again. Unless Judge Hull was predisposed to believe in the secular humanist conspiracy (and there was no reason to think he was), he was unlikely to read the essay as evidence of what Farris termed "a unified program in indoctrination of children." Proving such a scheme in court would require taking testimony from Holt editors and subpoenaing internal company documents, which would be costly and time-consuming. And, most important, the task was unnecessary in a free-exercise case. The Amish in *Yoder* didn't need to show that Wisconsin's mandatory schooling law was part of a plot against them; they needed to show only that it had a disproportionate impact on them because of their faith. As before, it appeared that Farris's impassioned beliefs were skewing his litigation strategy.

(The conspiratorial strain in Farris's memorandum soon gave it wide circulation. Promoting it as "an excellent insight into the philosophical bases for fundamentalist attacks on public schools," the National Coalition Against Censorship began selling copies for a dollar apiece. The group distributed "many hundreds" of copies, says Roz Udow, director of educational and public affairs. "We're still distributing them.")

Once again, though, Farris's mistake didn't prove decisive, for Judge Hull proceeded to make a mistake of his own. In his March 15 ruling, the judge agreed with the plaintiffs on most factual issues. He found that the Holt books did present a particular worldview, by seeking to instill "a broad tolerance for all of man's diversity, in his races, religions and cultures." In pursuing that goal, they "intentionally expose the readers to a variety of religious beliefs, without attempting to suggest that one is better than another." The plaintiffs, in contrast, "believe that Jesus Christ is the only means of salvation." They "reject for their children any concept of world community," as well as the notion "that all religions are merely different roads to God, finding this an attack on the very essence of the Christian doctrine of salvation." The judge added that he "does not doubt" that the Holt books offended the plaintiffs' sincere beliefs.

In sum, Judge Hull found that a government policy was offending the plaintiffs' sincere religious beliefs. Such a factual finding would ordinarily shift the burden of persuasion to the government.

Judge Hull, however, didn't take that step. Instead, he erroneously granted the defendants summary judgment—victory without a trial. In his mind, the constitutional issue was whether the books were neutral and unbiased toward religion. "From what this Court has read, it would appear that the Holt Basic Readings carefully adopt this constitutionally mandated neutrality," he wrote. Accordingly, nothing in the books "can be considered a violation of plaintiffs' constitutional rights."

But Judge Hull still didn't realize that neutrality isn't the issue in a free-exercise case. The language of the Wisconsin statute didn't discriminate against any religion; it required children of all faiths to attend school. As the Court said in *Yoder:* "A regulation neutral on its face may, in its application, nonetheless offend the constitutional requirement for governmental neutrality if it unduly burdens the free exercise of religion." Farris, who was convinced that the Holt books weren't even formally neutral toward religion, had failed to make Judge Hull understand that formal neutrality wasn't enough.

The judge had made a "fundamental error," Farris announced. He said he would appeal the case to the United States Court of Appeals for the Sixth Circuit.

In a letter, Farris told Vicki Frost and the other plaintiffs not to be discouraged. "We won each and every one of the factual battles before the court," he wrote. "It is far more important to win the factual battles in the trial court than to win the legal battles. . . . I would predict that Nat Coleman is sweating the outcome of this case. He is sharp enough to understand that he probably won the battle but is fixin' to lose the war. . . . I feel confident in the Lord that we will win on appeal."

Judge Hull "confused this case with an Establishment Clause case," Farris wrote in his brief to the Sixth Circuit. In a free-exercise case, the

Vicki Frost points to "secular humanism" in a textbook as her husband Roger looks on. She charged that Hawkins County's new reading textbooks promoted telepathy, witchcraft, evolution, and "women's liberation."

Three of the four Frost children were soon caught up in the controversy. Seventh-grader Marty and sixth-grader Rebecca were suspended for refusing to read the assigned textbooks. Vicki Frost tried to tutor second-grader Sarah on school grounds. Only kindergartner Lesha *(right)* took no part.

(GENE BRYANT, *TEA NEWS*)

Jennie Wilson avidly studied exposés of secular humanism and passed "juicy tidbits" to Vicki Frost. Some adversaries suspected Wilson of masterminding the protest. Here she and her granddaughter Vicky Baker picket an anticensorship seminar in 1984.

The protesters charged that secular humanism infected even fairy tales in their children's schoolbooks, inspiring this editorial cartoon featuring a Jennie Wilson lookalike.

(*KINGSPORT TIMES-NEWS*)

(*LEXINGTON HERALD-LEADER*)

Bob Mozert headed the protesters' organization, Citizens Organized for Better Schools. He is shown here with his children, Travis and Sundee, in 1986.

James Salley, the principal of Church Hill Middle School, excused children from reading the new textbooks because, he said, he "really wanted to avoid trouble."

Principal Jean Price of Church Hill Elementary refused to let Vicki Frost tutor her daughter on school grounds—which provoked an arrest and a lawsuit.

Principal Archie McMillan of Carter's Valley Elementary decreed that children must use assigned textbooks, not the 150-year-old *McGuffey's Readers*.

· · SCHOOL DEFENDERS · ·

Hawkins County Juvenile Judge G. Reece Gibson led the local fight against the protesters.

(PHYLLIS GIBSON)

(KINGSPORT TIMES-NEWS)

Left: At Volunteer High School, assistant principal Phyllis Gibson tried to keep students from turning vicious over allegations of drug use and debauchery.

Before an audience of nearly a thousand people, superintendent Bill Snodgrass railed against "outside agitators with their fat wallets."

(HAWKINS COUNTY ELEMENTARY YEARBOOK)

Texas textbook critic Mel Gabler gave the protesters his thorough critique of the disputed texts and testified for them at trial.

(GENE BRYANT, TEA NEWS)

Beverly LaHaye put her immense organization, Concerned Women for America, behind the Hawkins County parents.

(CONCERNED WOMEN FOR AMERICA)

Dubbed by the press the "Memphis Smut Raker," Larry Parrish represented Vicki Frost in a lawsuit charging school officials with conspiring to violate her civil rights.

(KINGSPORT TIMES NEWS)

(PEOPLE FOR THE AMERICAN WAY)

All in the Family creator Norman Lear
founded the powerful organization People
for the American Way to combat the
religious right.

(CAROLYN SALISBURY, NATIONAL EDUCATION ASSOCIATION)

Barbara Parker (right) of People for the
American Way counseled Hawkins
County school officials. She is shown here
accepting an award from National
Education Association president Mary
Hatwood Futrell.

(TONY PODESTA)

People for the American Way president
Tony Podesta was eager to get involved in
litigation. The Hawkins County lawsuit
proved to be the perfect opportunity.

(THOMAS G. HULL)

(DAVID GOODRUM, HARBINGER)

Representing the school district in court, cerebral Washington lawyer Timothy B. Dyk sometimes had trouble connecting with Judge Hull.

Thomas G. Hull, the folksy federal judge who presided over the textbook trial, often was guided less by legal doctrine than by common sense.

(CONCERNED WOMEN FOR AMERICA)

One of the religious right's leading lawyers, Michael P. Farris represented Vicki Frost and the other plaintiffs. He is shown here outside the courthouse after filing suit in 1983; Frost and Beverly LaHaye are behind him.

(VICKI FROST)

After the case was heard by the Sixth Circuit Court of Appeals in Cincinnati, some of the plaintiffs joined their lawyer for a group photo. *Back row:* Jennie Wilson, Michael Farris, James Baker, Jr. (holding James III), Rachel Baker. *Middle row:* Rebecca Frost, Vicki Frost, Brad Eaton, Sue Eaton, Jimmy D. Eaton. *Front row:* Rebecca Eaton, Lesha Frost, Sarah Frost, Heather Baker, Marty Frost, Roger Frost, Vicky Baker.

plaintiffs must "demonstrate that the books offend *their own* religious beliefs. That they have done." Farris devoted two pages to this crucial point, but only after spending seven pages repeating his analysis of the essay "More Than Reading."

The appeals process moved slowly. It was April 1985, more than a year after Judge Hull had dismissed the final count, when Farris stood up and presented his arguments to three appellate judges in Cincinnati. The judges proved indifferent to both the establishment-free exercise distinction and Holt's indoctrination plan. Instead, they challenged the wisdom of the plaintiffs' parenting philosophy. "How can you get children out of the house and exposed to anything without exposing them to something contradictory to their beliefs?" one judge asked. "We don't live in a narrow world," another judge said, and the schools ought to familiarize students with alien ideas.

The defense attorneys were exuberant afterward. The judges "jumped all over" Farris, Nat Coleman told his clients. Coleman thought, in fact, that one of the three judges was perhaps "the most eloquent advocate" for the defense in the courtroom. Another defense lawyer, Charles Hampton White, opined: "I really don't think there is much doubt that the Sixth Circuit will affirm Judge Hull's ruling of dismissal."

"We've lost three to nothing," Farris told the plaintiffs. They should steel themselves, he said, for seeking further review from the United States Supreme Court.

But the issue that had dominated oral argument, the plaintiffs' parenting philosophy, turned out to have nothing to do with the court's ruling. Two and a half months after oral argument, the Sixth Circuit judges issued a unanimous opinion ordering Judge Hull to hold a trial.

Summary judgment, the judges ruled, was appropriate "only if there is no genuine issue with respect to the material facts of the case." Here, the parties disputed whether the plaintiffs held sincere beliefs, whether exposure to the books offended those beliefs, and whether the schools could feasibly accommodate the plaintiffs' objections. The appellate judges expressed no view on whether the plaintiffs deserved to win at a trial; the point was only that the plaintiffs deserved to have one.

Just as Judge Hull had at the outset, the Sixth Circuit judges seemed to misapprehend the issues. Hull had held that even if the plaintiffs were sincere, religious, and offended by the Holt readers, they hadn't stated a credible constitutional claim because the books were religiously neutral. The Sixth Circuit never mentioned the fundamental flaw in this holding: that the establishment standard of neutrality didn't apply in a free-exercise case.

The reversal of Hull's summary judgment astonished the lawyers on both sides. "It just goes to show how powerful God is," declared Farris, "and how little we should rely on our own understanding. . . . The victory was very sweet because there was no question in my mind that it came from a source other than my efforts." "I am at a complete loss to explain this result," defense lawyer White told his clients.

Though it wouldn't get there for still another year, *Mozert v. Hawkins County Board of Education* was on its way to trial.

During these pretrial proceedings, People for the American Way was increasing its stake in the Hawkins County textbook controversy. At a Washington ceremony in January 1985, Norman Lear presented PAW's "Freedom to Learn" award to CARE president Reece Gibson. "CARE is deeply appreciative of the tremendous support, advice and encouragement that we received from the People for the American Way," Gibson said. "They came forward at a time when we were confused, unorganized and not sure of what was happening or why it was happening to our school system."

Then PAW took on a more prominent role. With *Mozert* headed for trial, PAW president Tony Podesta and Barbara Parker worried that Farris would outmaneuver the East Tennessee defense attorneys. At a dinner party hosted by Children's Defense Fund president Marian Wright Edelman, Podesta chatted with Washington lawyer Timothy Dyk. "We talked about People for the American Way," Podesta remembers. "Tim said, If you ever need any help, we do some *pro bono* stuff—just let me know. This was on a Thursday or Friday night. Monday morning I called and said, We have a case for you in Tennessee. I don't think he ever expected to hear from me again. It was let's-have-lunch stuff."

Dyk said he would like to learn more about the case. So, on a Friday night in the fall of 1985, Church Hill Elementary principal Jean Price flew to Washington. Meeting with PAW people, Dyk, and several other lawyers the next morning, she recounted the history of the controversy and answered questions. All the defendants had local lawyers, she said, and though she couldn't speak for the others, she would welcome additional help. She thought that the Tennessee lawyers didn't yet recognize "what they were up against." And, according to one of those Tennessee lawyers, Nat Coleman, Price was desperate: "Jean was emotionally very much involved in this case, appalled by the attempt to exercise censorship through the back door. She would've been a willing participant in *anything* that she thought would help to defeat Vicki Frost and that group."

Dyk had never litigated a religion case before, and he found the prospect intriguing. After more discussions, an agreement was reached between PAW and Dyk's law firm, Wilmer, Cutler & Pickering. Dyk and other Wilmer attorneys would represent the school defendants in the case. The attorneys would not charge for their professional services, but PAW would pick up their expenses.

Some of the Hawkins County school defenders, however, weren't sure about the wisdom of bringing in Washington lawyers. According to Barbara Parker's memo on the conversation, Reece Gibson told her that if PAW and Wilmer stepped in, "it will blow the argument that CARE has made all along—'that an outside group—CWA—came into Hawkins County and stirred up a ruckus.' " Parker replied that the case "will have implications that extend far beyond the boundaries of Hawkins County."

There was also a second concern. Supervisor of instruction Joe Drinnon says he phoned a Nashville-based "expert on this sort of thing" to ask about People for the American Way. The expert advised, Drinnon recalls, "You can bring them in but keep a safe distance, because they're kind of liberal." Gibson, according to his law partner, was also "a little bit uneasy" about PAW's politics. In implacably Republican Hawkins County, Podesta notes, "Hollywood, Norman Lear, Washington, D.C.—these were not good words." Later, when the plaintiffs charged that local officials were allied with Lear, a Hawkins County pastor deplored this "less-than-Christian" accusation.

But Jean Price, who was an individual defendant in the textbook suit (as were the board members, the superintendent, and three other principals), was afraid of being abandoned by her local allies. "If she is in the case for the long haul, she wants to be sure that she has unwavering legal support," Parker wrote in a memo after talking with Price. "She pointed out that the school board will change next year (there are two seats up for election) and that the Hawkins County superintendency is an elected position. As she said, 'right now the board and superintendent are behind me, but there might come a day when they're not.' " Price wanted Dyk to represent her.

Soon the other defendants in the case came around, too. In its November 1985 meeting, the school board voted to accept the offer of legal aid. Wilmer, Cutler & Pickering would represent the *Mozert* defendants *pro bono*. Leading the defense team would be Tim Dyk.

Born in Boston in 1937, Dyk graduated from Harvard College and Harvard Law School. In the 1961–62 Supreme Court term, he clerked for retired Justices Stanley Reed and Harold Burton; the following term he clerked for Chief Justice Earl Warren. At Wilmer, where he went to work in 1964, he developed a specialty in communications law. He has represented CBS and other media clients in regulatory and First Amendment suits, and he has taught First Amendment courses at Yale, the University of Virginia, and Georgetown. A contributor to the Gary Hart, Walter Mondale, Michael Dukakis, Paul Tsongas, and Bill Clinton presidential campaigns, Dyk explains his lack of government service by saying: "We haven't had enough Democratic presidents."

Cerebral and soft-spoken, Dyk is a highly respected appellate advocate. "Tim is a superb lawyer, a superb craftsman," says Judge Laurence H. Silberman, a Reagan appointee to the United States Court of Appeals for the D.C. Circuit and, though their politics differ, a friend of Dyk's. "He's got everything—brains, experience, and competitive urge." Henry Geller, a former FCC general counsel who has often opposed Dyk in court, considers him "brilliant" and "tenacious." "Everyone who's dealt with him says he's brilliant," says one of Dyk's associates.

Podesta was delighted to have Dyk handling *Mozert*. "He's a big-city lawyer, but he doesn't come off as a brash, braggart lawyer," Podesta told a reporter. "I knew this case required a surgeon, not an artillery unit."

Podesta was also delighted to have PAW at the center of a major lawsuit. "We were looking to develop a litigation expertise before the case came along," he remembers. Some people within the organization had argued that PAW should educate and let the ACLU litigate, but Podesta disagreed. "The ACLU had sat there and watched Mel and Norma Gabler screw up the textbooks of America for twenty years, saying there is no constitutional infirmity," he says. "Their view of litigation was different from ours. . . . We had a dozen communication professionals; the ACLU only had one part-time person. Part of the mission of our organization was public education, and we saw the litigation program as related to that."

To Podesta, the Hawkins County case had immense potential. "This one was made to order," he says. "Vicki Frost, Michael Farris, Beverly LaHaye, the Gablers—scriptwriters in Hollywood could not have invented a better cast of characters. It just seemed too delicious to believe."

In late 1985, Dyk and his Wilmer colleagues traveled to Hawkins County for pretrial depositions—the recorded testimony of parties to a lawsuit and other people with information bearing on the suit, conducted with the opposing lawyers but not the judge. The plaintiffs found Dyk and his colleagues daunting. "Vicki Frost told me about him the first day," remembers Jennie Wilson. "She called me from the armory—that's where they had decided was neutral ground for the depositions. 'Oh, Jennie!' she says. She named that firm, and of course we both knew it was tied up with the New Age." (According to Wilson, Lloyd Cutler, a partner in Wilmer, Cutler & Pickering and an adviser to President Carter, "is a New Ager, a bigwig helping bring about the one-world government.") Frost added, Wilson recalls, "that they had this fellow that taught law at Harvard or somewhere. It was a picture of gloom. . . . I said, Well, we've just got to pray. Let's just ask the Lord to move that fellow on out and down the road. We prayed on the phone, and lo and behold, he left at noon. We asked and the Lord heard us and he was gone."

Later, Dyk's colleague Judith Wish deposed Wilson. According to John Payton, another Wilmer attorney who attended the deposition, Wilson wouldn't answer questions until Michael Farris repeated them, and she studiously avoided looking at Wish. After a few minutes, Payton told Farris that the disrespect was intolerable, and Farris instructed Wilson to answer questions directly. Wilson obliged, in Payton's recollection, though she did archly ask Wish, "Who's taking care of your children while you're here?"

Reece Gibson's deposition was still more rancorous. At the outset, Farris announced that Tim Dyk had no right to attend the deposition because he had not yet registered with the court as a counsel of record. "I want you out of the room," Farris ordered. "Right now."

Farris finally relented and let Dyk remain, but the atmosphere remained tense. At various points during the hours that followed,

Farris accused Dyk of speaking "a naked little lie" and of making "the most ridiculous objection I have ever heard in my life." When Dyk asked Farris to explain the relevance of a particular issue, Farris snapped, "Not to you I won't." Later, when Dyk said that Farris's line of questioning was "the strangest thing I've ever seen," Farris replied, "Well, hang on to your hat. You haven't seen this afternoon yet."

At another point, when Dyk argued that Gibson's religious beliefs were immaterial, Farris said condescendingly, "I don't know how many religion cases you've ever been involved in—I do these all the time—and the position of other people's religion is important as it pertains to how they perceive my client's religion." Dyk responded with exasperated tact: "I think that you're an excellent lawyer. You have a very large reputation. But you are not the judge in this case."

"I was mad about a couple of things," Farris recalls. "One was that Tim Dyk and those guys walked in without any prior notice to us. They didn't have the courtesy to give us a call and let us know they were coming."

The other cause of Farris's anger was the person being deposed, Reece Gibson. "There are only two kinds of people in Hawkins County: rich white Republicans and poor white Republicans," says Farris. "The rich white Republicans, frankly, got mad at these parents because they didn't know their place. . . . It's a part of the rural South where they didn't like uppity folks. Well, *I* don't like people who don't like uppity folks. I really, genuinely believe in the downtrodden."

Gibson was the most prominent of the rich white Republicans. At one point during the deposition, when Dyk objected to a question, Farris exploded: "Good, I'm glad you object. I object too. I object to the fact that he threatened to have these people arrested. And I object to the fact that he . . . said he was going to have these kids investigated in his capacity as a judge. It's very objectionable, what he did."

Thanks in large part to Farris, *Mozert*'s pretrial battles were fierce. In late 1984, he lodged a complaint against Reece Gibson for violating professional ethics. Gibson had signed a People for the American Way fundraising letter, which was printed on Hawkins County Juvenile Court letterhead.

"Dear Friend," the letter began. "I'll never forget the night I decided I had to get involved in defending our local public schools from a series of censorship attacks. I had known for several months that a group called 'Citizens Organized for Better Schools' was challenging a new reading series adopted by our local school system. At first, judging by their name, I thought they were a *local* group interested in improving public education. But as time went by, I saw that this 'local group' was deeply connected to *national censorship groups* and was *working from a nationwide Radical Right agenda designed to impose their ultrafundamentalist ideology and beliefs on our schoolchildren.*" Gibson and others formed an anticensorship group, and when one member of it "wrote to many well-known groups asking for advice and help," only People for the American Way *"was really equipped to help us. . . . Without PEOPLE FOR THE AMERICAN WAY*, the censors could have struck a damaging blow to academic freedom and our children would have been the losers." PAW *"urgently needs your help."*

PAW people had been hoping to get Gibson to sign such a letter nearly from the outset. On February 3, 1984, less than a month after her first visit, Barbara Parker first raised the possibility in a note. She asked Gibson to read a prototype fundraising letter "and let me know if there is a possibility that you might sign a similar letter." Gibson responded that he would "have no hesitation," but "I feel that I must be somewhat careful in that it will probably find its way into the hands of the COBS. . . . They would love to catch me in an error or misstatement, no matter how slight."

Farris thought he had caught Gibson in a whopping error: a violation of the American Bar Association Code of Judicial Conduct, which decrees that a judge must not "solicit funds for any educational, religious, charitable, fraternal, or civic organization, or use or permit the use of the prestige of his office for that purpose." Farris filed a complaint against Gibson with the Tennessee Court of the Judiciary.

The Court of the Judiciary ultimately concluded that the complaint "did not have merit for disciplinary action." The court gave no explanation for its decision, and the judge who was presiding, Ben H. Cantrell, now says his files shed no light on the matter. The court may have been influenced by the fact that the letter sought "support" and "help" but not, in so many words, money.

Farris's hardball tactics—"They were behaving like a bunch of damned gangsters," says defense attorney Nat Coleman—provoked the opposition to respond in kind. Like Reece Gibson, Farris soon found himself brought before a judicial officer on charges of unprofessional conduct.

The charges stemmed partly from statements Farris had made at the Gibson deposition. At one point, Farris pressed the juvenile judge on the details of CARE's fundraising. Dyk objected that the issue was irrelevant.

Farris responded with a stunning revelation. "Well," he said, "we have information there was an attempt to bribe the federal judge in this case, and I want to know where the money came from."

"Mr. Farris," said Dyk, aghast.

"You laugh," Farris interrupted, "you're from Washington. If you were from East Tennessee, you might think differently."

"I'm sure that Judge Hull, if any attempt had been made to bribe him, he would have brought that to someone's attention."

"I don't know if it ever got to the state of communicating it to—"

"And if you're suggesting, Mr. Farris, that Judge Hull would not do that, I would object on Judge Hull's behalf to the suggestion you're making."

"Well, I'm not suggesting that at all," Farris said defensively. "What I'm suggesting is, the matter never got to Judge Hull's attention. It never got that far. But there was apparently some money trying to be collected for that purpose. So we want to know about that."

Dyk said Farris was ethically obligated to turn his information over to federal prosecutors and leave the investigation to them. Farris replied that he had already notified the FBI.

A moment later, after asking about CARE's fundraising, Farris returned to the bribe. He said he had heard, "about fourth-hand," that money was collected for the purpose of bribing the judge. "Have you ever heard of that effort before today?"

"Objection," said Dyk.

"Okay now, excuse me," Farris said. Though not a police officer, he proceeded to give Reece Gibson a *Miranda* warning, telling him that his statements could be used against him and that he had the right to a lawyer (because Gibson wasn't a defendant in the lawsuit, Dyk wasn't representing him). "Counsel," Farris said to Dyk, "would you like to in any way embellish on what I've said to him?"

"Well, I don't know whether Mr. Gibson's interested in the Fifth Amendment privilege here," said Dyk. "I object . . . on grounds of relevance. I think you have not performed your ethical obligation properly, reporting this to the U.S. attorney. . . . I do not think that you are, so far as I know, a member of the U.S. attorney's office. And I think that this is not the proper place to go into these, what you characterize as fourth-hand hearsay allegations. I suggest that you approach this by the proper route, rather than trying to introduce this red herring into this deposition."

"I'm trying, Counsel, to lay it aside," Farris replied. "I'm trying to separate the allegations of any bribery. I'm just trying to get it on the record that he doesn't know anything about that, which I assume will be his answer. And then we can leave that alone."

"Well, I object to those lines of questions."

Dyk and Gibson conferred. "All right," Dyk said, "the witness is saying he wants to answer the question, and I don't have the power to instruct him not to answer."

Gibson asked to hear the question again.

"The question is," Farris said, "have you ever heard before today of any talk about any efforts at all to raise money for a bribe?"

"No sir," said Gibson, "I have not."

"Okay."

"Not a bribe of a judge or anyone else," said Gibson.

Farris's source was a Volunteer High School student. She later wrote in an affidavit that a classmate "told me of a phone conversation she had participated in a few days previously. She answered her home telephone and a high-ranking school official asked for her father. . . . Her father answered on another extension and she listened to their conversation for a while. She was told in the midst of the conversation to hang up the extension. Before she hung up she heard the school official ask her father for money 'for the judge in the lawsuit.' After the conversation she was told by her father to go get his checkbook. My best recollection is that the girl told me that the amount requested was $1000.00.

"Approximately a week or a week and a half later," the affidavit continued, "Mr. Farris called me while I was at the home of one of the plaintiffs in this case. . . . I refused to give Mr. Farris my name and I made the plaintiff, in whose house I was, swear to me that she would not reveal my name either. I told Mr. Farris substantially the same information as I relate here. . . . Mr. Farris tried to convince me to go to the authorities but I felt I would be unsafe in doing that at that time." She subsequently went to the FBI in Knoxville and gave them "all the information that I had concerning this matter."

The affidavit did not identify the friend who eavesdropped or the school official who requested the money. It even omitted the name of the affidavit's author, using "Jane Doe" instead. "I fear for my safety if my real name is revealed in connection with this affidavit," she wrote. Frost and Farris say that they never learned the name of the eavesdropper, but that the overheard caller was supposedly superintendent Bill Snodgrass. ("That's preposterous," says Snodgrass. "I have no knowledge of anything like that.") And the affidavit's author was Joni Lynn Deel, a friend of the Frosts'.

Joni Deel was COBS's undercover operative at Volunteer High. In addition to the bribe story, Deel had provided the allegations about "Sexual Abuse & Sexual Permissiveness at Volunteer High" in the unsigned letter, written by Vicki Frost, that Mozert had given the school board. "She kept us informed about what was going on," says Jennie Wilson, "but she didn't want anybody to know that she was a friend of Vicki Frost."

The friendship was, however, an open secret at the school. "Let me tell you," says Phyllis Gibson of Volunteer High. "Joni Deel was in my English literature class. We knew that she was friends with Vicki Frost. Some kids would tell her things just for the heck of it, because they knew she'd run and tell."

Defense lawyer Nat Coleman didn't know where Farris had gotten the bribe story, but he thought Farris had gone too far in asking about it, and in browbeating witnesses and lawyers. "We finally said there's only one way we can slow him down and make him behave in a professional way," says Coleman. He and Ronald Woods, another of the Tennessee defense attorneys in the case, asked Judge Hull to reprimand Farris for conduct that "affronts the integrity of the Legal Profession." Judge Hull referred the matter to magistrate Joseph A. Tilson.

Farris responded contritely to the allegations of rudeness. He wrote in an affidavit that "I have apologized to counsel for said remarks, and I have written letters of apology to the two witnesses."

"Well, let me say this," the magistrate said at a hearing. "I'm perfectly aware of the fact that lawyers occasionally lose their tempers. Matter of fact, I've done it a time or two myself. Not proud of it, but it happens. Your remorse is duly noted, and will be considered, and is commendable."

Concerning the other issue, Farris said he hadn't accused Gibson of taking part in any bribery attempt, and "I certainly do not believe, nor have I ever suggested, that such a course of action ever reached the point of actually coming to the attention of this court in some improper fashion."

"You made some extremely alarming statements" based on an anonymous phone call, magistrate Tilson said. "That is disturbing."

"I didn't want to have to go into this," Farris replied, "but there was a threat to lynch me after one of the hearings." In the context of this and other threats, he thought a bribe attempt was perfectly plausible. His source, he said, seemed reliable.

Tilson was unpersuaded. "You didn't even know . . . the name of the person you were talking to. How can you state that you felt that it was reliable?"

"Well, your honor, it was a judgment call on my part, and I may have used poor judgment."

In a decision issued a month later, Tilson ruled that Farris had "sufficiently corrected and rectified the unprofessional conduct" of his discourteous remarks in depositions, but that he had violated professional ethics by asking Gibson about bribery. For this "gross negligence and utter irresponsibility," the magistrate concluded, "Mr. Farris deserves to be and is HEREBY SEVERELY REPRIMANDED." Farris appealed the issue to Judge Hull, who, much later, set aside the reprimand.

With time, Farris and his team concluded that they had misinterpreted Joni Deel's story. The "judge" who needed a thousand dollars, they decided, was probably not federal Judge Thomas Hull, but Hawkins County Juvenile Judge Reece Gibson. The money was for a CARE slush fund.

"I never heard that, but I think it is *fantastic*," says Phyllis Gibson, laughing. "That's so ignorant, I'm surprised Michael Farris even repeated it." CARE was financed, she maintains, by small donations— "most people gave ten bucks"—and, when that ran out, by "money out of our pockets."

Although CARE never held another public rally, the organization did continue to speak out against the protesters. "The COBS are no longer staging media events," Reece Gibson told CARE members in a January 1984 letter. The protesters had lowered their profile, he surmised, because "they have been countered by CARE in every publicity effort that they have made." Nonetheless, Gibson wrote, "they are still working quietly behind the scenes by making individual contacts. . . . WE

MUST NOT STOP AT THIS POINT." He closed by asking for contributions: "Many of you have indicated a willingness to support CARE financially and since we have hired an attorney who is working very closely with the School Board attorneys, we have incurred expenses. Anyone who can make a donation, no matter how small or large, please send it."

CARE paid a small retainer to a Kingsport lawyer, but he ultimately played no role in the lawsuit. "It became apparent that we were well represented legally," Gibson later told an interviewer. "It also became apparent that we *weren't* well represented as far as public opinion. . . . So what we did, we became the spokesman for the anti-censors against the COBS." In his estimation, "this type of thing is won in the court of public opinion."

Gibson kept busy trying to sway public opinion. During the month that he wrote the letter to CARE members, Gibson appeared on the CBS program *Nightwatch*, along with Barbara Parker, Michael Farris, and Vicki Frost. Afterward Gibson wrote to tell Parker that he was "quite pleased with the results." He added that he hoped Parker would be able to debate Farris one on one, because "you would show him up to be an idiot." Gibson also gave speeches all over East Tennessee. He reported to Parker that he had spoken to a Unitarian Church "and received a very enthusiastic response. . . . Talk about bright people!!!"

Most school people were happy to let Gibson be their public spokesman. Bill Cordell, the president of the elementary school PTA, wrote to tell Gibson that "I'm thankful you let us drop the ball in your lap—you're doing a heck of a job running with it!"

Publicity was a dicier matter for Vicki Frost and her fellow plaintiffs. Farris warned them that an ill-considered remark to a reporter could, if discovered by defense attorneys, complicate the case immensely. The protesters, however, weren't wholly obliging.

Bob Mozert continued to grant interviews, but Farris was forgiving. "Bob is Pentecostal and I'm not," he says. "He believed that God was wanting him to do some things that, if I'd had my druthers, he would not have done. . . . But I wasn't about to shut him up and be guilty of the same kind of religious bigotry as these other folks."

Farris also had scant leverage over Jennie Wilson. Because the school policy affected her grandchildren, rather than her children, she wasn't a party to the suit. "I think he got mad at me two or three times for being an old chatterbox," she recalls, "but after all, I wasn't a plaintiff." Frost says: "At CWA, they were somewhat embarrassed by Jennie."

Wilson continued writing incendiary letters to the editor. In one, she suggested replacing the American flags in front of county schools with United Nations flags, "to show their support of the one-world Holt philosophy." In another, she provocatively quoted the *Communist Manifesto* and then launched into a diatribe against People for the American Way; she never connected the two. In still another letter, Wilson linked PAW to *Playboy*, homosexuals, "Militant feminists," "Anti-nuclear advocates," and "TV and film producers," and closed: "People for the American Way—really?" This one provoked a response. Wilson's letter was "completely false and inaccurate," wrote PAW's Marcie Rickun. PAW "is a national nonpartisan citizens organization," with a board of directors chaired by "former Republican Congressman John Buchanan of Alabama."

The protesters' media efforts were unavailing. Opinion was solidly set against them. In a show taped after the trial, the *Donahue* audience snickered when protester Rachel Baker disputed the theory of evolution. "Now wait a minute," Phil Donahue chided. "Just 'cause they're from Tennessee, you think they don't know nothing. They love their children just like you do."

Even in fundamentalist Hawkins County, where no one would titter at talk of creationism, the protesters were pariahs. On behalf of CWA, Vicki Frost and Jennie Wilson conducted an informal telephone survey about a political issue in early 1985. "Didn't have anything to do with the textbook case," says Frost. "This one woman said, Well, I hope this is not like that COBS, 'cause they're trying to overthrow the government." Frost shakes her head in exasperation. "Here we were trying to *support* Americanism, patriotism, the Bible—but they thought we were doing completely the opposite!"

To Frost and her allies in Hawkins County and in Washington, these events and attitudes could only be the fruits of a conspiracy. Meanwhile, Frost's adversaries in Hawkins County and in Washington were concluding that they too must be victims of a monstrous conspiracy.

CHAPTER SEVEN

CONSPIRACY TO INTIMIDATE

"Through the whole process, you understand, these were good people involved," says Carter's Valley principal Archie McMillan. "Good *Christian* people. Yet the school system and the people in it were put in a situation where we were the bad guys against God, mother, and country. Every time we said something, it was turned and used to make us look like we were evil. . . . It was a terribly frustrating time."

Early on, the protesters did sometimes impugn their adversaries' faith or morality. After board member Larry Elkins said he didn't see any humanist taint in the Holt books, he recalls, Jennie Wilson informed him that he must not be a true born-again Christian. "I just didn't have a whole lot of regard for them after that," he says.

Once the suit was filed, though, the protesters avoided voicing such judgments about those who disagreed with them. They maintained that they wanted different readers for their own children, nothing more.

Some school people construed even this request as an affront. Roy T. Englert, Jr., a Wilmer lawyer who worked on the case before trial, says: "They couldn't quite understand—in part because it wasn't entirely true, but couldn't understand even to the extent it was true— that someone can object on religious grounds to what you're doing without saying you are a bad person. They all took it personally. . . .

This was not somebody coming in and saying, 'My religion is different from yours so I should get different treatment.' This was someone coming in and saying, 'My religion is the same as yours but you are not practicing it right.' "

The experience was especially hard on Church Hill Middle School principal James Salley. He had let children use alternative readers until the school board overruled him; then he had reluctantly suspended children whose parents wouldn't let them attend the Holt reading class. "It was an absolute nightmare for Coach Salley," remembers McMillan. "It permanently scarred Jay. . . . In his mind, it became a real monster. He blew it up." Nat Coleman, the Greeneville lawyer who was helping defend the textbook suit, says of Salley: "He was terrified by this lawsuit. I thought he was going to have to be hospitalized. . . . He really went through hell." Administrator Joe Drinnon says that the controversy "did much damage, in my opinion, to his physical and emotional well-being. Jay's a very moral person and, in my opinion, they did a great disservice to their cause, to *any* cause of the Judeo-Christian ethic, by assaulting people like that."

Jean Price, the elementary school principal whose dispute with Vicki Frost had led to Frost's arrest, also found the experience taxing. "What people think of me is very important to me," Price says. "I've always tried to live a Christian life, and to be an example to my faculty and to my students. . . . And then for somebody to come in and say that maybe I wasn't a Christian—that really was hard." "She took it very personal," says Phil Junot, the PTA officer at her school.

Salley and Price weren't alone. "There was times that I didn't sleep well at night," says McMillan. "It was a terribly traumatic time for everyone involved, because of the stress. You begin to think the irrational are taking over the world."

To be sure, being in the middle of a national conflict—and, in the press's eyes, being on the right side of it—had heady aspects too. "Would love to see you and discuss the many censorship cases that seem to be going on," Price wrote PAW's Barbara Parker in August 1985. "I tell everyone about our experience every time I get the chance." Joe Drinnon speaks proudly of feeling that "we had a battle to fight for more people than ourselves." "Honey," says Volunteer High's Phyllis Gibson, "this was the biggest thing that happened to Hawkins County since they had a lynching!"

But, Gibson goes on to say, the excitement lessened as the conflict dragged on. "A lot of people were just fed up," she remembers. "This lasted years. Now the first gallon of ice cream's good, but after that it gets a little gaggy."

The conflict affected the people on the other side too. Vicki Frost, seeking to remind her children that "we need to cleanse from our lives things that are hostile to the person of Jesus Christ," lit a bonfire in the backyard. As the children watched, she and Roger burned rock records and tapes, a Smurf that someone had given Lesha ("a Smurf is associated with the occult and magic," Vicki explains), and children's books that portrayed magic. "There's nothing wrong with burning something that's hostile to the person of Jesus Christ," Vicki says, "no matter who thinks it's extremist or radical or whatever."

Besides losing a Smurf and some books, the Frost children lost their television set. Their mother banished the TV to a storehouse, and for good measure cut the cord off. In a deposition, she explained: "I don't like the philosophies that come through on the television. . . . I feel about television in some senses the way I do about these Holt, Rinehart, Winston books."

The children also had other adjustments to make. "I kind of hated to change schools," says Marty. "At Cedar View they put me back a year. I'd been in seventh grade, and they put me in sixth." "I didn't like it at first because I hated to leave all my friends at Church Hill," says Rebecca, "and I was afraid to go into a Christian school because of all the things I've heard—that it was real hard and everything." Second-grader Sarah also had difficult moments. "I was riding the bus home one day," she remembers. "This fifth-grade boy goes, Is your momma Vicki Frost? I go, Yeah. He says, Your momma's *stupid.*"

The Frost children all left the public schools in December 1983, but several other plaintiffs' children stayed. At the middle school, Steve Whitaker was given an alternative reader for a few weeks after the board's Holt-only resolution, then he too was required to read the Holt book. During class discussions, he didn't point out what he considered to be errors in the Holt stories because he was afraid of being suspended again.

Some plaintiffs transferred their younger children from elementary and middle school but left their older children at Volunteer High (the Holt readers ended with eighth grade). Jan Whitaker says her high school son Chip had a rough time. Still incensed over the COBS letters

—one of which Jan Whitaker had written—students regularly threatened to beat him. "People would call this girl he was dating and tell her that they were looking for Chip and that he'd better not be caught walking around at the mall," his mother remembers.

High school classmates would sometimes chant "COBS! COBS!" when Angie Eaton, whose parents were also plaintiffs, passed by. "I went down there to pick her up one time," remembers Sue Eaton, Angie's mother, "and one girl lay down in front of our car. . . . It was a joke to some of her friends—your mom is one of *those* people." Later the Eatons did transfer Angie to a Christian school. "It was a hard change for her," her mother recalls. "She couldn't wear jeans, and girls made fun of her. Just a whole number of things. She was dating a boy at that time, and he told her that she wouldn't be able to get into college since she went to a Christian school. So she just got married. That was an easier out." Angie was fifteen at the time. The textbook conflict "changed Angie's whole life," her mother says.

"Peer pressure," says Jennie Wilson. "That's one of the things that's practiced in school. If you don't wear your little sneakers and your blue jeans and your knit shirt, you're different. . . . You're not in the right pecking order, and you ought to be pecked."

The adults had troubles of their own. Bob Mozert lost his job after a newspaper published the name of his employer. "Insurance companies are very conservative in nature," he says. "They want to keep a very low profile. They don't want any kind of controversy at all in the public eye. And I can understand the wisdom of that."

At one point Mozert got a call from a man identifying himself as Mel Gabler. "He told me how poor a choice we'd made by coming against these books, there are much worse things," says Mozert, "and he wished we'd never done this, wished we would drop our suit. . . . His impersonation was close to Mel Gabler's, except there was a spirit about it. His voice seemed to be more depressive, like an oppression from that individual that was speaking. Not an upbeat, positive type of voice like Mel Gabler's. Still I believed it was him; I just believed maybe he was having a bad day." Mozert later talked to Gabler, who denied having made the call.

Asked who could have done such a thing, Mozert thinks for several seconds and then says: "Anything that I would say would be purely speculative. . . . I know that the Hawkins County school board was joined by the misnamed People for the American Way, Norman Lear's

group—who crawled into bed with *Playboy,* started their organization
with a $40,000 grant from *Playboy.* That's the kind of opposition that
was against us, so I'm really not surprised by anything that was done."

Mozert and the other protest leaders no longer held public meetings
or attended school board meetings. COBS essentially disbanded, says
Mozert, for the protection of its members. He had read about the
1974 textbook protest in Kanawha County, West Virginia, which had
provoked shootings, beatings, and arson. As in Kanawha County, "I
saw the course of events headed toward violence."

The reason, he says, is clear: COBS was threatening the power
structure of Hawkins County. "The first week there were thirteen of
us. . . . The second meeting we had fifty. And the third meeting we
had a hundred. These are weekly meetings." (Mozert misremembers;
they were monthly meetings, and a reporter at the third one estimated
the crowd at seventy-five.) "At that time we started getting threats—
bomb threats, burning your homes, killing people, those kind of
things, from the opposition—because they saw how we were growing
in leaps and bounds. In three weeks it had increased from thirteen to
a hundred, so people were really beginning to see some things. Well,
they didn't want them to see some things."

Marion and Jennie Wilson and their daughter, Rachel Baker, faced
what they believe was a threat of imminent violence. As they were
driving one evening, two cars raced past, and a third one paused
alongside while someone shined a spotlight at them. The license plates
were covered. "They were fixing to do bodily harm to the wife and I,"
Marion Wilson says. "Either they would've forced us into running off
the road, or they would've blockaded us some way and maybe beat us
up." "But we confused 'em," says Jennie. "We wasn't in my car."
Instead they were in the Bakers' car, which the would-be assailants
hadn't seen before. The pursuers sped away.

The Wilsons were evidently a favored target, according to Jennie
Wilson. Several men approached their daughter's husband, James
Baker, at work and asked how he would feel if they came by with their
guns and "got rid of" his in-laws. He lived near the Wilsons, Baker
replied—and he had a gun too.

During the middle school suspensions in late 1983, plaintiff Sandra
Couch felt that the state might well try to take away her children. She
and the children left the county for a few days. "Even when we came
back home," she says, "we told them where to go if someone came to

the door and said, We're here to take your children. They knew which neighbor to go to, who would get them to family somewhere."

The protesters also felt alienated. Friends and even relatives stopped talking to her, Sue Eaton remembers. "Some of them don't even speak now." She adds that she grew close to the other plaintiffs, most of whom she hadn't met before the controversy began. "These became our only friends."

"You always feel like an outsider," says plaintiff Christine Meade. "When people find out you were involved in the textbook case, even now, unless they know what really went on, you're just looked at as a troublemaker, a fanatic. Most of the people don't understand to this day what really happened."

The stresses proved too great for several families. A relative who had worked for the Hawkins County schools harangued Brenda Sue Arnold for being a plaintiff in the suit. In addition, her husband Larry got a call from a fellow Mason. "He said, Larry, there's been a lot of talk at the lodge," Larry remembers. "He was trying to get me to be quiet about the textbooks." (Arnold subsequently resigned from the Masons, which he now denounces as "the largest cult in the world.") The Arnolds' son, Michael, also wanted to return to his friends in public school. So the Arnolds withdrew from the suit. "I think I made a big mistake," Larry Arnold reflects. "Probably I'd be a lot stronger Christian if I'd stayed in. If you're going to be a true believer in Jesus Christ, you're going to be hated."

Other families who dropped out of the suit included the Marshalls. Gina remained at the middle school, where she read an alternative book for the rest of her sixth-grade year and then used the Holt book in seventh and eighth grades. "I didn't want all the publicity from the lawsuit," Gina says. "If you're in sixth grade, you don't want that kind of attention."

Of all the anti-Holt activists, the Frosts endured the most. Volunteer High students, seething over the COBS letters, spoke openly about burning down the Frosts' house, slashing their tires, beating Vicki if they caught her alone, and even murdering her. Joni Deel, their high school friend, duly passed these remarks along to the Frosts. Worried that someone might poison their water, Roger put a lock on the wellhouse.

Volunteer High assistant principal Phyllis Gibson acknowledges that Deel's reports were accurate. "Insulting the school's reputation, that brought out the worst of them, you bet," she says. "The kids could've got vicious. . . . They could've done some really bad things." But, she says, she and principal Pat Lyons "asked them not to. We said this is not anything to get vicious over; you don't do that. . . . We talked to a lot of kids that we knew could pass the word." The students never made good on their threats.

Along with worrying over what the high school students might do, the Frosts were also sustaining countless slights and jibes. A woman screamed at Vicki in the grocery store—"You're trash! I'd be ashamed to show my face in public!"—until Vicki called the police. Once when she entered the Mountaineer Restaurant alone and sat down to eat, people at adjoining tables got up and moved. "I even went into Sears's bathroom," she says. "I guess the Lord was leading me." Inside, she found graffiti written in all three stalls: "Vicki Frost is a whore." When she went to the Mount Carmel post office to close the COBS postal box, a clerk asked whether mail to the box should still be forwarded to Wisconsin. Someone had evidently forged a change-of-address form.

In addition, the Frosts were targets of a series of rumors. According to one, Vicki had been arrested for storming into her daughter's elementary school classroom, hollering dementedly against the Holt books, and terrifying the young children. Another rumor had it that the Frosts belonged to a cult. According to another, Vicki was an accomplished troublemaker who had picketed a landfill and a nuclear plant; that's why she had been chosen to lead this protest. (Frost insists that she had never visited a nuclear plant or picketed anything.) Still another rumor claimed that Vicki and Roger Frost had separated; only Michael Farris's insistent intervention was keeping them from divorcing. (Though the Frosts' marriage had its difficult patches, "I knew of no troubles of that degree," says Farris. "I would talk to them both when they were discouraged, but in terms of direct marital counseling, I don't recall any.") The school system seemed to be behind the rumors' spread, if not their creation. Teachers passed the tales to one another and regaled students with them in class.

With all the publicity, the threats, and the hostility, Vicki Frost could no longer be the anonymous "homebody homemaker" she had been at the outset. "When I'd call to a drugstore or call about having my car fixed, they'd say what is your name—oh, I have to say my name!" she says. At one point, some twelve hundred people signed a petition against an X-rated video store in Hawkins County. Only

Frost's photo made the front page of the newspaper; the petition was portrayed as another Vicki Frost crusade. "If you can trace it back to Vicki Frost," she says ruefully, "you can discredit whoever else is involved."

"I've never seen anybody take such a barrage," says Larry Parrish, one of her attorneys. "What surprised me the most was how many of those people were aligned with her philosophically, religiously, scripturally. They had children in the public schools, and because she had taken hers out of public school, they took that as a direct slap. She thought she was better than they were, holier than they were. It was a statement by her of superiority, and they reacted accordingly. . . . She could hardly get out of her house without somebody jeering. . . . My heart broke for her."

The controversy was also onerous for Roger Frost. "Roger probably suffered more than anybody in the textbook case, because of his emotional makeup," says Vicki. In 1986, Larry Anderson, a Baptist preacher whose church the Frosts had previously attended, said in a letter to one of the *Mozert* plaintiffs: "In problems relating to my family it is definitely the responsibility of the man to take care of the situation, not the woman. If my child has a problem at school, or if I am disturbed about something which I don't approve, I won't permit my wife to be placed in a jeopardous situation." Roger felt that his manhood was being challenged. "That really hurt him," says Vicki. "Hurt his dignity. Roger had gone to Larry's church and supported him financially, and it hurt him for someone to make that accusation." There were also money worries. "He was under a tremendous financial burden to keep all his kids in Christian schools," Vicki remembers. They were able to do so only because Roger's parents lent them the money, interest-free, to pay off their mortgage.

Despite their sorrows, leaving Hawkins County was never an option. "This is home," Vicki says. "I've always lived in East Tennessee. Where could I go? If I moved up the road to Bristol, it's there. If I moved to Knoxville, it's still there. It was so broad, the attention and the media. Unless we moved completely away from our family—and we don't want to leave our mothers and our fathers."

The Frosts also didn't retreat because, to an extent, Vicki relished her woes. "It kind of gave me hope when I saw the enemy attacking," she says. "When you see the spiritual battle intensifying, you know you're on the path of truth."

Her suffering had another facet too. Even though she was confident that God had forgiven her—"God even loves murderers like me"—she felt profoundly guilty over her 1970 abortion. "I have a tendency to abase myself continually," she says. "In some respects I feel like I need to be punished. And when I'm badly treated, I more or less accept it as my due."

For people on both sides, the textbook controversy seemed so disruptive, so anguishing, that the underlying causes had to be monstrous. On each side, people perceived the muddled, improvised actions of their adversaries as elements of a sinister plan.

"This whole thing was made up out of whole cloth," says defense attorney Nat Coleman. "Concerned Women came down here, and it was just like a casting session—if you're going to produce a film, you go out and try to find actors to perform certain roles. And they very cleverly found Vicki Frost, because she fit the role that they wanted her to play perfectly. . . . This thing was contrived, it was manmade, it was orchestrated, it was not real from day one. . . . They scripted it very cleverly and cast it very well."

"I think Concerned Women for America had it all planned," agrees PAW's Barbara Parker. "That's why Church Hill was chosen." After finding a town with bedrock fundamentalism and an ongoing book protest, CWA convinced the protesters to drop their initial censorship request and then told Frost to get arrested to generate public sympathy. "I am totally convinced—and I know it sounds like a conspiracy theory—that this whole thing was set up," Parker says.

CWA's Michael Farris, however, maintains that the COBS strategy was fully developed long before he entered. His first contact with COBS came in Frost's phone call the day before her arrest. If there had been any earlier contact with CWA—Jennie Wilson says she wrote to the organization—Farris says he knew nothing about it.

In the CWA/COBS version, People for the American Way was the provocateur. Jordan Lorence, a CWA attorney who worked with Farris on the case, says that "Jean Price talked to People for the American Way officials, and they encouraged the Hawkins County officials to dig in their heels" by withdrawing the middle school accommodation. Vicki Frost says that PAW "moved into Hawkins County, setting up this Citizens Advocating the Right to an Education, providing them with materials." CARE, she charges, was essentially "a community outreach program of People for the American Way."

Not so, according to Parker. "They did have *Protecting the Freedom to Learn,* but there was no human contact until after Thanksgiving," she says. "That was what Farris kept trying to pin on us—that they could have handled everything fine but we went down and said the principals shouldn't be allowing this to be taking place. We did not do that."

Although scattered shards of evidence support each conspiracy theory, the bulk of the evidence supports each organization's account of its own entry into Hawkins County. The conflict was most likely local until late November, around the time of Frost's arrest.

The matching plots ultimately reveal less about the course of events in the fall of 1983 than about the magnitude and tenacity of the mutual suspicions. The Washington headquarters of PAW and CWA were only a few miles from each other, but the organizations' worldviews were light-years apart. The demagogic, take-no-prisoners rhetoric of each side's fundraising and public relations further impeded mutual understanding. In Hawkins County, the people on both sides generally shared a fundamentalist Christian worldview, but they too spoke past each other. The protesters were concerned about parental control of education and citizen control of government, about being treated with courtesy and respect by public officials, and about secular humanism and the New Age. The people on the other side were concerned about maintaining order in public schools and in public life, and about defending Hawkins County ways against attacks, especially attacks launched by outsiders.

The fierce suspiciousness produced subsets of matching conspiracy theories. "They were supposed to have arrested Vicki the day before, but they got mixed up down at the police station," says Jennie Wilson, referring to the school system conspirators. "The arrest was supposed to be the day before, and they got their wires crossed," says Phyllis Gibson, referring to the COBS conspirators. With time these conspiracy theories grew more solid, more elaborate, more fervent. The result was a second lawsuit.

On November 20, almost exactly one year after her arrest at Church Hill Elementary, Vicki Frost filed suit seeking a million dollars in damages. Her suit charged that the defendants—the city of Church Hill, former police chief Joe Ashbrook, the county school board, former school superintendent Bill Snodgrass, and Church Hill Elementary principal Jean Price—had conspired to "threaten and intimidate" her in order to squelch her constitutionally protected criticisms of the Holt textbooks. Because of the conspiracy to violate her civil rights, "Frost, since November 23, 1983, has continuously suffered mental anguish and anxiety and has been, and continues to be, held up to public scorn, derision and abuse." *Frost v. Hawkins County Board of Education* would be heard by the same federal judge who was presiding over the textbook case, Thomas Hull in Greeneville.

Money wasn't the goal, Frost explained in a letter to her lawyer just before the suit was filed. "I believe there is no recompense necessary, for we suffer gladly for Christ's sake—counting it joy (though many times our flesh becomes weak from the battle and we feel the fiery darts hurled about us)—knowing that there is an eternal reward. . . . We are entering the lawsuit so that judgment may be rendered upon those who have abused the constitution. . . . For these reasons we hope and pray that righteous judgment will be executed."

There was also, she acknowledges now, a more temporal stimulus behind her lawsuit: She felt that she had been treated disrespectfully. She wouldn't have filed suit, she says, "if they had said just one time, Mrs. Frost, we are sorry we have offended you."

If Frost was quick to see conspiracies before, now she seemed to see them everywhere—or, more precisely, she seemed to see nearly everything as evidence of an octopuslike scheme to destroy her. In a note to her lawyers entitled "Planned Strategies documented," she distinguished five levels of the plot. Plan A was to fail the students who refused to read the Holt books; Plan B, to charge parents with truancy for removing their children from class; Plan C, to arrest her; Plan D, to get a restraining order barring parents from removing their children from reading class; and Plan E, to prosecute the parents for contributing to the delinquency of a minor. Though her adversaries did publicly discuss each of these ideas (only the arrest actually came about), there's no evidence that anyone but Frost viewed them as preplanned, escalating responses.

Tormented, possessed, but also emboldened, Frost reanalyzed events and squeezed them into the conspiracy theory. Of the CARE rally, she wrote: *"School officials tried to incite a riot!"* Their idea, she believed, was that one of the protesters would be provoked to speak up in opposition, which "would have ignited the spark to create a riot and bodily injury and possibly death." Unraveling the web of intrigue, she surmised that the rally was held at the elementary school because she had been arrested there; this made it "the most strategically beneficial for achieving the maximum publicity and public appeal against me."

Frost also kept busy researching matters related to her case. She reviewed minutes of previous school board meetings to see if the board had ever imposed a time limit on anyone before COBS (it hadn't, at least according to the minutes). She examined records to see if General Sessions Court Judge Kindall Lawson routinely signed affidavits of complaint, as he had signed hers (he didn't). She viewed newspapers on microfilm to find articles about the textbook protest and arrest. She complained about Reece Gibson's role in the controversy to the state Court of the Judiciary—the body charged with supervising judicial ethics, to which Michael Farris had already complained about Gibson's PAW letter. When she got no reply, she had the post office investigate to ensure that her letter had been delivered. She added irate marginalia to her documents: "What a tale!" on a deposition, "Lies!" on a newspaper clipping.

Other people also helped keep Frost's attention focused on her mistreatment at the hands of Hawkins County officialdom. Beverly LaHaye brought her to CWA's 1984 and 1985 conventions. At one of them, Frost and CWA's other litigants stood on stage during a presentation called "Martyrs for Freedom." "I felt so loved, so accepted," Frost remembers. "Our people loved having them there," LaHaye says. "They'd been reading about them in the newsletter, praying for them, and here they were—just normal people like the rest of us! So that's why I thought of it. Kind of gave credibility to the case too."

Throughout the controversy, in addition, Frost got letters from strangers across the country. "Believe me," a South Carolina woman wrote, "if your local area is not that supportive, remember, WE are everywhere, pockets of strong believers who know we must stand for our Lord Jesus so that he will stand for us in the day of judgment." A jail inmate wrote to say that if there were more Vicki Frosts in the world, there would be fewer criminals. A ninety-seven-year-old Ohio man sent a letter of support, but took pains to stipulate that "I am no 'Lothario.' "

Not all correspondents were so friendly. An anonymous Hawkins County resident wrote, "If you would only look at you on TV and study it a little, I think you would smack the *sarcastic* smug look off and go crawl in a hole and pull the hole in after you. You are a disgrace to our county, state and universe." An anonymous North Carolina writer said: "If I gambled, which I don't, I'd give *1000* to *1* odds that you and your relatives eat Pork (bacon—ham—sausage etc.) yet proclaim you have the faith. Hypocrites, not Christians. . . . Why not SHUT UP."

"Yes, she has become obsessed," her lawyer later said in closing arguments at the trial. "She's become obsessed with the truth. When you read lie after lie after lie about yourself, it does something, it really does. . . . You become obsessed with exoneration."

For Vicki Frost, "Martyr for Freedom," Concerned Women for America was bankrolling the conspiracy case too. In this lawsuit, she was represented by Larry Parrish, a lawyer from Memphis who, like Frost, took the Bible literally.

While working as an assistant United States attorney in the mid-1970s, Parrish had achieved a measure of national recognition as (in *Newsweek*'s phrase) the "Memphis Smut Raker." Whether a film was legally obscene, and therefore not protected by the First Amendment, depended on "community standards." Ordinarily, a Memphis prosecutor would apply local standards to prosecute the local exhibitor of a film. Parrish developed a more creative approach. He targeted films that hadn't even been shown in Memphis, on the theory that they *could* have been; and he pursued everyone involved in a film's production and distribution, including those who had never been to Memphis and who had no control over the film's distribution. Scores of people were indicted, including Harry Reems, the actor who had made $100 for one day's work as the male lead in *Deep Throat;* Reems was convicted at trial but won a reversal on appeal. Before Parrish had completed his mission against pornography, Jimmy Carter won the presidency and appointed a new, more liberal U.S. attorney. Parrish resigned and entered private practice. At CWA's instigation, he (along with Michael Farris) represented Suzanne Clark, the Graham Bible College teacher whom the NEA had sued for libel.

Like Farris in the textbook case, Parrish and his associates in Frost's conspiracy case sometimes infuriated the opposing lawyers. Parrish took a deposition of Frost, which required the presence of several defense lawyers. The session ultimately reviewed Frost's life story for nearly seven hours without a lunch break. Indignantly, the defense lawyers said they had never *heard* of a lawyer deposing his own client—who should be willing to disclose information to her lawyer without a subpoena. The session must be some sort of "psychological tactic to drive us crazy," one defense attorney theorized. "In my wildest imagination," he added, "I cannot see whether this lady was in the Girl Scouts and the 4-H Club has anything to do with whether her constitutional rights were violated in 1983." Another accused Parrish of wasting time in order to inflate his fee. Parrish responded calmly: "Testimony preservation, as far as I am concerned, is an exceedingly important thing because nobody knows when the next Mack truck is going to run over them."

Another incident was more serious. Late one night shortly before Frost's case went to trial, defense lawyer Richard M. Currie, Jr., was working at his Kingsport office. The phone rang. He answered with the name of the law firm, and the caller stammered something. Recognizing the voice, Currie said, "Is this Mrs. Frost?" "Yes," she admitted. He chided her for calling so late.

"I had, by that time, gotten to know Mrs. Frost," Currie said later, "and other than the fact that we're diametrically opposed in this lawsuit, I get along pretty well with her. So we had kind of a half-joking conversation about the fact that she was calling me, and obviously didn't know who she was calling when she called."

Frost, it developed, had gotten publicly available phone records from the school district office and elsewhere, and then called the listed numbers, including Currie's, to see to whom they belonged. (Her phone bill for one month was $172.) She hoped that the patterns of calls might help prove the existence of the conspiracy. Then she and her lawyers subpoenaed other phone records, including those of Holt's regional salesman, CARE president Reece Gibson, the district prosecutor, a county judge, TV stations, newspapers—and Milligan, Coleman, Fletcher, Gaby, Kilday & Woods, the Greeneville law firm representing the county schools in the textbook case, whose phone number, unsurprisingly, had turned up several times in school records.

From a legal perspective, this process was flawed. Prior to trial, a party to a suit could at the time demand records from someone who isn't a party, such as the phone company, only by holding a deposition. Frost's attorneys had no intention of deposing the phone company representative; in fact, the subpoena directed that the records be delivered at 1:45 P.M. January 13, 1986, to 2401 Fort Henry Drive in Kingsport—a Kentucky Fried Chicken. Parrish says this practice was commonly used to get phone company records: "I had done the exact same thing hundreds of times, and I could probably identify dozens of attorneys who've done it too." But Judge Hull wasn't familiar with it, and neither were the lawyers on the other side.

Most important, Nat Coleman and his partners feared that their phone records might expose aspects of their litigation strategy. Some of the calls listed would relate to the case, and the very existence of the calls could be revealing. Such records "go to the heart of the attorney-client privilege," the lawyers argued. Even though there were two separate lawsuits involved—Frost's conspiracy attorneys had subpoenaed the records of the school's textbook attorneys—in both cases Frost was a plaintiff, CWA was funding her, the school board and Jean Price were defendants, and Michael Farris and Larry Parrish were listed as attorneys.

"I literally felt like I had been violated," says Coleman. "I had nightmares about it." It wasn't just the textbook case he worried about. Frost and her allies had called some of the numbers listed on the law firm's phone records. "We heard from our clients," says Coleman. "They would tell us, we received a telephone call from somebody, and how in the hell did they get our number? How in the hell did they know that you were our lawyer?"

Coleman moved to have Frost's attorneys sanctioned. Judge Hull referred the matter to magistrate Joe Tilson, who convened a hearing (the same hearing that addressed Farris's alleged misconduct in depositions). Parrish didn't attend—"I was otherwise occupied," he says—but he sent his associate, Fred McDonald.

At the hearing, defense attorneys tried to find out who was responsible for subpoenaing the phone records. Jennie Wilson, who had delivered some of the subpoenas, took the stand.

Coleman, who was questioning Wilson, thought she was Vicki Frost's mother (she is actually Rachel Baker's mother). "Are you related to Mrs. Vicki Frost?" he asked.

"Larry Parrish had told us how to reply," Wilson remembers. "He said think it over, make sure you know what he's saying. And I thought it over real good, and I decided there wasn't a way in the world I was her mother. So I finally said no."

Then Coleman asked if Wilson was related to Roger Frost.

"For five minutes I rolled that question around, and I finally decided nope, and I says no."

When Coleman moved on to the subpoenas, Wilson turned uncharacteristically vague. Did an attorney tell her how to deliver subpoenas? "I don't know." Did CWA's Cimron Campbell tell her? "I don't remember." Did Farris? "No, sir." Did Fred McDonald? "I don't remember." Did Parrish talk to her about subpoenas? "I believe so." What did he say? "I don't remember." Did any attorney explain how to serve a subpoena? "I don't remember." Did she give the phone records to any attorney? "I don't remember."

Frost proved more forthright. She had subpoenaed Coleman's phone records, she said, "because I found your phone number on the school board's records." But she couldn't remember whether McDonald or any of her other attorneys had known of the subpoena in advance. When the magistrate reminded her she was under oath, Frost replied, "I agree with you. That's why I want to be careful. I'm under obligation to God more so than this court."

Finally, McDonald himself cleared the confusion. He said he had directed Frost to prepare the subpoenas. "We were under a time crunch, and I may have overstepped the bounds," he said. "But I'm not real sure that I did or not."

Magistrate Tilson concluded that McDonald had indeed overstepped the bounds, by using subpoenas improperly and by failing to notify Coleman's law firm that its records were being subpoenaed. At day's end, two of Frost's attorneys, Farris and McDonald, had been rebuked for unprofessional conduct. Judge Hull later vacated the reprimand against Farris, but not the one against McDonald.

The conspiracy trial began in the federal courthouse in Greeneville on January 21, 1986. Roads between Hawkins County and Greeneville were sheathed in ice, and a frigid wind was roaring. "You couldn't even walk on the streets of Greeneville," says Marion Wilson. "Had to hold on to the buildings."

Parrish made his opening statement to the six jurors. Selection of the Holt books was "a bad decision, made for bad reasons," he said, and Frost and others had protested it. "Rather than say we made a bad decision—Hawkins County Board of Education and teachers and all —and instead of trying to rectify it, they circled the wagons and began to defend themselves. Began to say, we've got a right to make this decision, we own these children when they're in school. . . . And that sort of thing developed to the point where it became a conspiracy. It became, we've got to shut these people up, including Vicki Frost." Frost's arrest—"a matter of much notoriety" that inflicted on her "extreme mental distress"—was part of this plan.

As the trial got under way, Jennie Wilson was once again making mischief, this time unwittingly. She was chatting with another prospective witness in a waiting room when, she remembers, "along came a black man with a fatigue jacket on. Nice young black man." Wilson started talking with him. "I asked him, Are you a Christian? Oh, yes, and he told me about his salvation experience. I told him, Well, won't you pray with us? We need all the prayers we can get—we got a woman in there that the school arrested. Why, he said, I never *heard* of the school having somebody arrested! So we prayed." After a while, the man mentioned the reason for his presence at the courthouse: His wife was on the Frost jury.

Realizing that the conversation might look like an illicit attempt to influence a juror, Wilson sheepishly recounted it to Parrish. "He went and told the judge," says Wilson, "and Judge Hull said, Oh, it's all right, don't worry about it, nothing's going to slow me down. . . . He didn't care."

Hull did seem determined to get the case over with as quickly as possible. When one prospective juror said that a two-week trial— Parrish's estimate—might be an inconvenience, Hull said: "Well, I'm a little faster than most of them think we are. Won't be here that long." Hull instructed Parrish to prune down his witness list. "The clerk said you got 150 subpoenas," the judge said. "I want you to pick your ten best witnesses first. . . . In case we don't get to the rest of them, you'll have your best case in." Hull aimed to complete the trial, not in Parrish's two weeks, but in four days. "We don't want to stay here until next summer trying this lawsuit," he grumbled at one point.

Hull is a judge who likes to keep things moving. "When court opens," he says, "*somebody's* got to be in charge." He insists that lawyers appear on time, and he imposes fines against latecomers. He also forces lawyers to get to the point quickly. "He wants to get to the nub, what he calls the lick log," says Tom Wright, a lawyer who was Judge Hull's clerk during the trial.

Vicki Frost's testimony tried Hull's patience. Parrish had told her how to answer questions. "Say yes, no, or I don't know, basically, if you can," she recalls. But the skill eluded her. "The courtroom setting is different from sitting in your living room talking to someone," she says. "Larry Parrish told me to frame every word you're going to say before you say it. That's very difficult to do!" On the stand, she gave verbose, meandering answers to Parrish's questions.

Judge Hull chastised her several times. When his scoldings had no effect, he started questioning her himself, leaving Parrish standing by in silence.

Frost, already intimidated by the experience of testifying in court, became increasingly rattled by the judge's interrogation. "Vicki was just shaking," remembers Parrish. Finally she told Judge Hull: "You're making me nervous."

"You're making me nervous too," he replied.

Out of the jury's earshot, defense attorneys asked Hull to ease up on Frost. They were worried that his aggressive approach might make jurors feel sorry for her, or perhaps give her grounds for a new trial if she lost this one. Hull agreed.

"I'm an impartial observer, but I get impatient," he said, half-apologetically, to the jury. He told them not to let his behavior from the bench influence their opinions about the case.

"I'm probably impatient to everybody," says Judge Hull now. "And I guess, as I remember Vicki—she's a very nice woman, but if you ask her what time it was, she has a tendency to tell you how to build a clock."

On the fourth day of the trial, after conflicting testimony about the arrest and the events leading up to it, Roger Frost testified about its impact on his wife. He first described her prior to the arrest: "An excellent wife. I feel blessed that God give me a wife such as her. . . . She fixed well-prepared, nutritious meals. . . . She not only liked to keep the house thoroughly clean, but she did other chores as well. She loved to do wallpapering and different type work, hanging pictures, doing kind of home decorative stuff."

But her personality changed "immediately after the arrest," he continued. "She just became kind of introverted, withdrawn from the things that were normal—grocery shopping or shopping at the stores. There'd be people whispering and talking and pointing, and she kind of felt like they was talking about her. And we'd have to leave and come back home because she started getting upset with all these inner thoughts she was having."

She had withdrawn from home life too. "I do a lot of cooking now, and we order from fast-food restaurants," he said. "Her meals are not as well prepared, and not as often as they were. . . . She hasn't sewed anything, hardly. . . . Vicki's housekeeping is not like it once was. . . . She takes her clothes and throws them in the closet without hanging them up. Once she did the floor, wax and clean. She doesn't do it anymore."

In addition, he said, she had "gained a tremendous amount of weight" since the arrest. Though she had signed up for a weight-reducing program, she had subsequently dropped out. "Her emotions, she wasn't really able to carry through it like normal."

"Has it affected your husband-wife relationship?" Larry Parrish asked gently.

"Yes," Roger said. "Due to the fact she's had weight gain, and so self-conscious about that—as far as our sexual relationship, it's been where, you know, she just wants me to leave her alone."

Parrish then asked him to recount the events the day of the arrest. In particular, why had he stayed at work instead of rushing to bail his wife out of jail?

" 'Cause I was devastated. . . . I wanted to try to recompose myself and get my act together. . . . Another thing was, I had a fear that they had Vicki in jail. Was they trying to call me down there and trap me into doing something, in the state of mind I was in? If I went there and something was going wrong, and they were abusing Vicki or doing something that wasn't right with Vicki, what would I do? I had fears I would be locked up because I have a type of temperament, it being my wife."

On cross-examination, he was asked to elaborate on his type of temperament. He acknowledged suffering from psychological problems, "which," he stipulated, "is not uncommon of a Vietnam veteran." He had most recently been treated seven years earlier, in 1979, when he had spent two months in a VA hospital. The doctors, he said, had characterized his condition as "paranoia."

As the fourth day of trial ended, with what looked like one day to go, Vicki Frost and her allies were dejected. The cross-examination had humiliatingly breached Roger's privacy. "He was very upset," remembers Vicki.

Judge Hull, moreover, remained in a constant rush. Upon hearing that a witness would be a few minutes late, he announced: "If she's not here, we're not going to hear her. I have to wait for the witnesses or the witnesses have to wait for me, and it's going to be the witnesses waiting for me."

The judge also seemed to be irked at Larry Parrish. When Parrish said he wasn't sure how many more witnesses he would be calling, Hull replied: "You are an officer of this court, and I am expecting you to conduct yourself in such a manner you can properly get this case before this court. I'm expecting you to do it. You understand me?" Hull also berated Parrish over the phone company subpoenas (magistrate Tilson's hearing hadn't yet been held). "Highly improper for you to use those subpoenas to try to extract information from somebody," he said, "other than asking them to come into court and testify as witnesses where they can be cross-examined by the other side." "It was one of those moments in your practice that you remember," recalls Parrish. "Out of the blue he attacked. Rage in his face. He had to pause to get control of himself." In Jennie Wilson's assessment, Judge Hull seemed to resent Parrish for having "the audacity to come into this area of Tennessee and defend a hoodlum like Vicki Frost. He was *mad*."

"That night," Frost remembers, "we prayed: Lord, we've not been able to get all our witnesses; it just seems like we're overrun; we need a delay. I remember praying at a specific time at the hotel room."

Before morning, Hull was rushed to the hospital with abdominal pains. The rest of the trial was postponed, ultimately for two months, while he underwent and recovered from surgery.

"Judge Hull had made the comment I won't wait for you; you'll wait for me—and we waited," says Frost. "I'm not saying that the events that transpired were because of our prayer, but we did pray for God to intervene."

"When he came back he was a different person," says Wilson. "He had made a complete turnaround. He said, I don't care *how* long this takes, we're going to hear it out. . . . And we just thanked the Lord for that, 'cause we had asked that the Lord please intervene."

"It's been quite a while since I've been here," Judge Hull told the jurors when they reassembled two months later, on March 24, 1986. "I'm glad to see all of you again. Sure nice to be able to stand up and see you. Lots of things happened to me, but don't want to bore you with all the details."

Hull was ready to get back to work, but one juror, who had been in a car accident, was missing. Larry Parrish said he wouldn't consent to trying the case with just five jurors. Forcing the juror to appear under threat of contempt would also be unacceptable, Parrish said; the resentful juror might skew the result.

After lunch, Judge Hull announced that the missing juror had promised to come the next morning. "We have to press on," Hull told the other jurors. "As Longfellow said, let us all be up and doing with a heart for any fate, still achieving, still pursuing, learn to labor and wait. I'm not the best waiter in the world, but we'll wait this out. You are excused until nine o'clock in the morning. Don't talk to anybody about the case, but keep yourselves in shape. One of these days we're going to finish it and turn it over to you to make a decision."

The next morning, Hull seemed to retain his philosophical, indulgent mood. When a lawyer objected that one question—asking Doug Cloud why he had first run for school board—was irrelevant, Hull responded, "A little, but we'll let it in. Might be interesting."

Larry Parrish, however, felt that a full complement of jurors and an easygoing judge weren't enough. The two-month delay had irreparably harmed his case, he declared. He was moving for a mistrial, which would require impanelling another jury and trying the case anew.

"That's a judgment call," Hull responded. "I just don't feel like there's been any prejudice at all. . . . It hasn't been so long that memories fade on these matters. . . . If I felt prejudice on one side or the other, even though we got eight or nine days in this case, I would grant a mistrial. I don't feel like we do. . . . Overruled."

On March 27, the lawyers presented their closing arguments to the four-woman, two-man jury. The evidence adduced during the trial showed that Frost had been arrested, and that some of the defendants had spoken harshly to her or about her. There were some suggestive contradictions—Jean Price testified that superintendent Bill Snodgrass had told her to call the police the day before the arrest, when Frost and Sarah were sitting in their Jeep in the school parking lot; Snodgrass testified that he had said nothing about calling the police. There were also a few missing documents, implausible memory lapses, and far-fetched explanations. But there was no direct proof that anyone had conspired to deprive Frost of her constitutional rights.

Parrish tried to cast events in as sinister a light as possible. As the

COBS protest widened, the defendants concluded that "they've got to do something," he said. "And when they come to that decision, a plan develops. Now, this plan doesn't have to be written in a scroll and passed to everybody, but the plan is, make the objecting parents shut up. . . . The formulators of the plan, each of the individual school board members, I suggest, with Mr. Snodgrass and Mrs. Price, their thoughts started melding. Nobody sat down at a conference table and said, I think this. But the thoughts began to be put together. Then it's formed. That's the plan."

The first step, the November 16 suspensions of students, didn't quash the protest. Frost naively told Jean Price that she planned to start removing her daughter from reading class, and "next thing you know, Mrs. Price comes up with a penal statute." Then board member Doug Cloud and administrator Joe Drinnon "talk with Mrs. Price. . . . And do you think they didn't talk about this statute? Sure, they talked about the statute. . . . You are not supposed to be blind and stupid. You can infer things that make good common sense from the facts you know."

The next day, the day before the arrest, Frost returned to take her daughter out of school. "I submit to you that they expected to arrest Vicki Frost on Tuesday morning. Now, why didn't they arrest her? 'Cause Joe Ashbrook was late. . . . He testified he was dispatched there. There is no record. He showed up there unannounced. How did he know to show up there unannounced? I suggest 'cause he had been in collaboration before then. But Vicki came, got Sarah, and was in the car by the time he got there. So what do we do now? Tell her to leave."

As for the day of the arrest, the defense lawyers had emphasized that Frost herself had called the police. According to Parrish, however, this call was superfluous. "On the 23rd, he is dispatched there at 9:04, he gets there at 9:09. Five minutes. I suggest he was on his way anyway, that that dispatch just came in and gave him an alibi. He was on his way there anyway."

Concerning damages, Parrish directed the jury's attention to Frost, sitting at the plaintiff's table in the courtroom. "You are looking at a lady who is suffering right now in the most grievous kind of way." She had been virtually anonymous before the arrest. "Then they haul her off to jail. People are announcing that very day that you engineered your own arrest, called the police on yourself. And it gets bigger and bigger. A rally, a thousand people, December fifth. . . . She still hears it: She is a troublemaker, stirring up protest. The anguish of that, the emotional distress of that, you cannot know until you are in her shoes."

The defendants "drove Vicki Frost to court. She's trying to talk to them in every way she knows how, and they say no; they walk away. She comes again. They say no; they walk away. She comes again. They say no, walk away, and then they turn around and slap her in the face. She had to go to court to be heard. . . . If she comes in here and you all backhand her again, you all have enforced everything that has happened, this whole conspiracy. And I plead with you not to let this happen, for the good of yourself, for the good of the community."

When Parrish was finished, the defense lawyers gave their closing arguments. They laid heavy emphasis on the evidentiary gaps in Parrish's narrative.

"This conspiracy is a fantasy, folks," said Richard Currie, a balding, long-faced man. "It's not evidence. The fact that somebody talked to somebody some day is not evidence that anybody did anything wrong. . . . Mr. Parrish assumes that every time any of these defendants talk to each other, between the time Vicki Frost first went to the school board and the time that she was arrested, it was in some way plotting against her. . . . You just can't do that, folks."

Currie suggested that Frost's objections to the readers indicated a warped view of reality. "The strength of Mrs. Frost's beliefs, her zeal, her enthusiasm, have distorted the way she sees things. She's . . . been caused to see evils and plots and conspiracies that aren't there. . . . She remembers things how she thinks they were or wishes they were, not how they were. She stretches the truth."

As an example, he noted Frost's insistence that she only wanted alternative books for her own children. "Look at her actions; they speak much louder and more clearly." She had organized meetings, written letters to the editor, appeared on TV, and tried to get the National Rifle Association to oppose the readers. "She has every right to do this. She's exercising her free speech. But she comes here and tells you, all I wanted to do was for my children and my children alone."

Prior to the trial, Parrish had predicted that the defense lawyers would contend that Frost "loved" getting arrested because "she got her name in the paper." Now Currie made just that argument. "Vicki

Frost wanted publicity for her cause," he said. "She was not getting publicity. Her children had been suspended at the middle school, but once they were suspended and were home, there was no more publicity. She tried to get Mrs. Price to suspend her daughter to get some publicity that way. It didn't work. Went to the school and took her daughter out. That didn't get any notice either. She was intent on continuing until she got results, even if it meant getting arrested."

Defense lawyer Robert Cheek told the jury: "If there's conspiracy here, then I say it's on the part of the Concerned Women for America, selecting Vicki from over here in Hawkins County to lead their push against whatever it is they're trying to do." Cheek also cast doubt on the depth of Frost's suffering. "Vicki, I been around her, talked with her about damages: that she's been hurt, and that she's depressed," he said. "I been with Vicki now for a year—and I love Vicki, and her husband, and all of her children—but I never seen her depressed. She's always very happy. She's always gay and laughing and having a good time."

Another defense attorney, Charlton DeVault, said that if Frost had suffered, the arrest wasn't the reason. "Something else happened right after the arrest and before the preliminary hearing," something that "made all this difference in the atmosphere of Hawkins County and in Mrs. Frost's reputation." He was referring to revelation of the COBS letters, with their allegations about sex and drugs at Volunteer High. "After that report COBS ceased its meetings. They lost their credibility. This small organization of concerned citizens, who began in September with this Wicca petition objecting to witchcraft in the schools, escalated their charges to sexual misconduct in the schools. The community rose against them, and they disbanded."

He too doubted that Frost had suffered much. "Ladies and gentlemen of the jury, this lawsuit and the textbook lawsuit have made Mrs. Frost a star. It has changed her lifestyle. She is now a woman of the world, so to speak. She has twice gone to Washington, D.C., to attend the conventions of Concerned Women for America. . . . These expense-paid trips to Washington, D.C., the trips to Knoxville, the news broadcasts, the news interviews. . . . Bless her husband's heart, he's probably holding onto her coattails now, as she travels hither, thither, and yon in preparation for these lawsuits and talking to all these women's groups. I'm not saying that's bad. I think it's great. She's come out in the world. But I think she's chosen an improper means to achieve that. She's trying to do it at the expense of these defendants, these people that were just doing their job. We think that's wrong."

Frost cringed as she listened to the defense attorneys. "I would love to say that I had all the faith in the world and I just walked so strong and every time you saw me smile, that everything was of faith and no doubting," she says. "But no, there were moments that were very, very hard. . . . Mr. DeVault said that I was a woman dragging my husband around by my coattail. I was portrayed as a woman who had taken glory and loved my role as being a star. It was very disturbing."

After the attorneys finished their closing arguments, she says, "I went into the bathroom, getting down on my knees—not only on my knees, but probably had my hands on the floor too; I was *down*. And I said, Lord, I'm out here, I put you to the test. I'm out here on a limb, and unless you catch me—uphold me. Uphold me by your strong hand. I need your strength at this time. . . . And I prayed that God's will be done. To uphold me, to strengthen me, to help me, but whatever the outcome of the case was, be with me."

With the closing arguments complete, Judge Hull instructed the jury —one of the most crucial aspects of a trial. Here the judge must translate the talmudic distinctions of the law into layman's terms. According to Stephen J. Adler, an editor of the *Wall Street Journal* and the author of a book about juries, studies have found that jurors often are baffled by the instructions, with words—such as *tacitly* and *immaterial*—that come as second nature to lawyers but not to others. When they can't understand the law, Adler believes, jurors simply try to be fair. The law ordinarily promotes fairness, so jury rulings usually come out consistent with the law, but not always.

Thirty pages long, Judge Hull's instructions were not a model of clarity. One particularly unwieldy sentence was ninety-seven words long: "If it appears by a preponderance of the evidence in the case that the conspiracy existed, that the conspiracy alleged was willfully formed, and that the defendant about whom or which you are considering willfully became a member of the conspiracy, either at its inception or afterwards, and that one or more of the conspirators knowingly committed one or more overt acts in furtherance of some object or purpose of the conspiracy, then liability may be found if the conspirators succeeded in accomplishing part of their common object or purpose, even if they failed in total success." "If you can remember all of that, fine," says Jennie Wilson. "But I'm not sure that an East Tennessean could."

After lunch, the jury left the courtroom to deliberate. Larry Parrish acknowledged that he was pessimistic. "I'd be shocked if we win," he told a reporter. "We have very little chance of winning." He considered his case severely compromised by the two-month delay and by some of Judge Hull's rulings. He said, however, that he was confident of victory on appeal.

As the afternoon wore on, though, Parrish grew more optimistic. "The longer they stay, the better," he told Frost.

The other side, meanwhile, was growing fretful. "Old Reece Gibson had come in there all happy just about the time the jury went out," Wilson recalls. "But the longer they stayed, the more he sweated. He commenced a-pacing and a-sweating, a-pacing and a-sweating."

At five-twenty, the jurors announced their ruling: Frost had won. She was entitled to compensatory damages of $50,000 against the school board, they ruled, and punitive damages of $10,000 against superintendent Snodgrass and $10,000 against principal Price. They imposed no damages against Chief Ashbrook.

The ruling revealed that the jurors hadn't understood the instructions. Before they could impose any punitive damages against Snodgrass and Price, they had to find those defendants liable for compensatory damages. Defendants can't be punished for wrongdoing unless it has harmed the plaintiff.

"Ladies and gentlemen," Judge Hull explained to the jurors, "it's an inconsistent verdict as to punitive damages, and I'm going to have to send you back out after I tell you why it is inconsistent. In the charge, you may recall, the only time you can award punitive damages against any individual defendant is if you find that . . . they owe compensatory damages to that plaintiff. Since you found in your verdict only the board of education was to pay compensatory damages of $50,000, it's not proper for you to award punitive damages against Bill Snodgrass and Jean Price. Not only improper, but against the law. So you are going to have to renegotiate what you are doing."

The jury left the courtroom, and defense lawyers began protesting. "I object to your honor's sending them back with that instruction," said Currie, "because they have rendered their verdict." He evidently wanted the judge to declare a mistrial.

"You want to accept the verdict as it is, and not object to it being inconsistent?" said Hull.

Currie's clients were the school board ($50,000 compensatory) and Price ($10,000 punitive). "No, your honor."

"I just can't take a verdict or discharge a jury without trying to instruct them more," the judge continued, "and I'm sure they're in search of the truth and trying to do what they think is right. I think I have a duty to give them an opportunity."

At 5:48 P.M., the jurors sent out a note that they were confused by the judge's reinstruction. He brought them back in the courtroom, reread some of the original instruction, and explained their error again. "Where it's inconsistent so far is, you didn't find that Jean Price and superintendent Snodgrass were guilty and entitled to pay compensatory damages, and unless you do, you can't find that they owe punitive damages. . . . I hope I made that clear."

"Clear as the moon," the jury foreman replied jauntily. They returned to the jury room.

At 6:05, the jurors emerged again. This time they had gotten it right. They had assessed the entire $70,000 against the school board, all as compensatory damages. They had assessed no damages against Price or Snodgrass, whom they had earlier saddled with $10,000 each; or Ashbrook, whom they had never found liable; or the City of Church Hill, which Judge Hull had dismissed as a defendant before the jury began deliberating. Only the board was found liable.

"Thank you very much," Judge Hull told the jury. "A long trial. I got cut on a couple times while it was going on, by a doctor. A couple of you had a wreck. Thank you very much for your patience and your endurance and for pressing on with me. And the general public ought to thank you too. Thanks for a good job done. You may leave."

After the jurors had filed out, Hull addressed the lawyers. "Gentlemen, it's been nice to see you. Enjoyed the battle. Hope I haven't engaged in it too much."

"Just as soon not do it again," said Currie.

"Lord have mercy, your honor," said Cheek.

"Court's adjourned," said the clerk.

It was a victory, but a victory that Frost could have done without. The trial was "a very trying time," she remembers, having "all the things I had suffered through that two-and-a-half-year period being put before my eyes." Along the way, the family's privacy had been breached. Painful remarks that had previously been said in private, such as the allegation that she had engineered her own arrest, now were broadcast widely. And her standing in Hawkins County sank even lower when the current school superintendent, Robert Cooper, announced that three and a half teaching positions would have to be eliminated to pay the $70,000 judgment. "I guess that half a one was really worried," Frost says now.

In the end, though, the school district didn't have to pay a penny. "The evidence . . . points so strongly in favor of the Board," the Sixth Circuit Court of Appeals held in 1988, "that we think reasonable minds could not come to a different conclusion." Parrish and Frost had pointed to contradictions and ambiguities in the other side's accounts of events, but they had never amassed the evidence to prove that anyone had conspired to arrest Vicki Frost.

In contrast, considerable evidence, albeit all circumstantial or disputed, supports the notion the defense lawyers raised at the trial: that Vicki Frost had orchestrated her own arrest. On the morning of the arrest, for instance, Frost said, "They might try to arrest me today." She, not Jean Price, called the police that day. During the confrontation with Price and Ashbrook, Frost never told them that she planned to sign Sarah out and leave campus, though she now says that that was her plan. Price and Ashbrook assumed that she intended to violate school rules by tutoring Sarah on campus. After the arrest, Frost tried to take her daughter to jail with her—and the arrest of a mother and her second-grade daughter would no doubt make even bigger news than the arrest of a mother alone. Frost announced to Ashbrook that God had told her she might be arrested, and, before reaching the patrol car, she shouted, "Praise the Lord!"

Provoking an arrest is consistent with the protesters' other actions in the fall of 1983. Certain of the righteousness of their cause, they were briskly generating confrontations: at Carter's Valley, where Archie McMillan asked Jennie Wilson to leave the classroom and, according to the Wilsons, later expelled the two Baker children; at Church Hill Elementary, where Frost kept prodding Jean Price; and at the middle school, where children were suspended.

Even so, it seems unlikely that Frost plotted her arrest. To begin with, she doesn't come across as someone capable of orchestrating such a thing, lying about it, and then filing suit against the dupes. In addition, her actions on the day of the arrest don't amount to much provocation. Sarah was still in class at the time of the arrest; Frost hadn't yet violated any rules. Supervisor of instruction Joe Drinnon acknowledges that Ashbrook may have jumped the gun in making the arrest. "She was being confrontational to Jean, and he didn't know what to do," Drinnon says. "He was a little bit, appropriately, in awe of Jean, so he arrested her." Even Price, who says she has "no doubt" that the protesters planned the arrest, concedes that Frost didn't directly touch it off. "I was really surprised at the policeman when he arrested her," Price says.

Finally, it's difficult to conceive of Jennie Wilson and Vicki Frost savvily plotting *anything* to sway public opinion. Wilson tarnished the protesters' efforts by denouncing "Goldilocks" and "The Three Little Pigs." Later, during the textbook trial, Frost would become famous for believing that *The Diary of Anne Frank* and *The Wizard of Oz* would corrupt her children. However crafty they may be in other arenas, these women are hardly masters of public relations.

The trial of *Frost v. Hawkins County Board of Education* was over, but another courtroom engagement loomed. The textbook case, *Mozert v. Hawkins County Board of Education*, was scheduled to come to trial in a few months.

On the plaintiffs' side, Vicki Frost had the most important job of all. She would have to testify for hours, in comprehensive detail, about precisely what was wrong with the Holt reading books.

CHAPTER EIGHT

MORE THAN READING

"May I caution," Vicki Frost wrote in a draft letter to an area newspaper, "if you decide to investigate these county textbooks—you must be prepared with paper and pen and many hours of careful examination. Flipping through the pages will not uncover the rottenness therein."

Frost herself studied the books meticulously. "It's a very long process," she says, "because a lot of times you read a story and you may not understand an inference that could be made until you read something else." She pored over some volumes three times; "you had to remember what you read, and be real familiar with *every* story in there." By the July 1986 trial, she had devoted more than two hundred hours to the task. "I have been built up in my faith, and I know the Word of God enough to know the error," she says. "But a five-year-old, a six-year-old, a seven-year-old, they're like little twigs. They can be bent in the wrong direction because their minds are tender."

Frost didn't bother analyzing the kindergarten and first-grade readers. These books had been criticized in Jennie Wilson's widely mocked letter to the editor, signed with Bob Mozert's name; in a November 1983 letter to the editor written by Frost, which quoted and seemingly endorsed the Gablers' complaints about these early volumes; and in a draft affidavit that the plaintiffs prepared just after filing suit. By the trial, however, the kindergarten and first-grade volumes were no longer part of the lawsuit.

Accounts differ on why these textbooks were dropped. "Our attorney decided that," says Mozert. "And the reason why—and we agreed with it too—is that the first-grade reader would be a very weak case to present against humanism. There's really little in there. It starts in the second-grade readers." Michael Farris refers to the plaintiff families as "a cohesive, orderly group of plaintiffs that did whatever I told them to." When told of Mozert's recollection, however, Farris sketches a different picture. "The reality is that I could not shape these people very much," he says. "If they would've thought there was something wrong with the first-grade readers, we would've been battling the first-grade readers." Frost also says Farris didn't fine-tune their objections.

In any event, hundreds of objections remained. Frost organized them into sixteen categories: "futuristic supernaturalism, one-world government, situation ethics or values clarification, humanistic moral absolutes, pacifism, rebellion against parents or self-authority, role reversal, role elimination, animals are equal to humans, the skeptic's view of religion contrasting belief in the supernatural with science, false views of death and related themes, magic, other religions, evolution, godless supernaturalism . . . and specific humanistic themes." The plaintiffs maintain that these motifs weren't debasing education when *they* were in school in the 1950s and 1960s. Mozert remembers "Skip, Jerry, different people in the reader—they never taught a false religion."

The Hawkins County plaintiffs may be misapprehending the nature of the change, but there's little doubt that textbooks have changed enormously over the years. The changes are especially significant in the books' treatment of evolution, Christianity, morality, patriotism, and diversity—the plaintiffs' five basic objections.

Frost discovered twenty-four passages in the textbooks promoting the theory of evolution. An essay about Jane Goodall referred to the chimpanzee as "human's closest relative." According to another essay, thunderstorms may have helped create the "chemical building blocks from which life on earth emerged 3.5 million years ago." One story spoke of "the first man that stood on his hind legs and killed a bison," implying that his ancestors had walked on all fours. Each book did say, in small type at the end of the copyright acknowledgments, that "any material on evolution in this book is presented as theory, not fact." But the protesters doubted that most students read the acknowledgments. "Evolution teaches there's no God," Frost said at trial. "That violates my religious conviction."

Evolution has long been a prime target of fundamentalists' textbook protests. William Jennings Bryan, prosecutor of John T. Scopes, blamed the teaching of evolution for "all the ills from which America suffers." During the 1920s, twenty state legislatures considered fundamentalist-backed bills to ban the teaching of Darwin's theory, and five states enacted laws: Arkansas, Florida, Mississippi, Oklahoma, and Tennessee. Forty years later the Arkansas state teachers' association mounted a challenge to that state's law, which was still on the books though no longer enforced. In the 1968 case *Epperson v. Arkansas*, the Supreme Court struck down the statute. The law was unconstitutional, the Court said, because it barred the teaching of evolution "for the sole reason that it is deemed to conflict with a particular religious doctrine."

Partly in response to the *Epperson* ruling, fundamentalists set aside the goal of getting evolution out of the classroom, and began trying instead to bring creationism in. John Scopes "should not have been convicted," declared Jerry Falwell, because he was "teaching both points of view—evolution and creation." At San Diego's Institute for Creation Research (founded by Tim LaHaye) and other institutions, fundamentalists developed a secularized version of creationism called "creation science" or "scientific creationism." In the 1970s, state legislators introduced two dozen bills requiring teachers to devote equal classroom time to creation science and evolution. Bills became law in Louisiana and Arkansas, though both statutes were later struck down in court.

Textbook coverage of evolution has ebbed and flowed, according to Gerald D. Skoog of Texas Tech University. From the turn of the century to the early 1920s, books dealt with evolution succinctly but respectfully. One book spoke of the theory as "universally accepted by scientists as fact"; another declared that "all well-read biologists accept the doctrine." But the 1925 *Scopes* trial spooked textbook publishers, who, then as now, were eager to dodge controversy. Some books dropped evolution and Darwin entirely, and others omitted them from the index. In this sense, as Garry Wills notes, fundamentalists achieved some measure of victory at the "monkey trial."

Books devoted more attention to evolution as part of the post-

Sputnik revitalizing of science education, but fundamentalist opposition reignited—Mel and Norma Gabler led the fight in Texas—and textbook treatment of the topic once again fell off in the 1970s. One 1974 book spent about 2,000 words discussing the origins of life; the 1977 edition accorded the topic only 322 words, and the 1981 edition dropped it entirely. Then the pendulum swung once again. Science and civil liberties organizations mobilized during the 1980s, and textbook treatment of evolution gradually rebounded. "Currently, I'm pleased to say, it looks like evolution is back," asserts Eugenie Scott, executive director of the National Center for Science Education.

Even so, what's in the biology book doesn't always get taught in class. "It's often in the back of the textbook and, somehow, you just don't get to the back," Scott says. A 1988 study found that a quarter of introductory biology teachers in Texas weren't teaching human evolution at all, and another 50 percent were devoting less than half an hour to it.

While fundamentalists stand alone in many of their beliefs, creationism isn't one of them. According to polls, nearly half of Americans believe that "God created man pretty much in his present form at one time during the last 10,000 years," and seven in ten believe the public schools should teach creationism alongside evolution. The creationism position is generally most popular among Southerners, the less educated, the less wealthy, and people in small towns and rural areas—in sum, people like those of Hawkins County.

Besides evolution, the plaintiffs also objected to materials that denigrated Christianity and its central tenets. After a story about the devil, the teachers' edition advised, "Lead children to an understanding of the lack of logic inherent in the superstitious mind," implying that Satan doesn't exist. An essay asserted that "languages were not ordained in heaven," whereas the plaintiffs believed that God did ordain languages at the Tower of Babel. Several stories described death with no mention of the afterlife, or, in the case of a Navajo folk tale, with a non-Christian view of the afterlife that featured evil spirits astride horses.

The plaintiffs also protested materials indicating that all faiths are equally valid. The eighth-grade reader included the Hindu fable "The Blind Men and the Elephant," which ended: "So oft in theologic wars, / The disputants, I ween, / Rail on in utter ignorance / Of what each other mean, / *And prate about an Elephant* / *Not one of them has seen!"* The same volume contained a dramatization of *The Diary of Anne Frank*, in which Anne tells her friend, "I wish you had a religion, Peter." "No, thanks! Not me!" he replies. Anne responds: "Oh, I don't mean you have to be Orthodox, or believe in heaven and hell and purgatory and things. I just mean some religion, it doesn't matter what. Just to believe in something!" To the plaintiffs, who believe that Jesus is the only way to salvation, such statements were sacrilege.

In addition, the plaintiffs objected to descriptions of magic and the occult. After a play adapted from *The Wizard of Oz*, students were asked, "Are all witches bad?"; teachers were to mark the fundamentalist answer—yes—as wrong. A teachers' edition suggested having children write their own incantations, and one story urged children to use their imagination to "become part of" leaves and nature; the plaintiffs considered such practices satanic. Responding to the argument that these exercises were intended only to stimulate imagination and creativity, Jordan Lorence, a Concerned Women for America lawyer working on the case, observed that having children compose a prayer to Jesus might have the same salutary effect, but it would deeply offend people who hold different religious beliefs. The Holt exercises, Lorence maintained, offended the plaintiffs in precisely the same way.

Along with promoting unscriptural concepts, the Holt books ignored Christians and Christianity. Here the plaintiffs didn't rely solely on Vicki Frost's study of the readers. Paul Vitz, a New York University psychology professor who had studied textbooks' treatment of religion, analyzed the Holt series for the plaintiffs and testified at trial.

Of approximately six hundred stories and poems in the readers, Vitz found, not one depicted Biblical Protestantism. "There are no stories about life in the Bible Belt," he testified, "no stories about churchgoers, families or individuals who pray to God." The only story about Christianity dealt with a narrow aspect of Catholicism, with no mention of Jesus or the Bible. A Holt excerpt of Laura Ingalls Wilder's *Little House in the Big Woods* omitted a prayer. And while a teachers' edition quoted W. H. Auden's praise of narrative folk tales as "second only to the Bible in carrying on the western tradition," the series contained about thirty folk tales and not a single story from the Bible.

Non-Christian religions, in contrast, received respectful attention. In "Cherry Ann and the Dragon Horse," a Chinese girl prays to a horse idol. Other materials positively depicted Buddhism. Many stories portrayed American Indians, frequently with reference to their religious beliefs. And eighteen stories dealt with magic or the occult.

Two stories, Vitz said, disparaged Christianity. In "The Forgotten Door," a story set in the Smoky Mountains, a character remarks that a family at church "sang as loud as anybody" and "looked well fed" on what were probably stolen hams. In "The Scribe," the narrator says that his mother "has three Bible study certificates and is always giving me lessons from Bible history. I don't exactly go for all the stuff she believes in but sometimes it's interesting." Later he observes, "Jesus criticized the scribes but he needed them to write down his teachings." Not only was this statement critical of Jesus, Vitz said, but many scholars would consider it erroneous as well.

Unlike the 1983 Holt readers, early textbooks lavished deferential attention on Christianity. One study found that 85 percent of the space in colonial readers addressed religious matters. This religious content declined during the nineteenth century, as educators acknowledged the nation's growing diversity. Religious readings accounted for about a third of the 1837 edition of the *McGuffey's Third Reader*, 9 percent of the 1879 edition, and 6 percent of the last edition in 1901.

Even so, textbook Christianity didn't disappear. In each set of practice sentences, Webster's spelling books of the 1880s included at least one sentence about religion, such as "God created heaven and earth in six days." Arithmetic books of the era included such questions as "How many days is it since the birth of Our Saviour?" A 1955 study found that 93 percent of the texts used in one state, Missouri, contained religious references. Hundreds of the references dealt with prayer; hundreds more dealt with life after death.

Then came the Supreme Court's prayer rulings. While some schools were defying the Court, others were going overboard in trying to obey it. Some schools excised every mention of religion from the curriculum (such as by having students mark out the word *God* in textbooks), removed library copies of the Bible and other religious books, and, in one (possibly apocryphal) instance, disposed of the entomology collection's praying mantis. Teachers ordered students not to read the Bible on the bus or in class, and threatened to suspend children for "possession of Christian material." For praying silently to himself before an exam, one student was forced to write "I will not pray in class" five hundred times.

Though a few administrators mistakenly believed that the Supreme

Court had mandated such steps, others were simply trying to avoid the expense and controversy of a lawsuit. People offended by a whiff of classroom religion were indeed scurrying to court. Schools were sued over the mentions of God in the Pledge of Allegiance, "The Star-Spangled Banner," and Kurt Vonnegut's novel *Slaughterhouse Five*. To avoid litigation, educators began avoiding religion.

So did textbook publishers. Here too, some believed they were following the Supreme Court. One editor maintained that it would violate the First Amendment for a history textbook to mention Benjamin Franklin's prayer at the Constitutional Convention. Barbara Theobald, the supervising editor of the Holt reading series—who had met with Hawkins County school officials in 1983, as the COBS protest was gaining momentum—said in a deposition that identifying a character as a born-again Christian would "raise questions of the separation of church and state."

As with administrators, though, most publishers simply wanted to steer clear of controversy. "Anytime you have anything of a controversial nature in a textbook business, it gets around pretty fast," says Harry Hall, the regional Holt salesman who sold the reading series to Hawkins County. "As the school people start making decisions, whether or not it's something that might sway them one way or the other, I'm sure it's in the back of their minds." While choosing reading textbooks, administrators in other school districts phoned Hawkins County to ask about the conflict over the Holt readers, according to administrator Joe Drinnon. "Harry Hall, I'd say he'd just as soon we would've sent those books back," Drinnon surmises. Whereas the publishers of trade books often seem to believe that there's no such thing as bad publicity, textbook publishers seem convinced that there's no such thing as good publicity.

In the 1980s, several studies found that textbooks were grossly neglecting the role of religion in the United States. Paul Vitz, the *Mozert* plaintiffs' expert witness, conducted one inquiry; another was sponsored by People for the American Way. These and other studies found that, though some world history texts mentioned the Ten Commandments, hardly any listed them. One text included an excerpt of the Mayflower Compact that omitted all but one of the document's seven religious references. American history books described the Pilgrims as "people who made long trips," and noted that they "gave thanks" at Thanksgiving without saying whom they thanked; one teacher told students that they were thanking the magnanimous Indians. Books typically omitted the role of organized religion in the anti-slavery and civil-rights movements. As major sources of inspiration to Martin Luther King, they listed Thoreau and Gandhi but not Jesus. Some publishers even rejected photos of modern towns if church spires were visible. (Impelled by these studies, several states now require textbook publishers to give religion its historical due.)

Vitz found that the neglect of religion extended to basal readers. Like the Holt books, other readers rarely portrayed Christianity, occasionally portrayed Indian and Eastern religions, and frequently portrayed magic and the occult. Stories from the Bible almost never appeared, though books did feature stories based on Greek, Roman, and Eastern faiths. As in the Laura Ingalls Wilder story in the Holt reader, religion was sometimes excised. "Thank God" in an Isaac Bashevis Singer story became "Thank goodness" in a textbook.

Some authors resisted. In Barbara Cohen's story "Molly's Pilgrim," a teacher explains that the Pilgrims got the idea for Thanksgiving from the Jewish harvest holiday Sukkoth. Editors at Harcourt Brace Jovanovich initially removed every mention of Jews, Sukkoth, God, and the Bible. When Cohen refused to let her story appear in that form, a Harcourt editor pleaded with her: "Try to understand. We have a lot of problems. If we mention God, some atheist will object. If we mention the Bible, someone will want to know why we don't give equal time to the Koran. Every time that happens, we lose sales." The editor agreed to restore *Jewish* and *Sukkoth*, but not the other cuts. In the sentence "They read in the Bible about the Jewish harvest holiday," the words *in the Bible* still were omitted. Cohen fought to restore that phrase, but the editor was adamant: "We'll get into terrible trouble if we mention the Bible." With misgivings, Cohen acquiesced.

The Hawkins County plaintiffs also objected to materials that challenged their moral beliefs. A poem that began "Sarah Cynthia Sylvia Stout would not take the garbage out" encouraged children to disobey, in contravention of the scriptural mandate to respect one's parents. By saying that the truth "could cause needless trouble and suffering," a character in one story endorsed lying. Teachers' editions repeatedly recommended having students discuss whether lying and stealing aren't sometimes appropriate. These themes particularly distressed

Jennie Wilson. "That's unfortunate that a second-grade book would teach children that their mommas would lie to them," she said of one story. "Mommas have gone into the jaws of death to bring these children forth."

There was nothing new about raising moral issues in the classroom. Educators of the early twentieth century promoted moral education as a tool for assimilating the new immigrants—the "alien flotsam and jetsam," in the words of the alarmist 1913 tract *Moral Training of the School Child*. The National Education Association listed moral education as one of the seven fundamental goals of secondary education in 1918, and many schools implemented programs. By mid-century, virtually every public school in the United States was trying to teach moral values. Educators, remarked Jacques Barzun, evidently believed that each pupil had "the supremely gifted mind, which must not be tampered with, and the defective personality, which the school must remodel."

In moral education as in the other elements of the curriculum, the teacher told the students what they needed to know. Starting in the late 1960s, however, teachers began asking difficult questions and maintaining that there were no right answers.

"Values Clarification," developed by Sidney Simon of the University of Massachusetts and his colleagues, was designed to help the student "sort out all the pros and cons and achieve *his own* values." The teacher could state his own beliefs at the end of class, but he was to present himself as just another "person with values (and often with values confusion) of his own," whose morality "holds no more weight" than that of any student.

"It was an enormous rage," recalls Kevin Ryan, an education professor at Boston University. "Very good people who were concerned about values saw it as a way to deal with complex, important issues. They were told that all these good things would happen and they wouldn't have to play this old-fashioned role of being a rigid authority. Sidney Simon and his minions were all over the place having huge workshops for teachers. It struck exactly the right chord."

As it grew more popular, though, Values Clarification met with criticism on a number of grounds. The method implied that "clear, consistent, and soundly chosen" values were all that counted, as if a resolute Nazi were superior to a hesitant humanitarian. It seemed to trivialize moral issues by mingling them with personal preferences;

according to the book *Values Clarification,* the method would help students decide "Does religion have some meaning in my life, or is it nothing more than a series of outmoded traditions and customs?" as well as "Should I let my hair grow longer?" Some exercises seemed to invade privacy, as when students were asked whether they "regularly attend religious services and enjoy them" and whether they "ever had problems so bad you wished you could die so you wouldn't have to face them," as well as their views on divorce, premarital sex, and abortion.

Most important, studies found that Values Clarification wasn't working. The exercises might be thought-provoking and enjoyable, but they weren't affecting students' ethics. "Fortunately, because it was a pretty terrible idea," says Ryan, "the research showed that the claims they were making were totally incorrect."

But even as the formal Values Clarification methodology began to fall out of favor starting in the late 1970s, the underlying value-neutrality continued to color the curriculum. Home-economics textbooks of the early 1980s included these statements: "When you buy drugs illegally, you gamble on what you are getting and how they will affect you. It's your decision." "What is right and wrong seems to depend more upon your own judgment than on what someone else tells you to do." "Remember that adolescence is a time of trial and error. Too strict a conscience may make you afraid to try new ventures. . . . It may make you feel different or unpopular. None of these feelings belongs to a healthy personality."

As Vicki Frost charged, the Holt books sometimes adopted this no-absolutes approach. In "Such Is the Way of the World," a story based on an Ethiopian folk tale, a boy named Desta abandons the family's herd of cattle to chase his pet monkey, Jima. He finds the monkey, returns to the herd, and lets his parents believe that he has been there all day. Discussion questions after the story included: "Do you think Desta was wise to neglect the cows and search for Jima? Do you think he should have told his parents what really happened?" Answers to these questions, teachers were told, "will vary."

A similar tale appeared in the 1873 *Webster-Franklin Third Reader.* In "The Tempter," John is supposed to await his father at home, but a friend invites him out to play. John refuses. The friend persists. They will be gone only a few minutes; John's father will never know. "But I should know that I had done wrong," John says steadfastly, "and I should be sorry for it afterwards." The story concludes: "John did right. How much happier all boys and girls would be if they would do as John did when any one tempts them to do wrong!" Among the questions after the story was "Can you tell me why it is wrong to disobey your parents?" To the underlying question of whether disobedience was wrong, it seems, answers of the 1870s did *not* vary.

Frost also protested themes contrary to what she considered vital American principles. "The Forgotten Door" disparaged free enterprise by describing an advanced society without money, and it vilified the American military by saying that "no one knew the right or wrong" of the Korean War. The poem "Forgive My Guilt," which described a man's remorse over having once shot two birds ("They cried like two soft flutes, with jagged ivory bones where wings should be"), maligned hunting and advocated gun control. By harping on pollution, world population, hunger, and other planetary problems, Frost charged, the Holt books were promoting a one-world government that would erode American sovereignty. She also objected that the books presented environmentalism as the one and only moral absolute. All these teachings violated her faith.

Frost and the other plaintiffs would have preferred the vigorous patriotism of early American textbooks. Noah Webster's 1787 reader said on its cover: "Begin with the infant in the cradle; let the first word he lisps be Washington." Some spelling texts featured a "Federal Catechism," designed to inculcate a worshipful attitude toward the nation. An author closed his 1859 history text by saying that the rise of the United States "to so towering a height of power and prosperity . . . is a beautiful and a wonderful subject to write about, and I wish, for your sake, that I had written the story with more skill." Through the early 1960s, textbooks presented the United States as, in Frances FitzGerald's words, "the greatest nation in the world, and the embodiment of democracy, freedom, and technological progress."

After 1965, though, textbooks began to reflect society's growing discord and self-doubt. Books discussed poverty, imperialism, and pollution; emblematically, the word *progress* in one edition sometimes became *change* in a subsequent one. In basal readers, materials with patriotic themes virtually disappeared. A history text spoke of the American past as "a gnarled experience involving problems, turmoil, and conflict."

The new thinking was encapsulated in *Looking at History*, the text-book review sponsored by People for the American Way in 1986. Although its findings about religion in history texts attracted the most publicity, the study concentrated on other matters. Announcing that they preferred books that included "the 'warts' on our forefathers' and foremothers' skins," the five academics on the PAW panel praised texts for discussing the inferior rights of women in colonial society, the "brutal" treatment of the Indians, and Woodrow Wilson's belief in white supremacy. Books were faulted for defending American involvement in the Mexican Revolution, failing to question President Johnson's explanation of the Gulf of Tonkin episode, and neglecting to mention the National Organization for Women, the Equal Rights Amendment, Cesar Chavez, the United Farm Workers, and pollution. The reviewers criticized one book for portraying American society as "truly democratic and egalitarian," and another for its "veiled patriotic bias." A generation earlier, a complaint about "patriotic bias" would have been virtually inconceivable.

Feminist themes in the books also offended the plaintiffs. One essay approvingly described the 1848 Seneca Falls convention, including its declaration that "the history of mankind is the history of repeated injuries and usurpations practiced on the part of man toward woman." Girls or women broke into all-male preserves in "The Revolt of Mother," "Young Ladies Don't Slay Dragons," "The Queen Who Wouldn't Make Spice Nuts," and several other stories. "Where's one story," asked Frost at trial, "where a little girl makes a dress for a doll?" She stresses now that she didn't object to particular stories in isolation, but only to the overall mix. "There's nothing wrong with a woman holding what society would consider to be a male-dominated job in itself," she says. "It's just the terrible imbalance."

Frost also criticized a poem about brotherhood. "All men are not brothers," she asserted in a deposition. "In the Christian belief, brothers are those who have received Jesus Christ as their Savior, who have been born again, are of the family of God. That's what makes us brothers. We are not brothers of every religion." At trial, this was as close as any plaintiff came to criticizing the books' portrayals of ethnic and racial minorities. Earlier, Mozert had been more disparaging in a letter to the editor ("And doesn't it strike you rather odd that all five characters in this story are depicted as being of the black ethnic group?'') and in a deposition (a black child's remark that "white folks had done lots of bad things to our folks," Mozert said, could bring about "situations like the Black Panthers").

The Holt readers and other modern texts do depict a far different universe from that of earlier books. Numerous but passive in *McGuffey's Readers*, girls and women in today's readers, as journalist Larry Van Dyne writes, "pound nails, change the oil in their cars, repair telephone lines, drive race cars, play softball, ride in rodeos, and serve as doctors and mayors." Encyclopedia Brown, the boy detective featured in a popular series of children's mysteries, has been transformed into a girl detective in reading textbooks. Girls beat boys at nearly every game. Most women go to work—according to a 1987 study, a woman depicted in a basal reader is less likely to be a stay-home mother than to be a spy, shepherd, or anthropologist—and men often remain at home and keep house.

The presentation of blacks has also changed. Early books were contemptuous. An 1851 geography text spoke of blacks as "destitute of intelligence," and an 1863 Confederate math text included a problem based on the predicate that "5 white men can do as much work as 7 negroes." By the middle of the twentieth century, disdain had given way to condescension and neglect. Illustrations rarely included blacks, and almost never featured blacks and whites together. A New York history book, published in 1956 and still used a decade later, mentioned blacks only in a chapter called "How People Live on a Tropical Island." A 1966 study of American history texts found that blacks virtually disappeared between Reconstruction and the 1954 school desegregation decision.

Near the end of the 1960s, Frances FitzGerald notes, George Washington Carver and Ralph Bunche popped up as positive role models, as if textbook editors had taken "a sudden and overwhelming interest in peanuts and the United Nations Secretariat." A short time later, blacks were appearing more routinely. Indeed, in some drawings, faces that had been white in earlier editions became black.

The pace of textbook change increased in the 1970s and 1980s. Particular books now ignored Indians' massacres of whites in favor of whites' massacres of Indians, displayed illustrations of cowboys in which blacks outnumbered whites, and, as Van Dyne noted, devoted more attention to Shirley Chisholm than to the Chisholm Trail. Whereas blacks had appeared in almost no urban or suburban illustrations in the 1950s, they appeared in nearly two-thirds in the 1970s. Black sharecroppers disappeared, replaced by black laboratory technicians. Of role models highlighted for special attention in sidebars in several social studies books, more than half were women, and all the men were Hispanic, Indian, or black; not a single white male was included.

These textbook changes serve pedagogical ends. Many educators believe that students feel better about themselves, and in turn learn more readily, when they identify with the characters in their schoolbooks. Positive role models, according to one educator, make it likelier that "minority students will successfully buy into the educational process."

When the curriculum slights the child's group, in contrast, the child feels alienated. The National Education Association warns against books filled with "suburban families of four with briefcase-toting fathers and nonworking mothers," on the theory that children from different backgrounds may "quite understandably decide that reading is not for them." Maryland's textbook guidelines say that a black character's portrayal as "bad or cowardly," unless adequately explained, "may contribute toward the failure of a black child to develop a healthy self-image." South Carolina's guidelines call for curricular materials to "counteract stereotypes that hinder women and minorities from achieving their full potential in science and mathematics education."

Along with boosting self-esteem, textbooks aim to make students more tolerant. A curriculum that ignores minorities' contributions, according to the New York "Curriculum of Inclusion" report of 1989, "gives European American children . . . inappropriate encouragement to disparage children of other cultures." Holt instructed its authors to be sure that books "contribute to the development of positive, respectful images of others"; in particular, portrayals of minority groups "must not depict differences in customs or life-styles as undesirable and must not reflect an adverse value judgment of such differences."

This teaching seeks not only to help students learn more effectively but also to transform society. Educator Pauline Gough wrote in 1976 that "we can only hope" that a curriculum free of sexism will produce "the kind of androgyny that will permit full expression of each child's potential." The Council on Interracial Books for Children said in 1980:

"We have no desire to see children's books that would solely help the dominated get a bigger piece of the pie. We don't like the pie, period. . . . We should not study merely the few women who have overcome sexist barriers, but examine the very standards that have excluded other women's actions from being considered 'accomplishments.' " A speaker at a 1974 National Council of Teachers of English workshop urged teachers to ask themselves whether they were seeking to eliminate linguistic sexism in order to align the language with reality, or in order to "make the power structure say uncle." She added: "Either motive is acceptable, but it is important to recognize which is which."

Considerable evidence indicates that curricular materials do alter attitudes of students, particularly young students. After assessing more than seventy studies, one review of the literature concludes that students exposed to "sex-equitable" materials are more likely to "(1) have gender-balanced knowledge of people in society, (2) develop more flexible attitudes and more accurate sex-role knowledge, and (3) imitate role behaviors contained in the materials." Another research summary finds that "multicultural readings produce markedly more favorable attitudes toward nondominant groups than do all-white curricula."

In fact, scarcely anyone disputes that the public school curriculum affects students' attitudes. From the right, Mel Gabler says textbooks "mold nations"; from the left, the Council on Interracial Books says books "mold minds." Concerned Women for America believes that teaching about homosexuality "destroy[s] family values" and "stimulates experimentation"; the American Association of University Women contends that *not* teaching about homosexuality is "a form of discrimination . . . that has an indelible impact on the roughly 10 percent of our youth who are homosexual or bisexual."

The teachers' editions of the Holt readers addressed the attitudinal issue in "More Than Reading," by Holt senior vice-president Thomas J. Murphy (the essay that Michael Farris would rely on during the early stages of *Mozert* litigation). "When we think about reading programs used in the schools over the last hundred years," Murphy wrote, "we can readily see that more than reading skills acquisition was and is involved." *McGuffey's Readers* "emphasized a Judeo-Christian values system." Readers of the Dick-and-Jane era depicted "a model family environment."

Modern programs, Murphy continued, emphasize humor, reality, and, most important, heterogeneity: "These programs convey the diversity of our people, heretofore presented as a homogeneous group. We are, after all, old and young and middle-aged; handicapped and richly endowed physically. We're all colors; we're tall and short, fat and skinny, and 'just right.' . . . We are the same as all humans everywhere, yet proud of our nation and of its diversity.

"It could be assumed," he added, "that this new generation of reading programs had the concept of diversity in focus when the programs were conceived. I don't think that is the case at all. Increased participation in matters of schools and schooling by an alert and interested citizenry has played and continues to play a very significant role in the content of all text materials."

On the involvement of the "alert and interested citizenry," Murphy and his colleagues at Holt could speak from tempestuous, wearying experience.

As soon as it was published in 1973, the series called Holt Basic Reading was a great success. Teachers liked the fact that it contained excerpts of children's literature rather than materials written expressly for teaching. "We used the best literature, the best materials on linguistics and language," says senior author Bernard J. Weiss, a school superintendent and former schoolbook publishing executive. The innovative series dominated the reading market through much of the 1970s, generating over $50 million in sales by the end of 1981. Though Weiss declines to comment, one knowledgeable source says that Weiss's royalties may well have exceeded a million dollars.

Despite the ultimate success of the series, the first edition was barely off the press when the "alert and interested citizenry" began finding fault with it. Charging that the Holt series slighted women, Texas feminists urged the state to reject it, and the Task Force on Sexism called for its prompt "ELIMINATION." As the date for California's book adoptions neared, Holt sales representative Carl J. Pendleton predicted that "we may squeeze through this time with only a minimum amount of changes, but by the next adoption, we will not be so fortunate."

The Pendleton memo is among 2,261 pages of internal Holt files subpoenaed in the Hawkins County case. These documents offer a rare glimpse into the process of textbook development—a process, as Frances FitzGerald observes, characterized by intense secrecy and an almost pathological fear of controversy. The files show how editors strived to preempt protest whenever possible, worked to appease critics when protest did break out, and scrambled to keep up with the perceived demands of the marketplace.

"There, of course, has been some criticism of *sexism*—and we are guilty to a point," conceded senior author Weiss in a 1974 memo. He and his co-authors, along with staff editors at Holt, had been working on the books since 1967—"before the strong emergence of the Women's Movement," as one memo noted. In the books and accompanying filmstrips of 1973, consequently, women and girls "are generally relegated to the background."

In the background, moreover, females rarely strayed from stereotypic niches. The workbook for the first-grade reader declared that books called *Dolls* and *Dresses* were "for girls," and asked who should read *Trains* and *Planes;* the right answer, according to the teachers' edition, was boys. Illustrations showed boys running, playing rambunctiously, and working with tools, while girls baked cookies, drew pictures, and cut out paper dresses. During development and production of the series, says Thomas Murphy, "nobody thought about how sexist the damn stuff was. . . . Women designers, women editors, women authors—nobody."

The depiction of race and ethnicity raised problems too. In California in 1974, the Standing Committee to Review Textbooks from a Multicultural Perspective detected racism in such phrases as "the afternoon turned black," "it's going to be a black winter," and "the deputy's face darkened." Other California critics faulted the books for referring to a Hopi rain dance as "strange and primitive," for calling a European folk tale "American" but a Japanese folk tale "Japanese" (such "racist logic is related to the internment of Japanese-Americans during World War II"), and for saying that "the people of Gascony are noted for their sly cunning and the people of Normandy for their greed" ("a definite insult to the French people").

Revising the series slightly for 1977, staff editor Barbara Theobald drafted new guidelines. At least 50 percent of the characters in text and illustrations should be female. Materials "should depict a society in which men and women share privileges, responsibility, and opportunities for personal growth." Stories should include one-parent households. A black woman should be "the owner of a car or airplane." Elderly characters should be "capable of some activity demanding agility." The 1977 changes to the series, Murphy says, constituted "a very political revision. We were counting heads as to whether we had 50 percent females, whether we had every minority group represented."

Later guidelines grew more elaborate. Opening with a Walt Whitman epigram—"The Female equally with the Male I sing"—one version stipulated that women should be woodworkers and truck drivers, and men should be nurses, hairdressers, and airline cabin attendants. Men should not be "brutish, violent, crude, harsh, or insensitive," and women should not be "fearful, squeamish, passive, dependent, weepy, mechanically inept, frivolous, shrewish, nagging, [or] easily defeated by simple problems." Girls should work with electricity, study insects, and solve math problems. Boys should read poetry, chase butterflies, and "pay attention to personal appearance and hygiene." Women and girls should sometimes be "larger, heavier, physically and emotionally stronger, and more aggressive than the men or the boys around them." Words to avoid included *manmade* (use *synthetic*), *workmanlike* (use *competent*), *plainsman* (use *plainsdweller*), *statesman* (use *diplomat*), and *letterman* (use *student who has won a school letter*).

The guidelines were equally punctilious when it came to other groups. Blacks must not be "in low-paying jobs, unemployed, or on welfare," but rather "in professions at all levels." American Indians should be "involved in the American mainstream" rather than on reservations, and they too mustn't be "in low-paying jobs, unemployed, or on welfare." ("Unfortunately," Theobald observed in a memo, "the reality for the Indian in our society falls into all of the *avoids*.") Asian Americans and Hispanics must speak English. Jews must not work in "stereotypical occupations," such as "diamond cutters, doctors, dentists, lawyers, classical musicians, tailors, shopkeepers, etc." Minority children should not be shown "playing only with toys from the mainstream or only with toys from their own culture," but with both types of toys. Older people should not be in "nursing homes, with canes, in wheelchairs," or "in rocking chairs, knitting, napping, and watching television." "When selecting authors and stories and when writing art and photo specs," the guidelines directed, "be sure to familiarize yourself with the latest U.S. population figures so that your materials reflect current statistics."

Editors prepared elaborate tally sheets and instructions. "Count number of children (under 21), adults, and older people (over 65) and indicate M or F. . . . Indicate predominant make-up of crowd with regard to sex and ethnicity. . . . Indicate the occupations or roles of featured people. This will help determine the balance of leadership roles." Concerned with authors as well as characters, the sheets included a genre column "to insure that minorities are contributing a variety of selections and not just selections of a certain type."

"Counting and chart-keeping should not be regarded as a useless editorial exercise," the guidelines admonished. "Careful tallies and analysis of how people are represented will reduce the need for costly reprint corrections and may prevent the loss of an adoption." One memo reported on a particular volume: "The in-house count shows 146 female and 146 male characters, or a ratio of 1:1. Animal characters were not included in this count."

To improve the balance, characters sometimes changed gender or ethnicity from one edition to the next. The story "Freddie in the Middle," featuring Mrs. Jay, became "Maggie in the Middle," featuring Mrs. Chang.

More often, materials by or about white males were replaced with new materials. But finding the replacements wasn't easy, as one memo (concerning a Holt literature series) explained: "1. The body of Western literature . . . is made up primarily of works written by and often focused upon Caucasian males. 2. Many of the older works written by and about ethnic minorities and women which may be considered good literature reflect traditional prejudices and would tend to offend some people. . . . 3. The forthright language and candid subject matter in many of the best modern works by and about members of these groups make them unacceptable in many high school classrooms. Attempts to have authors modify such works have rarely met with success." Combining ethnic and gender goals further complicated the task. "We simply could not find a good story with an Asian-American female lead," one editor lamented.

The Holt files indicate that gender and ethnicity sometimes trumped other considerations. Theobald observed that a particular story was "not great literature" but "we gain two points—a female leading character and characters with Spanish-American names." Another editor agreed that the story had "very little literary merit," but "it does help us to achieve some ethnic balance in a very *unbalanced* book." "Two girls may be featured," Weiss remarked of one selection, "but that's the only positive statement I can make about this play." Of another, he wrote: "I'm sorry, but I still do not see much merit in this story—aside from the ethnic aspect."

Weiss also dissented from some of the linguistic mandates. "I feel we are reflecting too much paranoia in eliminating a word like 'mankind,' " he wrote in one letter; in another, he impishly used *peoplekind* rather than the Holt-decreed *humankind*. He also resisted changing *man-eating shark* to *flesh-eating shark;* "being an Hors d'oeuvre," he reasoned, "is not sexist." One staff member grumbled that Weiss's "attitude generally about the material we sent him by and about women and minorities ill befits the author of a modern reading series."

Holt's strenuous efforts, however, didn't placate the critics. Seattle's Ethnic Bias Review Committee judged the 1977 edition "unacceptable" because, "while Blacks are emphasized, it is a narrow representation of those in athletics and music," and because the series contained an intolerable stereotype, a black waiter. In the Texas textbook hearings in 1980, feminists disputed Holt's claim that the readers manifested a perfect gender balance. With animals included in the count (Holt had omitted them), males outnumbered females nearly two to one. "Children of this age," Judith Bergum testified, "are influenced by a story about Mr. Rabbit just as much as they are by a story about Mr. Jones."

During the same hearings, NOW representative Twiss Butler denounced a story in which a boy initially dislikes his new female teacher ("I don't want to go to any gal teacher"), but later, after seeing her hit a home run, excitedly announces that she "can play on my side anytime." The boy's initial hostility, Butler testified, was "the same old story: A mere schoolboy can oppose a woman's right to hold a job if he feels threatened by her competence." His turnabout also connoted patriarchy: "Well, her credentials are worthless until she meets the standards that he sets for approval."

"Some of the selections which we perceive to be positive responses end up being criticized most severely," Theobald observed. "We obviously have to read every selection at least once from the point of view of some of these critics." She suggested that Holt ask Butler and the director of the Council for Interracial Books to review the company's antibias guidelines.

In other instances too, Holt deferred to the views of outsiders. Explaining why a particular story was eliminated from a revision, an editor said that it "is the example used by many 'cultural' advisory councils of what *NOT* to do. We didn't *dare* leave this one in!" "With regard to the offensive portrayal of Negroid facial characteristics on page 22 . . . " another editor wrote, "the artist is himself a Negro.

When we questioned his interpretation, he was very vocal in defending what he did. We didn't think we could impose our white eyes on his artistic interpretation." Holt staff members met with the California multicultural committee, a Hispanic group, black ministers, and others. In thanking a college professor for sending a student's analysis of sexism in the Holt readers, one Holt staff member confessed that "some of our prejudices are so ingrained it is difficult to recognize them."

In fact, out of the 2,261 pages of in-house documents, only one memo exhibits clear-cut animosity toward the feminists and multiculturalists. In 1974, sales representative Carl Pendleton wrote that Japanese-American activist Jeanette Arakawa, who was associated with the Palo Alto multicultural committee, had criticized Holt books on TV. "We even met with [Arakawa] in June," Pendleton fumed. "We are trying to cooperate with these people—talking to them and getting their input, making changes, etc. and then they turn right around and pull a Pearl Harbor on us. It just goes to show you, you can't trust any of them."

Conservatives, meanwhile, were also complaining about the new Holt series. Indianapolis parents faulted the books for excessively using the word *hate*, describing two boys sleeping together, and depicting children lying, disobeying, scheming, and starting a business without their parents' permission. In Minnesota, one group of parents blasted the books as "anti-white" for containing too many minorities; another group condemned one volume for being "anti-parental in many respects," portraying "alien" philosophies, and advancing the march of "Atheistic Humanism in the Schools." In Texas, the Gablers criticized the series for slighting phonics, invading students' privacy, encouraging rebellion, and promoting evolution and situational ethics. California parents announced that, using "high-powered magnifying glasses," they had detected a girl wearing a "transparent skirt" in one illustration —like the swastika and the upside-down cross that the Hawkins County protesters would later find.

Sometimes Holt editors acceded to conservative demands. In response to the 1973 Indianapolis protest, Barbara Theobald recommended getting rid of *hate* in most places, replacing the story that showed boys sleeping together, and eliminating some depictions of ill-behaved children. But she drew the line at having the children consult their parents before starting a business. This criticism, she declared, represented "an intrusion on an author's or publisher's prerogatives."

Conservative influences were evident elsewhere too. The in-house guidelines urged authors not to refer to evolution, not to invade students' privacy, and not to include "any subtle propagandizing for communism." With conservative sensibilities in mind, one memo warned that a proposed illustration showing a mixed-race couple "would make some people very nervous." In 1980, Holt even brought in a prominent conservative critic to address the staff: Kris McGough of Columbia, Maryland, a Catholic mother who had testified before a congressional committee, written a monthly column for the journal of the National Council for the Social Studies, and served on Maryland's Values Education Commission.

Still, Holt people had only so much patience for conservative criticisms. After McGough's talk, for example, when staff members sent their reactions to Theobald, one declared that publishers shouldn't be "intimidated" by such a "reductionist, simplistic, and reactionary" argument; another said that McGough represented a "dangerous" and "paranoid minority" whose members opposed independent thinking because it would "threaten their control"; another urged that Holt "not lose sight of the long-range goals of education in the face of any one group's self-serving interests, however vocal it may be"; and still another wondered what possessed people to "feel threatened by a question or an idea in a textbook"—sentiments that the staff never voiced concerning liberal critics.

Another Holt staff member vented his ire in 1973, when a small Texas newspaper, evidently inspired by the Gablers, published a negative item about a Holt book. "Is this article grounds for a suit for misrepresentation?" wrote regional sales manager Don C. Hale. "It sure as heck cannot do us any good. And I am tired of sitting back and taking it. Maybe CBS could do a news report on the Educational Research Analysts (The Gablers) of Longview, Texas, and expose their true qualifications as educators?" At the time, CBS owned Holt. *60 Minutes* did air a feature about the Gablers, but it was relatively innocuous, and it didn't appear until nearly seven years after Hale wrote his memo.

Holt editors viewed Mel Gabler, Kris McGough, and other conservative critics as fundamentally different from Twiss Butler, Jeanette Arakawa, and other liberal critics. In a 1981 speech, Theobald denounced the Eagle Forum, the Moral Majority, the Gablers, and other

conservatives as the sort of "censors" one finds in "totalitarian socie-
ties." In the next section of her speech—a section entitled "Positive
Pressure Groups"—she said: "At the other end of the spectrum
we have other groups . . . who seek to improve our educational institutions and textbooks in a positive manner." To Theobald, it
seemed, critics who wanted schoolbooks to feature more women were
"positive pressure groups," whereas those who wanted fewer women
were "censors."

In attracting critics from the left, the Holt books weren't unique. Black
organizations and parents sought, sometimes successfully, the removal
of *The Adventures of Huckleberry Finn*—one protest occurred at Mark
Twain Intermediate School in Fairfax County, Virginia—and other
books containing the word *nigger*. The District of Columbia refused to
purchase any songbook that contained the word *darky* in Stephen Foster lyrics (and Georgia in turn refused to buy any book that changed
the lyric to *brother*). Parents in Amherst, Massachusetts, tried in 1987
to get rid of a textbook for, among other things, characterizing Reconstruction policies as "harsh" and failing to describe Columbus's en-
slavement of the Indians. In 1988, one critic decried the "cultural
arrogance" in a novel about an eleven-year-old boy's anxieties over
moving: The book flagrantly ignores "the existence of the millions of
eleven-year-olds in this world who are too hungry or too poor to face
problems as relatively frivolous as those facing Peter." "Literature,"
another critic demanded in 1984, "*must accurately* portray the disabled"; as unacceptable portrayals, she cited *The Hunchback of Notre
Dame, Peter Pan, A Christmas Carol, Heidi, Treasure Island*, and *Richard III*.
    Complaints about fairy tales weren't the exclusive province of the
right, either. The Council on Interracial Books for Children and other
critics condemned *The Tale of Peter Rabbit* as sexist (the only disobedient character is male), ageist (the crotchety farmer is old), "racist by
omission" (all the bunnies are the same color), and materialistic (Peter
is hunting for food). The council also called on "concerned parents and
educators" to get rid of such stereotype-ridden stories as "Cinderella,"
"Little Red Riding Hood," and "Hansel and Gretel." In 1992, a California school board dealt with a different objection to "Hansel and
Gretel": two self-proclaimed witches complained that it teaches children that "it is all right to burn witches and steal their property."
    Just as Theobald does, many people distinguish liberal "positive

pressure groups" from conservative "censors." Pressures to include women and minorities in textbooks "are not censorship," Dorothy C. Massie of the NEA wrote in 1984; rather, they are "forms of affirmative action sorely needed to promote equity and accuracy in classroom instruction." "Opposition to sexist, racist, or religious stereotypes is surely different from what moral monopolists have in mind," David Bollier contended in a 1982 People for the American Way book. "They want to *impose* their restrictive, rigid stereotypes on everyone else, while minority groups are usually seeking to *break down* derogatory stereotypes and expand materials available."

Such arguments follow a pattern that's common in schoolbook protests. They define a seemingly neutral boundary, proclaim it a democratic imperative, and condemn protesters for crossing it. Many of these arguments arose in the Hawkins County conflict and shaped the public's perception of it.

The trouble with the first of these arguments—the "stereotype" distinction drawn by Massie and Bollier—is that disparagement lies in the eye of the beholder. What PAW considers a derogatory, hidebound portrayal of women, Concerned Women for America finds positive and appropriate. And if the crucial difference is that the right improperly reinforces existing attitudes whereas the left properly eliminates them, the result is a ratchet that permits only change. The director of the Council on Interracial Books made this point explicitly, saying that censorship can arise only where the goal is "to protect the status quo and the orthodoxy."

To be sure, liberals often seek to rebut offensive materials with other materials, while conservatives often want to remove offensive materials entirely. Racist and sexist books, Massie writes, can be used as "teaching tools," with the teacher pointing out their "defects."

But the left-right split here isn't absolute. The Hawkins County plaintiffs would have dropped many of their objections if teachers had used the "defects" of the Holt books, as diagnosed by Vicki Frost, as teaching tools. And for their part, liberals are sometimes as eager to excise as conservatives. When a United Church of Christ board called for banning creationism from the public schools, no alarms went off at the National Coalition Against Censorship. Instead, the coalition's *Censorship News* lauded the church for its "historic commitment to the public schools, excellence in education and academic freedom."

When it comes to censorship, such double standards are common. Marc Stern, a lawyer with the American Jewish Congress, recalls that he once wondered about his own organization's record in criticizing schoolbooks. He found a file labeled "Censorship," but it only contained accounts of other groups' attacks on books. "I knew, because I had worked here as a law student, that there were cases in which *we* had objected to things in textbooks," he says. "We had a very good librarian, and I sent her off to the file room and said, Find me where we objected to stuff. And she did. It was kept, literally, a city block away, in a different file room. Well, the stuff that *others* took out that we liked was called 'censorship.' The stuff that *we* wanted to take out because we didn't like it was called 'defamation.' "

Under another distinction often drawn by People for the American Way, right-wing censors are trying "to push American public education back to the dark ages with an approach that tells students *what* to think instead of teaching them *how* to think."

Schools, however, constantly teach students what to think. They acclaim knowledge, punctuality, obedience, self-discipline, cooperation, tolerance, and hard work. They teach evolution without creationism, racial equality without William Shockley's ideas about genetics, and the Holocaust without fringe groups' theories that it was a hoax (in fact a Colorado teacher was demoted in 1991 for raising the hoax hypothesis in class). State education codes are chockablock with one-sided mandates. Tennessee schools must teach "the contribution of black people to the history and development of this country and of the world," "the evils of intemperance," and "the importance of . . . planting and cultivating flowers." In California textbooks, according to state guidelines, "the practice of thrift should be encouraged." One model curricular policy says that classroom materials must present "different points of view," and that they must "foster respect for minority groups, women, and ethnic groups"—or, as restated by education professor Kenneth A. Strike of Cornell, "the values of the marketplace of ideas shall be in force in our schools except when the topic is minorities or women." In these and many other areas, schools vigorously teach students what to think.

Still another distinction constrains the parent's authority. "I think that, as a parent, my rights extend solely to my children, and not to all of the children in the school or the community or the nation," a leading censorship chronicler, Edward B. Jenkinson of Indiana University, wrote in 1989. "So if I want an alternate assignment, I have the right to request that."

Parents, however, are also citizens, voters, and taxpayers. They care not only about their children's upbringing, but also about government efficiency, tax rates, and community mores. If they can properly complain that funds earmarked for a golf course should be spent on a homeless shelter instead—and do so without being told that, inasmuch as they will be free to stay away from the golf course, they have no right to protest it—why can't they complain about a school library stocked with Harlequin romances but no Shakespeare? (In any event, Jenkinson backed off his endorsement of alternatives when confronted with the Hawkins County case. If these protesters were to get separate textbooks, he said, other parents across the country would demand different books in every grade and every subject; public education would grind to a halt.)

In a 1981 book, First Amendment scholar Robert M. O'Neil suggested a different limit to parents' authority. Because school boards are democratically elected, "a single parental challenge to a unit or course that has been approved by an elected board (or its appointed surrogates) is antidemocratic," even if the parent "seeks to have only a single child excused." The Hawkins County CARE petition declared similarly that teachers and administrators ought to have "sole authority over book selection," for "this process is the most democratic way, the basis on which this country was founded."

But while voting may head any list of fundamental democratic rights, it hardly exhausts the list. To begin with, the First Amendment guarantees the right to petition the government. Some of these petitions result in special treatment for the petitioner—antidemocratic in a sense, but hardly scandalous. The First Amendment also protects the right to criticize government, even intemperately, and the right to form associations with others. How can the COBS protest against the Holt books be any more antidemocratic than, say, a Physicians for Social Responsibility protest against nuclear arms?

There is one difference, of course. Censors seek to close off access to the ideas that fuel our political discourse. Free speech advances a society toward political, social, and artistic truth, or so we believe. Consequently, the government is largely forbidden from regulating speech based on its content. In nonspeech areas, the government faces no such constraints; it need not await any "clear and present danger" before banning a medicine, automobile, or toy. Speech is special.

School, however, is also special. Students are a captive audience assembled by the state. They can escape the public school only by enrolling in a private school or, in those states that permit it, by studying at home with their parents—options that require more resources than some families can muster. Children, moreover, lack the intellectual sophistication and emotional maturity of adults. Parents and educators assume that some expressions of some ideas will harm children, an assumption that is subject to heated dispute concerning adult audiences.

Most important, the mission of public education forces the government to do what the First Amendment as a rule frowns on: select particular ideas, package them, and present them with the imprimatur of the state. Schools must choose phonics or whole-word sight-reading. They must decide whether to allocate limited class time to sex education, peace education, death education, drug education, or something else. Such official choices, virtually forbidden in other spheres, are inescapable in the public schools—which has led some imaginative constitutional scholars to argue that modern public education violates the First Amendment's free-speech guarantee.

If government can't avoid assembling the curriculum, how do we distinguish permissible selection from impermissible censorship? Is it censorship when a school library declines to subscribe to *Hustler?* "It would be good, positive censorship, in my opinion," says Hawkins County principal Jean Price. But if that's censorship, then everyone is a censor.

Under one common distinction, refusing to purchase *Hustler* is selection, and taking it off the shelf is censorship. Students have a First Amendment case against a school that removes a library book because of the ideas in it, but not against a school that refuses to buy the controversial book to begin with. In a moment of excessive zeal, the American Library Association once considered publishing a blacklist of librarians who complied with demands to remove books; it never contemplated a similar list of librarians who selected books timorously.

This is a peculiar distinction, akin to prohibiting racial discrimination in firing but not in hiring. Most likely it reflects the disparity of exposure: Removal of a book is sometimes a public act, whereas refusal to buy a book is almost always a private one. Whatever its basis, the double standard operates to make school people even more cautious as they select books. To avoid the potential hullabaloo and litigation that may result from removing a book, it's better not to buy any book that poses even a slight risk of unsuitability. Demonizing book removal may, perversely, impose a chilling effect on book selection.

Under another typical distinction, a *Hustler* opponent isn't a censor if he's an accredited educator. As one of the "basic differences between censors and selectors," Edward Jenkinson lists: "Censors rely on the reviews of other censors to get rid of books. Selectors rely on reviews published in professional journals." From one angle, the distinction fades to nothing: Censors read censors; selectors read selectors. From another angle, though, it makes a dubious but potent assertion: The child's education should be left to professionals. A *Los Angeles Times* editorial about the Hawkins County case illustrates this approach by asserting that "parents have a right to oversee their children's education, but they may not substitute their biases for the pedagogic judgments of professional educators." Parents have biases; educators have pedagogic judgments.

In keeping with this emphasis on credentials, educators sometimes try to shift book battles onto their turf. When an Arizona couple contended that a book had harmed their child, the school instructed them to explain fully, with documentation, "the nature and extent of the damage to your children" and "precisely how (i.e., the sequential, mechanistic process)" this damage had come about.

Similarly, when parents disparage a book's contents, educators often concentrate on its pedigree. In Montgomery County, Maryland, a group of parents complained that ninth-graders shouldn't be required to read James Dickey's grim novel *Deliverance*, with its scene of homosexual rape. School administrators responded by listing the prizes that the book and its author had won. As board member Harriet Tyson later wrote, the two sides spoke past each other. The parents "were clearly questioning the wisdom of requiring a 14-year-old to read a book with such explicit and negative sexuality. Their question, it seemed to me, was 'When is the twig bent?' The staff had avoided that complex and sensitive question entirely, smugly calling upon institutional prerogatives and expert literary judgment."

All of these distinctions—how to think versus what to think, selecting versus censoring, educators' pedagogic judgments versus parents' biases—serve to shut out, and often to shut up, complaining parents. Instead of saying that protesters are advancing faulty complaints, their opponents accuse them of violating the democratic covenant by daring to complain at all. The implication is that reckless statements *in a* schoolbook are sacrosanct, whereas criticism *of* a schoolbook is disgraceful if not unconstitutional. Instead of talking about values, educators and their allies talk about procedures (as when the Hawkins County school board stressed that the Holt books had been selected by dedicated local teachers) or expert prerogatives (as when Barbara Theobald assured the Hawkins County school people that the readers contained only "established, accepted literature").

Indeed, educators go to considerable lengths to sidestep the values questions. The NEA condemned the Reagan administration for "inflam[ing] passions regarding prayer in the schools, sex education, censorship, creationism and other issues which complicate the politics of publicly financed schooling." In a fact sheet called "Dealing with the Smear Tactics of the Far Right," the NEA also denounced a conservative group for having advised school board candidates to "divide the voters on ideological lines—for example, a strategy based on a conservative vs. a liberal view." From this perspective, education should be left to professionals, and kept away from impassioned parents and ideologically inclined politicians.

It's refreshing, then, when an educator grapples with the fundamental issues. In an article published in 1983, Dorothy Massie of the NEA observed that "the conflict that engages public education today is a conflict of values and, ultimately, of two opposing visions for the future." Referring to Tim LaHaye's *Battle for the Mind*, she went on to describe this conflict in dire terms: "The preachers, politicians, and ideologues of the Radical Right seem to view with regret the pluralistic nature of our society. . . . Their kind of schooling would instill in the children a kind of ethical and cultural protectionism antithetical to the democratic principles on which our nation was founded. The public schools *should* be the central arena in LaHaye's battle for the mind. That LaHaye and his kind should ever be permitted to win the battle is unthinkable."

Slanted as her analysis is—"I happen to be, I guess, what you might call a lefty," says Massie—at least she recognizes what's at stake. She sets forth an argument to which conservative schoolbook critics can respond by arguing about the purposes of public education, the realm of parental control, and the values that undergird American society.

Though the proper direction of the public schools always lurked in the background, however, the Hawkins County lawsuit addressed slightly different issues. Whatever they requested at the outset, in court the protesters sought different books for their own children only. So far as other children were concerned, the curriculum would remain unchanged.

Is it, then, unthinkable that *any* child should grow up thinking like Tim LaHaye? How can we reconcile our commitment to the values that Massie catalogued, particularly our belief that differences among citizens contribute to social progress, with the rights of those who don't share those values? Must the schools, as one longtime school administrator contends, "tolerate all creeds except intolerance"? These questions lay at the heart of *Mozert v. Hawkins County Board of Education,* a case that, in the crescendo of news coverage, was being labeled "Scopes II."

SCOPES II

On July 14, 1986, television camera crews and newspaper photographers lined the Main Street sidewalk in downtown Greeneville. Whenever anyone rounded the corner and headed for the federal courthouse, the media pack sprang into action, shutters popping and minicams whirring. Plaintiffs, lawyers, spectators, people pursuing their own courthouse business—all were chased like celebrities. "You take the pictures now and sort out the names later," one cameraman said.

People attending the trial of *Mozert v. Hawkins County Board of Education* passed through a metal detector just inside the courthouse doors, climbed a flight of stairs, and entered the high-ceilinged courtroom. In the rear spectator section were a dozen hardwood pews, seating about seventy people. Two bas-relief wood sculptures—Work Projects Administration products of a pre-feminism era—hung on the back wall: a woman with child entitled "The Resources of Nature," and a robust man entitled "Man Power."

Vicki and Roger Frost, Jennie Wilson, and some of their allies had visited the courtroom a few days earlier. "Judge Hull doesn't know this, and I hope we won't get in trouble now," says Vicki. "But we were all over that courtroom! I remember Roger being up at the seat of Judge Hull, praying for God to give him wisdom. And then I remember Jennie Wilson going over and praying—I don't mean for this to sound as extreme as it may—but she prayed over in the defendants' part of the room out of Psalms, that consternation, confusion, chaos, and calamity fall upon those who would come against truth."

There was no jury to pray for. The outcome of the case would depend principally on the application of the First Amendment to facts that the two sides had stipulated in advance, so the lawyers had agreed to have Judge Hull decide the case.

Now, with the trial about to begin, the lawyers took their places. On his side, Farris had two other CWA lawyers and a law student. Working with Tim Dyk were four other lawyers from Wilmer, Cutler & Pickering, along with five paralegals, a law student, a secretary, three local lawyers representing the defendants, and an attorney for the State of Tennessee, which had intervened to voice its concerns. Farris told reporters that *Mozert v. Hawkins County Board of Education* was starting to look like *David v. Goliath.*

Indeed, the two lead counsel could hardly have been more different. Thirty-four-year-old Farris, wearing a light blue seersucker suit, could have slid comfortably into a Greeneville law firm. The same couldn't be said of forty-nine-year-old Dyk, with his downtown Washington gray suit and professional reserve. Farris's law degree was from Gonzaga; Dyk's was from Harvard, and he taught part-time at Yale and Georgetown. Farris was a devoted Republican and a former Moral Majority leader; Dyk was a devoted Democrat and a member of the board of the Migrant Legal Action Program. Farris says his CWA salary was about $50,000; though Dyk declines to say, several other Washington lawyers estimate his 1986 law firm compensation at between $300,000 and $400,000. Farris's wife, Vickie Farris, a former schoolteacher, spent her days home-schooling their five daughters; Dyk's wife, Sally Katzen, was (like her husband) a Wilmer partner who taught part-time at Georgetown. Farris and his *Mozert* team stayed at a Holiday Inn; Dyk and his senior aides took over a bed and breakfast that was opulent by local standards.

Barbara Parker, who by then had left People for the American Way, and a few other spectators amused themselves one day by casting *Inherit the Wind II*. To play Farris, they envisioned Michael J. Fox. For Dyk, they pictured Alan Alda, though reporters suggested that Walter Matthau was a closer match. "I think Tim liked Alan Alda better," says Parker.

The two lawyers' advocacy styles also differed. Farris could be witty, adroit, and inventive, but he could also be brash and peevish. In depositions and at trial, Farris recounted personal experiences, badgered witnesses, and tried to engage defense lawyers and witnesses in debate. Dyk, in contrast, was measured, soft-spoken, calculating, and impersonal.

Personal conviction had brought Farris into the Greeneville courtroom to begin with. He dedicated his legal skills to the conservative causes he cared fervently about. Dyk, in contrast, was a professional advocate whose personal views didn't dictate the cases he took or the arguments he presented. That's not to say that he and his colleagues viewed *Mozert* in soulless abstract. Dyk says he believed from the start that a victory for the plaintiffs would be "a disaster for the public schools."

Another member of the defense team remembers perceiving the case in national terms. "It was very much *Concerned Women for America versus People for the American Way*. The local school board officials and the local plaintiffs, while not pawns, were somehow less important." To the defense lawyers, this source recalls, "the enemy was really not Frost or Mozert, but Falwell, lurking in the background."

Responsible for explaining the intricate objections to the Holt readers, Vicki Frost was the plaintiffs' most important witness. She detested the role, she says. "I *dreaded* having to be the spokesperson for listing the objections to the book. I didn't mind to do the research and put it all together. . . . But I dreaded getting up and speaking."

She also offers another reason for her reluctance to testify: "I dreaded so bad to get up in front of people because I'm overweight." Her weight, previously around 175, had climbed to 215 since her arrest. "I've learned since that time that I have thyroid disease, and probably had it at that time but didn't know it," she says. "Course, your thyroid reacts to stress, and your thyroid controls your metabolism."

Her obesity left her open to excruciating derision. Strangers raised the topic in letters to her. "Being fat while others go hungry," one wrote, "is far worse than any of these textbooks." The *Kingsport Times-News* published a letter to the editor that said: "Mrs. Frost, I believe we are told it is a sin to overdo anything whether it be drinking, eating, or whatever. From what I see, maybe you should consider a vegetarian diet."

"I just hated to put myself up to suffer any more in that regard,"

Frost says. "I would worry, what am I going to wear? Those things may seem vain. But because I'm overweight, people would make fun. . . . I just dreaded it."

She had other worries too. A couple of months earlier, Roger had moved to their farm in Sneedville for several weeks. "We weren't really separated," says Vicki. "Roger has suffered from problems with his nerves since he got back from Vietnam." The conspiracy trial had taken its toll on him. "He had to be at court and listen to the lawyers say that he was just being drug around and hanging on to my coattail. That hurt him as a man. With his personality, rather than just brushing it off and laughing at it, it bothered him." Now he was feeling better, living at home, and taking time off from work to accompany her to court.

Vicki had met with Farris the night before the trial began in order to go over her testimony, but she couldn't concentrate. "He knew I was having a hard time," she recalls. "So we just stopped and prayed. It was just difficult for me, with all that I had on my mind, all that I had to do. My mind was tired; my body was tired. . . . I was so tired!"

Driving to Greeneville the next morning, panicky over the prospect of taking the witness stand, she had to pull over to the side of the road and throw up. She hurried into the courtroom with just five minutes to spare.

"Call Mrs. Vicki Frost," said Farris.

Wearing a blue plaid dress, her hair held back with barrettes, Frost sat down in the witness box. However queasy she may have felt, she seemed poised and unruffled as she testified, speaking animatedly and gesturing with a yellow highlighter.

She seemed so composed, in fact, that several observers thought she had to be speaking from a script prepared by someone else. Volunteer High assistant principal Phyllis Gibson dismisses her as "a little robot" on the stand, and observes pointedly: "Mrs. Wilson is a very bright, educated woman." "It was clear that Vicki didn't prepare her own testimony," says Barbara Parker. "I always thought it was the Gablers, that she was just reading directly. . . . She had every movement down pat. I'm sure she was rehearsed time and time again, she appeared so calm and cool and collected."

Frost and her allies are adamant that the testimony was all her own. "She has a photographic memory," Sue Eaton says admiringly. Frost maintains that she spent more than two hundred hours studying the books and preparing her objections. She initially got some guidance from the Gablers' literature, but her own final objections were far more elaborate than theirs. "The Bible, the holy preacher, is the source that helped us to determine what was in error in these books," she says. "It was the Bible. No outside source, not Mel Gabler from Texas, not any other organization. The Holy Bible was our source."

Rumored mastermind Jennie Wilson provided scarcely any help, according to both Frost and Wilson. "Those old schoolbooks, they depressed me," Wilson says. "That may sound foolish to you, but really they did. They made me so sad. I tried to help her, but I just couldn't stand it."

Whatever assistance she may have had, Frost managed to keep her testimony clear and straightforward, but not succinct. As she had at the conspiracy trial, she gave wordy responses to her lawyer's questions. The crowd, standing-room-only at the beginning, thinned out, and Judge Hull grew irritated. "I think," Frost apologized at one point, "I'm wanting to talk too much."

Farris had instructed his witnesses to give simple, direct answers. "If it was 51 percent yes, then answer yes without going into all the exceptions," Bob Mozert recalls. "Vicki Frost did not do that. . . . It would have violated her conscience to say yes or no when there is large portions that she did not believe to be correct, so she placed the extra burden on herself to go back in and give an explanation in detail."

Not until the second day of trial did Farris finish questioning Frost. Now Tim Dyk stood up to cross-examine her—and Frost's answers lengthened even more. With interruptions, the cross-examination would continue for three days.

Dyk focused on apparent contradictions in Frost's account. The plaintiffs had stipulated that another reading series approved for use in Tennessee schools, published by Open Court, would not offend their religious beliefs. The Open Court books, unlike the Holt readers, contained stories from the Bible.

But, as Dyk pointed out, the Open Court books also contained material about imagination, the supernatural, feminism, and other topics that the plaintiffs found intolerable in the Holt series. The plaintiffs did want their children excused from reading some Open Court stories with this material, but not all of them. Why was that?

"You are comparing things that don't come near close," Frost answered. The Holt series "is so polluted, there is no system or method that I could possibly work out to make it acceptable. There is just not any way at all." The Open Court books were entirely different, with far less objectionable material and a superior overall philosophy. To Frost, it was simply a matter of balance. She could tolerate an Open Court story in which a child disparages adults, because the books have an "overriding theme" of "respect for family." A girl playing baseball in Open Court was "not offensive"; similar stories in Holt were offensive because of Holt's "overemphasis on nontraditional roles."

Dyk tried to find the boundary. Would her religious beliefs be violated if a teacher or textbook said something in favor of gun control?

"I wouldn't go ask for my child to be taken out of the class."

"Would it violate your religious belief?"

"It would be offensive."

What about a single antimilitary statement?

"I stated on the last statement it would be offensive," she replied. "I can deal with small offenses. I can't deal with burdens. . . . It moves from offense to burden."

But where, Dyk asked, is the dividing line? How many unscriptural stories is too many?

"It would have to be evaluated by the book you had."

Dyk tried again. Was it correct, he asked, that a single statement praising the National Organization for Women "would offend your religious beliefs, but wouldn't cause you to take your children out of public school?"

Frost started to explain her opposition to feminism.

"True-false question," Judge Hull grumbled. "It's not essay-type."

"It would be offensive," Frost said, "but . . . not to the point that I would have to go down and ask for my child to be removed from class."

Dyk next asked about particular stories in the Open Court book. In one story, a frog turns into a prince. Why was this acceptable?

Because, Frost said, it didn't mention magic.

Dyk noted that she objected to "distorted realism" in the Holt books. "You think it's perfectly realistic for the frog to be turned into a prince?"

No, said Frost, but this was "fantasy," not distorted realism.

It was increasingly evident that Frost hadn't given much thought to distinguishing tolerable offenses from intolerable burdens. Asked if she would remove her children if the schools required them to read the Open Court books with no stories excepted, she said, "I don't know."

But she *had* given considerable thought to her objections. Some of the concepts were so horrendous to her that, sitting on the witness stand, surrounded by lawyers, reporters, and spectators, the very thought of them made her lose her composure. "You say Equal Rights Amendment, but ERA is part of the feminist movements. It is *not* equal rights," she said, her voice starting to crack. "It is gay rights, lesbian rights, and woman's right to have an abortion. That violates the word of God. I don't want my daughter growing up to be a feminist. I will not put up with it!" She was fighting back tears. "I don't mean to get emotional, but this is so ungodly, this feminism!"

At one point Dyk tried to turn Frost's murky answers to his advantage. "You are having a little trouble making me understand your point of view—would you say that's accurate?"

"I don't know," Frost said. "I mean, we're having communication problems."

"Okay," said Dyk. "Now, let's suppose that a teacher in public schools had an acceptable book and she's teaching away. Do you think maybe you would have a little bit of difficulty in explaining what the teacher could do and what she couldn't do, consistent with your religious beliefs?"

Sensing trouble, Frost backed off. "The primary objection in this whole lawsuit is the contents, the philosophical contents of the stories themselves."

"My question to you is, don't you think it might be rather difficult for you to explain to this teacher what your religious beliefs would permit and what they would not permit?"

Frost stammered for a moment, then asked Dyk to repeat the question. "You're going to have to make it very simple," she said.

"I'm trying to," he replied. He asked again if Frost wouldn't have a hard time telling the teacher what topics would be forbidden in classroom discussions.

She assumed that teachers would follow the teachers' edition, she said. When she was in school, teachers asked about comprehension, not about "how this relates to gun control or women's role in society."

Frost had evaded the question, but Dyk had made his point. The schools couldn't be expected to anticipate her numerous and at times incomprehensible objections (though Farris would later insist that they wouldn't have to do so).

Dyk made other points too. He demonstrated that Frost's objections went beyond textbooks. Frost said she would be offended if a teacher made a feminist remark, or if another student expressed beliefs contrary to Scripture. "There is no way," Dyk told Judge Hull, "this woman can attend public school and *not* have her religious beliefs violated in some way or other."

Dyk also sought to demonstrate that censorship, not accommodation, was the plaintiffs' ultimate goal. He tried to introduce in evidence a letter from Farris to a potential expert witness. Farris objected, and Hull ruled it inadmissible.

So, without making the letter a part of the court record, Dyk read it and asked Frost if she agreed. A victory in the lawsuit, Farris had written, would establish that "textbooks which teach the religion of secular humanism cannot be forced onto children. Although this finding will not directly require the judge to throw the textbooks out of the public schools, it will be a major building block in the effort to force the public schools to remove such books and practices. Such a finding can be widely publicized to demonstrate that a federal court made a finding that an ordinary textbook was teaching the religion of secular humanism."

"That's not my object in this case," said Frost.

"Things are going real well," defense attorney Nat Coleman told a reporter during a break. "We'll just let her dig her own grave."

As commonly occurs in free-exercise cases, the defense had conceded before trial that the plaintiffs' beliefs were sincere and religious—two steps in the judicial inquiry. During Frost's cross-examination, Farris repeatedly objected that Dyk was violating the sincerity stipulation by probing for inconsistencies in her beliefs. Gesturing toward the reporters who were sitting in the jury box, Farris said that if the question of sincerity remained open, "we have the wrong people sitting in the jury box"—the trial would require a jury to decide this factual issue. "We're going to have to start this thing over."

"No, I'm not going that way," said Judge Hull. He asked Dyk whether he was attacking Frost's sincerity.

No, said Dyk; the stipulation didn't go that far. In his view, the

Holt books didn't burden Frost's beliefs. She was saying that a topic is "okay in one context and not okay in another context," Dyk told the judge, "and it depends on how much of it there is or how little of it there is." Where objections are so contextual, he said, no cognizable burden exists. The free-exercise clause doesn't apply when someone says that "at fifteen percent, that book doesn't violate my religious beliefs, but at twenty-five percent, it does."

Part of Dyk's argument, pressed throughout the trial, was that the Constitution protects only the *central* tenets of religious faith, and not the lesser tenets. A centrality requirement would enable the defense to box Frost in. If she objected only to the Holt readers, and didn't apply her religious principles to the Open Court books or the rest of the school curriculum, then her beliefs weren't central. If she did apply her principles to the entire curriculum, then she would have to object to far more than the school could reasonably accommodate. Either way—because her beliefs were too insubstantial to be central, or because they were too far-reaching to be accommodated—she would lose.

After hearing the lawyers' arguments, Hull ruled that Dyk could continue questioning Frost about apparent inconsistencies in how she interpreted the Holt and the Open Court books.

Later Dyk asked about other inconsistencies in the application of Frost's faith. "Is it true," he said, "that you had a television set until the time this controversy arose, at which time you took it out of your house?"

Farris objected that the issue was irrelevant.

Dyk said it was relevant in light of the Supreme Court's only free-exercise case involving the public schools, *Wisconsin v. Yoder.* "The Amish," Dyk said, "had created a separate community in which they rejected all worldly influences. It relates to the issue of burden in this case. . . . We have children here who watch programs like *The A-Team.* . . . If *The A-Team* and these other programs have scenes which these plaintiffs say are objectionable in public schools but they will tolerate them on television, then it may violate their religious beliefs but not to the point it becomes unconstitutional. The Constitution does not give you a right to go home and watch things on television while complaining about the same things in public schools."

Farris responded that Dyk was construing the free-exercise clause so narrowly as to cover only the Amish; "anybody that has buttons or zippers can't have constitutional rights." He added that he had represented people in home-schooling cases who have "beliefs essentially identical to Mrs. Frost."

But had he, Judge Hull asked, confronted the argument that Dyk was making about the inconsistent application of beliefs?

"Nobody has ever had the audacity to do what Mr. Dyk is doing," Farris declared, "and that is trying to prove people's religious beliefs are not true."

Hull replied, "Hard for me to believe that somebody, somewhere, does not have as much audacity as Mr. Dyk."

Dyk tried again to explain the relevance of the Frosts' TV. "We're dealing here with people who do not care strongly enough to shield their children," he said.

"It's awful hard to shield anybody, isn't it?" mused Hull. "Doesn't mean you don't have a right to try, though, does it?"

When dealing with public education, Dyk replied, "there has to be some rather strong showing of burden on the religious beliefs."

Hull said, "You really want to go in and try to determine . . . how zealously these people adhere at other places what they claim they're adhering to in the school system?"

"Yes, your honor."

"I don't believe you can do that. I don't think that's a defense. At least, I'm not going to let you do it this afternoon."

The inconsistency issue arose again the next day. William Farmer, a bespectacled thirty-eight-year-old lawyer representing the State of Tennessee, offered a different reason why inconsistencies were relevant. They didn't cast doubt on the sincerity of Frost's beliefs, but only on the feasibility of accommodating the beliefs. "Anybody could come here and say that what we're doing—if we're teaching children phonics, it violates the First Amendment," he said.

No, said Hull. "It's got to be grounded in her religion. But she comes along and says she's a Christian, and the Christian doctrine is harder than anybody can attain. I know something about it." Hull was a Methodist who said grace before meals and attended services at a church across the street from the courthouse.

Farmer argued that the two sides of the constitutional analysis— the religious burden on the plaintiffs, and the state's interest in refusing to accommodate them—were interrelated and inseparable. "We have a state interest in teaching these children how to be citizens in the modern world and—"

Hull interrupted: "In a uniform manner only? That is the question." Hawkins County, he added, "even got like the Bible on Christianity: 'Holt, Rinehart is the way and the only way.' " In his view, the state interest and burden questions were not intertwined. "The first thing is, she's entitled to nothing if her religious beliefs have not been violated. And that may be unkind, but that's the first question." That, Hull said, was what Dyk's talk of centrality was getting at: "They're not burdened because many other times these children are exposed to the same or similar subjects in other walks of life, and no objection is made." He added that he anticipated Dyk would argue that Frost is "entitled to nothing because the world is so big that she can't isolate herself and her family from it even if she wants to."

Farmer said that Frost couldn't isolate her children even at school, because health, social studies, science, and other courses included the same topics as the Holt books. First-graders learned about pollution, second-graders about hunger, and third-graders about family disputes. "It goes on and on. . . . Reading is not the only issue in this lawsuit. It's much, much broader than that."

The judge noted that the plaintiffs weren't asking for public schools tailored to their faiths; they were asking only to avoid the Holt books —a request that sounded manageable to Hull. "This great big system, isn't it big enough, broad enough, smart enough to be able to take this in? I'll be the devil's advocate; nobody else is arguing. All the facilities the state has, all the educators, the minds of the world, can't we take care of thirteen children over there who don't want to go to class and want to learn some other way? . . . Surely in this broad, diverse country of ours, there's more than one way of doing things, isn't there?"

"Yes, sir," said Farmer.

"How many ways did Hawkins County decide they'd do it in?"

"You have to address that to Hawkins County people."

"It's one," said Hull. "They say, one way."

Though he had granted the defendants summary judgment two years earlier, Hull now seemed to be favoring the plaintiffs. During pretrial hearings, he had urged school officials to give in and accommodate the children. "If I was a taxpayer of Hawkins County, I don't know whether I would want to make any law or not," he had said at a July 1985 hearing, and added: "The fact is, I think the case ought to be settled."

Now Farris stood up to respond to Farmer. Inquiring into the Frosts' TV habits would extend the trial's duration by "three or four months," he announced, a prospect that he knew wouldn't appeal to the restless Judge Hull. "I have never watched *The A-Team*," Farris said. "I don't know if this court has watched *The A-Team* or not." To rebut the implications of Dyk's proposed questions, the plaintiffs might need to bring in scripts from the show as evidence, or even subpoena *A-Team* star Mr. T, "if he professes to be a Christian," to testify that he saw nothing unscriptural about *The A-Team*. (Mr. T was indeed a Christian; he had appeared on Jim and Tammy Bakker's TV program.) Going off on such tangents would be "ridiculous," Farris said. The plaintiffs had stipulated that the Open Court books would satisfy them, and "who is to question that?"

"I have enjoyed the debate very much," said Hull, "but let's get back to getting some evidence in." He said that despite his misgivings, he would allow Dyk to ask Frost about TV.

"I knew it was going to be appealed," Judge Hull remembers, "and I just thought I'd let everything in." He didn't want his ruling to be reversed because he had erroneously excluded evidence, which would require him to convene another trial. "I didn't want another trial," he says.

Although Frost's cross-examination wasn't yet complete, Judge Hull allowed another witness for the plaintiffs to testify first: Paul Vitz, the New York University professor who had studied the content of the Holt textbooks. Vitz testified out of order because he had to return to New York later in the day.

The fifty-year-old Vitz had traveled a long spiritual path from his liberal Protestant roots. As a sophomore at the University of Michigan, "I read Bertrand Russell, announced I was an atheist, and took considerable pride in my hard-won independence," Vitz writes. His militant atheism lasted a few months, followed by "a long agnostic indifference to religion." Then Vitz, "a totally unprepared, recalcitrant, secularized psychologist who thought that the only natural direction of change was exactly in the opposite direction," became a Christian in the early 1970s, and a Catholic in 1979.

Vitz is one of a handful of academics at prestigious mainstream institutions who share the concerns and the terminology of the religious right. "The secular humanists have been able to dominate and control education," he declared during an interview for a Heritage Foundation newsletter. He named as leading secular humanists John Dewey,

Thomas Paine, the Unitarians, and the signers of the Humanist Manifestos—a list well known to readers of *Battle for the Mind* and Tim
LaHaye's other works.

In the Greeneville courtroom, Vitz summarized his study of the
Holt books. Because the books neglected Protestant Christianity, he
said, students would come to view Protestantism as "relatively exotic
and foreign, and not something characteristic of everyday American
life today."

As Farris had done when first filing the suit, Vitz compared the
fundamentalist plaintiffs to downtrodden blacks. "My position here is
based on the arguments, with which I agree, that were made in reference to the effects of leaving out black history and black heritage and
black culture from our schools," he said. "It was argued that this had
negative effects on black children because they were not acknowledged, and their history and heritage was not acknowledged. I think
this is generally accepted—to leave out one's heritage and history is to
make one feel somewhat embarrassed or ashamed of it; at least, not to
value it."

After Vitz had completed his testimony, Vicki Frost returned to
the stand. Dyk tried to show that Vitz's empirical study of the Holt
books was irrelevant. "Do you agree with Dr. Vitz that Biblical Protestantism ought to be a central theme of public education?" he asked.

"That's not my objection that we have come to court for," she said.
"We have come saying—"

"*No* is the answer," Hull interrupted. "What is the next question?"

Dyk asked whether the absence of religious themes concerned her.

"I have given lengthy testimony as to what violates our scriptural
conscience," Frost said.

Hull leaned over. "He's got a right to cross-examine you and challenge your thinking," he said. "He's asking you a question. Please stay
on track and answer it."

"I will do the best I can," Frost said, "but I don't want you to
make me say something I don't believe."

"Don't say anything you don't believe," said Hull.

Finally Frost conceded that, "as I can understand" the question,
her objections did not rest on the books' exclusion of Biblical Protestantism, the point of the Vitz testimony.

With that issue resolved, Dyk returned to TV.

"We have a television set, but that is in a storehouse," Frost said.

Before December 1983, it had been in the house, and the family had sometimes watched it. They no longer did.

"Is it not true that you object on religious grounds to your children watching *Sesame Street?*"

Frost said she once saw one character call another a "fool" on the program, "and that was offensive." Thereafter she didn't let her children watch it.

Dyk moved on to a different topic. After the lawyers' lengthy arguments over whether TV was relevant, *Sesame Street* was the only program he asked about.

"Parent banned 'Sesame Street,' " the *Cincinnati Post* headlined its article on the trial's events that day. The *Knoxville Journal* titled its front-page account " 'Sesame Street' 'offensive,' says fundamentalist." The information elicited by Dyk's question didn't help Judge Hull, but it did appeal to the reporters sitting in the jury box.

Coming from all over the United States and from Australia, Germany, and England, the reporters did constitute a jury of sorts, and a powerful one. Judge Hull would define *Mozert* for the few hundred lawyers who kept up with free-exercise law. The reporters would define the case for everyone else.

Like the Mencken-based character in *Inherit the Wind*, the *Mozert* reporters seemed to view the fundamentalists sardonically. Chatting among themselves, the reporters "tended to scoff at Vicki," says Mike Dye, who covered the trial for the *Kingsport Times-News*. When one reporter left a "SAVED" sign in his chair, he added at the bottom: "i.e., reserved; not born-again."

At every break, the reporters mobbed the major players. "You couldn't walk a step," says Beverly LaHaye, who attended part of the trial. "When you came out of that courthouse, there were probably seven or eight steps going down. You'd hit that first step and, boom! They were right there." "It was like ants swarming onto a morsel of food," says plaintiff Sandra Couch.

Inevitably, the media attention attracted pranksters and eccentrics. A teenage boy marched in front of the courthouse with a fake snake wrapped around him. He carried a sign that said, "HAWKINS COUNTY SCHOOLS SHOULD TEACH SNAKE HANDLING." David Brand, Reece Gibson's law partner, admits that he was responsible. "Cost me fifty dollars," he says, chortling.

No one, however, had hired Zevs Cosmos, a disheveled, bearded man who held up a sign saying "NUDE CHRISTIAN CHURCH . . . REPENT IN THE RAW" and distributed pamphlets containing a nude photo of himself. "One day he jumped in front of Mrs. Frost," remembers Volunteer High's Phyllis Gibson. "I guess one of her trademarks was that smile; no matter what was going on, she smiled. So he jumped in front of her and said, Mrs. Frost, where do you put your horns at night? *That* wiped the smile off her face. I thought she was going to hit him."

The lawyers generally obliged the TV reporters with a few remarks. In contrast to Dyk's circumspect comments—he wanted to avoid telegraphing his strategy to the other side—Farris sometimes offered frenzied sound bites. If the defendants won, he predicted, "major civil unrest" might follow. "Blacks in South Africa will have more rights" than Christians in the United States; concentration camps could be on the horizon. John Payton, a black Wilmer lawyer working with Dyk, denounced the South Africa comment as "deplorable." Dyk, ever cautious, said only, "The government here is considerably better than the one in South Africa."

At times Farris suspected that Dyk was playing to the press inside the courtroom. Farris charged that Dyk asked about *Sesame Street* "for the purpose of embarrassing the witness." A question about "Cinderella," Farris complained at another point, was intended only "to embarrass her and make headlines," because "these people"—he motioned to the reporters—"are going to go out of here and report that she objects to 'Cinderella.' "

"Does she care whether they report that or not?" said Hull. It was an astute question: Frost presumably wasn't ashamed of her religious beliefs—but CWA, Farris's employer, desperately wanted the plaintiffs to come across as mainstream Christians.

Farris knew that "Cinderella" would appeal to the press, because ABC, CBS, the *Washington Post,* the *Philadelphia Inquirer,* and *USA Today,* among others, were already emphasizing Jennie Wilson's objections to "Goldilocks" and other materials in the kindergarten and first-grade readers, which were not at issue in the lawsuit. "ABC News put on the first-grade reader, showed pictures," remembers Farris, "even though we had told them that's not true, there's no substance to it. They *knew* it, they *verified* it, and they still did it anyway." Focusing largely on these objections to fairy tales, Russell Baker and Lewis

Grizzard devoted satirical columns to the *Mozert* plaintiffs. "You've really arrived when Lewis Grizzard writes about you," says Phyllis Gibson.

There were other prominent media inaccuracies, nearly all of which tarnished the plaintiffs. "Some parents want to ban textbooks that teach evolution and what they call 'anti-Christian values,' " Dan Rather told *CBS Evening News* viewers, as if the plaintiffs were suing to keep the books from all children. The *Christian Science Monitor* reported that Frost had been arrested "when she barged into her daughter's classroom and charged that a number of textbooks . . . violated her child's religious upbringing"; actually she had been arrested for arguing with the principal in the school office. Several newspapers reported that the parents objected to *Macbeth;* actually they objected to the modern poem "Your Thing," which begins with lines from the *Macbeth* witches' chant.

Consistent with the derisive tone that dominated the coverage, reporters—especially TV reporters—often pursued Vicki Frost rather than Bob Mozert. Frost was a large woman with a deep accent, imperfect grammar, bright red lipstick, an omnipresent smile, and no college degree; Mozert was an articulate former business-college professor with a master's degree. Frost better fit the stereotype of a sanctimonious Bible-thumper straight out of Mencken. A born-again-Christian journalist who followed the trial theorizes that Americans are bigoted against fundamentalists and against overweight people; a fat fundamentalist is doubly afflicted. "As far as just physical looks go, she's somebody that people want to point their finger at and say she's weird," says Tom Wright, Judge Hull's clerk during the trial. "She was a great big woman, dressed very modestly. . . . It just made a perfect picture, her coming down the courthouse steps with 'Scopes II' over her head in the newspaper."

That label, widely used in the press, also carried implications. It suggested that the *Mozert* fundamentalists were using the law to force their religious beliefs on others, as the *Scopes* fundamentalists had done. As a law review article pointed out, *Mozert* could instead be called "Barnette II," in reference to the 1943 Supreme Court case excusing Jehovah's Witnesses from reciting the Pledge of Allegiance in school.

After reviewing some of the coverage, the *St. Louis Journalism Review* suggested that *Mozert* provides "a case study in media hype gone wild." Major media, the article said, "seem guilty of sensational, oversimplified reporting of a complex case." After reviewing several examples of misreporting, the article closed with a quotation from Vicki Frost: "I don't have much hope that truth about this case will ever be printed."

The magnitude and tenor of the coverage owed something to People for the American Way. "This organization started as a commercial," says PAW president Tony Podesta, referring to Norman Lear's TV ad criticizing the religious right. "Media wasn't just an auxiliary function; it was our purpose." In *Mozert*, he says proudly, "We framed the debate. Censorship rather than religious freedom. 'Scopes II'? We invented the term, then all of a sudden you see it in *Time* and *Newsweek*. We really worked the press very hard." He adds with a laugh: "CWA didn't know what hit them."

CWA did try to fight back against what it termed PAW's "disinformation" campaign. In a *USA Today* guest column, Farris asserted that belittling fundamentalists is akin to "calling blacks 'Sambo' and depicting them as shiftless, lazy shoeshine boys." "This is *Scopes* upside down, backwards," he told reporters. "The Christians are now the persecuted minority, and the ones who believe in evolution are now the persecutors." In his unmodulated style, Farris also wrote to PAW to complain about its newsletter's coverage of the case: "I could call you liars but that probably would not offend you. . . . Your petty anti-Christian drivel shows you to really be nothing more than religious bigots."

It was a lost cause, though. "Every evening when we turned on the television news, we felt we were in a foxhole and being bombarded," says CWA's Mark Troobnick. "I have never been in a case where the media was so antagonistic and so one-sided. PAW seemed to control the kaleidoscope through which the press perceived the case."

Tim Dyk, beneficiary of the one-sided news coverage, also finds fault with it. "The press should have explained the issues, instead of just presenting them as nuts," he says. In his view, the press misrepresented the trial as something humorous, when it was actually quite serious. Here Dyk was echoing an earlier advocate who had complained that the press had treated his case "as a farce instead of a tragedy": Clarence Darrow, counsel to John T. Scopes.

Nearly every article and editorial about *Mozert* prominently cited two of the plaintiffs' objections. "Just going through the newspapers, you'd think our whole case was to get *The Wizard of Oz* and *The Diary of*

Anne Frank banned," says Frost. These two objections had a devastating impact on public opinion. "Judy Garland and Anne Frank?" says
CWA attorney Jordan Lorence. "They've *got* to lose! Those are American heroes, icons."

The Anne Frank complaint was the most damning. In truth, the
plaintiffs objected to a single assertion: "I wish you had a religion,
Peter. . . . Oh, I don't mean you have to be Orthodox, or believe in
heaven and hell and purgatory and things. I just mean some religion,
it doesn't matter what. Just to believe in something!" Albert Hackett
and Frances Goodrich, the MGM screenwriters who adapted the diary
for the stage, evidently based this dialogue on part of the diary entry
for July 6, 1944: "[Peter] has no religion. . . . People who have a
religion should be glad, for not everyone has the gift of believing
in heavenly things. You don't necessarily even have to be afraid of
punishment after death; purgatory, hell, and heaven are things that a
lot of people can't accept, but still a religion, it doesn't matter which,
keeps a person on the right path." To the plaintiffs, such indifferentism
—the view that religions are interchangeable—flatly contradicts the
scriptural teaching that Jesus is the only path to salvation.

By reporting without further detail that the plaintiffs objected to
The Diary of Anne Frank, however, the press hinted that they must be
anti-Semitic. Trying to avoid being lumped in with the Holocaust-is-
a-hoax groups, CWA issued a press release explaining the actual objection and adding plaintively: "CWA and the parents do not dislike
Jewish people."

Frost received hate mail over the Anne Frank objection. One writer
likened her to the Nazis. Another, observing that he had visited the
Frank family's attic hideout, declared that Frost was surely bound for
hell; he signed off, "Cordially yours."

Even more unsettling were the fan letters that the Anne Frank
objection generated. "WAKE UP ARYAN AMERICA," admonished
a flyer sent by "The Phoenix Movement" of Sacramento. "Judeo-
Freemasons are GANGSTERS! WE MUST NEUTRALIZE THEM!"
Frost also heard from members of the Christian Identity movement,
which teaches that the Israelites spoken of in the Bible are actually
Caucasians, and that the people now masquerading as Israelites are
offspring of the "seed of Satan." From Mariposa, California, an Identity follower sent Frost a series of letters, videotapes, audiotapes, and
books, including a tape of a 1961 talk by Identity founder Wesley A.

Swift. Though the sender didn't mention it, Swift had been active in the KKK and the Christian Defense League, and he had ties to the paramilitary Minutemen and American Nazi leader George Lincoln Rockwell. "As he sent information I began to see that he held views that were offensive to me," Frost says, and she stopped corresponding with him. "If I understand *anything* about Scripture, you're not to hate anyone."

Shortly after the trial, Jordan N. Gollub of Bristol, Virginia, announced that his KKK chapter would march through Rogersville to show "support for Christian parent Vicki Frost." Recognizing another public relations catastrophe, Farris sent a mailgram to the Klan leader: "PLEASE DO NOT HAVE A RALLY TO 'SUPPORT' THE PARENTS IN THE HAWKINS COUNTY TEXTBOOK TRIAL. IT WOULD HURT OUR CASE TREMENDOUSLY AND PLAY INTO THE STRATEGIES OF THE LEFT." PAW, to its credit, refrained from exploiting this juicy opportunity. Instead it joined CWA in issuing a statement saying that the organizations "condemn the bigotry and violence of the Ku Klux Klan and . . . abhor their entry into this controversy." On the appointed day, Gollub grumpily canceled the parade when he was the only Klansman to appear.

"You just couldn't get people's eyes off Anne Frank," says Marc Stern, a lawyer with the American Jewish Congress. "In Jewish audiences, people still talk to me about the case where they tried to suppress Anne Frank. And I'll go through this whole rigmarole about how they didn't suppress Anne Frank; they just objected to the fact that the only thing they read in Anne Frank was this one excerpt. The textbooks picked a very small piece of Anne Frank, and what piece did they pick? The piece that said it doesn't matter what religion you have; you just have to have some religion. These textbooks aren't neutral."

Given the opportunity to change the plaintiffs' objections, Michael Farris says, "I'd have taken out Anne Frank and *The Wizard of Oz.*"

PAW might be prevailing in the press, but Farris seemed to be holding his own in court. Not only did Judge Hull appear to think the schools should accommodate the plaintiffs; to some observers, the judge also seemed hostile to Tim Dyk.

At the end of the second day of trial, Hull instructed Dyk to provide a list of "what questions you intend to ask all the rest of the witnesses for the plaintiff, as they come on, and what your reason is for asking

such questions, and also what is the evidence that you're going to put
on these issues"—a massive assignment. Gesturing toward the jam-
packed defense table, Hull said, "You've got a whole staff of people
over here. Put some of them to work." The subtext, PAW's David
Crane remembers, was: "You think you're hot shit? Well, you're on
my turf now."

Hull has the reputation of being a down-to-earth judge comfortable
with a range of legal issues, but no intellectual. He is intuitive rather
than scholarly. "He's got a raw sense of what's right," says Tom
Wright, his clerk during the *Mozert* trial. "My experience in working
for him was, a lot of times he would tell me what the result should be
in a case without doing any legal research, and then leave it to me to
do the legal research. And the legal research would end up backing
him up. Nine times out of ten, that's the way it is with him. He's going
to reach the same result the court of appeals would reach, but without
reading all the opinions and knowing their reasoning." Another former
associate says of Hull: "His down-home, country, common-sense approach would never be approved by Yale or Harvard, but it's a good
approach for a rural area."

Dyk, in contrast, specializes in presenting complex legal arguments
to appellate judges—the sort of lawyering that Dyk's friend Judge
Laurence Silberman terms "a business for legal intellectuals." In
court, Silberman says, "Tim comes off as a Harvard College–, Harvard
Law School–educated, sophisticated Washington lawyer, because
that's what he is." In Greeneville, Dyk was dry, formal, at times
condescending. A British reporter found him "persistently calm and
sneering."

Some school defenders worried that Farris had the better rapport
with the judge. David Crane thought Judge Hull had a chip on his
shoulder when it came to Dyk, "Yale professor of constitutional law,
hotshot lawyer from Washington and his staff." Joe Drinnon remembers Farris as a "Southern courtroom lawyer" with the style of a "fire-
and-brimstone preacher," in contrast to Dyk's "fairly monotoned
style." William Farmer, the attorney representing the State of Tennessee, says, "We had an East Tennessee judge listening to the proof, and
I think he was more of a kindred spirit with Farris than Dyk. Farris
didn't come across as a Washington lawyer; he came across more as a
friend of the people."

The school defenders took some solace from the fact that Farris's angry side occasionally emerged in the courtroom. "You never knew when he was going to just flip his lid," says Barbara Parker. "He did a couple times. He just would go bonkers, just a crazy person." At one point, says Phyllis Gibson, "He was like a kid. He threw a temper tantrum. You wanted to jerk him up and smack him and say calm down."

"There *was* one point during the trial where Michael started to lose his cool," acknowledges his colleague Mark Troobnick. "He came back to the table, and Jordan and I said, Mike, you've got to calm down—relax. He said, Yeah, I just lost it for a second there. Then he was calm. There was only that one instance that I can remember where he lost his temper. It was something that Tim Dyk had said."

Judge Hull also seemed hostile to another of the defense lawyers. After Bob Mozert testified about the scriptural bases of the plaintiffs' objections, plaintiff Rachel Baker took the stand. Judith Wish, Dyk's Wilmer colleague, cross-examined her.

Wish tried to show that the Bakers had known about the Holt books before moving to Hawkins County. Judge Hull interrupted several times, asking why the issue was relevant. Then Wish asked Baker what church she attended, an issue that the attorneys had stipulated in advance. "I know about it," Judge Hull complained. "I read the stipulation. Wish I hadn't, if we're going to prove them again anyway. I wasted my time." During the rest of the cross-examination, Hull continued to snipe at Wish.

"Judge Hull doesn't like women lawyers," says Jennie Wilson. "He hated Wish. . . . He was blasting her. I mean, he was inhuman."

Phyllis Gibson had the same impression, and, she says, she did something about it. She went to Hull's chambers during a break, got admitted to see him, and said, "Judge Hull, I wish you'd give the women in there some credit for having some sense. You're very ugly to the female lawyers, who are much more brilliant than those other turkeys." Hull was unreceptive, Gibson recalls. "He got really pissed, and told me he'd conduct his courtroom the way he wanted to."

When asked, four years after the trial, about his apparent antagonism toward Wish, Judge Hull seems bewildered. He now has, he says, three clerks—he holds up three fingers—of whom, he adds, all three—he holds up the fingers again—are women. "I *like* women," he insists. "I try to hire somebody smarter than I am." He adds that he can't remember any female attorneys taking part in the *Mozert* trial.

Farris called Mel Gabler to the stand. The defense had earlier objected that Gabler had nothing to add. "Mr. Gabler claims to be a textbook expert," said Dyk, but the issue facing the court was whether the books offended the plaintiffs, not whether they offended any experts.

Judge Hull asked what made Gabler an expert. "Did he graduate from the textbook school?"

"I think I was careful to say he 'claims to be,' " Dyk sniffed. "I do not regard him as one."

Farris said the testimony would be relevant because the Gablers' criteria matched the plaintiffs'. As for Gabler's status as an expert, Farris said, "You can ask the People for the American Way—they think he's an expert and they recognize him as an expert."

Unenthusiastically, Hull agreed to allow the testimony. "I have regretted every ruling I have made because it seems to lengthen the trial," he said.

On the stand, Gabler explained the background and scope of his textbook review operations. He testified that some of the humanistic material in the 1983 Holt books, the ones used in Hawkins County, had been removed from the 1986 editions.

Dyk cross-examined him. He first asked if "your primary objective has been to oust the objectionable textbooks from the public schools."

Farris objected that the question was argumentative.

Overruled, said Hull. "He can field the questions."

Dyk complained, "I do object to Mr. Farris's objections when I'm trying to cross-examine the witnesses."

"Our system," shrugged the judge. "I have to let him object. I can't silence him, can I?"

Dyk said, "I have no comment on that, your honor."

"Tolerate it as well as you can," said Hull. "I object to all objections. I like to sleep up here rather than rule on it. Go ahead."

Gabler answered that he had not sought to have books removed from schools. "We participate in the process before the books are adopted. Basically what we've done, these twenty-five years, is just show the general public what is in the books, because we find most of the people do not like what they see."

Dyk held up a copy of James Hefley's book *Textbooks on Trial*, a sympathetic account of the Gablers' work which the Gablers sold from their Longview home. The book jacket referred to "Mel and Norma Gabler's on-going battle to oust objectionable textbooks from public schools and to urge publishers to produce better ones."

Gabler responded: "Probably poor choice of words by the publisher's PR department. . . . Some people who use our material do go to the schools and get books thrown out that are already in. But our thrust is to prevent the books from being adopted when they do not meet mainstream American values."

Several other expert witnesses also testified for the plaintiffs. Patrick Groff, a professor of education at San Diego State University, said that the plaintiff children would learn better from the Open Court books than from the Holt ones. "If a child reads something in school that is quite offensive to what they have been taught at home or elsewhere, they find that difficult to comprehend. They are not motivated by it." Ray Powell, the former superintendent of schools in South St. Paul, Minnesota, said that his school system routinely offered alternative assignments to religiously offensive material.

A Hawkins County teacher also bolstered the plaintiffs' case. Evelyn Rodriguez, who had taught first grade at Carter's Valley Elementary in the fall of 1983, said she always used supplemental materials in class. She also described the county's program that took special-needs students out of the regular classroom for thirty minutes a day. The students left behind in the regular class, she said, didn't ask to go to the special-needs class, or tease the students who leave.

On cross-examination, Rodriguez agreed that the plaintiffs' accommodation would complicate the task of teaching. "For one thing, I wouldn't know what they had been going over, the skills they had been taught, and I wouldn't be able to incorporate it into my other subjects that I would have to teach during the day." She said she would be worried that she couldn't mention topics from the regular reading class when they arose at other times in the school day. The accommodation would also be difficult because when students were particularly enthusiastic about a story, she sometimes let them continue reading past the usual end of class.

Judge Hull had a question. How would she respond if the school board ordered her to give a different reading book to a few students in her class?

"If I were ordered to do it," she said, "I would find a way to do it."

Finally, fourteen-year-old Rebecca Frost testified that she agreed with her parents that the Holt books were contrary to the Bible. Because the Bible instructs Christians to keep apart from evil, "reading the Holt books would be doing the opposite of what the Bible teaches."

After Dyk said he had no questions for Rebecca, Farris announced: "Plaintiffs rest." On Monday the defense would begin to present its case.

The first defense witness was Robert L. McElrath, the state commissioner of education. A bald man with sharp features, McElrath declared: "I would fight and die for a person's right to believe in the religion of their choice. The question is, can the public schools accommodate? After long and prayerful thought, I'm of the opinion that there are several reasons why this is impossible." Echoing Evelyn Rodriguez, he contended that "reading is not taught in isolation." A teacher might refer back to stories in the reader when, for instance, the same vocabulary words arise in other subjects. In addition, the teacher would have to stop the class and consult religious students about whether some discussion topics offend their beliefs; younger children might be unable to make this determination. Finally, he said, "if we did it for three students or fourteen students in one reading class, I think soon we would be doing it in science classes and for other religious groups in the school."

On cross-examination, Farris asked McElrath a series of hypotheticals. Would he require black students to read a racist book, pending the state textbook commission's reassessment of the book?

After trying to evade the question, McElrath responded, "I would not accommodate them."

"Would you make Jewish students eat ham?"

"We don't make youngsters eat food. We offer them a choice."

"Would you make Jehovah's Witness students salute the flag?"

"No. The Supreme Court has ruled on that, in terms of separation of church and state."

"Would you make a conscientious objector take ROTC training in high school?" Farris had in mind a case in which the Sixth Circuit Court of Appeals—the court whose decisions were binding in Tennessee—had upheld a religious student's right to refuse to participate in ROTC.

"I would not, because I would consider it not that important in terms of the curriculum."

"If a choir was putting on a Christmas concert," Farris asked, "would you force a Jewish student or atheistic student to sing Handel's 'Messiah' or the 'Hallelujah Chorus,' if they had objections on a religious basis?"

"No, I would not."

If United Pentecostals objected to mandatory co-ed physical education because of the students' "immodest" clothing, would McElrath force them to attend? Again Farris had in mind a case in which a federal court had crafted a free-exercise exemption.

"Yes, I would," McElrath said. "But I would address the dress issue by allowing the youngster to choose alternative dress."

"What if their complaint was not the way they were dressed . . . but the fact that they were having to watch other students who were in immodest apparel, in their opinion? Would you let them opt out then?"

"I had situations like that when I was in high school. The answer is no."

When Farris was finished, Judge Hull asked a question of his own. "Why is it impossible to let . . . the Christian objectors read out of the Open Court book, and the rest of them read out of the Holt books, and the teachers teach out of both of them? Why can't that be done?"

"I testified earlier that I think it's just very unfair to hold teachers accountable," said McElrath.

"We're paying them to be accountable there in the schoolroom," said Hull. "Got a raise last year. . . . Why, other than being hard on the teachers, which I don't mean to be, but why can't they teach four students out of one book and sixteen out of another set of books? What would be the bad result, if any, to either the four or the sixteen, if that's done? And why would it affect the cause and objectives of the State of Tennessee to do that?"

"I think it would affect both groups, relative to achievement scores, because of the division of time."

"What leads you to come to those conclusions?" said Hull. "Those are conclusions that you have come to. What facts do you have that would lead you to those conclusions?"

McElrath was unable to specify any facts.

· · ·

After lunch the defense called Faye Taylor, the director of elementary education for the state. She testified that the plaintiffs' objections went well beyond reading. All day long, teachers would have to take care to avoid topics that might offend the plaintiffs.

Farris objected, provoking a lengthy argument over the magnitude of the lawsuit. "The plaintiffs present a very simple scenario: We don't want these books, we will take these other books," he said. If Taylor testified about how the plaintiffs' objections might apply to the rest of the curriculum, "I could imagine my cross-examination taking several hours on this. . . . I think we should stay on reading and reading only, and not go off into the other areas of the curriculum."

Hull said he was inclined to agree.

"To me this is a critical issue, absolutely critical," said Dyk. "What we have here is a case which Mr. Farris is trying to make about a book. It is not a case about a book." A student in class might raise a question about the Equal Rights Amendment, even though the topic didn't appear in the textbook. "What is the teacher going to do, stop and phone Mrs. Frost and say, Is this okay, Mrs. Frost?"

"You take the position that the public schools are not available to them," said Hull, "because of the religious beliefs they have got?"

Earlier Dyk had suggested that no religious burden existed. Now he said that the burden was so immense that it couldn't be accommodated. "That is correct. The public school is not the place for these plaintiffs. If the state is going to teach these people, they have to do the things which they find objectionable. . . . There is no way these people can go to public schools and get the kind of education that the public schools are there for." Only home-schooling or a religious school could accommodate such "sweeping religious beliefs."

Wasn't Dyk, Hull asked, essentially saying that the plaintiffs ought to object to more than they do?

"No, no," said Dyk. "We are relying on the specific testimony, the exact testimony." According to Frost's testimony, some objections were limited to the Holt books, but many others were more general. "Her world views and religious views are so sweeping that it goes way beyond the Holt books to all sorts of other books and to every aspect of the curriculum."

But, said Hull, did the plaintiffs' lawsuit challenge anything other than the Holt books?

"That will be the next lawsuit, your honor," said Dyk.

"Well," said Hull, "we can only take them one at a time."

"But the point is, your honor, this court should consider what is going to happen in the future, other objections that will come up. . . . This is not a case about a book, really. . . . It is about the way the discussion takes place in the class. It is about exposing children to controversial issues. It is about using the methodology of role playing. It is about exposing them to family conflict, drug abuse, and child abuse. . . . And it is shot through the whole curriculum."

Judge Hull said he didn't see how he could look beyond the Holt books. "What the plaintiffs are saying is, We object to these textbooks —not for the general masses, but for our children—and all we want is an alternative textbook for this particular class," he said. "How can I expand the lawsuit to say, Well, you probably mean the next class and the next class and the next class, ad infinitum, world without end, amen?" He asked Farris to respond.

To Farris, the very idea that the plaintiffs couldn't be accommodated was un-American. "It means we violate the fundamental principle upon which this country was founded, and that is no taxation without representation. We take the taxes from these people and say we are entitled to operate the public school system in a way that systematically violates your religious belief system —systematically violates the religious belief system of a whole bunch of people, not just these plaintiffs."

Why, Hull asked, couldn't the defense talk about the other parts of the school day that the plaintiffs' objections would seem to address?

Because the First Amendment flatly forbids it, Farris answered. If Taylor was going to testify that the plaintiffs object to science and other studies, "she has become an arbiter of scriptural interpretation, and courts have said consistently that the government cannot be an arbiter of scriptural interpretation." It was "a First Amendment violation, in and of itself, to let a government official come in and say, I better understand your religion than you do, and you really don't understand your religion."

"If Mr. Farris is right," Dyk responded, "this whole trial is unconstitutional. How can they be accommodated if we're not allowed to inquire in this courtroom or the public schools?" He noted that Frost objected to a Holt story for saying dinosaurs lived millions of years ago, a point that would come up in science class.

"Which is not before us," said Hull.

"It *is*, your honor," Dyk insisted. "It *has* to be before us." Teaching evolution in reading class is no different from teaching it in science class. Afraid of controversy, teachers would back off from teaching evolution or the other forbidden topics in class.

"Isn't that going on now?" said Hull, referring to Vitz's testimony. "They're afraid to say anything about religion."

"I think that's exactly the problem," Dyk agreed. "We're going to broaden it beyond the teaching about religion to teaching other subjects. A teacher is going to be afraid of getting sued. . . . You're going to put the teacher in the situation of where she's quaking in her boots every time she goes into the classroom. Oh my goodness, I have one of Mrs. Frost's children. . . . What am I supposed to do? Am I going to teach her something today that is going to result in a lawsuit against me?"

Hull called a recess to consider the issue. When court resumed a few minutes later, he said he would allow Taylor to apply the plaintiffs' objections to the rest of the curriculum.

Unable to bar Taylor's testimony, Farris tried to show that it was erroneous. Taylor had spoken of the age of fossils as a fact. "Are you aware," Farris asked her on cross-examination, "of the presupposition of the carbon-14 dating system that the bombardment of radioactive waves upon the isotope of carbon-14 has always been constant?"

"No, sir."

"Are you also aware that there is evidence that there was a universal flood about four to five thousand years ago, that is evidenced by the finding, for example, of a mastodon in Siberia flash-frozen in an instantaneous wall of water? Are you aware of that?"

"No, sir."

Farris asked more questions about evidence that, in the minds of "creation scientists," casts doubt on Darwin's theory. Defense attorney John Payton remembers the exchange as "better than *Inherit the Wind*."

The defense continued to apply the plaintiffs' Holt objections to the rest of the curriculum. Gay Grabeel, a Hawkins County teacher who had addressed the CARE rally, testified that the objections would impinge on social studies, health, science, English, and other topics, as well as class discussions, supplementary reading material, and students' oral presentations.

Farris repeatedly objected. By interpreting the plaintiffs' beliefs, he said, the defendants were "trying to create a perfect world for the plaintiffs, and we're not asking for a perfect world."

Hull replied that he wasn't convinced of the relevance of the testimony, but he wanted to create a full record. "We're all going to put this case to bed here this time, as far as I'm concerned."

Grabeel also testified that excusing some students from class would create problems. It might stigmatize the student in class who brought up a forbidden topic, if other students had to leave the room. Students who stayed in the class might wonder, "What's wrong with them? What's wrong with me?" Such comings and goings would "foster bias and prejudice."

Farris chose an unorthodox approach for impeaching Grabeel's testimony. On cross-examination, he asked if she taught spelling.

Yes, she said.

He held up her handwritten notes of the speech she had given at the CARE rally. "Did you spell Tennessee correctly?" he asked.

"No, I didn't," she said.

Judge Hull asked why her spelling ability was relevant.

"Well, your honor," said Farris, "she is portrayed as a professional educator qualified and competent in all sorts of educative subjects. We are going to show all sorts of words this lady can't spell."

Hull turned to the witness. "Can you spell or not?" he asked.

"I didn't think I was going to be *graded*," Grabeel said. "This is a speech. It was for me. You told me—I got a subpoena and it said bring everything you have relative to the case. So I opened the kitchen drawer and pulled out this. This is for me, it wasn't for anybody else at the time. . . . I thought it was a fairly good speech myself, and I thought I would keep it."

Hull told Farris to proceed.

"Let me just give you a list of words that you misspelled, Mrs. Grabeel," he said.

"Go right ahead."

He listed *exist, multifaceted, superintendent,* and *governor.*

Grabeel offered a surprising defense for a spelling teacher: "Mr. Farris, if you could read them, then they weren't that badly misspelled."

Roger Farr, a professor of education at Indiana University and a reading expert, testified that in his opinion, no basal readers approved in Tennessee would suit the plaintiffs. The Open Court books, he said, contained far more objectionable material than the plaintiffs had listed.

With any reader, he added, omitting some stories would hinder the educational process. "In the development of a basal reader, the objectives for teaching reading are cycled through the program. Every story includes some objectives that are introduced, some that are practiced, some that are retaught. To eliminate stories at random, or under whatever conditions they are eliminated, is to eliminate those objectives."

Most authorities, Farr added, believe that schools must teach "critical reading," which he defined as "understanding the point of view in articles, understanding contrasting ideas, evaluating material that has been read." Teaching critical reading and respecting the plaintiffs' objections would be "almost impossible." Critical reading requires exposure to uncongenial ideas and values, as well as role-playing, the use of imagination, and discussion of students' own experiences.

Dyk asked about the opt-out program as it had worked at Church Hill Middle School, with children leaving the classroom and reading alone. "Seems to me it was an abdication of teaching by the school district," said Farr. Reading instruction requires "direct teaching by teachers," and it requires the students to "share opinions and ideas" in a classroom discussion.

After a recess, Farris cross-examined Farr. First he demonstrated that even devout Christian children could perform critical thinking. "I want you to assume as a hypothetical—which isn't a hypothetical, but we have to assume it because we're not going to call my daughters in to testify—that I have very similar religious beliefs to the plaintiffs, and we teach our daughters at home, and we teach them in a method that is consistent with our religious beliefs," he said. "Now our fifth-grade daughter last year, when she was being tested for the fourth grade, was given an SRA examination. When she came to a science question that had an evolutionist base, she spotted the fact that the question called for an evolutionary answer and said, I'm not going to answer that question because it calls for me to speculate on the nature of evolution. Did she demonstrate critical reading in that scenario?"

"Yes, she did."

Farris turned to the issue of imagination. Farr was mistaken in saying that the plaintiffs object to imagination as such; they object only to "imagining themselves participating in sins." Would such limitations impede critical reading?

"Mr. Farris, if you can tell me how to limit someone's imagination, I would be very pleased to hear it."

Farris obliged. "Dr. Farr, what you do is memorize a lot of Scripture. You have Scripture rolling over in your mind constantly, so that you become rooted in and grounded in the word of God. When you do that, then you can limit your imagination and not participate in mental sin."

"Nor participate in public education."

"You say you have to participate in mental sin to participate in public education?" said Farris. *"That's* the price of participating in public schools?"

"That was your definition of what you just described, not mine."

Farris read excerpts from a book Farr had co-written in 1979, *Teaching a Child to Read,* which recommended that teachers consider the child's interests and background in designing a reading program, and that they assign individualized material rather than relying exclusively on a basal reader. Why, Farris asked, should teachers consider the student's background, age, sex, and race, but not his religion?

"My understanding of the separation of church and state—I cannot develop materials that meet the religious needs of that particular group of children," Farr said.

As their final witness, the defense attorneys called Robert Coles. Coles was a showstopper: winner of the Pulitzer Prize; author of some fifty books, including the five-volume Children of Crisis series that examines how children cope with extraordinary stress; a Harvard professor best known for an anguished, self-scrutinizing course that students nicknamed "Guilt"; and, not least of all, a reflective, introspective Christian unafraid to talk about judgment, redemption, and sin. One member of the defense team recalls, "There was a deep respect for him among the lawyers at Wilmer, this true expert, truly thoughtful person, a *mensch* . . . a morally wonderful person." No one could accuse psychiatrist Coles of being callous to children. If he said the schools need not accommodate the plaintiffs, it would carry considerable weight.

A troubled-looking man with a taut face and deep-set eyes, Coles testified that the plaintiffs' objections collided with essential functions of the public school, including teaching critical thinking, inculcating tolerance, and exposing children to such topics as death and divorce. If the plaintiff children were permitted to leave the room, they would grow apart from their peers, "setting the stage for all kinds of invidious feelings, I regret to say, not to mention a sense of perplexity, loneliness, and confusion." The children who remained would be mystified and confused by the departures; they might become "distant, uncomprehending, perhaps truculent."

As Coles spoke, recalls Barbara Parker, "Vicki and Roger could hardly contain themselves—they'd never heard a Boston accent."

During cross-examination, Farris tried to get Coles to concede that the plaintiff children had suffered and that, if forced to leave the public schools, they would suffer further.

Coles disagreed. "The school has to assert its intellectual sovereignty," he said. "That's what a school does. It sets up its rules and regulations." Being forced to attend private school wouldn't harm the plaintiff children, he said. He also suggested that if they remained in the county schools, the Holt books wouldn't diminish their faith.

When Farris was done, Judge Hull addressed Coles. He asked whether a child would suffer if he felt religiously alienated in the public school, but his parents couldn't afford to send him to a private school.

Yes, Coles said, but suffering has its value. "From what I have seen in all of my work with children, this would be a moment of opportunity for their families to teach them what they believe and to remind them this is their belief and encourage them in this regard. I quoted in the deposition . . . an important passage to me that George Orwell gave us many years ago. He asked this question: Why is it that some of the characteristics we most admire in people take place in those who have known pain, suffering, and hardship? I think this would be a hardship for these families, but I think it could also be an opportunity for them."

The ennobling effect of suffering is a prominent theme in Coles's writings. In *Children of Crisis* he wrote that "many children facing war, prison life or nuclear holocaust showed astonishing resourcefulness and precocity before disaster," and he quoted Martin Luther King as saying: "Undeserved suffering is redemptive." Tragedy, Coles wrote in *The Moral Life of Children*, sometimes "becomes a handle for vision, for personal examination, for the momentary dissipation of fearfulness through bold moral confrontation." In the essay "Moral Energy in the Lives of Impoverished Children," he observed (attributing the thought to George Eliot) that "out of sorrow a redemptive moment or two might be rescued, even an entire life somehow redeemed."

Hull said, "I guess anybody that is a little different in any society pays a price."

"We do," said Coles, "and that is what part of this country is about, paying the price and in return becoming a part of America."

With that, the defense rested.

Farris said he had two rebuttal witnesses, plaintiffs Sue Eaton and Rebecca Frost.

Eaton testified that the defense witnesses had been wrong in asserting that the plaintiffs would object to things outside the Holt books. She had two children in the public schools, and she never had a religious objection to anything in the classroom except the Holt readers.

Farris asked Rebecca Frost how she had felt when the school permitted her to read the alternative textbook.

"I felt good about it," she said.

"Why was that? Why did you feel good about it?"

"Because I was not violating my religious beliefs and my convictions toward God."

"Rebecca, how would you feel if you knew that the government schools said that you cannot come here unless you are willing to have us teach you contrary to your religious beliefs?"

"Well, I would feel like I . . . wouldn't be allowed to have any religious beliefs in the country anymore, because that is what this country was founded upon. They came over across on the *Mayflower* for their religious beliefs so that they could be free to believe what they wanted to believe. I think I should have that right."

"Rebecca, how did you feel when you were kicked out of school?"

"I was scared."

Farris said he was done. Dyk had no questions, and Rebecca left the stand. "I was scared" became the last line of testimony in the eight-day trial.

As the Frost family wormed through a crush of reporters outside the courthouse, Roger Frost smiled and said, "God bless America."

Dorothy Massie of the NEA, who attended the *Mozert* trial, likens the conflict to a proxy war. "People for the American Way had its own purposes," she says. "It made headlines and raised money on these poor benighted people in Tennessee. . . . I don't think there was any question that People For's arguments were right, and I'm glad they did what they did. Nevertheless, they were using these people."

Similarly, some of the plaintiffs' supporters believe that Vicki Frost was exploited. "Concerned Women wanted publicity, and I felt like they used her," says Pam Cox, a journalist who was close to the Frosts. "I worried about how she would be impacted and affected after it was all over and those people were finished with her. . . . It was hard on *all* the parents. They weren't a bunch of nuts! Maybe a little bit overboard, but they had their kids' well-being at heart. They didn't set out to start what ended up happening. It snowballed, and Concerned Women of America used them to a certain degree."

"I didn't feel used," Frost responds. "I knew it was beneficial for CWA to have a case of this nature. There were times when we didn't hear from them for a while, and we desired to hear from them. But they were busy, and they called as they could." As for the media coverage, she says: "I cannot fault CWA at all. We were all swamped. It's like throwing up a bag of feathers and trying to catch them—you couldn't catch all the lies."

Some of Pam Cox's points, however, are echoed by Tony Podesta of People for the American Way. "I felt sorry for Vicki Frost," he says. "She really believed what she was feeling, and she was kind of unprotected by Farris and then ridiculed by the press. . . . She wasn't very well prepped. She was easy to tear apart—and we did. But I felt ambivalent about it. She wasn't a political organizer; she was a parent who cared about her kids and thought that relativism was really a problem. Probably she is right.

"The funny thing about these people," Podesta continues, "is that they do have a point. It's hard to look at the teenage pregnancy rate, the STD rate, the illiteracy rate, the high school graduation rate, and say that everything is great. At least these people care passionately about these problems and want to do something about them. . . . They serve a purpose in helping liberals and civil libertarians and First Amendment people understand that *traditional values* is not a code word for oppression. They have raised some valid issues. It's a good thing that they're there. But it's also a good thing that they lose."

Two months after the trial ended, the lawyers and litigants reconvened in Greeneville for closing arguments. In the hallway outside the courtroom, Frost ran into Podesta. She and the other plaintiffs were confident of victory, she told him. "And," she added, "we love you."

"I'm glad to hear that," Podesta replied.

Inside the courtroom, the two sides grappled over who was championing diversity and who was subverting it. "We're asking for diversity in choice; they're asking for uniformity in coercion," declared Farris. If the plaintiffs won, he stressed, Hawkins County classrooms would have *more* books, *more* diversity.

"I think it is clear," responded Dyk, "that it is the public schools who are in favor of diverse education, and the plaintiffs in this case who are fundamentally against it."

The competing diversity claims might sway public opinion, but Judge Hull had to weigh more complicated issues. Did the Holt books burden the plaintiffs' religious beliefs? And, if so, could the public schools lift the burden?

CHAPTER TEN

DAYS OF JUDGMENT

The case consumed Judge Thomas Hull. "I walk about two miles a day around a track, and I would think about it," he says. In church, he would listen to the sermon for a few minutes "and then I go back to the lawsuit." During nearly every waking hour, in fact, "I was thinking, Well, *what's* the solution to this thing?"

Several eccentrics were eager to help. In a series of letters bearing the salutation "Dear Honorable Hull," a Virginia woman sought leave to file a brief in *Mozert*. She would provide, she said, evidence of "seditious conspiracy" and other "CRITICAL MATERIALS VITAL TO AN IMPARTIAL TRIAL FOR THE PLAINTIFF." When Judge Hull ruled against her motion to intervene, she responded that his order violated the Constitution, "patronize[d] the usual strategies of disinformation," and constituted the impeachable offense of giving "AID AND COMFORT TO THE ENEMY."

No walls, it seemed, could keep people from hearing about *Mozert* and sharing their thoughts with the judge. A prison inmate wrote that if the plaintiffs believed the Holt books would damage their religious faith, they "might do well to shop around for a sturdier article." A South Carolina woman related that in 1975 "I turned from all outside distractions to the word of God." Since then, she had lived an eremitic existence, without TV, radio, books, newspapers, or telephones. But the textbook trial had managed to penetrate her solitude; in her view, the books should be banned.

These kibitzers weren't much help on the legal issues confronting Judge Hull. The defendants had stipulated that the plaintiffs' beliefs were religious and sincere, leaving three free-exercise questions in dispute: Did reading the Holt textbooks burden the plaintiffs' religious beliefs? If so, did the state have a compelling interest? If so, could the state excuse the children from reading the books without undermining that compelling interest?

Did the Holt books burden the plaintiffs' religious beliefs?

Yes, said Michael Farris. He maintained that the *Mozert* plaintiffs, like the applicant for unemployment insurance in *Sherbert v. Verner*, had been forced to choose between a public benefit and allegiance to religious principles. Hawkins County had told them that if they wanted a free public education, they would have to sin.

Timothy Dyk and his colleagues for the defense responded that no burden existed because, among other reasons, reading the Holt books wouldn't alter the students' religious beliefs. This argument held some appeal for Judge Hull. "Most of these people go to church three or four times a week, and they teach their kids a strong doctrine," he says. "I could've held, and believed it was right, that the dominance of these parents would outweigh any kind of influence that the teacher would've had in the class for an hour a day." But he thought that schooling would still exert some influence. "I concluded that being compelled to read for eight years something that was foreign to what your parents told you *had* to be a burden."

In his ruling, Judge Hull wrote that the plaintiffs believed that "after reading the entire Holt series, a child might adopt the views of a feminist, a humanist, a pacifist, an anti-Christian, a vegetarian, or an advocate of 'one-world government.' " ("Ridiculous? Perhaps . . ." an early draft of the opinion added.) Further, he said, the plaintiffs' religious beliefs "compel them to refrain from exposure to the Holt series." The school board had made reading the books a condition of obtaining a free public education. Because the plaintiffs were put to a choice between enjoying a public benefit and living by their faith, "this case is clearly in line with" *Sherbert* and the other precedents.

Did the state have a compelling interest?

To Judge Hull, this was the simplest question. "Once I got past the burden question," he recalls, "I got past compelling interest pretty fast. *Of course* there's a compelling interest to educate people."

Could the state still pursue that interest and, at the same time, excuse children from reading the Holt books? "I stuck there for a while," Hull remembers.

Here the plaintiffs focused singlemindedly on the Holt books. Farris emphasized that the parents objected only to the readers, and not to teaching methods, classroom discussions, or other courses. Excuse them from the Holt readers, he said, and they will be satisfied.

The defense disagreed. "You have to look at how the whole controversy here started," Dyk recalls. "It wasn't that they were monitoring the books in the schools. It was that a child—Vicki Frost's daughter, I guess it was—brought home a schoolbook and asked a question. And Frost said, My goodness, we have a problem with this story. The more they looked, the more problems they found." In Dyk's view, Frost "had more problems than she yet realized."

There was something to this point. As Dyk notes, most of the plaintiffs hadn't systematically reviewed their children's textbooks before the fall of 1983. By the time of the trial, they had closely examined the Holt readers and the other reading series approved for use in Tennessee, and they had found objectionable material in every one of them. Even the Open Court series, the plaintiffs' favored alternative, contained material that they would not permit their children to read. (Frost now maintains that she had no objections to the alternative books that the middle school had given her children, but those were only two grades' worth; she acknowledges that other volumes in those series might have offended her.) The plaintiffs seemed to find intolerable material wherever they looked—and they hadn't yet looked at their children's schoolbooks in math, science, and other courses.

This argument, however, didn't sway Judge Hull. When Dyk contended at closing arguments that the plaintiffs objected to far more of public education than the Holt books, the judge responded: "I guess maybe their desire would be to win the whole world for Christ, totally the way they see him, but are they *in this lawsuit* saying anything other than we don't want our children to attend this forty-five minute session?" "When he said that," Farris remembers, "I knew we had driven our point home."

In his decision, Hull wrote that "the plaintiffs have drawn a line," with the Holt series on one side and the rest of the curriculum on the other side. "The defendants may not justify burdening the plaintiffs' free exercise rights in this narrow case on the basis of what the plaintiffs might find objectionable in the future."

The defense lawyers also raised other arguments about the feasibility of accommodation. They portrayed reading class as the fulcrum of education in Tennessee. They claimed that children who left the room during reading class would be stigmatized, and that religious divisiveness would poison the student body.

Judge Hull was unswayed. In one draft opinion, he (or his clerk) suggested that the Hawkins County school board was in no position to be singing paeans to tolerance. "The real danger to the state interest in education," the draft said, "lies not in allowing five school children an alternative reading textbook, but in the cavalier treatment of the plaintiffs' objections and requests by local officials. The School Board basically said, 'Read the Holt books or get out.' . . . It seems unlikely that any amount of teaching could overcome this negative lesson given by the School Board on the topic of tolerance and respect for the beliefs of others." This paragraph was dropped from the final opinion, which exhibited a relatively dispassionate tone.

The defense also emphasized the mechanics of the public school. Reading isn't generally taught as a separate course in grades one to four, Dyk noted (though, as Farris responded, all five remaining student plaintiffs were now in middle school). Even the higher grades use an integrated curriculum, in which the themes from reading class may arise throughout the school day. "Moreover," the defense argued, "skills taught in the reading class are reinforced in the other subjects, and the reading lesson is used to help teach skills that are part of the other subjects."

The factual record, however, undercut these arguments. Church Hill Middle School had excused a group of students from the Holt books for several weeks, yet the defense introduced no evidence that this accommodation had harmed anyone. A member of the defense team remembers James Salley, the anguished principal responsible for the excusals, as the "weak link" in their case. The defense didn't call Salley to testify about the accommodation, a second member of the defense team recalls, because "he's not the kind of witness that you'd look forward to putting on the stand. . . . There are people who get so nervous when they have to testify that they can't think straight." Attorney Nat Coleman says the defense lawyers were "terrified" by the prospect of Salley on the stand, and "what he was going to say or whether he was going to break down." So Dyk relied on expert witnesses who testified about the hypothetical effects of excusal, rather than the actual effects of the middle school excusals.

Hull found the omission significant. "There was no testimony at trial that those arrangements resulted in any detriment to the student-plaintiffs," he wrote in his opinion. "In fact, those children still received above average grades for that period." He observed that even after the school board's no-accommodation vote, Salley had continued to accommodate two students, Steve Whitaker and Gina Marshall.

Along with arguing that these plaintiffs couldn't feasibly be accommodated, the defendants also contended that scores of others might seek excusals from part of the curriculum; "widespread chaos" would follow. This is a stock argument in free-exercise cases. "Behind every free exercise claim is a spectral march," writes law professor Ira C. Lupu of George Washington University; "grant this one, a voice whispers to each judge, and you will be confronted with an endless chain of exemption demands from religious deviants of every stripe."

Hull responded that the "very legitimate concern" about hordes of future claimants "seems unlikely." So far as the evidence showed, nobody in Hawkins County had ever sought such an accommodation before. The county was mostly conservative Protestant, so, if other groups *did* lodge requests, the requests would probably be similar to the plaintiffs'. Accordingly, the judge wrote, accommodating this "small group of students" probably would not "wreak havoc in the school system by initiating a barrage of requests for alternative materials."

In sum, Judge Hull concluded, the evidence introduced at trial "overwhelmingly" demonstrated that "uniform, compulsory use of the Holt series . . . is by no means essential to furthering the state's goals."

The defense raised one additional argument: that the accommodation, which the plaintiffs said was required by the First Amendment's free-exercise clause, was forbidden by the First Amendment's establishment clause. If the plaintiffs were given alternative books and a separate reading class, Dyk contended, the reading teacher would have to confer extensively with the parents in order to know what textbook materials would exceed "the limitation of scriptural authority." The result would be "entanglement" between religion and government, which violates the establishment clause's separation of church and state.

Farris responded that teachers wouldn't need to understand anybody's faith. The parents, he said, "are willing to list acceptable books and acceptable stories, and they will get out of the way and let the school do their thing. They're not asking to erect a religious, invisible shield around their children, like we used to see on Crest toothpaste commercials. They're simply saying, Here are the books and the stories that we think systematically violate our beliefs."

Once again, the two sides were disputing the magnitude of what the plaintiffs' faith demanded. Nothing but excusal from the Holt books, said Farris; much more, said Dyk. Dyk's position was bolstered by the fact that the plaintiffs couldn't accept, in toto, any reading textbook series approved for use in Tennessee. It seemed unlikely that the plaintiffs were offended by every reading series and yet not offended by any other textbook in the Hawkins County curriculum.

Farris recognized this as a potential problem, but he couldn't do anything about it. "If I would've shaped their case," he says, "I would've had them say these books are objectionable, but last year's books or some other set of books are perfectly fine. They wouldn't say that. I'm proud of them for sticking by their convictions. As a Christian, I agree that they should stick by their convictions. But as a lawyer, it would've been nice to shape them up a little bit."

On this establishment clause issue, Judge Hull sided with the defendants. Because "no single, secular reading series on the state's approved list would be acceptable to the plaintiffs without modifications," reading teachers would have to tailor assignments to the plaintiffs' beliefs—and "the average reading teacher might not readily recognize those portions of the texts which offend the plaintiffs' beliefs." The result would likely violate the establishment clause. Indeed, Judge Hull added, "it is hard to imagine" that the schools could offer any reading program satisfactory to the plaintiffs without creating establishment clause problems. The schools, he decided, owed the students an accommodation—but not the one that the plaintiffs were seeking.

. . .

Under section 49-6-3050 of its state laws, Tennessee allowed parents to teach their children at home. "The State of Tennessee has provided a complete opt-out, a total curriculum alternative, in its home schooling statute," the judge wrote in his opinion. "The Court perceives that this alternative could also work effectively for a single subject."

Students, as Hull envisioned it, would sit in study hall or the library during reading class, and then learn reading at home from their parents. As with all-day home-schooling, the county would administer standardized tests to make sure that the students were learning. "The Court finds," Hull wrote, "that these children are bright and capable of completing such a program without serious detriment to their reading skills or citizenship."

This solution would lift the plaintiffs' religious burden. It would avoid the administrative complexities and constitutional ambiguities of tailoring a reading curriculum to the plaintiffs' beliefs. It would save the schools from having to provide books and teachers for a special reading class. And it would require the parents to shoulder some of the burden themselves, through the home-schooling obligation, rather than foisting it all on the schools. In all, it was a pragmatic, common-sense compromise typical of Judge Hull. "It hasn't got much to do with constitutional law," he acknowledges, "but since the legislature of the State of Tennessee had authorized home school, I thought it was pretty reasonable."

Having outlined his opt-out approach, Judge Hull closed the remedy portion of his opinion on a cautious note: "This opinion shall not be interpreted to require the school system to make this option available to any other person or to these plaintiffs for any other subject. Further accommodations, if they must be made, will have to be made on a case-by-case basis by the teachers, school administrators, Board, and Department of Education in the exercise of their expertise, and failing that, by the Court."

This limiting language was important, Judge Hull remembers. "It's one thing to say that the state, which has a compelling interest in education, can accommodate twelve people with an opt out. If there were going to be eighty percent of the student body opt out, I'd have to take a rereading on that."

At closing arguments, Judge Hull announced that he would issue his opinion within thirty days. "The press was wanting to know, and I thought, Well, I'll give them a date," he remembers. "It kind of rushed me a little bit." As the deadline approached, he and the clerks polished and shortened the opinion. An early draft was about forty pages; as issued, the opinion was twenty-seven pages. "I've looked at it later," the judge says, "and it ought to have been fifteen."

As Hull and his clerks finished the opinion, several people involved in the lawsuit had some inkling of the outcome. By the end of testimony, says Tim Dyk, "we thought we were going to lose." "I have a strong feeling there will be some kind of relief for them," Hawkins County school superintendent Robert Cooper told a reporter. "It's scary to think what Judge Hull could do," said school attorney Nat Coleman.

On the other side, Vicki Frost announced that defeat was inconceivable. "Too many people are praying across the country for Judge Hull not to come back with a favorable decision."

On the morning of October 24, 1986, *Mozert v. Hawkins County Board of Education* once again appeared on the docket of the Greeneville federal court. Nearly three years after the lawsuit was filed, and three months after the trial, Judge Hull was scheduled to issue his ruling.

The two lead lawyers, Michael Farris and Timothy Dyk, awaited word in their respective Washington offices. Vicki Frost stayed home in Church Hill. Bob Mozert came to the courtroom to give the plaintiffs' reaction to the crowd of reporters.

Minutes before the opinion was released, one reporter leaned over and asked Mike Dye of the *Kingsport Times-News* for his forecast. Dye, who had tried in his coverage to emphasize the legal issues rather than the plaintiffs' unorthodox beliefs, said he expected that the parents would win some kind of relief. This prediction astounded the other reporters, Dye remembers; they couldn't imagine someone with Vicki Frost's views winning *anything*.

At ten o'clock, court employees distributed photocopies of Judge Hull's decision. Dye, who was on a tight deadline, turned to the final pages to see what the judge had ordered. "The plaintiffs are therefore entitled to opt out of the Hawkins County public school reading program," he read, "while still enjoying the benefit of the rest of the curriculum."

The plaintiffs had won, but, just as Dye had predicted beforehand, not unequivocally. Judge Hull had given them the right to keep their children from reading the Holt books, and the obligation to teach the children reading at home. The plaintiffs had wanted the right without the obligation. They had wanted the county to provide alternative reading books and separate instruction, or—this was a long shot—to pay their tuition at religious schools. Although Farris had mentioned partial home-schooling in his closing argument, he had told a reporter afterward that it would be "less than the ideal solution."

But that's not how Farris depicted Judge Hull's decision now. "It's a wonderful victory. We are ecstatic," Farris proclaimed. "Except for a sentence or two, we couldn't have written it better ourselves." Religious students would now be free to opt out of sex education, biology, and other courses, explained Farris—who at trial had urged Judge Hull not to trouble himself with the potential consequences of his decision.

Farris's employer also portrayed the decision as a monumental triumph. "This ruling is far better than anything we could have imagined," said Beverly LaHaye. "When we heard the news this morning we were absolutely overjoyed. In my heart I thought we'd win a little but this is far more than I expected."

On the other side, PAW president Tony Podesta presented an equally hyperbolic assessment. The ruling, he said, represented "a recipe for disaster for public education . . . that will invite every sect in the country to pick and choose which parts of the curriculum it will accept." He contended that "the schoolhouse door will have to be converted into a revolving door as different sects participate in the public school curriculum in differing degrees."

Judge Hull tried to present a more nuanced explanation. "The opinion was getting kicked around pretty much," he remembers. "I probably shouldn't have done it, but I got on the television a time or two to try to explain what I'd done. You would've thought the opinion should've done that, and did." Indeed, in a footnote of the decision he had responded to the news coverage: "Despite considerable fanfare in the press billing this action as 'Scopes II,' it bears little relation to the famous 'monkey trial' of 1925. These plaintiffs simply claim that they should not be forced to choose between reading books that offend their religious beliefs and forgoing a free public education."

But a footnote in Hull's opinion was no match for the two Washington organizations. Each side had every incentive to exaggerate what had happened. CWA could thrill its constituents with a huge victory, and PAW could panic *its* constituents with a huge defeat.

"I've been just covered up with reporters and all I can say is Praise God!" Beverly LaHaye wrote in a fundraising letter. But, she added, "we have a *long road ahead*. The ultra-liberal organization, People for the American Way (PAW), and Norman Lear's 150 high-powered lawyer staff have appealed. . . . I don't even want to think of what it will be like if the TV reporters were to say, 'The case has been dropped for lack of financial support.' "

"We all know the story behind the original 'Scopes Monkey trial,' " Podesta wrote in a PAW fundraising letter. "Scopes II," he continued, "will prove to be far more threatening" than the original monkey trial, "because in 1987 the issue no longer is limited to evolution or one school teacher. This time the intolerance is taking deadly aim at entire reading programs that include *The Diary of Anne Frank* and *The Wizard of Oz*. . . . These attacks are being made by the Religious Right in an attempt to force one intolerant version of 'God's law' on everyone. . . . So far—unbelievable as it must seem—the Religious Right is winning."

As they had throughout the litigation, the news media echoed PAW's interpretation of events. Editorial pages termed the decision "peculiar" *(Atlanta Constitution)*, "preposterous" *(Baltimore Sun)*, "absurd" *(Philadelphia Inquirer)*, "outrageous" *(Boston Globe)* and "off the deep end" *(Roanoke Times & World-News)*. "Some judges," scolded the *Cleveland Plain Dealer*, "seem unable to grasp such basic ideas as the freedom of religion and the separation of church and state." The New York *Daily News* suggested that Judge Hull "try a little light reading. He can start with the Constitution. Then 'The Wizard of Oz.' It might help his thinking. It certainly can't hurt."

Syndicated columnists were equally appalled. Just what were the plaintiffs seeking protection *from*, George Will wrote: "Literature? Science? The 20th century?" The free-exercise clause, he added, "is not a guarantee of intellectual spiritual serenity." "A greater disservice to children," James J. Kilpatrick declared, "scarcely could be imagined." Judy Mann charged that the ruling would "open the doors of the public schools to religious zealots." To Richard Cohen, Hull's ruling amounted to nothing short of "child abuse." On the whole, liberals denounced the opinion as part of the religious right's crusade to Christianize public education, while conservatives denounced it as judicial activism.

Most of the critical commentary noted that the plaintiffs found

The Wizard of Oz objectionable. Coverage also frequently mentioned "Cinderella," "Jack and Jill," *Macbeth*, and other materials that weren't at issue in the suit. And virtually every article, column, and editorial said that the plaintiffs disapproved of *The Diary of Anne Frank*.

That particular objection generated its own backwash. The Anne Frank Center in New York held a news conference to condemn the Hull decision and other "attempts to ban *The Diary of Anne Frank*." Eli Wallach, the actor who had performed in the stage adaptation of the diary, told reporters that the Reagan administration had paved the way for the despicable ruling by spreading the canard that "the left—liberals—have been forbidding religion in the schools." He pledged to help raise funds to overturn Judge Hull's decision. Lending their names to the effort were Senator Alfonse D'Amato, New York City Mayor Ed Koch, and playwrights Wendy Wasserstein and Christopher Durang.

A few weeks later, theatrical producer Robert Mellette of North Carolina announced plans to stage *The Diary of Anne Frank* at Volunteer High in Hawkins County, with proceeds going to People for the American Way. Concerned Women for America offered to help sponsor the production so long as PAW wasn't the beneficiary. Before Mellette had responded to that offer, however, Hawkins County school superintendent Robert Cooper said that Mellette couldn't use Volunteer High. With profits going to PAW, Cooper said, "the other side" —the *Mozert* plaintiffs and CWA—"would probably want equal time." The *New York Times* and other newspapers reported the "equal time" justification without explaining that it referred to PAW and ticket proceeds, and thereby left the impression, yet again, that the plaintiffs were anti-Semitic crackpots. "Equal time for what?" fumed Alan Dershowitz in his syndicated column. "A pro-Holocaust play?"

Even George Bush felt compelled to stand up for Anne Frank. "There is no reason *The Diary of Anne Frank* should not be read," the vice president told the National Religious Broadcasters in February 1987. "Closing our children off from the outside world will not protect them."

On both sides, the *Mozert* litigants' responses to Judge Hull's ruling were mixed. Although Vicki Frost spoke of it as "a joyful morning," Bob Mozert seemed subdued. "We feel pleased with the basic outcome of the judgment," he told reporters. But, he added, he didn't believe that alternative readers would violate the establishment clause, as Judge Hull had held. "My attorneys tell me we will file a counter-appeal" on that ground, Mozert said. (Farris now says he gave scarcely any thought to appealing.) A day later Mozert said, "I feel it was rather anticlimactic for us. Regardless of the decision, we knew there'd be an appeal. . . . We still have a ways to go."

Mozert's muted response may have reflected the fact that most plaintiffs had decided to leave their children in private schools. Mozert was principal of a new Christian school in Kingsport, and he planned to keep his children there. Rachel Baker refused to say whether her two daughters would go back to public school; Jennie Wilson, Baker's mother, now says they would never have returned.

Vicki Frost said she hadn't decided whether to send her children back to the county schools. "I would have some concerns about putting them back into public school," she told a reporter at the time. Now she says that those concerns were overriding; the atmosphere in the county schools was too hostile. And, she adds, she was once again growing more discerning: "How can God accept compromise? Does he want his children in a system where they'll be given a compromise? A system that is hostile to him, where he'll just be one among many gods?" Just as Dyk had predicted during the trial, Frost gradually concluded that her children didn't belong in the public schools, with or without Holt readers.

Jean Price had no way of knowing of Vicki Frost's change of heart, though. "Today I could not handle Vicki bringing Lesha, who would be in the 3rd or 4th grade, back to my school as a student," Price wrote to Barbara Parker the day after the decision came down. "Yet by Monday I will prepare myself for that."

Once again, Price and her Washington benefactors suspected hidden forces. "We heard rumors that one of the law clerks was a fundamentalist," says PAW's David Crane, "and he was the one who had really convinced Hull he could be a hero and have a sort of moderate position. Who's to say—that was the rumor." "That's why Jean Price was convinced that they were going to lose the case," says Parker, "because he did have a fundamentalist clerk."

Hull's clerk Tom Wright was indeed a born-again Christian who had worked for Campus Crusade for Christ. "I'm a real regular guy," says Wright, a burly, gregarious man. "I just happen to have had an experience with Jesus Christ that changed my life." As for his leverage over the judge, Wright says firmly: "Judge Hull has his own mind. He decided the case; I didn't decide it. . . . The people in Hawkins County may think that we had a bias towards the plaintiffs, but we didn't. We thought they were just as goofy as everybody else."

Price and PAW might perceive Judge Hull's ruling as a total defeat, but not all defenders of the Hawkins County schools agreed. CARE president Reece Gibson told a reporter that he thought the ruling was a reasonable compromise, designed "to minimize disruption of the school system." In fact, given that the plaintiffs had sought alternative textbooks, "it's a victory for our side."

Judge Hull himself considered the ruling a compromise. "Both sides won and both sides lost," an early draft of the opinion said. "Neither party prevailed fully." "If they hadn't been wanting to make some law," Hull says now, "probably everybody would have settled for it. It wasn't a bad situation."

But PAW and the Washington-based defense attorneys did want to make law. They wanted a splashy, precedent-setting victory. Within hours of the issuance of Hull's decision, the defendants filed a notice of appeal in the Sixth Circuit. "We intend to take this case as far as is necessary to get this decision reversed," Tim Dyk declared.

Judge Hull had concluded that the school board had violated the plaintiffs' constitutional rights. The next question was the amount of money owed as compensation.

"These are supposed to be love-thy-neighbor Christians," defense attorney Nat Coleman said before the hearing, "but let me tell you, these people are out for every dime they can get." The plaintiffs' damages for pain and suffering, he said, could "bankrupt" the school system.

At the December 15 hearing, however, Farris and the plaintiffs sought only reimbursement for actual expenses—tuition at the private schools, transportation, books, the higher cost of school lunches, lost wages due to attending the trial, and other costs—and not any compensation for pain and suffering or for damage to reputations. "We could have asked for millions," Farris told a reporter. "But we were fighting for principle." After the two-and-a-half-hour hearing, Judge Hull announced that he was awarding damages totaling $50,521.59.

· · ·

As they worked on the appeal, the defense lawyers tried to attract amicus support. An amicus curiae ("friend of the court") is an organization that, though not a party to a suit, is interested enough in the issues to file a brief on behalf of one of the parties. The brief can offer additional legal arguments or underscore particular implications. No less important, it can tell judges that the party to the suit isn't alone; his legal theory is backed by a respectable organization.

Although amicus briefs are ordinarily reserved for the Supreme Court, the *Mozert* defense lawyers campaigned for amicus support in the Sixth Circuit appeal. Dyk's law firm sent a memorandum to potential amici, warning that "the very essence of the public school curriculum" was at stake.

Education groups readily signed on. One brief, prepared by Yale law professor Burke Marshall, was submitted by the National School Boards Association, the New York State Education Department, and more than a dozen other organizations. The National Education Association filed a brief too.

The defendants also sought support from religious liberty groups. "With a religiously based challenge against them, they wanted to get mainstream religion wrapped all around them," says Oliver S. Thomas, a church-state lawyer with the Baptist Joint Committee. "That way, the judges would say, Look, here's my denomination— *everybody's* on the side of the school board."

About a month after Judge Hull's ruling was announced, representatives of denominations and religious liberty organizations convened in the Baptist Joint Committee's conference room in Washington to discuss *Mozert*. "People for the American Way requested the meeting," Thomas remembers. "Because I am viewed as a sort of a centrist and a moderate in this very volatile church-state field, they asked me to convene it."

Attending the meeting were officials of the American Civil Liberties Union, Americans United for Separation of Church and State, the American Jewish Committee, the American Jewish Congress, the National Council of Churches, and the Christian Legal Society, among others. With the exception of the Christian Legal Society, most of the groups represented were "strict separationists"—that is, they favored the rigorous separation of church and state. As a result, they fought the religious right on school prayer, aid to religious schools, and other recurrent church-state issues—just as People for the American Way did. Knowing of this common ground, Tim Dyk and PAW president Tony Podesta "came in thinking this was going to be a cakewalk," one participant remembers. But it wasn't.

"Tony Podesta told us that the press was going crazy with this case, and that People for the American Way had struggled to limit the press coverage," remembers Marc Stern of the American Jewish Congress. Stern had with him a hyperbolic PAW fundraising letter, which he read aloud. "I said, How can you tell us you were trying to limit the press when you were obviously *inciting* it?"

Then, going around the long table, people summarized their views of Judge Hull's opinion. "You know what they said, basically?" recalls the Baptist Joint Committee's Thomas. "We think it's a good decision. Look, this is a state where they have home-schooling, and the state has approved a number of textbooks, not just one. . . . So a number of people were saying, Hey, what's wrong with letting them read that book and take a standardized test?"

When the discussion turned to the legal arguments the defendants were advancing, Thomas recalls, "it was like a cold bath" for Dyk and Podesta. Stern of the American Jewish Congress was particularly outspoken. "Their brief had said that the public schools are under no obligation to accommodate religious belief, and there were strong intimations that any effort to accommodate religious belief would be an establishment of religion," Stern remembers. "I pointed out that, for example, the Jewish community has long insisted on exemptions from Christmas plays. 'We never said that'—Dyk said that to me in a way that it suggested that I shouldn't make things up. So I read him a passage of his brief and said, 'Well, what does it mean? It doesn't mean what it says?' 'Don't bother me with that, kid,' was the attitude. . . . We had a very heated discussion."

Among other arguments he advanced at the meeting, Dyk endorsed a new free-exercise doctrine that three Supreme Court justices had proposed a few months earlier. Under this approach, the government would win by showing that it was pursuing a "legitimate public interest" via "a reasonable means"—a much lower threshold than the existing test, "compelling state interest" and "least-restrictive means." In practice, this modification would virtually eliminate free-exercise exemptions.

"People went off the wall!" says Thomas. "I was one of them. I said, Wait, you can't do that! . . . We feared its application in other areas." Dyk—the lawyer who had repeatedly urged Judge Hull to contemplate the effect of his ruling on future litigants—evidently hadn't considered the destructive effect of *his* legal theory on future free-exercise claimants, not all of whom would be fundamentalist Christians.

Sam Ericsson of the Christian Legal Society was incensed. "What Tim Dyk displayed at that meeting was a very arrogant antifundamentalism," Ericsson remembers. "Those of us who are in the trenches battling for religious liberty—whether it's Jewish, Catholic, Muslim, Christian, whatever—we do not take kindly to somebody who is not religious coming in and dumping on quote-unquote fundamentalists. . . . He came in here thinking that the intellectual elite was going to be in his corner, because his perception was that truly religious people are sort of dum-dums. That's the tone. And it didn't play well."

Ericsson's description of the meeting is echoed by Lee Boothby, a lawyer representing Americans United for Separation of Church and State. "Most of us were very unhappy around the table," Boothby remembers. "They came to our group probably thinking that we agreed with them because a number of us were separationists. But they did not understand that we were not separationists in the sense that we were antireligious. . . . I had the feeling that they were more in that mindset. . . . They were kind of appalled that we thought those people had some rights."

Dyk may not have realized going in, but he and PAW approached *Mozert* differently from many other strict separationists. In the mid-1980s, PAW opposed fundamentalist Christians in politics across the board, or nearly so; and it concerned itself exclusively with enforcing one religion provision in the First Amendment, the establishment clause. Americans United, the American Jewish Congress, and other organizations agreed with PAW on church-state separation under the establishment clause, but, unlike PAW, they valued religious liberty under the free-exercise clause too. They also strove to focus on principles, recognizing that a judicial precedent that dispossesses fundamentalists of religious liberty will ultimately harm the adherents of other faiths. As Marc Stern noted, if the establishment clause prohibited schools from accommodating fundamentalists, it must also bar schools from accommodating Jews.

Some religious liberty groups ultimately sided with Dyk's clients. But, as the meeting at the Baptist Joint Committee showed, scarcely any lawyers who specialized in religious liberty thought *Mozert* was—as Dyk says—"an easy case."

Another strict-separationist organization, the American Civil Liberties Union, also found *Mozert* difficult. Because the ACLU had opposed school prayer, creation science in the classroom, and publicly funded nativity scenes, Tim LaHaye had termed it "one of the most harmful organizations in the history of America," and Bob Mozert had referred to it as the "Anti-Christian Liberties Union." But the ACLU was accustomed to championing the rights of people who despised it, including Nazis, white supremacists, and Reagan administration officials. A vocal group of ACLU officials was prepared to back Mozert and his fellow plaintiffs.

ACLU executive director Ira Glasser summarized the case in a memo to the organization's executive committee. "I am reminded of a New York case in the early seventies," he wrote, "in which a Native American woman removed her daughter from the history class at her local public school because of her objection to the way Native Americans were portrayed. She had no wish, nor could she afford, to remove her child entirely to private school, but endeavored to teach her history at home. She was cited for neglect and violation of the compulsory attendance laws. The case was resolved before the [ACLU's New York affiliate] became involved, but in discussions at the time, we had decided to file an *amicus* brief in support of her claim." *Mozert* differed "because the request comes against a background of a widespread fundamentalist attempt to impose their religious beliefs on the schools," Glasser noted. But, he continued, "that is not involved in this case. Indeed, it is possible to view this case as a civil libertarian way to respond to the grievances of fundamentalist parents."

The ACLU executive committee assigned *Mozert* to a special committee. This committee ended up disagreeing with Glasser; in its view, public education is "a package" that parents can't alter, and "mere exposure to ideas contrary to a student's or parent's faith is not a violation of the free exercise clause." The committee recommended adding these provisions to official ACLU policy.

At the January 1987 ACLU board meeting, however, board member Nadine Strossen spoke out strongly against the committee's proposed policy language. Strossen, then a professor at New York University Law School (she is now at New York Law School), had just written a law review article dealing with religious challenges to the curriculum. She thought the *Mozert* committee had paid too little heed to free-exercise rights.

"She found it disingenuous to say that the students' rights could be fulfilled by giving up the right to a free public education," according to the minutes of the board meeting. "She stated that in the past the ACLU has opposed the government conditioning the receipt of public benefits upon a waiver of constitutional rights. She acknowledged that most Board members, from their liberal perspectives, would be supportive of the school board position. However, in our civil liberties capacity, we have to recognize that some activities of school systems can be very threatening to civil liberties. Ms. Strossen asserted that in this context, we have to protect the right of the minority." Strossen proposed substitute policy language, under which exposure to contrary ideas could be a free-exercise violation if and only if the claimant "could show a particular belief, which is sincerely held and centrally important, specifically prohibiting such exposure."

"I thought it was one of the most, if I may say so, eloquent statements I ever made," recalls Strossen, who went on to become the ACLU's first female president. "I remember citing the *Barnette* decision, *Sherbert versus Verner*—all these cases where the ACLU had defended the right of free exercise."

During the ensuing debate, those who backed the committee's language focused on the purposes of public education and the risk that opt-outs might influence the curriculum. Those who backed Strossen, according to the minutes, "saw the *Mozert* case as a religious freedom case, rather than an attempt to establish religion."

The two hours scheduled for the discussion elapsed, and the board voted. Strossen's substitute policy language was defeated on a voice vote, and the committee draft was passed by a vote of 38-24.

"I felt crushed," says Strossen. "A longtime member of the board came up to me afterwards and she said she had never seen me looking so despondent."

On July 9, 1987, *Mozert* returned to the Sixth Circuit Court of Appeals in Cincinnati. In this argument, Timothy Dyk would try to persuade the judges that Judge Hull's analysis was fatally flawed, and Michael Farris would defend the judge's ruling.

Behind the bench sat three judges, all relatively conservative.

A 1979 Carter appointee, Cornelia Kennedy was sixty-three years old. She had reached the appellate bench over the opposition of the NAACP, which had discovered that as a trial judge she had ruled against the plaintiffs in every civil rights case to come before her, about a hundred in all. A strong believer in judicial restraint, she sometimes compared her philosophy to that of Chief Justice William H. Rehnquist.

Like Kennedy, forty-two-year-old Danny J. Boggs believed deeply in judicial restraint. Unwise policies aren't necessarily unconstitutional, he maintained; he spoke sometimes of having a rubber stamp made that would say "STUPID BUT CONSTITUTIONAL." A 1986 Reagan appointee, Boggs had the reputation of being incisive and well prepared at oral arguments, and of having wide-ranging interests. In choosing law clerks, in fact, he had applicants fill out a long cultural-literacy quiz, which included such questions as "Distinguish Irving Babbitt from George Babbitt."

Presiding over the hearing was a 1972 Nixon appointee, sixty-five-year-old Pierce Lively, the chief judge of the circuit. A former clerk remembers him as courtly, hardworking, and scholarly. Constitutional law was his specialty.

"Mr. Dyk," Chief Judge Lively said, "you may proceed."

Dyk presented a smooth, cautious argument. Judge Boggs asked several difficult questions: Could the free-exercise clause ever exempt a student from part of the core curriculum? Was it unconstitutional under the establishment clause to let home-schooling students take courses at public schools, as the State of Washington did? Dyk gracefully evaded such questions, and the judges didn't press him for answers. Sitting down at the end of his initial argument, Dyk was smiling.

After a short statement by Michael Cody, Tennessee's attorney general, it was Michael Farris's turn. Wearing a beige coat and brown slacks, rather than the dark blue or gray suit favored by more seasoned appellate lawyers, Farris stepped up to the podium. In the audience section, Jennie Wilson bowed her head and closed her eyes for a brief prayer.

For the next forty minutes, Farris toughed out a remarkably contentious interrogation. Chief Judge Lively in particular seemed hostile to Farris's arguments, and at times hostile to Farris himself.

Farris opened by referring to an earlier question. "I'd like to start with the observation, in answer to the question Chief Judge Lively posed to General Cody, and that is, is the hybrid system permissible under Tennessee law? In our brief, we cited the Washington State system—"

Chief Judge Lively interrupted: "I didn't ask about Washington State. I asked if there was any authority under the *Tennessee* law that this was permissible."

"I was just going to apologize to the court for only mentioning Washington," Farris said. He reported that the Tennessee home-schooling statute also permitted partial home-schooling, though only at the discretion of local school officials.

A moment later, Judge Boggs asked Farris about the nature of the religious burden in *Mozert*. "Do your people argue that not reading the Holt series is mandated by their religious beliefs?"

"That is correct," said Farris. "Because of the content of the Holt series, they cannot in good conscience, consistent with their religious beliefs, read the Holt series."

Chief Judge Lively thought Farris was evading the issue. "What does this core curriculum require them to believe? *Anything?*"

"If this was a right to believe case, we wouldn't even be talking," Farris said, referring to the fact that the Supreme Court has said that people have an absolute right to believe as they wish.

"Well, you tell me a free-exercise case which neither involved a requirement of belief or stating that a person believed something, or some practice that offended their religion," said Lively. "Which case does that?"

"We think it's—"

"Mere exposure I have not found until I got to this case. Now I want you to tell me what the basis of it is. *Constitutionally.*"

"*Spence versus Bailey,* your honor, is exactly the same kind of case," Farris said, referring to the case in which the Sixth Circuit exempted a religious objector from otherwise mandatory ROTC training in high school.

"*Exactly* the same kind of thing?" said Lively.

"*Exactly* the same kind of case," Farris said, unfazed. "The only difference is, it's core curriculum versus . . . physical education. What's the constitutional basis for such a distinction? There is none."

"It seems to me," said Judge Kennedy, "that your clients are assuming that these things are being taught in a literal sense. Their religion doesn't require them to read stories in a literal sense that are not religiously related, does it?"

"Your honor," Farris replied, "you misunderstand the religion, as your question states it. Their views are clear. The Bible says touch not the unclean thing. The Bible says to avoid even the appearance of evil. Have nothing to do with the fruitless deeds of darkness, but rather expose them. They're not supposed to be involved in these things."

Farris went back to *Spence*. The claimant there believed it was wrong to fight a war, Farris said, but the state wasn't making him fight a war. "They were just teaching him to *study* about war."

"No," said Judge Kennedy. "They were training him to participate in a war."

Judge Lively broke in: *"Engage* in the training. We didn't say be *exposed* to the idea that there is military training in the world."

With the judges growing more combative, Farris tried a different argument. Public education doesn't merely expose students to ideas, he said; indeed, the defense had conceded that the schools seek to change children's beliefs. "They say so in their briefs. They say, We want to inculcate these certain beliefs in children." Farris may have had in mind the defense brief's statement that the schools seek "to break down sexual stereotypes" through the reading program.

But Lively wasn't persuaded. "Not the certain beliefs," he said. "The idea that there is pluralism in the world, and that tolerance is one of the qualities that we promote. They don't say you have to believe anything. They say you should be exposed to the idea that there are other people who sincerely believe other things. That is a burden, to be exposed to that?"

"All I can say, your honor—"

"Constitutionally?" Lively added.

"Constitutionally," Farris said, "every case that has ever looked at this has never required a compulsion of belief to create—"

"There's no belief!" shouted Lively, misconstruing Farris's partial answer. "What are they required to believe here?"

"I'm not saying—that's not the standard. I'm saying—"

"What *is* the standard?" the chief judge demanded.

"The standard is that they are required to engage in conduct that is contrary to their—"

"What's the conduct here?"

"Reading these books."

"Oh, my," said Lively, exasperated. "Reading the books, requiring them to read the book, is engaging in conduct that is the equivalent of saluting the flag. Is that what you're saying?"

Farris, still unrattled, replied: "That is what we're saying, your honor."

"Well," Lively said, referring to the Supreme Court decision allowing dissenters to refuse to salute the flag, "why weren't the flags taken out of the room in *Barnette,* then, so that they wouldn't be exposed to the flag and the other children saluting the flag? Why wasn't that what was required, rather than just telling them *you* don't have to salute the flag?"

"That's what we're asking for," Farris replied. "We're asking for the exact same remedy in *Barnette.* We're asking for the right to opt out. We're not asking for the removal—"

"Oh, no," interrupted Judge Lively. "They stayed in the room and watched the others. They were exposed to other people affirming this patriotic idea."

Rather than responding to Judge Lively's point, Farris quoted a recent establishment clause case and then, inexplicably, launched into a discourse on Anne Frank. "Anne Frank has been subject to a lot of dispute in this case," he said. *"The Diary of Anne Frank,* by the way, does not even appear in these books. It's a play. . . . The passage objected to by the plaintiffs in this case does not even appear in *The Diary of Anne Frank."* In fact, he suggested, the plaintiff families were just like the Frank family: "Anne Frank's own parents reviewed all the books that Anne Frank read and refused to let her read books that violated their belief system."

"Did they educate her at home?" asked Chief Judge Lively.

"Apparently they did."

The audience laughed.

"Well, then, that's a different proposition," the chief judge observed.

Farris's tranquil demeanor seemed to slip for a moment. "The alternative was to send her to *Nazi* schools," he said.

A moment later Farris disputed Dyk's claim that the defendants exemplified tolerance. "What he's talking about is toleration, but what he really means is homogenization," Farris charged. "They want to turn children into cookie-cutter models, just like they think that they should be."

"How can you say that," said Lively, chuckling, "in view of the fact that your clients want only one point of view on any subject presented? . . . *You* seek, it seems to me, to impose on the schools your point of view."

"The reason is, who's the government?" Farris said. "They're the government, and they're the ones that have the power of coercion."

Judge Boggs wondered who should decide whether the Holt books "teach" the ideas that they present to students. "We may think it's loony to believe that they do. Can we make that judgment?"

"I don't think so," replied Farris. "I think these people are entitled to their belief, and their particular belief is sincere."

A moment later he went further. The judges, he said, should gauge the existence of a First Amendment burden by the plaintiffs' actions— their refusal to read the books. The content of their religious beliefs was irrelevant. (Farris had come a long way since filing the case in December 1983, when he had declared that the books "teach" witchcraft and secular humanism.) "The plaintiffs said our religion will not allow us to read the Holt books. . . . That's their belief," he said. "And the consequences are clear. The factual consequences are, if you don't read it, you're out of the school. You're kicked out. *That's* the burden right there."

Judge Kennedy thought the burden inquiry addressed a different point. "The burden is not their being kicked out of school," she said. "The burden we're talking about here is the burden on them of being exposed to these stories." One factor for the court to consider in evaluating the burden, she continued, was the fact that the plaintiffs accepted topics elsewhere in the curriculum that they found objectionable in the Holt books.

Farris's voice remained calm, but his words were heating up: "It's not the burden of being exposed to the stories, because the parents aren't going to let you expose their kids to the stories. No matter what you order, the kids will not read these books. The burden is whether they're going to be allowed to attend the public schools or not, in the face of their religious belief."

When his time was up, Farris returned to his seat. Dyk, who had reserved seven minutes for rebuttal, stood at the podium.

Having recognized the subtext in the judges' questions, Dyk said: "I'd like to begin by making clear, if it's not clear already, that the public schools are not asking these children to believe everything they read in these books. The reason to have diverse viewpoints is so they can discuss them and criticize them and engage in critical thinking. And we're not trying to change anybody's religious beliefs, even in the area of tolerance."

"Thank you, Mr. Dyk, Mr. Farris, General Cody," Chief Judge Lively said when Dyk was finished. "The case is submitted. The court will now stand in recess."

Farris was disheartened as he walked outside. "I knew we were dead meat five minutes in," he remembers. "Except I wasn't sure about Boggs." Farris's colleague Jordan Lorence says he felt that Lively and Kennedy "had just read PAW press releases instead of the briefs."

Dyk was jubilant. He recalls of Farris: "I thought he was angry a large part of his argument . . . and I was delighted."

Mobbed by reporters outside the courthouse, the best-known plaintiff was keeping her peace. "As about a dozen reporters milled around her on the sidewalk, barking questions and thrusting out microphones," the *Greeneville Sun* reported, "Mrs. Frost merely smiled and said nothing, creating a sequence of question, silence, question, silence, etc., until the reporters finally gave up." Bob Mozert and his family stood nearby, largely untouched by the media mob.

With the oral argument complete, the three Sixth Circuit judges retired to a conference room to deliberate. Their discussion, Judge Boggs recalls, "was certainly lengthier than average, but not unusual for a case of major import." After circulating draft opinions, the judges met for a second conference a few weeks later.

"It seems hardly possible to question the fact that the plaintiffs' free exercise rights have been burdened," Judge Hull had written in his decision. But two of the three appellate judges found questioning that fact to be quite easy. On August 24, 1987, six weeks after the oral argument, the Sixth Circuit judges announced their decision. The plaintiffs had lost, for reasons that the argument had foreshadowed.

What the plaintiffs found objectionable, Chief Judge Lively wrote for the court, didn't amount to any burden on religious freedom. "The plaintiffs did not produce a single student or teacher to testify that any student was ever required to affirm his or her belief or disbelief in any idea or practice mentioned in the various stories. . . . The plaintiffs appeared to assume that materials clearly presented as poetry, fiction and even 'make-believe' in the Holt series were presented as facts which the students were required to believe. Nothing in the record supports this assumption." Furthermore, no evidence showed "the conduct required of the students was forbidden by their religion." The plaintiffs had testified that "reading the Holt series 'could' or 'might' lead the students to come to conclusions that were contrary to teachings of their and their parents' religious beliefs"; this, the majority ruled, "is not sufficient to establish an unconstitutional burden."

"Mere exposure," the Sixth Circuit judges held, didn't implicate the First Amendment's free-exercise clause. The claimants in the Supreme Court's unemployment compensation cases were being compelled "to engage in conduct that violated [their] religious convictions," which the *Mozert* plaintiffs were not. "The requirement that students read the assigned materials and attend reading classes, in the absence of a showing that this participation entailed affirmation or denial of a religious belief, or performance or non-performance of a religious exercise or practice, does not place an unconstitutional burden on the students' free exercise of religion."

The majority opinion conceded that *Yoder*, the case exempting the Amish from compulsory education beyond eighth grade, did involve "exposure without compulsion to act, believe, affirm or deny." But, the judges added, *"Yoder* rested on such a singular set of facts that we do not believe it can be held to announce a general rule." The Amish "separate themselves from the world and avoid assimilation into society," and compulsory education threatened to destroy the Amish community. The *Mozert* plaintiffs did not separate themselves from the world; the Holt books did not imperil their religious community; and they had alternatives—private school and home-schooling—to meet their religious obligations.

Stipulating that this was not the holding of the case—that, in other words, the observation was mere "dictum" that would not bind future courts considering the issue—the majority also observed that the plaintiffs' objections were mind-boggling in their scope. Frost had testified that evolution, feminism, magic, and other themes "could not be presented in any way without offending her beliefs." Such testimony "casts serious doubt on their claim that a more balanced presentation would satisfy their religious views." Rather, the record indicated that in some spheres the plaintiffs would accept "only accommodations that would violate the Establishment Clause."

The plaintiffs having "failed to establish the existence of an unconstitutional burden," Chief Judge Lively saw no need to reach the other issues.

"It was a difficult case," Judge Lively says now. "But I've been twenty years on the bench, and I've had a lot of difficult cases."

Unlike Judge Lively, Judge Kennedy believed that the other issues raised by the defendants merited discussion. While agreeing fully with the chief judge's analysis, she wrote separately to say that even if the plaintiffs' beliefs *had* been burdened, "I would find the burden justified by a compelling state interest."

Teaching students about "complex and controversial social and moral issues," she wrote, "is . . . essential for preparing public school students for citizenship and self-government." In her view, the defendants had amply demonstrated that "mandatory participation in reading classes using the Holt series or some similar readers is essential to accomplish this compelling interest." She added that the case implicated other compelling interests too, such as avoiding classroom disruption and avoiding religious divisiveness. If many other students requested excusals from courses, public education would become "impossible to administer."

Judge Boggs reached the same result as his two colleagues—victory for the defendants—by a far different path.

He began his concurring opinion by saying that "I approach this case with a profound sense of sadness." The Hawkins County parents and principals had "in most cases reached a working accommodation." Then, facing "what must have seemed a prickly and difficult group of parents," the school board withdrew the accommodation. He noted that the board had presented no evidence that the accommodation had harmed anyone. The situation, he wrote, reminded him of Edwin Markham's poem "Outwitted":

> He drew a circle that shut me out—
> Heretic, Rebel, a thing to flout.
> But Love and I had the wit to Win:
> We drew a circle that took him in!

Judge Boggs then proceeded to knock away the underpinnings of Chief Judge Lively's majority opinion. The plaintiffs, Boggs wrote, had testified that "they object to the overall effect of the Holt series, not simply to any exposure to any idea opposing theirs," and Judge Hull had reached the same conclusion. He chided the majority for "focusing narrowly on references that make plaintiffs appear so extreme that they could never be accommodated."

"Under the court's assessment of the facts," he added, "this is a most uninteresting case. . . . The extent to which school systems may constitutionally require students to use educational materials that are objectionable, contrary to, or forbidden by their religious beliefs is a serious and important issue. The question of exactly how terms such as 'contrary,' 'objectionable,' and 'forbidden,' are to be assessed in the context of religious beliefs is a subtle and interesting one. But this decision, as I understand it, addresses none of those questions." The court, he said, should "take plaintiffs' claims as they have stated them —that they desire the accommodation of an opt-out, or alternative reading books, and no more."

Judge Boggs next disputed the majority's view that "mere exposure," by its nature, cannot be conduct forbidden by faith. He noted that before Vatican II, a Catholic committed a mortal sin by reading any book listed in the *Index Librorum Prohibitorum*. "I would hardly think it can be contended," Boggs wrote, "that a school requirement that a student engage in an act (the reading of a book) which would specifically be a mortal sin under the teaching of a major organized religion would be other than 'conduct prohibited by religion.' " *Mozert*, he thought, was legally indistinguishable from this hypothetical. "I would think it could hardly be clearer that [the plaintiffs] believe their religion commands, not merely suggests, their course of action."

Judge Boggs next addressed Judge Kennedy's contention that even if no burden existed, the school system's Holt-only position narrowly pursued a compelling state interest—namely, instilling the skills of critical reading. The plaintiffs were willing to have their children take any skills tests, Judge Boggs noted, but the defendants maintained that critical reading is difficult to evaluate. "Their view," Boggs observed, "seems to be that if we are teaching it in the state classrooms, critical reading must be happening, but if plaintiffs are learning reading outside that class (and testing as well as, or better than, the average state student), it must not be happening." He likened this approach to Justice Potter Stewart's notorious remark about obscenity, "I know it when I see it." To Judge Boggs, the defendants hadn't met the "quite strict" test for determining whether an interest is compelling.

Having disputed the principal foundations of the Lively and Kennedy opinions, Judge Boggs proceeded to offer a different rationale for the outcome. In his view, the school curriculum is virtually sacrosanct. "A constitutional challenge to the content of instruction (as opposed to participation in ritual such as magic chants, or prayers) is a challenge to the notion of a politically-controlled school system." Requiring school boards to come up with a compelling interest whenever they refuse to accommodate students would constitute "a significant step" and "a substantial imposition on the schools." The Supreme Court hadn't taken that step. *Sherbert* and the other unemployment cases, in his view, rested on such a "thin" constitutional basis that they should not be "extended blindly." Judge Boggs saw no evidence that the framers envisioned free-exercise rights going so far.

"Therefore," he wrote, "I reluctantly conclude that under the Supreme Court's decisions as we have them, school boards may set curricula bounded only by the Establishment Clause. . . . Pupils may indeed be expelled if they will not read from the King James Bible, so long as it is only used as literature and not taught as religious truth. . . . Jewish students may not assert a burden on their religion if their reading materials overwhelmingly provide a negative view of Jews or factual or historical issues important to Jews, so long as such materials do not assert any propositions as religious truth, or do not otherwise violate the Establishment Clause."

"It may well be that we would have a better society if children and parents were not put to the hard choice posed by this case," Judge Boggs mused. "But our mandate is limited to carrying out the commands of the Constitution and the Supreme Court." In his interpretation, those commands meant that "the school board is indeed entitled to say, 'my way or the highway.' "

"This case was certainly harder than most of our cases for me," Judge Boggs says now, "and, I am sure, for the other judges."

"We're not surprised," Farris told reporters. Loss in the appeals court, he said, was "just a whistle stop on the way to the U.S. Supreme Court." He predicted that the Sixth Circuit's "absolutely novel view of constitutional law" would be "easily reversed" by the Supreme Court justices.

People for the American Way president Tony Podesta said he was "thrilled" by the ruling, which he considered "a real victory both for religious pluralism and educational excellence."

Judge Hull came before TV cameras again to defend his opinion.

"If I erred at all," he said, "I erred—and I'm proud to have done so —on behalf of individual freedom."

On one ground, Judge Boggs was remarkably prescient. He said that "the constitutional basis" of the unemployment compensation cases was "sufficiently thin that they should not be extended blindly." In 1990, after *Mozert* was over, the Supreme Court pruned these precedents back to the roots, and in the process upended decades of free-exercise doctrine.

In *Employment Division v. Smith,* a drug rehabilitation organization had fired two counselors for ingesting peyote during a ceremony at their Native American Church. The state denied their applications for unemployment benefits on the ground that they had been fired for misconduct on the job.

The Supreme Court could have applied its traditional compelling-state-interest test to these facts and plausibly have reached either outcome. It could have ruled that religious freedom bars government from penalizing the sacramental use of peyote, or that the government has a compelling interest in barring the use of hallucinogens without exception.

Instead, though, the Court revamped its doctrine. The free-exercise clause, Justice Antonin Scalia wrote for the Court, exempts someone from a government requirement only under two circumstances: if the program at issue already takes account of the applicant's particular situation, as unemployment compensation systems do; or if the program burdens another constitutional right along with religious free exercise, such as freedom of speech or "the right of parents . . . to direct the education of their children." This approach enabled the Court to avoid overruling any precedents. *Sherbert* and the other unemployment cases fall in the first category; *Yoder,* concerning parents' supervision of education, falls in the second. (*Smith* itself might seem to fall in the first category, given that the issue was whether the two counselors could get unemployment benefits. But the Court instead viewed it as a case about the application of the criminal law, and ruled that the counselors had to abide by the same rules as everyone else.)

Smith represented an enormous change. Previously the Court had treated the unemployment cases and *Yoder* as applications of a general rule (with narrow exceptions) of religious accommodation. *Smith* redefined them as tiny islands in a sea of nonaccommodation.

A case like *Mozert,* where a parent raises a religious objection to part of public education, might land on one of those islands. The *Yoder* exception, for cases that combine religious freedom and the parental supervision of education, would seem to include such cases. By the same token, though, *Smith* demonstrates the Court's distaste for free-exercise exemptions. With that subtext in mind, judges today might look at a *Mozert*-like case even more skeptically than the Sixth Circuit did in 1987.

Because of the changed and as-yet-uncharted legal landscape, the Sixth Circuit opinions in *Mozert* don't merit exhaustive analysis. But a few points should be made.

First, "mere exposure" doesn't violate the free-exercise clause in most circumstances. Few people relish having to confront information that undermines their religious beliefs, but government can't be expected to adjust its expressions to the sensibilities of thousands of different faiths. George Will and the ACLU, who rarely agree on anything, agree on this point.

But that's not the end of the analysis. To begin with, the law imposes criminal penalties against parents who don't send their children to school. Many parents can't afford private school or home-schooling; their children are legally compelled to attend public school. For those children, what Lively brushed off as "mere exposure" could with equal validity be called "forced exposure."

Moreover, though exposure to religiously unpalatable teachings is merely unpleasant to some people, it is sinful to others. The *Mozert* plaintiffs fall in the latter category. They believe that the Bible commands Christians to avoid exposure to such teachings. They made this point at trial, though they also made a number of other points that weakened it.

With his *Index Librorum Prohibitorum* example, Judge Boggs showed that exposure could constitute sin, which would ordinarily amount to a free-exercise burden. Rather than responding to this argument, Chief Judge Lively observed that the Holt books "appear to us to contain no religious or anti-religious messages." This is akin to telling Adele Sherbert, the Seventh Day Adventist claimant in one of the unemployment cases, that working on Saturday "appears to us" to have no religious significance. What "appears to us" makes no difference in a free-exercise case; what matters is how the act appears to the religious claimant.

In another sense too, Lively and Kennedy seemed to be applying their own spiritual yardstick to the plaintiffs. Many people "start with the assumption that all ideas have to be examined and debated, and the best idea in the marketplace of ideas will ultimately triumph," Marc Stern of the American Jewish Congress points out. "But not all religious groups start with that proposition. . . . A whole series of faiths take the position that adherents should not pay attention to things defined as heresy. They have a religious obligation to avoid those things." The Sixth Circuit, in emphasizing that students must understand different peoples and beliefs, failed to understand the plaintiffs and their beliefs.

In any event, the court undercut its holding by trying to distinguish *Yoder*. The judges seemed to be saying that only an exposure that threatens the survival of a separatist religious community is unconstitutional. In this regard, the court may have been hinting that a central tenet of the faith must be offended. Avoiding exposure is central to the Amish faith, but not to fundamentalist Christianity—as the court seemed to be saying when it noted, without explaining the relevance of the fact, that "other members of [the plaintiffs'] churches, and even their pastors, do not agree with their position in this case."

In 1980, Chief Judge Lively had written a decision rejecting a free-exercise claim on the ground that it wasn't central. Although Judge Boggs says that "I certainly recall a good deal of discussion of centrality in our preparation," the Sixth Circuit opinion in *Mozert* never mentions centrality.

If centrality is an unacknowledged pillar of the ruling, it is a pillar that has subsequently been demolished. In 1988, after the *Mozert* litigation was finished, the Supreme Court ruled that a centrality requirement "cannot be squared with the Constitution or with our precedents, and . . . it would cast the judiciary in a role that we were never intended to play."

Chief Judge Lively's observation that the plaintiffs disagree with "even their pastors" is problematic on another level too. In a free-exercise case, the focus is on the individual, not the church. Noting that "intrafaith differences . . . are not uncommon," the Supreme Court held in a 1981 case that "the guarantee of free exercise is not limited to beliefs which are shared by all of the members of a religious sect." If the Sixth Circuit placed any reliance on the divergence of beliefs between the plaintiffs and their pastors, it was misplaced.

· · ·

Second, as the Lively and Kennedy opinions indicated, the plaintiffs' "balance" argument was perplexing. To begin with, "balance" implies a flexibility not ordinarily associated with religious faith. "Here I stand, I cannot do otherwise," Martin Luther declared—in contrast to the plaintiffs' contention that their faith permitted a few feminist stories but not as many as the Holt books contained.

In addition, the plaintiffs never explained why they assessed balance only between the covers of the Holt books. Why not also weigh the other lessons imparted during the school day, some of which might mitigate the Holt themes? If the parents wanted the Holt tales of female dragonslaying balanced with tales of girls playing house, moreover, why couldn't they supply the missing material at home? Judge Kennedy made this point when she wrote that "I question how an omission can constitute a burden."

The legal relevance of Paul Vitz's study was also murky, as Dyk pointed out at trial. The issue was the plaintiffs' subjective analysis of the books, not a professor's objective, empirical analysis of their balance. It was as if a Jewish plaintiff, seeking alternatives to pork in the school lunch menu, called an expert witness to testify that eating pork raises one's cholesterol—perhaps interesting, but irrelevant to the legal inquiry.

(To be sure, the Vitz study had a counterpart on the other side: Robert Coles's testimony that reading the Holt books wouldn't affect the children's religious faith. When it comes to Rebecca Frost's upbringing, American law and tradition confer greater authority on college dropout Vicki Frost than on Pulitzer-winner Coles. As Leo Pfeffer, a respected First Amendment lawyer and an ardent church-state separationist, has written in a related context: "No non-Jew has the moral right to act on the assertion that it will not harm the Jewish child to sing christological carols or participate in Nativity plays. . . . Such a decision can be made only by the child, his parents, and his spiritual adviser.")

The imbalance argument introduced so many contradictions and inconsistencies that it weakened the plaintiffs' case. An absolute objection to a few particularly repugnant aspects of the Holt readers, as Sam Ericsson of the Christian Legal Society had recommended at the outset, would have created a more compelling burden than the plaintiffs' contextual objections to broad themes. The plaintiffs couldn't have hoped to win excusal from the entire Holt reading series, but that in itself

would have strengthened their hand. "It would have been a very different case," Dyk says, "if they had said we find these three stories
objectionable, we would like to have our children excused, and that's
going to take them out of class fifteen minutes on two days of the school
year."

Farris, however, disagrees. "A person who objects to reading one
story about witchcraft is silly," he says. "A person who objects to a
whole series of books that, day in, day out, have the same themes,
that's a more sensible objection." At any rate, he adds, the plaintiffs
weren't willing to modify their objections.

Third, Judge Boggs's ultimate conclusion—that the court must defer
to school boards in this sphere—isn't persuasive. Boggs never explained what makes free-exercise cases special. Such an explanation
was due, because the Supreme Court has frequently meddled with
schooling in the name of other constitutional provisions.

In establishment clause cases, for instance, the Court has barred
school prayer, devotional Bible readings, a moment of silence for
prayer or meditation, the posting of the Ten Commandments on the
classroom wall, the teaching of creation science, and a prohibition
against the teaching of evolution. The evolution and creation science
cases directly affected the curriculum; the other cases brushed against
it, because educators defended the practices in part on pedagogical
grounds.

Enforcing other provisions of the Constitution, the Court has told
school administrators that they must tolerate student protests, exempt
objectors from pledging allegiance to the flag, convene hearings before
expelling students, and—in the most far-reaching decision of all—
desegregrate the public schools. As University of Colorado law professor Betsy Levin observes, the Court has now intervened in "nearly
every major area of educational policy."

Finally, the Sixth Circuit's "mere exposure" holding points to a dis-
maying waste of time and resources. Dismissing eight of the nine
counts in 1984, Judge Hull wrote that the plaintiffs weren't accusing
the schools of "attempting to coerce the school children into per-
forming any symbolic act, subscribing to any particular value, or professing any particular form of belief." Instead, the plaintiffs seemed to
be contending that "the mere exposure to this broad spectrum of ideas

and values which they find offensive amounts to a constitutional violation." Not so, Hull ruled: "The First Amendment does not protect the
plaintiffs from exposure to morally offensive value systems or from
exposure to antithetical religious ideas." The Sixth Circuit reversed
this ruling and ordered Judge Hull to hold a trial.

Defense attorney Nat Coleman says of Hull's "mere exposure"
decision of 1984 and the Sixth Circuit's "mere exposure" one of 1987:
"You look at those two opinions, and put them up against the wall and
compare them—they're about the same. And you wonder why in the
world did we go through the agony of having to try this? You can't
imagine how hard it was on the parties involved."

On February 22, 1988, the *Mozert* litigation, four years and three
months old, reached an end. The Supreme Court refused to grant a
writ of *certiorari*—the Court's legal process for accepting such a case
for review. As is their ordinary practice, the justices gave no explanation, and no justice recorded his dissent from the decision. Chief Judge
Lively's opinion would remain binding law in the Sixth Circuit—Tennessee, Kentucky, Ohio, and Michigan—and persuasive but nonbind-
ing law in the rest of the country.

The plaintiffs' lawyer had been confident that the Supreme Court
would hear *Mozert*. "Mike Farris was devastated," says Vicki Frost.
"I'm of the opinion that he even cried." After learning of the Court's
decision, Farris angrily told reporters: "It's time for every born-again
Christian in America to take their children out of public schools, and
the quicker the better, to protest this decision." "I was really, really
devastated," he says now.

Tim Dyk was gratified by the final outcome. "I thought it was a
very good opinion," he says of the Lively decision. He says he never
expected the Supreme Court to grant review, because the Sixth Circuit
had properly disposed of the issues.

Judge Hull, who like Farris had expected the Supreme Court justices to hear *Mozert*, maintains that he wasn't bothered when they
didn't. "They say a judge goes through three stages," he observes.
"The first year he's worried to death he's going to be reversed on
everything he does. The second year he thinks he's so good that there's
no way he could ever be reversed. And the third year and thereafter,
he doesn't care whether he's reversed or not. I've long since gotten to
the last stage."

"The state has exiled us," Vicki Frost told reporters when her defeat was final. "They've put us outside and legally separated us from the public domain. . . . We believe all this is falling right in with God's plan. He says there is a great persecution to come. I see this as part of the persecution. And we're to rejoice in the persecution."

CARE president Reece Gibson printed up custom-made bumper stickers. He put one on his car and handed others to friends. The stickers said: "FROST LOST."

In early 1984, Jennie Wilson told Roberta Hantgan, the filmmaker who was secretly working for People for the American Way: "We can't lose. Jesus is on our side."

"The Lord just took this through so beautifully," Wilson says now. "You're thinking, You crazy old woman, you lost the battle. No: We won. The world thinks we lost, but we won. . . . Our children are out. They're getting a fine education, learning their heritage, how this great nation was built on Judeo-Christian principles. They're learning that there are penalties for misbehavior and rewards for right behavior. They're learning to be good citizens. They're learning to think, a lost art. . . . It was the best blessing that ever happened, having these children expelled from public school."

She returns to the topic a moment later: "This battle, maybe you think it was lost, but the nice part is that the Lord has already told us the things that are going to come to pass. . . . We're convinced the Lord's coming back any moment and take us out of this mess and let these people be all the humanists they want to be." She adds, laughing gaily: "It'll serve 'em right."

CHAPTER ELEVEN

BEYOND PROVIDENCE

W hen they decided to reverse Judge Hull's ruling, the Sixth Circuit judges had before them an amicus brief from the National Education Association. Hull's "unprincipled" and "destructive" opt-out plan, the teachers' union charged, "substitutes segregation and intolerance for the democratic values that public education is designed to foster."

In a similar controversy a dozen years earlier, however, the NEA had engineered an opt-out plan of its own. After studying the Kanawha County, West Virginia, schoolbook protest of 1974, an NEA committee recommended giving the fundamentalist protesters alternative English and math classes, which would use older, inoffensive textbooks. If these special classes attracted a majority of students, the NEA report said, then entirely separate schools "might be a reasonable means of meeting the legitimate needs and desires of the communities." (Kanawha County did create alternatives, first by letting students opt out of books they found offensive, and then by authorizing separate schools; by that time, though, the protest had subsided, and the special schools never opened.)

Dorothy Massie, who wrote the NEA's Kanawha County report in 1974 and attended the *Mozert* trial in 1986, believes that the disparate treatment makes perfect sense. Kanawha County represented "a true conflict between a truly old mountain culture and an urban one," she says. "They were true believers, these mountain men. Whereas in Tennessee, this Vicki Frost had a checkered background. She and her husband were latecomers to religion. They had certainly gone astray. . . . They did not epitomize the struggle between religious fundamentalism and modern secularity. They simply didn't."

But Massie's characterization of the plaintiffs isn't the major difference between the two conflicts. The crucial difference is timing.

From the NEA's perspective, fundamentalists of the mid-1970s were quaint anachronisms being knocked about by the modern state. Giving them special books or schools would be like landmarking an old building: rescuing a rickety, picturesque structure from the wrecking ball of progress.

By the mid-1980s, however, fundamentalists had re-entered politics, and, to the NEA's horror, one of their goals was to remake the public schools. Through an "interlocking network of special interest groups," the NEA reported in 1986, the religious right was waging "warfare against public education," seeking "not to *improve* public schools, but to discredit and ultimately destroy them." An NEA publication called "Preserving Public Education," issued a month before the *Mozert* trial, devoted its full nine pages to Concerned Women for America, the Moral Majority, the Heritage Foundation, the John Birch Society, Lyndon LaRouche, advocates of school choice, Reagan's judicial nominees, and conservative protests against sexually explicit books —as if the only threats to public education came from the right, the far right, and especially the religious right.

For People for the American Way too, the involvement of the religious right seemed to determine which side in Hawkins County deserved support. Had *Mozert* involved the Amish, says Barbara Parker, "People for the American Way might have *defended* their right" to opt out of an offensive class, because "I don't think the Amish were hooked into this whole political philosophy." In the same vein, PAW-procured defense lawyer Tim Dyk urged the *Mozert* judges to abandon the compelling-state-interest test in favor of a test that the government could win much more easily; later, though, when the Supreme Court *did* greatly weaken the free-exercise clause in *Employment Division v. Smith*, PAW endorsed legislation to undo the decision. The about-face may have owed something to the fact that *Mozert* involved fundamentalist Christians, whereas *Smith* involved members of a Native American faith.

The other side had its share of paradoxes too. With religious freedom as with other civil liberties, conservative Supreme Court justices tend to side with the government, and liberal justices tend to side with the individual. Had Michael Farris succeeded in getting the Supreme Court to hear *Mozert*, Chief Justice William Rehnquist, Justice Antonin Scalia, and pending nominee Robert Bork—three men whose nominations the religious right had exuberantly supported—almost certainly would have voted against the fundamentalist plaintiffs. Liberal Justices William Brennan, Thurgood Marshall, and Harry Blackmun men whose deaths some hard hearted fundamentalists had been praying for—might well have ruled for them.

The public debate about *Mozert* seemed equally topsy-turvy. Conservatives often complain that multicultural education and its variations will erode the crucial base of knowledge and values shared by all citizens. Liberals, in contrast, are leery of assimilation and a common base of knowledge; they want students to revel in the diversity of American society. Conservatives speak of a melting pot; liberals speak of a multicultural mosaic. In *Mozert*, though, it was *National Review* that spoke (perhaps tongue in cheek) of "picking and choosing" as "the American Way," and the *Washington Post* that extolled "the common ground on which this country is based and which has been its greatest strength."

Similarly, civil libertarians rarely worry about governmental efficiency—but they did in *Mozert*. As Nadine Strossen recalls, some ACLU board members argued that Judge Hull's approach would unduly disrupt the public schools. "My own view is that not only is there not an affirmative civil liberties interest in maintaining public education per se," Strossen says, "but if anything, there are civil liberties arguments against it. . . . There certainly have been great libertarians, John Stuart Mill being a prime example, who argued that compulsory public school education is inherently inconsistent with individual liberty. I don't think I would go that far. . . . But when you have the government serving as educator and inculcator, and requiring students to attend, and requiring citizens to finance education, you have to be particularly protective of voices dissenting from the government-imposed orthodoxy."

In another dispute that arose during the *Mozert* litigation, a dissenting voice won a great deal of public attention: Jenifer Graham, a California high school student who refused to dissect a frog in biology class. Like the Tennessee protesters, Graham wouldn't perform a

school assignment as a matter of conscience. Like them, she suffered
for her stand: Teachers berated her; classmates ridiculed her. But
unlike the Tennesseans, Graham engaged the public's sympathies. She
appeared on Joan Rivers's talk show, starred in an Apple Computer
commercial, and was the subject of a TV movie. After stipulating that
he was neither an antivivisectionist nor a vegetarian, a *Boston Globe*
columnist wrote of his "sneaking admiration" for this high school
student "willing to stand up for her principles."

Scarcely anyone took the Voltairean position of disagreeing with
Vicki Frost's views but defending her right to live by them. Her saga
inspired no movies. Her support, in fact, came almost exclusively from
fellow fundamentalists and their organizations. Any wider backing
seemed to be barred by the widespread assumption that fundamentalists, whatever they might say, are always conniving to force their beliefs
on others and create a Christian nation.

The *Mozert* plaintiffs and their lawyers may not have been pursuing a
Christian nation, but they were seeking something more than alternative readers for a handful of children. The protesters initially wanted
to ban the Holt books outright, and to ban several library books as
well. Had they succeeded, they probably would have targeted additional books. While the first Sixth Circuit appeal was pending in the
summer of 1984, the Frost family burned a pile of "ungodly" children's books and rock-and-roll records (along with a Smurf) in their
backyard. (Vicki took photos of the bonfire. "So long, Elvis!" she
unrepentantly labeled one.) Jennie Wilson's husband Marion burned
his Mason book and paraphernalia when he left the lodge. Had the
protest continued, it's conceivable that the COBS leaders would have
torched a pile of Holt textbooks in public.

Concerned Women for America had goals of its own. In a letter to
a potential expert witness, Michael Farris predicted that victory in
Mozert would constitute "a major building block in the effort to force
the public schools to remove" humanist books from the classroom.
The agenda may have been even broader: Like some other religious
right activists (as well as some libertarians), Farris opposed the very
idea of state-run public schools. "It is very, very dangerous to have the
machinery called public schools," he said at CWA's 1987 convention,
according to a PAW transcript. "In fact, I believe . . . that public
schools are per se unconstitutional. You can't run a school system

without inculcating values. . . . Since inculcation of values is inherently a religious act, what the public schools are doing is indoctrinating your children in religion, no matter what." Consistent with this goal, Farris argued in court that, if the Hawkins County schools couldn't accommodate the plaintiff children, the county should pay their tuition at religious schools.

The plaintiffs and their lawyer, in sum, wanted more than the right to opt out of reading class. The Tennesseans wanted book banning, and conceivably book burning. Their Washington lawyer wanted public education denuded of its anti-Christian elements, and conceivably dismantled.

Can one, then, conclude that Judge Hull's opt-out approach was just? In my view, yes.

To begin with, the breadth of our rights doesn't ordinarily depend on our motives in asserting them. Madalyn Murray may have wanted to wipe religion from the face of the earth, and she may have seen her lawsuit as Step One in doing so, but courts assessed only the legal issue she raised. Flag-burners and cross-burners may want to do away with the Constitution, but its protections nonetheless extend to them. As one of Judge Hull's draft opinions in *Mozert* noted: "Although plaintiffs would probably like to see use of the 1983 Holt series discontinued for what they perceive to be the good of the community, the nation, and the souls of the school children, they have not sought such a remedy."

Moreover, what fundamentalists often want—schools that mirror their values—is unexceptional. In *Jefferson on Religion in Public Education*, Robert M. Healey writes that "the kind of religion which Jefferson believed had a place in public education corresponded exactly with his own beliefs." Starting in the 1840s, Horace Mann exhorted schools to teach "common core religion," which turned out to match Mann's own Unitarianism. Parents and communities often want the public school curriculum to reflect their beliefs, and they're troubled when it promotes others' beliefs. Eugenie C. Scott, the physical anthropologist who heads the anticreationism National Center for Science Education, says she worries about "New Age crackpots" in the Berkeley, California, public schools. "Should my daughter get some flaky teacher who wants to introduce transcendental meditation or some such nonsense," Scott says, "I will be on that teacher's desk!"

One solution is to keep ultimate truths—anyone's ultimate truths—out of the classroom. Fundamentalists might protest that such a rule discriminates against them, because they want religion to permeate every aspect of their lives and their children's lives. In a sense they're right: A classroom silent about religious matters *is* more congenial to religious liberals than to religious conservatives. But, as church-state scholar George R. LaNoue has observed, one could say the same of the First Amendment itself.

The more serious problem is that the schools regularly and perhaps unavoidably breach the no-ultimate-truths rule. It doesn't take a fundamentalist, for instance, to believe that a sex-education book is conflating sin with psychology when it says: "Some religions or families believe that all masturbation is wrong or immoral. Persons taught these values may experience guilt if they were to masturbate." Another textbook counsels against premarital sex, but for a strikingly narrow reason: "Most experiences in premarital sex take place in less than ideal settings. The danger of being discovered inhibits feelings of relaxation and enjoyment. The security of marriage allows freer expression of love, thus sexual experiences between spouses are usually more satisfying." A home-economics textbook counsels students on how to help a young child cope with a family death: "Do not say, 'God took Daddy away because He wants Daddy to be with Him in heaven.' Not only is this confusing, but it causes the child to fear and hate God for taking the father away." Instead, one should say that "death is a normal part of life."

Harriet Tyson, a former member of the board of education in Montgomery County, Maryland, and a widely published commentator on educational topics, detects a more pervasive conflict. She writes: "Schools, in harmony with 'polite' society and academic fashion, do in fact have a world view, unconscious though it may be. . . . Contrary to the claims of the Religious Right, this world view is not the 'religion of secular humanism.' Rather, it is a mixture of philosophies, *isms,* and *ologies:* humanism, scientific materialism, behavioral psychology, a pop version of humanistic psychology, and the kind of 'scientific management' faddish in American industry a generation ago. It values objectivity over subjectivity, favors a behaviorist interpretation of reality over any other, and is more comfortable with scientific explanations than with philosophic ones. It celebrates the new and the up-to-date over the old or 'irrelevant.' . . . In sum, it is a world view not consciously hostile to religion but intrinsically antagonistic to it and to the values it holds dear."

Over the years, educators have often minimized the conflicts between curriculum and religious faith. "I think it would be good for a youngster to have to do something they don't want to do," Hawkins County superintendent Bill Snodgrass said in a deposition. Twenty-five years earlier, a Baltimore school administrator told Madalyn Murray's son that, just as he found praying distasteful, other students disliked foreign languages; the school couldn't please everyone. A century before that, the Maine supreme court ruled that daily readings from the King James Bible were "no more an interference with religious belief" than readings from Greek mythology. (Anticipating Chief Judge Lively's opinion in *Mozert*, the Maine court stressed that "no one was required to believe or punished for disbelief.")

For some religious believers, however, faith is more than a personal preference. Some American Indian languages have no word for *religion;* their concepts of the holy are fully intertwined with life and culture. "My religion was a seven-days-a-week affair," writes Joe Wittmer, an author raised in the Old Order Amish. Vicki Frost says that the Bible dictates *"all* my life."

Adherents of such faiths recognize that other people hold different visions of ultimate truth. But they don't want the other visions laid out before their young children as equally valid alternatives. The word *heresy* is rooted in *haeresis,* meaning "choice."

The Holt books were not only laying out alternatives; they were also trying to influence students' choices. To be sure, as Chief Judge Lively ruled, students didn't have to believe what they read. Some students no doubt disbelieved the feminist materials in the 1983 Holt readers and emerged with their traditional values intact—but then, some students surely disbelieved the sexist materials of the 1973 edition and emerged with their feminist values intact. Holt expunged the sexism based on the conviction that "mere exposure" to textbooks *does* affect students' values.

Schools are often fastidious about the messages reaching students, and sometimes teachers as well. Various schools have banned T-shirts showing beer mascot Spuds McKenzie, "underachiever" Bart Simpson, a Confederate flag, a dismembered fetus, a handgun, a condom, a statement that abortion is murder, and the exclamation "Drugs Suck!" An expert witness in one of the school prayer cases testified that overhearing the Lord's Prayer and Bible verses was "psychologically harm-ful" to Jewish children. Opponents of Channel One, the TV newscast for classrooms, maintain that exposure to school-sponsored commer-cials will harm students; a California judge ordered schools to allow students and teachers to leave the classroom during the newscast. A federal statute protects teachers from "mere exposure" to uncongenial ideas: Under the Equal Access Act, which permits students to organize religious and political clubs on campus, administrators must not "com-pel any school agent or employee to attend a school meeting if the content of the speech at the meeting is contrary to the beliefs of the agent or employee."

Scarcely anyone disputes that schoolbooks affect the students who read them. "Young children assimilate the content and values of read-ing materials with little conscious thought," observes the Civil Rights Commission. "The words and pictures children see in school," the Association of American Publishers says, "influence the development of the attitudes they carry into adult life." Textbooks have the capacity to "indoctrinate children in societally prescribed behaviors," according to the NEA. Pierce Lively and Cornelia Kennedy notwithstanding, federal judges often believe that books change attitudes, even adults' attitudes; that's why cross-burners have been sentenced to read the civil-rights chronicle *Eyes on the Prize* and *The Diary of Anne Frank*.

While conceding that the curriculum collides with some people's reli-gious values, some educators maintain that we can't expect schools to alleviate the conflict. Writing in the *Chronicle of Higher Education*, C. Glennon Rowell of the University of Tennessee declares that "the heart and soul of public education . . . is group-oriented instruction using core materials." In his view, a request for excusals or alternative books, as in Hawkins County, amounts to "an abuse of the First Amend-ment."

In truth, though, public education has been moving steadily away from Rowell's Procrustean uniformity. To begin with, the schools have vastly increased the number of choices available to students. The high school of the 1890s taught about forty separate subjects. High schools of the 1990s offer many times that, even in small towns. For instance, Cherokee High in Rogersville offered 132 courses in 1990, including Cherokee history, computer drafting, housing and home furniture, cosmetology, horticulture, and "single survival." The new concerns sometimes elbow aside traditional ones. In Pasadena, California, the school resource guide once asserted: "In the tenth grade, study is concentrated on the growth of democracy, and especially on the form of government which developed. Such a study should be brief and to the point, in order to allow time for the unit on Driver Education."

Schools have also tried to make students with physical differences feel welcome. Under federal law, school districts must provide individually tailored educations to all handicapped children. For handicapped students "mainstreamed" into regular classrooms, teachers often must develop special assignments, discussion questions, activities, and tests, and they must adjust grades to reflect the students' physical conditions. Owing to all this special treatment, a year's schooling for a handicapped student costs on average 2.3 times as much as a year's schooling for a nonhandicapped student. When the local public schools can't provide an education tailored to a child's handicap, the district must send him to a suitable private school, whatever the cost—and it can approach $100,000 per year per student.

Many other programs tailor education to students' differences. Students lacking fluency in English spend the day in bilingual education units set apart from the rest of the school. Pregnant students get prenatal care, and students with infants get day care; in some cities, these students attend special schools. Some districts provide schools-within-schools for students fighting drug or alcohol addiction, the children of alcoholics, and chronic troublemakers or gang members. In Philadelphia in 1991, about ten children whose parents were members of the activist group MOVE didn't attend school at all; they studied with a city-paid MOVE tutor. New York City and Los Angeles have special high schools for gay students. Atlanta, Philadelphia, Newark, and other districts have implemented "Afrocentric" curricula, some of whose advocates speak of tailoring education to blacks' "special learning patterns" through, for example, "ethnomathematics," which presents problems in a narrative style.

In 1986, the year of the *Mozert* trial, the National Education Association endorsed alternative programs for a wide variety of students, including "displaced students of desegregated districts; pushouts; disruptive students; disabled readers; gifted, talented, and creative students; students of low academic ability; underachievers; students socially promoted; pregnant students and teenage parents; and students who do not qualify for or have no desire to pursue a college program."

Given this context, I find it hard to take seriously People for the

American Way's alarm over "cafeteria-style education" resulting from Judge Hull's ruling, or the NEA's talk of insurmountable "educational and administrative problems." Educators seem eager to adjust the education to the individual in countless respects.

There's an equity issue too. Special education, bilingual education, and many other programs operate on the principle that disparate treatment is sometimes the only way to produce equal outcomes. A high school library may be open to everyone, for instance, but narrow passages, high shelves, and stairs can effectively bar the disabled. If disabled students are to use the library, they will have to be given special treatment, such as an employee who brings books to them. The accommodation will cost money, and a few nondisabled students may feel rankled that they don't get the same customized service. But such unequal treatment is essential to make the library equally accessible to all.

The same principle applies to people whose religious obligations conflict with official requirements. An Orthodox Jew who refuses to eat pork in the school cafeteria isn't just being contrary; he is acting in accordance with his deepest, constitutive beliefs. Though it may seem unflattering, perhaps we should treat such a refusal as the administrative and legal equivalent of a disability. Justice John Paul Stevens, who is not ordinarily hospitable to free-exercise claims, suggested this approach in the 1986 Supreme Court case *Bowen v. Roy*. Noting that welfare officials were required to help applicants who had "mental, physical, and linguistic handicaps," Stevens reasoned that a "religious inability"—a father's belief that, by writing his daughter's social security number on a form, he would imperil her spirit—"should be given no less deference."

The feasibility and equity of accommodation writ large aren't the only issues. Some administratively workable accommodations collide with the central missions of public education. The *Mozert* defense lawyers maintained that letting students opt out of the Holt readers fell in this category. Without reading the Holt books, the defense attorneys suggested, students wouldn't be equipped for adulthood in "a multiracial, multicultural and multireligious society." (The lawyers also maintained that students were utterly free to disbelieve what they read.) Or, as a *Dissent* writer declared, a "tolerant, broad-ranging" curriculum, such as Hawkins County's, "is the only one a pluralistic society can accept."

Tolerance and pluralism may well be the dominant themes in the modern curriculum. "Pluralism is celebrated as a supreme institutional virtue," the authors of *The Shopping Mall High School* write, "and tolerating diversity is the moral glue that holds schools together." One study of American history books found toleration presented as "the only 'religious' idea worth remembering." What was being tolerated, often as not, was omitted.

Tolerance can be an expansive and sometimes elusive concept, though. When a Jewish girl in Yonkers, New York, asked to be excused from singing Christmas hymns in 1949, her teacher scolded her. Refusing to sing, the teacher said, would be terribly intolerant of her. A decade later, a Baltimore administrator told Madalyn Murray that her son need not pray. To be tolerant of other students, however, he would have to "stand with the rest, maintain an attitude of reverence, and just move his lips as if he were saying prayers."

A more common abuse is to equate toleration with indifferentism. When *Mozert* came before the Sixth Circuit in 1987, Judge Danny Boggs distinguished civil toleration (the notion that adherents of all faiths deserve equal rights as citizens) from religious toleration (the notion that all faiths are equally valid as religions). Civil toleration means that all religions are equal in the eyes of the state; religious toleration means that all religions are equal in the eyes of God.

It's a vital distinction, and one that educators don't always grasp. An NEA publication says that teachers must inculcate "a respect for the . . . validity of divergent religious beliefs." In the Holt books, "The Blind Men and the Elephant" and *The Diary of Anne Frank* dramatization suggested that all faiths are equal spiritually, not just civilly.

"I hear teachers telling kids, 'It doesn't matter how you pray, just pray,' or, 'It's wonderful to have faith, and does it really matter which one?' " says Charles C. Haynes, who, as executive director of the First Liberty Institute at George Mason University, trains public school teachers to deal with religious topics in the classroom. "But that kind of well-meaning relativism is destructive to the faiths of the kids. It undermines what parents are teaching, that it *does* matter to whom one prays and how one prays. It doesn't just matter; it matters ultimately." Many teachers, Haynes adds, believe that "a commitment to certain absolutes is an intolerant position."

From the school's perspective, another problem arises. According to one model policy, the school must "foster respect for minority groups, women, and ethnic groups." What happens when parents, for religious reasons, don't want their children learning to respect minorities and women? Accommodating such objections—for instance, by letting children out of a book or course—may give other students the idea that the school endorses sexist or racist beliefs. "It is a mission of public schools," writes school administrator Frederick W. Hill, "*not* to tolerate intolerance."

There are, I think, two weaknesses in this position. First, tolerating everything except intolerance is circular. As Tom Lehrer once put it, "I know there are people in this world who do not love their fellow men. And I hate people like that." This circularity becomes more obvious in an era of multicultural education. British educators Philip H. Walkling and Chris Brannigan observe: "What makes a particular culture identifiably that culture might include essentially sexist or racist practices and principles. . . . Sexism can be, in theory, rooted in beliefs which are among the most strongly held and which are crucial to cultural identity. That is, they can be the very sort of belief which those of us who value a multicultural society think that minorities have the right to preserve."

Second, a bedrock principle of civil liberties is that the state must allow a great many things that majorities disapprove of: Jehovah's Witnesses distributing anti-Catholic literature in Catholic neighborhoods, Nazis marching through a predominantly Jewish suburb, protesters setting fire to an American flag. The Constitution generally *does* tolerate intolerance. The schools ought to teach that principle, and operate in accordance with it, in order to prepare students for their lives as democratic citizens.

Boundaries exist, of course.

Parents can't expect the public schools to teach religious dogma, and they can't expect the schools to insulate religious objectors from other children all day long (as New York City did by building a wall between Hasidic Jewish students and other students, until a court ruled the approach unconstitutional). But parents can reasonably request secular alternatives to religiously offensive assignments. Or, as Judge Hull suggested, they can ask to have their children sent to a study hall, and take over responsibility for part of the curriculum themselves.

Parents can't expect teachers to make religious judgments on their behalf. But they can expect teachers to respect the parents' judgments

—unlike the teacher in the Midwest who told Jehovah's Witnesses that their parents were wrong, God wanted them to participate in the classroom Halloween party; unlike the kindergarten teacher who told an atheist's daughter that her mother was wrong, God does exist.

Some materials are indispensable; parents can't expect to have their children excused from reading them. But as former Massachusetts education official Charles Glenn writes concerning *Mozert,* "The number of specific texts that are truly essential to carrying out the mission of public education is surely very limited: the Declaration of Independence, the Bill of Rights, the Gettysburg Address, a handful of others. We have no business making a free public education dependent, as it was in Hawkins County, upon a willingness to have one's children read the *Wizard of Oz!"*

The courts may limit accommodations to cases where parents can show, with greater clarity than the *Mozert* plaintiffs, that their faith specifically forbids their reading about particular concepts. But administrators shouldn't require that showing. For one thing, the values of religious liberty are jeopardized whenever the state draws children away from their parents' faith. Although First Amendment doctrine may not recognize the resulting harm, administrators should. For another thing, state employees shouldn't be interrogating people about the intricacies of their religious beliefs unless absolutely necessary.

We can differ over how far schools ought to go to accommodate religious objections to the curriculum—whether schools ought to release students only from supplementary books, or from single textbooks and courses (as in *Mozert*), or from multiple textbooks and courses. My point is that the presumption ought to be in favor of accommodation, rather than, as in Hawkins County, against it.

Although he is reluctant to criticize Hawkins County officials, one school administrator with a substantial interest in the case says *he* would never have forced the children to read the Holt books: Bernard J. Weiss, senior author of the Holt series. "If a book is anathema to them, and they're willing to read something else instead, what's the problem?" says Weiss, who is now superintendent of schools in East Baton Rouge Parish, Louisiana. Though he believes that the Hawkins County parents misinterpreted the Holt materials, he would have given their children alternative books. "I don't think we should force our beliefs on parents," he says. "Society is not homogeneous, and a difference of opinion is legitimate."

When the public schools *won't* bend, fundamentalists often are driven elsewhere—to religious schools or, where permitted, to home schooling. Unable to opt out of part of the curriculum, they opt out of all of it. Such alternatives have repeatedly dismayed supporters of public education. "The true end of American education is the knowledge and practice of democracy—whatever other personal ends an education may serve," Dallas Lore Sharp wrote in his 1922 book *Education in a Democracy*. Sharp—along with the American Legion, the Ku Klux Klan, and Vicki Frost's nemesis, the Masons—called for the abolition of private schools. Oregon did prohibit private schools, but the Supreme Court struck down the law. "The greater the proportion of our youth who fail to attend our public schools and who receive their education elsewhere, the greater the threat to our democratic unity," Harvard president James Bryant Conant wrote in 1952. "Letting subcultural groups split off and form their own private schools," writes James Moffett, an educator who has developed several reading programs, "will seriously deepen community and national divisions." In Moffett's view, "America needs to accommodate plurality *within* unity, so that various parties can pursue, on the same sites, the ramifications of their goals and values and discover where these lead."

If we truly believe that pluralistic public education is an essential foundation of a peaceful multicultural society, then we should do what we can to keep fundamentalists (and other religious dissidents) in the public schools. Even skipping the occasional book or class, they benefit from and contribute to the democratic mission of public education. They acquire information and attitudes that they wouldn't otherwise get. (In a 1993 study, Albert J. Menendez asserts that textbooks used in fundamentalist schools "create a permanent ghetto of the mind.") By their presence, fundamentalists also give other students an object lesson in diversity. We shouldn't panic when the differentness manifests itself, as when some students leave the room or read a different book. Embracing diversity but forbidding its public expression is a crabbed form of pluralism.

The end result in *Mozert* was to drive members of a religious minority—fundamentalists who interpreted Scripture differently from their neighboring fundamentalists—out of the public schools. In Christian schools or home schooling, the plaintiff children encountered less diversity than before. With the plaintiff children out of the classroom, public school students likewise encountered less diversity than before. It's hard to see how this outcome represents, as PAW chairman John Buchanan declared it, "a tremendous victory for pluralism and diversity."

Aggrieved by the intolerant Puritan state, a band of seventeenth-century American colonists set sail for another new world. At first they planned to organize a community off the coast of Nicaragua, on the Isle of Providence, but they found that Spaniards had already claimed the island. Some of the settlers returned to New England, and others journeyed to a different island. This new settlement (its name and location are lost to history) endured for a few hardscrabble months and disappeared. While it lasted, it mandated absolute religious toleration: Speaking a harsh word against anyone's religion was punishable by death.

The same prohibition sometimes seems to govern our public life. In the name of respecting our differences, it tells us to suppress them. In pursuit of civil peace in a religiously heterogeneous nation, it tells us to behave as if we were religiously homogeneous. This approach, as the journal *First Things* observed in 1990, "is not pluralism at all. It is the opposite of pluralism. It is the monism of indifference. . . . Pluralism is the civil engagement of our differences and disagreements about what is most importantly true."

Part of the confusion stems from a common misapprehension of the Constitution. The First Amendment requires the *state* to treat all faiths as equally valid. But *citizens* aren't obliged to follow suit. On the contrary: The separation of church and state is intended to safeguard each citizen's liberty to believe that his faith is valid and, if he chooses, that all others are heretical. As James Madison wrote in his "Memorial and Remonstrance," church-state separation keeps government from trying to "extinguish Religious discord, by proscribing all difference in Religious opinion."

"Accommodations," University of Chicago law professor Michael W. McConnell writes, "are a commonsensical way to deal with the differing needs and beliefs of the various faiths in a pluralistic nation." Accommodations can also act as safety valves, lessening the sort of provocations that induce religious groups to pursue far-reaching policy goals (such as government funding of religious schools) and political goals (such as born-again-Christian "takeovers" of school boards).

In a variety of ways, many schools now accommodate Muslims,

Amish, Plymouth Brethren, Mennonites, Orthodox Jews, and other religious minorities. "The interesting thing I find," says Charles Haynes of the First Liberty Institute, "is that the resistance to accommodation almost always comes at the point when the request is from a Christian religious group. That is when heels are dug in. 'Censorship,' 'pressure tactics,' these kinds of charges begin to be hurled." There's a reason for this response, Haynes notes, the same reason that motivated the NEA to shift its stance between the Kanawha County protest and the Hawkins County protest: "Those people are giving the schools the hardest time."

Indeed they are. Among the defining characteristics of fundamentalism, sociologist James Davison Hunter lists "the deep and worrisome sense that history has gone awry" and "a quality of organized anger." Angry malcontents bent on rectifying history can be unpleasant to deal with. They may announce outright that those who disagree with them aren't true Christians (as Jennie Wilson told one school board member), or they may imply it (as Vicki Frost did at times). Fundamentalist protesters may advance endless demands, supported by unfathomable arguments, in a tone of exasperating self-righteousness. Nonetheless, educators should try to respond with forbearance and reason. Smearing the supplicants as communists and carpetbaggers, as the administrators of Hawkins County did, subverts the constitutional values of pluralism, liberty, and tolerance.

"It still stands out in my mind, seeing Vicki Frost on television complaining about great works of literature," says Oliver S. Thomas, the church-state lawyer who hosted the meeting where Tim Dyk solicited amicus support. "It was easy to make fun of her. And that was unfortunate, because what lay behind *Mozert* is a very significant problem: How do we live together with our deep religious differences?" Vicki Frost's lawsuit is over, but that problem endures.

EPILOGUE

C BS, Inc., announced the sale of *Holt, Rinehart & Winston* to Harcourt Brace Jovanovich on October 24, 1986—coincidentally, the day that Judge Hull issued his decision. A week later a Holt spokesman declared that the controversy wouldn't affect the content of the readers. In truth, however, the 1986 edition of the series already omitted some of the materials targeted in the Hawkins County suit, including a teachers' edition essay entitled "Humanism in Teaching Reading" and a question about how the Declaration of Independence and the Constitution reflected "humanistic ideals."

Once the most popular reading series in the nation, Holt Basic Reading today is on the verge of extinction. Harcourt no longer promotes it, and sales are few—mostly replacement copies for districts that adopted the series in the 1980s. "It will vanish in a short period of time," says senior author Bernard J. Weiss. In his view, the highly publicized Hawkins County case contributed to the demise. "This has been a very severe disappointment," he says.

Mel and Norma Gabler continue to review schoolbooks in Longview, Texas. The final outcome of *Mozert*, Mel believes, reflects the anti-Christian bias of the judiciary. "If you are before a humanistic judge, there is no way he's going to see the Christian side; it's just impossible," he says. "And I would say 75 percent of our judges are totally humanistic, so Christians in the public school are having a hard time. They are almost a persecuted minority. Oh, man, it's sad."

Beverly LaHaye remains president of Concerned Women for America. "Even though we lost, I would go back and do it again," she says of the Hawkins County lawsuit. "We still believe that parents should have the right to determine what their children are taught. . . . And I personally get energized when I can help another family." She notes that CWA also benefited: "The case promoted us to more of a national position. It was a PR success for us—we were quickly identified as a friend of the family."

Tony Podesta left People for the American Way in 1987 to become a lobbyist and political consultant in Washington. He considers *Mozert* an unmitigated success for PAW. "Lots of other organizations do hundreds of cases a year and never end up with two pages in *Newsweek*," he says. "It generated a lot of interest in the organization on the part of lawyers, which is useful. It helped the cause of intellectual freedom in schools. And it became the lens through which people saw these issues. People had a different view after this case; that was more important than whether we won or lost. I don't think there was a down side."

Timothy Dyk left Wilmer, Cutler & Pickering to become head of appellate litigation at another large law firm, Jones, Day, Reavis & Pogue. "I've had a number of Supreme Court arguments that have been significant, and some arguments in other cases," Dyk says. "But I suppose that in terms of personal satisfaction, the Tennessee case is the most satisfying case I've worked on. . . . Whenever you're doing something that you think is important, there's a special satisfaction in it. I got to work with a lot of interesting people, and I learned a lot about that part of Tennessee. It was an educational experience. I thought we did a good job in the case; that's always satisfying. And we won. That was nice."

Michael Farris left Concerned Women for America after *Mozert* to work as president of the Home School Legal Defense Association. In 1993, he sought and won the Republican nomination for lieutenant governor of Virginia. "Since I was a little kid, I've believed that someday I would run for office," he explains. "I'm a person that's interested in public policy." *Mozert*, he says, "is the case of a lifetime in many different ways. At this point in my life I would say that it shaped me and shook me and encouraged me and discouraged me more than any case I've ever had."

Thomas G. Hull continues to hear cases in the federal courthouse in Greeneville. In 1991, he was recommended for the Sixth Circuit Court of Appeals, but the Bush Justice Department refused to consider him; at sixty-five, he was too old. "It was an interesting lawsuit," Judge Hull says of *Mozert*. "I'd have to say it was the most celebrated case that I've ever been a judge in or a lawyer in. I don't know why, but it was—more media attention, more attention in the populace. It was a case of a school board, a governmental entity, just crushing children, seven to twelve years of age. . . . I think that the best result that could've come out of it was the one that I suggested, the Sixth Circuit to the contrary notwithstanding."

Hawkins County schools dropped the Holt readers in 1989 in favor of a series published by Macmillan. After six years with the Holt books, school officials say, it was time for a change. They maintain that the lawsuit had nothing to do with it.

Officially sanctioned religious activities in the schools ceased during the *Mozert* litigation. "We had a parent in the Clinch School, which is very rural, and he didn't want his child to go to Bible classes," says Robert Cooper, who was superintendent at the time. "All the other children were going, and this parent didn't want his child to be the only one left behind. So we consulted with our attorney, and he advised that it would be best to discontinue it." Guy Tilley, the pastor who ran the Bible classes, says *Mozert* lay behind the school district's capitulation: "Because of the textbook thing, they couldn't afford another lawsuit. Hawkins County didn't have the money." Even though organized Bible classes are no longer held, several administrators say they wouldn't be surprised to learn that individual teachers still pray or read Scripture in class.

Bill Snodgrass, defeated in the 1984 superintendent election, works as an educational consultant for the State of Tennessee. "I can't say that it changed my life in any way," he says of the lawsuit. "It was unpleasant—just an aggravation you had to deal with. You could've spent the time more useful, more constructive, doing something else."

Joe Drinnon is still supervisor of instruction for the county schools. "I'm sure glad we did it just like we did it," he says. "I'm thankful for some little coincidences that fell together—for example, getting in touch with the American Way people, because I believe they would've ground us into the ground with local help. We just didn't know the scope of it."

Archie McMillan, the Carter's Valley principal who refused to let Jennie Wilson's granddaughters use alternative textbooks, now is principal of Church Hill Elementary. "I'm just kind of glad it's over," he says. "It was one of those things where you experience a tremendous amount of anxiety because you don't know what's going to happen next."

James Salley, the Church Hill Middle School principal who permitted children to use alternative readers, retired in 1989. "I don't want to get into it," he says when asked about the textbook controversy. "I spent three or four years of my life on that."

Jean Price, the Church Hill Elementary principal in whose office Vicki Frost was arrested, moved to Texas with her husband in 1987, and then returned to East Tennessee in 1992. She is now principal of Haynesfield Elementary in Bristol. "Hopefully I'll never have to go through this kind of experience again," she says of the textbook controversy. "You always worry about your reputation in the community when things like this start. But after the big meeting we had at the school, I would go out to the grocery store and it wasn't unusual for somebody to come up and hug me and say they were thinking about me. It was just *amazing,* the support of the people. That helped tremendously."

Juvenile Judge *Reece Gibson,* the head of the anticensorship group CARE, died of cancer in 1989. "I got pretty mad at God for a while," says his widow, *Phyllis Gibson,* who is still assistant principal of Volunteer High. "I didn't talk to him. Then I realized that this was his plan, and I couldn't change it." Of the textbook controversy, she says: "Things like this are good sometimes. They make us wake up and think about what we value, what we believe in, what we're willing to fight for." Now, she says, "We're watching every day. Every day! . . . I read everything I can get my hands on—Phyllis Schlafly, Don Wildmon. I feel like I have to take up where Reece left off. I have to be the watchdog."

Bob Mozert moved to Dover, Delaware, in 1989. He runs his own insurance-adjustment firm there. His son Travis is a prelaw student at

Delaware State College, and his daughter Sundee attends a public high school.

Mozert has no regrets about the case that bears his name. "I did what I should have," he says. "I would do nothing differently, except a few things that I might do more wisely, having had the experience. Just employ perhaps some different tactics and strategies, a finer edge on it than what was done." He says he looks on his subsequent success in business as "a reward for a job well done in the textbook case."

After nineteen years in Church Hill, *Jennie Wilson* has put her house on the market. Her husband, Marion, died of cancer in 1991, and her older sisters have invited her to move in with them in southern Mississippi.

Asked about the impact of the textbook controversy, she says: "I sometimes wonder if it contributed to my husband's death. He felt that the right thing would be done, and he was disappointed." Her voice quakes, and tears roll down her cheeks. "Emotional blows like that sometimes trigger those radical cells. Sometimes I think about that. But I know where he is. It didn't catch the Lord unaware, and if that's the way he willed it, well, that's all right."

She wipes her face and continues. "But as for myself, it was interesting. I enjoyed it. I think somebody had to do it, and I am pleased that I could have had a finger—although I often think, My goodness, all you did was do wrong. 'Cause there weren't any changes in the schools. I must've done something wrong, or surely *somebody* would've seen the light." A moment later she adds with a shrug: "I was frustrated when everybody didn't see it my way, but, gracious, they didn't see things Jesus's way when he was here either. If this were heaven, what would we have to look forward to?"

Vicki Frost lives in the same Church Hill house as before, but Roger no longer does. He moved out in 1990, and they were divorced in 1993; at the divorce hearing, he testified that he was living with another woman. Vicki says the divorce grieves her, but not unbearably: "I consider myself to be a daughter of God. *That's* my most important relationship."

Marty and Rebecca have graduated from high school; both now work at Kingston Warren, an automotive-related plant in Church Hill. Marty got married at nineteen and became a father two years later, making Vicki a grandmother at forty. Sarah graduated from Kingsport Christian School in 1993 as valedictorian of her fifteen-student class;

she hopes to attend college. Lesha is a sophomore at Kingsport Christian.

The divorce isn't the only change in Vicki's life since the textbook trial. To help pay her children's tuition, she now works the graveyard shift at a factory, bending tubing. She attends Shekinah, a nondenominational charismatic church; though she hasn't yet spoken in tongues, she says she's open to it. She is working toward a college degree through her church, and she says she has "a little bit of a yearning" to learn Russian and become a missionary to the former Soviet Union. At her request, the divorce judge restored her maiden name, Vicki Leslie. "I don't plan to live passively," she asserts. "So, if there's any conflict or trouble, I don't want it to be associated with the Frost family."

She says of the textbook controversy: "God was merciful to wake me up out of my sleep. Now I'm more discerning of everything. Everything! What I see, what I hear, I'm more discerning—discerning the good and the evil, discerning the right and the wrong. And I pray that God not stop. I *want* to know truth. I seek God's truth."

·· SOURCES ··

Most of my information about the Hawkins County controversy comes from three sources: my interviews with participants (the interviews are listed in the Acknowledgments); the court records of *Mozert v. Hawkins County Board of Education* and *Frost v. Hawkins County Board of Education*, including depositions, exhibits, briefs, rulings, and trial transcripts; and news coverage, particularly in the *Kingsport Times-News* and the *Rogersville Review*.

Several other sources proved helpful throughout the book: internal memos and other documents at People for the American Way and Concerned Women for America; the personal papers of Vicki Frost, Phyllis Gibson, and Barbara Parker; People for the American Way's film about Hawkins County, *Censorship in Our Schools;* and David W. Dellinger's " 'My Way or the Highway': The Hawkins County Textbook Controversy" (Ed.D. diss., University of Tennessee, 1991).

I omit those sources, as well as most newspaper articles, newsmagazine articles, and reference works, from the chapter-by-chapter source lists that follow.

CHAPTER ONE
SECULAR HUMANISM IN HAWKINS COUNTY

"A Visit to Mars," by John Kier Cross, appears in Bernard J. Weiss, Loreli Olson Steuer, Susan B. Cruikshank, and Lyman C. Hunt, *Riders on the Earth* (New York: Holt, Rinehart & Winston, 1983).

The books that influenced Frost and Wilson are Tim LaHaye, *The*

Battle for the Mind (Old Tappan, N.J.: Fleming H. Revell Co., 1980); and Constance E. Cumbey, *The Hidden Dangers of the Rainbow: The New Age Movement and Our Coming Age of Barbarism* (Lafayette, La.: Huntington House, 1983).

I learned about the Gablers and their influence from interviews with them and with Barbara Parker, and from Joan DelFattore, *What Johnny Shouldn't Read: Textbook Censorship in America* (New Haven: Yale University Press, 1992); Carol Flake, *Redemptorama: Culture, Politics, and the New Evangelism* (New York: Penguin, 1984), pp. 39–40; James C. Hefley, *Textbooks on Trial* (Wheaton, Ill.: Victor Books, 1976); Edward B. Jenkinson, "How the Mel Gablers Have Put Textbooks on Trial," in James E. Davis, ed., *Dealing with Censorship* (Urbana, Ill.: National Council of Teachers of English, 1979); William Martin, "The Guardians Who Slumbereth Not," *Texas Monthly*, November 1982; Barbara Parker, "Your schools may be the next battlefield in the crusade against 'improper' textbooks," *American School Board Journal*, June 1979; "Profile of a New Right Group: Educational Research Analysts," *TEA PR-gram* (Tennessee Education Association), 11/9/81; Arnie Weissmann, "Building the Tower of Babel," *Texas Outlook*, winter 1981–82; and the Gablers' own publications.

For East Tennessee history, I relied on Stanley J. Folmsbee, Robert E. Corlew, and Enoch L. Mitchell, *Tennessee: A Short History* (Knoxville: University of Tennessee Press, 1969); *Goodspeed's History of Tennessee*, East Tennessee ed. (Nashville: Charles & Randy Elder, Booksellers, 1972; orig. publ. 1887); J. G. M. Ramsey, *The Annals of Tennessee to the End of the Eighteenth Century* (Knoxville: East Tennessee Historical Society, 1967; orig. publ. 1853); Clara Smith Reber, *Church Hill, Tennessee Area History 1754–1976* (Church Hill: privately published, 1976); Jim Stokely and Jeff D. Johnson, eds., *Encyclopedia of East Tennessee* (Oak Ridge: Children's Museum, 1981); Samuel Cole Williams, *History of the Lost State of Franklin* (New York: Press of the Pioneers, 1933); George Henry Alden, "The State of Franklin," *American Historical Review* 8 (January 1903): 271–89; and Eric Foner, "The South's Inner Civil War," *American Heritage*, March 1989.

CHAPTER TWO
GOD IN PUBLIC SCHOOLS AND PUBLIC SQUARES

On the history of religion and American education, I relied heavily on Robert Michaelsen, *Piety in the Public School: Trends and Issues in the Relationship Between Religion and the Public School in the United States* (New York: Macmillan, 1970); Leo Pfeffer, *Church, State, and Freedom* (Boston: Beacon, 1953); and Anson Phelps Stokes and Leo Pfeffer, *Church and State in the United States*, rev. ed. (New York: Harper & Row, 1964).

I also consulted American Textbook Publishers Institute, *Textbooks in Education* (New York: American Textbook Publishers Institute, 1949); Hillel Black, *The American Schoolbook* (New York: Morrow, 1967); Samuel Windsor Brown, *The Secularization of American Education* (New York: Russell & Russell, 1912); Richard B. Dierenfield, *Religion in American Public Schools* (Washington, D.C.: Public Affairs Press, 1962); William Kailer Dunn, *What Happened to Religious Education?: The Decline of Religious Teaching in the Public Elementary School, 1776–1861* (Baltimore: Johns Hopkins, 1958); Adrian Augustus Holtz, *A Study of the Moral and Religious Elements in American Secondary Education up to 1800* (Menasha, Wisc.: George Banta Publishing, 1917); Albert J. Menendez, *The December Dilemma: Christmas in American Public Life* (Silver Spring, Md.: Americans United for Separation of Church and State, 1988); Richard John Neuhaus, genl. ed., *Democracy and the Renewal of Public Education* (Grand Rapids, Mich.: Eerdmans, 1987); Diane Ravitch, *The Great School Wars: A History of the New York City Public Schools* (New York: Basic, 1974); A. James Reichley, *Religion in American Public Life* (Washington, D.C.: Brookings, 1985); Theodore R. Sizer, ed., *Religion and Public Education* (Boston: Houghton Mifflin, 1967); Joel Spring, *The American School 1642–1985* (New York: Longman, 1986); James C. Carper, "A Common Faith for the Common School?: Religion and Education in Kansas, 1861–1900," *Mid-America* 60 (1978); David B. Tyack and Thomas James, "Moral Majorities and the School Curriculum: Historical Perspectives on the Legalization of Virtue," *Teachers College Record* 86 (1985): 513–37; and *Commonwealth v. Cooke*, 7 Am. L. Reg. 417 (1859).

On the history of fundamentalism, see Jeffrey K. Hadden and Anson Shupe, *Televangelism: Power and Politics on God's Frontier* (New York: Henry Holt, 1988); Genevieve Forbes Herrick and John Origen Herrick, *The Life of William Jennings Bryan* (Chicago: John R. Stanton Co., 1925); James Davison Hunter, *American Evangelicalism: Conservative Religion and the Quandary of Modernity* (New Brunswick, N.J.: Rutgers University Press, 1983); Walter Lippmann, *American Inquisitors: A Commentary on Dayton and Chicago* (New York: Macmillan, 1928); George M. Marsden, *Fundamentalism and American Culture: The Shaping of Twentieth-Century Evangelicalism, 1870–1925* (New York: Oxford, 1980); Leo P. Ribuffo, *The Old Christian Right: The Protestant Far Right from the Great Depression to the Cold War* (Philadelphia: Temple University Press, 1983); R. A. Torrey, A. C. Dixon, and others, eds., *The Fundamentals: A Testimony to the Truth*, 4 vols. (Grand Rapids, Mich.: Baker, 1988; orig. publ. 1917); Phillip E. Hammond, "The Curious Cause of Conservative Protestantism," *Annals of the American Academy*, no. 480 (July 1985); and Martin E. Marty, "Precursors of the Moral Majority," *American Heritage*, February-March 1982.

I also consulted several general works on religion in the United States, including Sydney E. Ahlstrom, *A Religious History of the American People*

(New Haven: Yale University Press, 1972); George C. Bedell, Leo San-
don, Jr., and Charles T. Wellborn, *Religion in America* (New York: Macmillan, 1975); Edwin Scott Gaustad, *A Religious History of America*, rev.
ed. (San Francisco: HarperSanFrancisco, 1990); Martin E. Marty, *Pilgrims in Their Own Land: 500 Years of Religion in America* (New York:
Penguin, 1985); and Garry Wills, *Under God: Religion and American Politics* (New York: Simon & Schuster, 1990).

The Supreme Court's school prayer decisions—*Engel v. Vitale*, 370
U.S. 421 (1962); and *School Dist. of Abington Township v. Schempp*, 374
U.S. 203 (1963)—are discussed in Kenneth M. Dolbeare and Phillip E.
Hammond, *The School Prayer Decisions: From Court Policy to Local Prac-
tice* (Chicago: University of Chicago Press, 1971); Paul A. Freund and
Robert Ulich, *Religion and the Public Schools* (Cambridge: Harvard Uni-
versity Press, 1965); John Herbert Laubach, *School Prayers: Congress, the
Courts, and the Public* (Washington, D.C.: Public Affairs Press, 1969);
William K. Muir, Jr., *Prayer in the Public Schools: Law and Attitude
Change* (Chicago: University of Chicago Press, 1967); Leo Pfeffer, *Reli-
gion, State, and the Burger Court* (Buffalo, N.Y.: Prometheus, 1984);
David M. Ackerman, "School Prayer: The Congressional Response,
1962–1988," Congressional Research Service, 10/25/88; Richard B. Dierenfield, "Religious Influence in American Public Schools," *Clearing House*
59 (1986): 390–92; Frederick Fox, "My Day in Court," *Theology Today*,
October 1977; Erwin N. Griswold, "Absolute Is in the Dark," *Utah Law
Review* 8 (1963): 167–82; and Philip B. Kurland, "The Regents' Prayer
Case: 'Full of Sound and Fury, Signifying . . .' " in Philip B. Kurland,
ed., *Church and State: The Supreme Court and the First Amendment* (Chicago: University of Chicago Press, 1975). The *New Republic* editorials
were published 7/9/62 and 6/29/63. Books and articles about the history of
religion and American education, cited above, were also helpful.

On Madalyn Murray O'Hair, see William J. Murray, *My Life Without
God* (Nashville: Thomas Nelson, 1982); Madalyn Murray O'Hair, *Bill
Murray, the Bible, and the Baltimore Board of Education: An Atheist Epic*
(Austin, Tex.: American Atheist Press, 1970); and Lawrence Wright,
"God Help Her," *Texas Monthly*, January 1989.

On the religious right, I consulted Steve Bruce, *The Rise and Fall of
the New Christian Right: Conservative Protestant Politics in America 1978–
1988* (New York: Oxford, 1988); Flo Conway and Jim Siegelman, *Holy
Terror: The Fundamentalist War on America's Freedoms in Religion, Politics
and Our Private Lives* (Garden City, N.Y.: Doubleday, 1982); Dinesh
D'Souza, *Falwell: Before the Millennium; A Critical Biography* (Chicago:
Regnery Gateway, 1984); E. J. Dionne, Jr., *Why Americans Hate Politics*
(New York: Simon & Schuster, 1991); Jerry Falwell, *Strength for the Jour-
ney: An Autobiography* (New York: Simon & Schuster, 1987); Frances
FitzGerald, *Cities on a Hill: A Journey Through Contemporary American*

Cultures (New York: Simon & Schuster, 1986); Robert C. Liebman and Robert Wuthnow, eds., *The New Christian Right: Mobilization and Legitimation* (New York: Aldine, 1983); Richard John Neuhaus and Michael Cromartie, eds., *Piety and Politics: Evangelicals and Fundamentalists Confront the World* (Washington, D.C.: Ethics and Public Policy Center, 1987); Kevin P. Phillips, *Post-Conservative America: People, Politics, and Ideology in a Time of Crisis* (New York: Random House, 1982); Robert Wuthnow, *The Struggle for America's Soul: Evangelicals, Liberals, and Secularism* (Grand Rapids, Mich.: Eerdmans, 1989); Perry Deane Young, *God's Bullies: Native Reflections on Preachers and Politics* (New York: Holt, Rinehart & Winston, 1982); Richard John Neuhaus, "What the Fundamentalists Want," *Commentary*, May 1985; Clyde Wilcox, "The Christian Right in Twentieth Century America: Continuity and Change," *Review of Politics* 50 (1988): 659–81; and James E. Wood, Jr., "Religious Fundamentalism and the New Right," in John F. Wilson and Donald L. Drakeman, eds., *Church and State in American History*, 2d ed. (Boston: Beacon, 1987).

On secular humanism, see John L. Kater, Jr., *Christians on the Right: The Moral Majority in Perspective* (New York: Seabury, 1982); Tim LaHaye, *The Battle for the Mind* (Old Tappan, N.J.: Fleming H. Revell Co., 1980); Tim LaHaye, *The Battle for the Public Schools: Humanism's Threat to Our Children* (Old Tappan, N.J.: Fleming H. Revell Co., 1983); Tim LaHaye, *The Hidden Censors* (Old Tappan, N.J.: Power, 1984); Onalee McGraw, *Secular Humanism and the Schools: The Issue Whose Time Has Come* (Washington, D.C.: Heritage Foundation, 1976); Geoffrey Aronson, "The Conversion of Beverly LaHaye," *Regardie's*, March 1987; Samuel I. Blumenfeld, "Is Humanism a Religion?" in Beverly LaHaye, ed., *Who Will Save Our Children?* (Brentwood, Tenn.: Wolgemuth & Hyatt, 1991); James Davison Hunter, " 'America's Fourth Faith': A Sociological Perspective on Secular Humanism," *This World* 19 (1987): 101–10; Tim LaHaye, "The Religion of Secular Humanism," in Stanley M. Elam, ed., *Public Schools and the First Amendment* (Bloomington, Ind.: Phi Delta Kappa, 1983); National Education Association, "Inquiry Report: Kanawha County, West Virginia: A Textbook Study in Cultural Conflict" (1975); J. Charles Park, "The New Right: Threat to Democracy in Education," *Educational Leadership* 38 (November 1980): 146–49; J. Charles Park, "The Religious Right and Public Education," *Educational Leadership* 44 (May 1987): 5–10; and John W. Whitehead and John Conlan, "The Establishment of the Religion of Secular Humanism and Its First Amendment Implications," *Texas Tech Law Review* 10 (1978): 1–66.

The Humanist Manifestos appear in Paul Kurtz, ed., *Humanist Manifestos I and II* (Buffalo, N.Y.: Prometheus, 1973). "A Secular Humanist Declaration" is in Paul Kurtz, *In Defense of Secular Humanism* (Buffalo, N.Y.: Prometheus, 1983).

Judge Hand's opinion in *Smith v. Board of School Comm'rs of Mobile County* can be found at 655 F. Supp. 939 (S.D. Ala. 1987); the appeals court's reversal of it is at 827 F.2d 684 (11th Cir. 1987).

About the New Age movement and the fundamentalist critique of it, I consulted Eric Buehrer, *The New Age Masquerade: The Hidden Agenda in Your Child's Classroom* (Brentwood, Tenn.: Wolgemuth & Hyatt, 1990); Constance E. Cumbey, *The Hidden Dangers of the Rainbow: The New Age Movement and Our Coming Age of Barbarism* (Lafayette, La.: Huntington House, 1983); Michael P. Farris, *Where Do I Draw the Line?* (Minneapolis: Bethany House, 1992); Joseph Brown, "A Lie by Any Other Name," *Fundamentalist Journal*, February 1988; Ronald Enroth, "The New Age Movement," *Fundamentalist Journal*, February 1988; Edward Jenkinson, "How an Imaginary Movement Is Being Used to Attack Courses and Books," *Educational Leadership* 46 (October 1988): 74–77; Paul Kurtz, "The New Age in Perspective," *Skeptical Inquirer* 13 (summer 1989): 365–67; M. G. "Pat" Robertson, "Breaking Counterfeit Religion," *Charisma and Christian Life*, September 1990; and Lys Ann Shore, "New Light on the New Age," *Skeptical Inquirer* 13 (spring 1989): 226–40. For a general overview of the movement, see Russell Chandler, *Understanding the New Age* (Dallas: Word, 1988).

In addition to the sources on secular humanism and the New Age, sources that illuminate the role of conspiracy theories in fundamentalism include Harold Brunvand, *The Choking Doberman* (New York: Norton, 1984), pp. 169–86; John H. Bunzel, *Anti-Politics in America: Reflections on the Anti-Political Temper and Its Distortions of the Democratic Process* (New York: Knopf, 1967); Jim Castelli, *A Plea for Common Sense: Resolving the Clash Between Religion and Politics* (San Francisco: Harper & Row, 1988); Richard Hofstadter, *The Paranoid Style in American Politics and Other Essays* (New York: Vintage paperback, 1965); George Johnson, *Architects of Fear: Conspiracy Theories and Paranoia in American Politics* (Los Angeles: Jeremy P. Tarcher, 1984); Hal Lindsey with C. C. Carlson, *The Late Great Planet Earth* (Grand Rapids, Mich.: Zondervan, 1970; Bantam paperback, 1973); and Pat Robertson, *The New World Order* (Dallas: Word, 1991).

My understanding of religion's shifting role in American public life comes from John Murray Cuddihy, *No Offense: Civil Religion and Protestant Taste* (New York: Seabury, 1978); George Gallup, Jr., and Sarah Jones, *100 Questions and Answers: Religion in America* (Princeton: Princeton Research Center, 1989); Will Herberg, *Protestant-Catholic-Jew: An Essay in American Religious Sociology*, rev. ed. (Garden City, N.Y.: Anchor, 1960); Richard John Neuhaus, *The Naked Public Square: Religion and Democracy in America* (Grand Rapids, Mich.: Eerdmans, 1984); Mark Silk, *Spiritual Politics: Religion and America Since World War II* (New York: Simon & Schuster, 1988); Robert Wuthnow, *The Restructuring of American Religion: Society and Faith Since World War II* (Princeton:

Princeton University Press, 1988); Daniel Yankelovich, *New Rules: Searching for Self-fulfillment in a World Turned Upside Down* (New York: Random House, 1981); Theodore Caplow, "Religion in Middletown," *Public Interest,* summer 1982; George Gallup, Jr., "Commentary," *Gallup Reports,* March 1984; Stephen Hart, "Privatization in American Religion and Society," *Sociological Analysis* 47 (1987): 319–34; and Martin E. Marty, "Hell Disappeared. No One Noticed. A Civic Argument," *Harvard Theological Review* 78 (1985).

On the religious right's efforts to abide by the new rules, see Allen D. Hertzke, *Representing God in Washington: The Role of Religious Lobbies in the American Polity* (Knoxville: University of Tennessee, 1988); David Snowball, *Continuity and Change in the Rhetoric of the Moral Majority* (New York: Praeger, 1991); and Arthur H. Miller and Martin P. Wattenberg, "Politics from the Pulpit: Religiosity and the 1980 Elections," *Public Opinion Quarterly* 48 (1984).

John Hick discusses the innate superiority claims of religion in *Problems of Religious Pluralism* (New York: St. Martin's, 1985).

CHAPTER THREE
CITIZENS ORGANIZED

Mary Anne Raywid's book is *The Ax-Grinders: Critics of Our Public Schools* (New York: Macmillan, 1962).

The film *Let Their Eyes Be Opened* can be found at People for the American Way; Paul Kurtz discusses it in his *In Defense of Secular Humanism* (Buffalo, N.Y.: Prometheus, 1983), pp. 270–71.

The library books that COBS opposed were Norma Fox Mazer, *Up in Seth's Room: A Love Story* (New York: Delacorte, 1979); and Erich Segal, *Oliver's Story* (New York: Harper & Row, 1977).

Wilson and Drinnon read Benjamin Hart, *Poisoned Ivy* (New York: Stein & Day, 1984).

CHAPTER FOUR
CHRISTIANS IN JAIL

The description of Sam Ericsson as "obsessed with moderation" comes from Allen D. Hertzke, *Representing God in Washington: The Role of Religious Lobbies in the American Polity* (Knoxville: University of Tennessee Press, 1988), p. 184.

On the NEA's libel suit against Suzanne Clark, see Clark's own *Blackboard Blackmail* (Memphis: Footstool, 1988), as well as Beverly LaHaye, *Who But a Woman?* (Nashville: Thomas Nelson Publishers, 1984), pp. 79–85.

In addition to my interviews with Beverly LaHaye, I consulted Flo Conway and Jim Siegelman, *Holy Terror: The Fundamentalist War on America's Freedoms in Religion, Politics and Our Private Lives* (Garden City, N.Y.: Doubleday, 1982); Sara Diamond, *Spiritual Warfare: The Politics of the Christian Right* (Boston: South End, 1989); Carol Flake, *Redemptorama: Culture, Politics, and the New Evangelism* (New York: Penguin, 1984); Beverly LaHaye, *The Spirit-Controlled Woman* (Eugene, Ore.: Harvest House, 1976); Beverly LaHaye, *The Restless Woman* (Grand Rapids, Mich.: Zondervan, 1984); Beverly LaHaye, *Who Will Save Our Children?* (Brentwood, Tenn.: Wolgemuth & Hyatt, 1991); Tim LaHaye, *The Battle for the Mind* (Old Tappan, N.J.: Fleming H. Revell Co., 1980); Geoffrey Aronson, "The Conversion of Beverly LaHaye," *Regardie's*, March 1987; Janet R. Buffington, "Concerned Women for America leader has polish," *Moral Majority Report*, April 1984; Jim Buie, "Tim LaHaye: Shadow on the Capitol," *Church and State*, October 1985; Edward Cone and Lisa Scheer, "Queen of the Right," *Mirabella*, February 1993; "An Interview with Beverly LaHaye," *Fundamentalist Journal*, April 1984; Beverly LaHaye, "Whose Ethics in the Government Schools?" *Kappa Delta Pi Record*, spring 1987; Holly G. Miller, "Concerned Women for America: Soft Voices with Clout," *Saturday Evening Post*, October 1985; Connie Paige, "Watch on the Right," *Ms.*, February 1987; and Carolyn Weaver, "Unholy Alliance," *Mother Jones*, January 1986.

In addition to my interviews with Michael Farris, I consulted his book *Where Do I Draw the Line?* (Minneapolis: Bethany House, 1992) and his article "My Client Is the Moral Majority," *Barrister*, spring 1982, as well as "Profiles in Education: Michael Farris," *Education Update* (Heritage Foundation), fall 1987; *Library Journal*, 6/15/81, pp. 1273–77; and newspaper coverage of Farris's Washington State activities. His lawsuit over Gordon Parks's *The Learning Tree* (New York: Harper & Row, 1963) resulted in the decision *Grove v. Mead School Dist. No. 354*, 753 F.2d 1528 (9th Cir.), *cert. denied*, 474 U.S. 826 (1985). His Supreme Court victory came in the case *Witters v. Washington Dep't of Services for the Blind*, 474 U.S. 481 (1986).

CHAPTER FIVE
THE SUPERPOWERS

"Lights set on a hill" comes from Oliver P. Temple, *East Tennessee and the Civil War* (Cincinnati: Robert Clarke Co., 1899), p. 64.

The People for the American Way book is Barbara Parker and Stefanie Weiss, *Protecting the Freedom to Learn: A Citizen's Guide* (Washington, D.C.: PAW, 1983).

On Norman Lear, see Kathryn C. Montgomery, *Target: Prime Time—Advocacy Groups and the Struggle Over Entertainment Television* (New York: Oxford, 1989); Norman Lear, "Nurturing Spirituality and Religion in an Age of Science and Technology," *New Oxford Review*, April 1990; Norman Lear, "People vs. Falwell," *Moment*, November 1984; Leah Rozen, "Desperately Seeking Seriousness," *Spy*, June 1989; United States Commission on Civil Rights, *Characters in Textbooks: A Review of the Literature* (Washington, D.C.: Government Printing Office, 1980), pp. 23–24; Geoffrey Wolff, "Shortcuts to the Heart," *Esquire*, August 1981; and news coverage of PAW's creation.

On John Buchanan, see John H. Buchanan, "Guerrilla War in America's Streets," *Manion Forum*, transcript of broadcast no. 626 (South Bend, Ind.), 10/2/66; Shirley Christian, "Foreign Danger," *Atlantic*, October 1983; and news coverage of his 1980 defeat.

Most other information about People for the American Way and Concerned Women for America comes from my interviews with Tony Podesta, David Crane, and Barbara Parker of PAW; my interviews with Beverly LaHaye, Michael Farris, and Jordan Lorence of CWA; several confidential sources; the two organizations' publications, fundraising letters, and internal documents; and news coverage.

CHAPTER SIX
RELIGIOUS BURDENS

The free-exercise cases discussed are *Sherbert v. Verner*, 374 U.S. 398 (1963); and *Wisconsin v. Yoder*, 406 U.S. 205 (1972). See generally Laurence H. Tribe, *American Constitutional Law*, 2d ed. (Mineola, N.Y.: Foundation, 1988), pp. 1242–75; and Stephen Pepper, "Taking the Free Exercise Clause Seriously," *Brigham Young University Law Review* (1986): 299–336. On the burden requirement, see Ira C. Lupu, "Where Rights Begin: The Problem of Burdens on the Free Exercise of Religion," *Harvard Law Review* 102 (1989): 933–90; and Note, "Burdens on the Free Exercise of Religion: A Subjective Alternative," *Harvard Law Review* 102 (1989): 1258–77.

Judge Hull's rulings dismissing the case are published at 579 F. Supp. 1051 (E.D. Tenn. 1984); and 582 F. Supp. 201 (E.D. Tenn. 1984). The Sixth Circuit ruling that sent the case back for trial is at 765 F.2d 75 (6th Cir. 1985). The Sixth Circuit's misconstrual of Judge Hull's reasoning is noted in Nadine Strossen, " 'Secular Humanism' and 'Scientific Creationism': Proposed Standards for Reviewing Curricular Decisions Affecting Students' Religious Freedom," *Ohio State Law Journal* 47 (1986): 342–43.

Tim Dyk's background comes from Dyk's vitae; *Broadcasting*, 4/25/

88, p. 95; *Legal Times*, 7/28/86, p. 3; and Federal Election Commission records.

CHAPTER SEVEN
CONSPIRACY TO INTIMIDATE

On the conflicting worldviews held by the religious right and its opponents, see James Davison Hunter, *Culture Wars: The Struggle to Define America* (New York: Basic, 1991); and W. Barnett Pearce, Stephen W. Littlejohn, and Alison Alexander, "The Quixotic Quest for Civility: Patterns of Interaction Between the New Christian Right and Secular Humanists," in Jeffrey K. Hadden and Anson Shupe, eds., *Secularization and Fundamentalism Reconsidered* (New York: Paragon, 1989), pp. 152–77.

Stephen J. Adler spoke about jury instructions at an Annenberg Washington Program seminar, Washington, D.C., 4/10/92.

The conspiracy verdict was overturned in *Frost v. Hawkins County Bd. of Educ.*, 851 F.2d 822 (6th Cir.), *cert. denied*, 488 U.S. 981 (1988).

CHAPTER EIGHT
MORE THAN READING

On evolution and creationism, I spoke with Gerald Skoog and Eugenie Scott, and I consulted Steve Bruce, *The Rise and Fall of the New Christian Right: Conservative Protestant Politics in America 1978–1988* (New York: Oxford, 1988); Peter Irons, *The Courage of Their Convictions: Sixteen Americans Who Fought Their Way to the Supreme Court* (New York: Free Press, 1988); John L. Kater, Jr., *Christians on the Right: The Moral Majority in Perspective* (New York: Seabury, 1982); Edward J. Larson, *Trial and Error: The American Controversy Over Creation and Evolution*, updated ed. (New York: Oxford, 1989); Dorothy Nelkin, *The Creation Controversy: Science or Scripture in the Schools* (Boston: Beacon, 1982); Ronald L. Numbers, *The Creationists: The Evolution of Scientific Creationism* (New York: Knopf, 1992); Garry Wills, *Under God: Religion and American Politics* (New York: Simon & Schuster, 1990); "Evolutionists vs. Creationists," in *The Gallup Poll: Public Opinion 1982* (Wilmington, Del.: Scholarly Resources, 1983), pp. 208–14; Judith V. Grabiner and Peter D. Miller, "Effects of the Scopes Trial," *Science* 185 (9/6/74): 832–37; Rodney A. Grunes, "Creationism, the Courts, and the First Amendment," *Journal of Church and State* 31 (1989): 465–86; Wayne A. Moyer, "How Texas Rewrote Your Textbooks," *Science Teacher*, January 1985; Karen O'Connor and Gregg Ivers, "Creationism, Evolution and the Courts," *PS: Political Science and Politics*, winter 1988; Gangar Shanbar, "Factors Influencing the Teaching of Evolution and Creationism in Texas Public High School Biology Classes" (doctoral diss., Lubbock, Tex.: Texas Tech University, 1989); Gerald Skoog, "The Coverage of Evolution in High School Biology Textbooks Published in the 1980s," *Science Education* 68 (April 1984): 117–28; Gerald D. Skoog, "The Coverage of Evolution in Secondary School Biology Textbooks, 1900–1989," in John Herlihy, ed., *The Textbook Controversy* (Norwood, N.J.: Ablex Publishing, 1992), pp. 71–87; *Edwards v. Aguillard*, 482 U.S. 578 (1987); *Epperson v. Arkansas*, 393 U.S. 97 (1968); and *McLean v. Arkansas Board of Educ.*, 529 F. Supp. 1255 (E.D. Ark. 1982).

On how textbooks and schools have treated religion, see Association for Supervision and Curriculum Development, *Religion in the Curriculum* (Alexandria, Va.: ASCD, 1987); Richard B. Dierenfield, *Religion in American Public Schools* (Washington, D.C.: Public Affairs Press, 1962); William Kailer Dunn, *What Happened to Religious Education?: The Decline of Religious Teaching in the Public Elementary School, 1776–1861* (Baltimore: Johns Hopkins, 1958); Ruth Miller Elson, *Guardians of Tradition: American Schoolbooks of the Nineteenth Century* (Lincoln, Neb.: University of Nebraska Press, 1964); Charles R. Kniker, *Teaching About Religion in the Public Schools* (Bloomington, Ind.: Phi Delta Kappa Educational Foundation, 1985); Theodore R. Sizer, ed., *Religion and Public Education* (Boston: Houghton Mifflin, 1967); Harold A. Pflug, "Religion in Missouri Textbooks," *Phi Delta Kappan* 36 (April 1955): 258–60; Loreli Olson Steuer and Susan Simonton Steddom, "From McGuffey to the Eighties: American Basic Reading Programs," *Teacher*, May-June 1979; the regular feature "Religious Practices and Influences" in the journal *Religion and Public Education; Smith v. Denny*, 280 F. Supp. 651 (E.D. Cal. 1968), app. dism'd, 417 F.2d 614 (9th Cir. 1969) (Pledge of Allegiance); *Sheldon v. Fannin*, 221 F. Supp. 766, 774 (D. Ariz. 1963) ("Star-Spangled Banner"); and *Todd v. Rochester Community Schools*, 41 Mich.App. 320, 200 N.W.2d 90 (Ct.App. 1972) (*Slaughterhouse Five*).

Research showing how textbooks neglect religion includes Charles C. Haynes, "Teaching About Religious Freedom in American Secondary Schools," Americans United Research Foundation (1985); O. L. Davis, Jr., Gerald Ponder, Lynn M. Burlbaw, Maria Garza-Lubeck, and Alfred Moss, *Looking at History: A Review of Major U.S. History Textbooks* (Washington, D.C.: People for the American Way, 1986); and Paul C. Vitz, *Censorship: Evidence of Bias in Our Children's Textbooks* (Ann Arbor, Mich.: Servant Books, 1986). See also Barbara Cohen, "Censoring the Sources," *American Educator*, summer 1987; Paul Gagnon, "Democracy's Jewish and Christian Roots," *American Educator*, fall 1987; Paul C. Vitz, "Religion and Traditional Values in Public School Textbooks," *Public Interest*, no. 84 (summer 1986); and Jeffrey L. Pasley, "Not-So-Good Books," *New Republic*, 4/27/87.

On moral education, I talked with Kevin Ryan and Harriet Tyson, and I consulted Leland W. Howe and Mary Martha Howe, *Personalizing Education: Values Clarification and Beyond* (New York: Hart, 1975); Larry C. Jensen and Richard S. Knight, *Moral Education: Historical Perspectives* (Washington, D.C.: University Press of America, 1981); F. G. Martin, *Moral Training of the School Child* (Boston: Gorham, 1913); Kevin Ryan, *Questions and Answers on Moral Education* (Bloomington, Ind.: Phi Delta Kappa Educational Foundation, 1981); Sidney B. Simon, Leland W. Howe, and Howard Kirschenbaum, *Values Clarification: A Handbook of Practical Strategies for Teachers and Students* (New York: Dodd, Mead, 1978; orig. publ. 1972); Harriet Tyson-Bernstein, "The Values Vacuum," *American Educator*, fall 1987; and Ivor Pritchard, "Moral Education and Character," report on conference sponsored by Office of Educational Research and Improvement, U.S. Department of Education (1988). "The Tempter" appears in G. S. Hilliard and L. J. Campbell, *The Webster-Franklin Third Reader* (New York: Taintor Bros., Merrill, 1878), pp. 26–27.

On patriotism in the curriculum, see Davis, Ponder, Burlbaw, Garza-Lubeck, and Moss, *Looking at History;* Frances FitzGerald, *America Revised: History Schoolbooks in the Twentieth Century* (Boston: Little, Brown, 1979); Diane Ravitch, *The Schools We Deserve: Reflections on the Educational Crises of Our Time* (New York: Basic, 1985); Joel Spring, *The American School 1642–1985* (New York: Longman, 1986); and David B. Tyack and Thomas James, "Moral Majorities and the School Curriculum: Historical Perspectives on the Legalization of Virtue," *Teachers College Record* 86 (1985): 513–37.

Sexism and racism in the curriculum are discussed in several of the patriotism sources, as well as in American Association of University Women Educational Foundation, *How Schools Shortchange Girls* (Washington, D.C.: AAUW, 1992); Hillel Black, *The American Schoolbook* (New York: Morrow, 1967); Council on Interracial Books for Children, *Guidelines for Selecting Bias-free Textbooks and Storybooks* (New York: Council on Interracial Books for Children, 1980); Pauline Gough, *Sexism: New Issue in American Education* (Bloomington, Ind.: Phi Beta Kappa Educational Foundation, 1976); Susan S. Klein, ed., *Handbook for Achieving Sex Equity Through Education* (Baltimore: Johns Hopkins University Press, 1985); Lloyd Marcus, *The Treatment of Minorities in Secondary School Textbooks* (New York: Anti-Defamation League, 1961); United States Commission on Civil Rights, *Characters in Textbooks: A Review of the Literature* (Washington, D.C.: Government Printing Office, 1980); Patricia B. Campbell and Jeana Wirtenberg, "How Books Influence Children: What the Research Shows," *Interracial Books for Children Bulletin* 11 (1980): 3–6; Mary E. Hitchcock and Gail E. Tompkins, "Basal Readers: Are They Still Sexist?" *Reading Teacher*, December 1987; Patricia Johnson, "Traditional offerings won't cut it," *American Educator*, March 1991; Robert Lerner, Althea K. Nagai, and Stanley Rothman, "Filler Feminism in High School History," *Academic Questions* 5 (winter 1991–92); and Larry Van Dyne, "Whatever Happened to Dick and Jane?" *Washingtonian*, April 1982.

Several publishers' and states' textbook guidelines can be found in Holt, Rinehart & Winston documents turned over to the *Mozert* plaintiffs during discovery. John T. Ridley of Houghton Mifflin sent me several others. See also New York Education Department, Commissioner's Task Force on Minorities: Equity and Excellence, "A Curriculum of Inclusion" (1989).

My understanding of the Holt series' history comes from the in-house Holt documents, and from interviews with Thomas J. Murphy, Bernard J. Weiss, and a confidential source.

My discussion of schoolbook criticism relies on Stephen Arons, *Compelling Belief: The Culture of American Schooling* (New York: New Press, 1983); David Bollier, *Liberty and Justice for Some: Defending a Free Society from the Radical Right's Holy War on Democracy* (Washington, D.C.: People for the American Way, 1982); Lee Burress and Edward B. Jenkinson, *The Students' Right to Know* (Urbana, Ill.: National Council of Teachers of English, 1982); Arnold Burron, John Eidsmoe, and Dean Turner, *Classrooms in Crisis: Parents' Rights and the Public School* (Denver: Accent, 1986); *Censorship: Managing the Controversy* (Alexandria, Va.: National School Boards Association, 1989); Stanley M. Elam, ed., *Public Schools and the First Amendment* (Bloomington, Ind.: Phi Delta Kappa, 1983); Nat Hentoff, *Free Speech for Me—But Not for Thee* (New York: HarperCollins, 1992); Edward B. Jenkinson, *Censors in the Classroom: The Mind Benders* (Carbondale, Ill.: Southern Illinois University Press, 1979); Jack Nelson and Gene Roberts, Jr., *The Censors and the Schools* (Boston: Little, Brown, 1963); Robert M. O'Neil, *Classrooms in the Crossfire: The Rights and Interests of Students, Parents, Teachers, Administrators, Librarians, and the Community* (Bloomington, Ind.: Indiana University Press, 1981); Martin Eger, "A Tale of Two Controversies: Dissonance in the Theory and Practice of Rationality," *Zygon* 23 (September 1988): 291–325; Frederick W. Hill, "On Textbook Battles: Celebrate—don't censor—our differences," *American School and University* 59 (July 1987): 12–15; Michael Hudson, "Censorship Threatens Education," *Kappa Delta Pi Record* 23 (spring 1987); Dorothy C. Massie, "Censorship and the Question of Balance," *Social Education*, February 1984; Dorothy C. Massie, "A Conflict of Values," *e/sa forum* [engage/social action], January 1983; Carol Ann Moore, "Portrayals of the Disabled in Books and Basals," *Reading Horizons* 24 (summer 1984); Joseph Nocera, "The Big Book-Banning Brawl," *New Republic*, 9/13/82; Perry Nodelman, "Cultural Arrogance and Realism in Judy Blume's *Superfudge*," *Children's Literature in Education* 19 (winter

1988); Daniel Okrent, "History Is Mush," *New England Monthly*, February 1989; Kenneth A. Strike, book review, *Harvard Educational Review* 50 (August 1980); "United Church of Christ Board: 'Fight Creationism in Public Schools,' " *Censorship News*, fall 1983; and *Board of Education, Island Trees Union Free School Dist. No. 26 v. Pico*, 457 U.S. 853 (1982).

CHAPTER NINE
SCOPES II

For background on Paul Vitz, see Vitz's book *Psychology As Religion: The Cult of Self-Worship* (Grand Rapids, Mich.: Eerdmans, 1977); and *Human Events*, 5/17/86, pp. 426–27 (reprinting article from *Education Update*).

"Barnette II" as an alternative to "Scopes II" is suggested in John G. West, Jr., "The Changing Battle over Religion in the Public Schools," *Wake Forest Law Review* 26 (1991): 390.

Press coverage of the case is criticized in Ted Gest, "Media Bias, Sloppiness Mark 'Scopes II' Coverage," *St. Louis Journalism Review*, February 1987.

On the Christian Identity Movement and Wesley Swift, I spoke with Gladys Segal of Group Research, and I consulted Sara Diamond, *Spiritual Warfare: The Politics of the Christian Right* (Boston: South End, 1989), pp. 140, 264; Benjamin R. Epstein and Arnold Forster, *The Radical Right: Report on the John Birch Society and Its Allies* (New York: Vintage, 1966), pp. 45, 214; Arnold Forster and Benjamin R. Epstein, *Danger on the Right* (New York: Random House, 1964), p. 35; and L. J. Davis, "Ballad of an American Terrorist," *Harper's*, July 1986, pp. 53–62.

Cases discussed include *West Virginia St. Bd. of Educ. v. Barnette*, 319 U.S. 624 (1943) (flag salute); *Spence v. Bailey*, 465 F.2d 797 (6th Cir. 1972) (ROTC); and *Moody v. Cronin*, 484 F. Supp. 270 (C.D.Ill. 1979) (PE).

The examples of Robert Coles on suffering come from his *Children of Crisis: A Study of Courage and Fear* (Boston: Little, Brown, 1967), pp. 325–26; *The Moral Life of Children* (Boston: Atlantic Monthly Press, 1986), p. 132; and "Moral Energy in the Lives of Impoverished Children," in Timothy F. Dugan and Robert Coles, eds., *The Child in Our Times: Studies in the Development of Resiliency* (New York: Brunner/Mazel, 1989), p. 51.

CHAPTER TEN
DAYS OF JUDGMENT

Judge Hull's opt-out opinion is published at 647 F. Supp. 1194 (E.D. Tenn. 1986). With Judge Hull's permission, his former clerk Tom Wright gave me copies of drafts.

Ira C. Lupu writes of the "spectral march" in "Where Rights Begin: The Problem of Burdens on the Free Exercise of Religion," *Harvard Law Review* 102 (1989): 947 (footnote omitted).

On the small network of religious liberty lawyers, many of whom attended Tim Dyk's presentation at the Baptist Joint Committee, see *National Law Journal*, 1/18/88, pp. 1, 40–41. Their organizations are discussed in Leo Pfeffer, "Amici in Church-State Litigation," *Law and Contemporary Problems* 44 (1981): 83–110.

Three justices proposed changing the test for free-exercise cases in *Bowen v. Roy*, 476 U.S. 693, 707–8 (1986) (Burger, C.J., joined by Powell and Rehnquist, JJ.).

My understanding of the ACLU's deliberations comes from interviews with Nadine Strossen and John M. Swomley, as well as the organization's minutes and internal memoranda. See also Samuel Walker, *In Defense of American Liberties: A History of the ACLU* (New York: Oxford, 1990), p. 345.

On the backgrounds of the three appellate judges, I consulted Ethan Bronner, *Battle for Justice: How the Bork Nomination Shook America* (New York: Norton, 1989), pp. 118–19; Barnabas D. Johnson, ed., *Almanac of the Federal Judiciary* (Chicago: LawLetters, 1989), vol. 2, Sixth Circuit; and *National Review*, 7/20/92, p. 21; I also spoke with former Sixth Circuit clerks.

The Sixth Circuit decision is *Mozert v. Hawkins County Bd. of Educ.*, 827 F.2d 1058 (6th Cir. 1987), *cert. denied*, 484 U.S. 1066 (1988). Analyses include George W. Dent, Jr., "Religious Children, Secular Schools," *Southern California Law Review* 61 (1988): 863–941; Ronald B. Flowers, "They Got Our Attention, Didn't They?: The Tennessee and Alabama Schoolbook Cases," *Religion and Public Education* 15 (1988): 262–85; Nomi Maya Stolzenberg, " 'He Drew a Circle That Shut Me Out': Assimilation, Indoctrination, and the Paradox of a Liberal Education," *Harvard Law Review* 106 (1993): 581–667; Don Welch, "The State as Purveyor of Morality," *George Washington Law Review* 56 (1988): 540–57; Note, "Appealing to a Higher Law: Conservative Christian Legal Action Groups Bring Suit to Challenge Public School Curricula and Reading Materials," *Rutgers Law Journal* 18 (1987): 437–62; and Note, "Of Textbooks and Tenets: *Mozert v. Hawkins County Board of Education* and the Free Exercise of Religion," *American University Law Review* 37 (1988): 985–1012.

Several articles written before *Mozert*'s final disposition also proved useful, including G. Sidney Buchanan, "Accommodation of Religion in the Public Schools: A Plea for Careful Balancing of Competing Constitutional Values," *UCLA Law Review* 28 (1981): 1000–1048; Mary-Michelle Upson Hirschoff, "Parents and the Public School Curriculum: Is There a Right to Have One's Child Excused from Objectionable Instruction?" *Southern California Law Review* 50 (1977): 871–959; and Nadine Strossen, " 'Secular Humanism' and 'Scientific Creationism': Proposed Standards for Reviewing Curricular Decisions Affecting Students' Religious Freedom," *Ohio State Law Journal* 47 (1986): 333–407.

The Supreme Court rejected a centrality inquiry in *Lyng v. Northwest Indian Cemetery Protective Ass'n*, 485 U.S. 439, 457–58 (1988). The Court spoke of "intrafaith differences" in *Thomas v. Review Bd.*, 450 U.S. 707, 715–16 (1981).

Leo Pfeffer discusses Christmas carols in *Church, State, and Freedom* (Boston: Beacon, 1953), p. 406.

Betsy Levin speaks of judicial intervention in public education in "Educating Youth for Citizenship: The Conflict Between Authority and Individual Rights in the Public School," *Yale Law Journal* 95 (1986): 1650 n.10.

CHAPTER ELEVEN
BEYOND PROVIDENCE

The recommendations for Kanawha County come from the NEA's "Inquiry Report: Kanawha County, West Virginia: A Textbook Study in Cultural Conflict" (1975), pp. 63–64. Kanawha County's actual policy comes from *Library Journal*, 3/15/75, p. 542; *Library Journal*, 6/1/75, p. 1068; and an interview with James Moffett, author of a book about the controversy, *Storm in the Mountains: A Case Study of Censorship, Conflict, and Consciousness* (Carbondale, Ill.: Southern Illinois University Press, 1988). Other NEA publications quoted include "Dealing with the Smear Tactics of the Far Right," February 1986, and "Preserving Public Education," June 1986.

On the Jenifer Graham case, I relied on Animal Legal Defense Fund, "Objecting to Dissection: A Student Handbook" (n.d.); *National Law Journal*, 10/16/89, p. 43; *People*, 5/27/87, p. 109; newspaper coverage; and an interview with Graham's mother, Pat Graham.

The quotation about Jefferson comes from Robert M. Healey, *Jefferson on Religion in Public Education* (New Haven: Yale University Press, 1962), p. 17. On the similarity between Mann's faith and his notion of proper classroom religion, see Robert Michaelsen, *Piety in the Public School: Trends and Issues in the Relationship Between Religion and the Public School in the United States* (New York: Macmillan, 1970), p. 69; and Charles L. Glenn, " 'Molding' Citizens," in Richard John Neuhaus, genl. ed., *Democracy and the Renewal of Public Education* (Grand Rapids, Mich.: Eerdmans, 1987), p. 39.

Jesse H. Choper argues that the schools should abstain from teaching ultimate truths in "Defining 'Religion' in the First Amendment," *University of Illinois Law Review* (1982): 611–12. George R. LaNoue's point about neutrality and religious liberalism comes from "The Conditions of

Public School Neutrality," in Theodore R. Sizer, ed., *Religion and Public Education* (Boston: Houghton Mifflin, 1967), p. 34.

The examples of schoolbook passages that seem to conflict with religious faith come from Larry Van Dyne, "Whatever Happened to Dick and Jane?" *Washingtonian*, April 1982, p. 168; Warren A. Nord, "The Place of Religion in the World of Public School Textbooks," *Educational Forum* 54 (1990): 255; and *New York Times*, 3/10/87, p. C11.

Harriet Tyson's quotation comes from "The Values Vacuum: A Provocative Explanation for Parental Discontent," *Religion and Public Education* 16 (1989): 383. Will Herberg raised some of the same issues in "Religion and Education in America," in James Ward Smith and A. Leland Jamison, eds., *Religious Perspectives in American Culture* (Princeton: Princeton University Press, 1961), pp. 11–51.

The Bill Murray and Maine supreme court incidents come from Madalyn Murray O'Hair, *Bill Murray, the Bible, and the Baltimore Board of Education: An Atheist Epic* (Austin, Tex.: American Atheist Press, 1970), p. 86; and *Donahoe v. Richards*, 61 Am. Dec. 256, 263–64 (Maine 1854).

Jack F. Trope, an activist for Native American religious freedom, spoke of languages lacking a word for *religion* in an address to the Religious Liberty Committee of the National Council of Churches, Washington, D.C., 6/5/92. The Joe Wittmer quotation comes from "Be Ye a Peculiar People," *Contemporary Education* 54 (1983): 179. Martin Marty pointed out the root of *heresy* in *Context*, 3/15/92, p. 1.

The banned T-shirts and the Channel One limitation come from newspaper coverage. The expert witness's testimony is cited in *Abington School Dist. v. Schempp*, 374 U.S. 203, 209 (1963). The Equal Access Act quotation is from 20 U.S.C. § 4071(d)(7).

The Civil Rights Commission and the American Association of Publishers quotations about textbooks' influence are from United States Commission on Civil Rights, *Characters in Textbooks: A Review of the Literature* (Washington, D.C.: Government Printing Office, 1980), pp. 13–14. The NEA quotation is from Patricia B. Campbell and Jeana Wirtenberg, "How Books Influence Children: What the Research Shows," *Interracial Books for Children Bulletin* 11 (1980): 3.

C. Glennon Rowell analyzed *Mozert* in *Chronicle of Higher Education*, 11/26/86.

The Pasadena school guide quotation comes from Robert M. Hutchins, "Is Democracy Possible?" *The Center Magazine*, January-February 1976, pp. 3–4.

On special education, see 20 U.S.C. 1401 §§ *et seq.;* Joel Spring, *The American School 1642–1985* (New York: Longman, 1986), p. 331; G. Mann Phillips, "Mainstreaming and Its Implications," in Bernard J. Weiss, Loreli Olson Steuer, Susan B. Cruikshank, and Lyman C. Hunt, *Freedom's Ground* (New York: Holt, Rinehart & Winston, 1983), teachers' ed., p. 856; U.S. Department of Education, Office for Civil Rights, letter of finding to Hawkins County Schools, 11/20/89; Decision Resources Corp., Washington, D.C., "Patterns in Special Education Service Delivery and Cost" (1988); and *Newsweek*, 9/14/92, p. 11.

On other accommodations, I relied on Ricardo L. Garcia, *Fostering a Pluralistic Society Through Multi-Ethnic Education* (Bloomington, Ind.: Phi Delta Kappa Educational Foundation, 1978); Arthur G. Powell, Eleanor Farrar, and David K. Cohen, *The Shopping Mall High School: Winners and Losers in the Educational Marketplace* (Boston: Houghton Mifflin, 1985); Diane Ravitch, *The Schools We Deserve: Reflections on the Educational Crises of Our Time* (New York: Basic, 1985); Abigail M. Thernstrom, "Bilingual Miseducation," *Commentary*, February 1990; *New Republic*, 4/15/91, p. 22; and news coverage.

The NEA endorsed a range of alternatives in its Resolution B-10, "Alternative Programs for Students with Special Needs" (1986).

Justice Stevens referred to a "religious inability" in *Bowen v. Roy*, 476 U.S. 693, 720–22 (1986) (Stevens, J., concurring in part and concurring in the result) (footnote omitted). See also John H. Garvey, "Free Exercise and the Values of Religious Liberty," *Connecticut Law Review* 18 (1986): 798–801, which likens the Constitution's treatment of religious obligations to the insanity defense in criminal law.

On pluralism in the schools, see Powell, Farrar, and Cohen, *Shopping Mall High School*, p. 3; *American Teacher*, November 1989, p. 7.

The misapplications of tolerance come from Leo Pfeffer, *Church, State, and Freedom* (Boston: Beacon, 1953), p. 407; Rita Warren with Dick Schneider, *Mom, They Won't Let Us Pray* (Old Tappan, N.J.: Chosen, 1975), p. 136; and NEA, "Special Alert: Phyllis Schlafly's 'Bill of Student Rights,' " March 1986, p. 2.

The Philip H. Walkling and Chris Brannigan quotation is from "Anti-sexist/Anti-racist Education: A Possible Dilemma," *Journal of Moral Education* 15 (January 1986): 21–22.

The case about the wall separating Hasidic students is *Parents' Ass'n of P.S. 16 v. Quinones*, 803 F.2d 1235 (2d Cir. 1986).

The examples of teachers "correcting" students' religious beliefs come from William K. Muir, Jr., *Prayer in the Public Schools: Law and Attitude Change* (Chicago: University of Chicago Press, 1967), p. 46; and Dindy Robinson, "Where to Draw the Line," *Humanist*, January-February 1989, p. 35.

The Charles Glenn quotation is from "Religion, textbooks, and the common school," *Public Interest*, no. 88 (1987): 47.

On public school advocates' concern over the private school alternative, see Michaelsen, *Piety in the Public School*, p. 134; Moffett, *Storm in the Mountains*, p. 211; Dallas Lore Sharp, *Education in a Democracy* (Boston: Houghton Mifflin, 1922); and Barbara Bennett Woodhouse, " 'Who

Owns the Child?': *Meyer* and *Pierce* and the Child as Property," *William and Mary Law Review* 33 (1992): 995–1122.

The study of textbooks used in fundamentalist schools is Albert J. Menendez, *Visions of Reality: What Fundamentalist Schools Teach* (Buffalo: Prometheus, 1993). See also Alan Peshkin, *God's Choice: The Total World of a Fundamentalist Christian School* (Chicago: University of Chicago Press, 1986).

The Isle of Providence tale comes from Larzer Ziff, *Puritanism in America: New Culture in a New World* (New York: Viking, 1973); I'm indebted to John H. Mansfield for directing my attention to it. Other quotations in the closing paragraphs come from "Putting First Things First," *First Things*, March 1990, p. 8; Michael W. McConnell, "Accommodation of Religion: An Update and a Response to the Critics," *George Washington Law Review* 60 (1992): 694; and James Davison Hunter, "Fundamentalism in Its Global Contours," in Norman J. Cohen, ed., *The Fundamentalist Phenomenon: A View from Within; A Response from Without* (Grand Rapids, Mich.: Eerdmans, 1990), pp. 59, 63.

For this chapter, I also consulted Nicholas Appleton, *Cultural Pluralism in Education: Theoretical Foundations* (New York: Longman, 1983); Robert A. Dahl, *Dilemmas of Pluralist Democracy: Autonomy vs. Control* (New Haven: Yale University Press, 1982); William A. Galston, *Liberal Purposes: Goods, Virtues, and Diversity in the Liberal State* (New York: Cambridge University Press, 1991); Amy Gutmann, *Democratic Education* (Princeton: Princeton University Press, 1987); James Davison Hunter, *Culture Wars: The Struggle to Define America* (New York: Basic, 1991); David Moshman, *Children, Education, and the First Amendment: A Psycholegal Analysis* (Lincoln, Neb.: University of Nebraska Press, 1989); Art Must, Jr., ed., *Why We Still Need Public Schools: Church-State Relations and Visions of Democracy* (Buffalo, N.Y.: Prometheus, 1992); Henry J. Perkinson, *The Imperfect Panacea: American Faith in Education 1865–1976*, 2d ed. (New York: Random House, 1977); F. Clark Power and Daniel K. Lapsley, eds., *The Challenge of Pluralism: Education, Politics, and Values* (Notre Dame, Ind.: University of Notre Dame Press, 1992); Patrick Welsh, *Tales Out of School: A Teacher's Candid Account from the Front Lines of the American High School Today* (New York: Penguin, 1986); Stephen L. Carter, "Evolutionism, Creationism, and Treating Religion as a Hobby," *Duke Law Journal* 1987: 977–96; Gregory Gelfand, "Of Monkeys and Men—An Atheist's Heretical View of the Constitutionality of Teaching the Disproof of a Religion in the Public Schools," *Journal of Law and Education* 16 (1987): 271–338; Michael W. McConnell, "Accommodation of Religion," *Supreme Court Review* (1985): 1–59; and Stephen Macedo's book manuscript entitled *The Only Sure Foundation: Public Schooling and American Liberalism.*

·· ACKNOWLEDGMENTS ··

Most of the players in the Hawkins County protest and litigation graciously shared their time and recollections with me. I thank them: Larry Arnold, Conley Bailey, L. W. Bailey, Jr., Heather Baker, Danny J. Boggs, Al Clark, Suzanne Clark, Kimberlee W. Colby, Nat Coleman, Robert Cooper, Bill Couch, Sandra Couch, David Crane, Joe Drinnon, Timothy Dyk, Sue Eaton, Larry Elkins, Roy T. Englert, Jr., Samuel E. Ericsson, William H. Farmer, Michael P. Farris, Marty Frost, Roger Frost, Sarah Frost, Vicki Frost, Mel Gabler, Norma Gabler, Edward McGlynn Gaffney, Jr., Phyllis Gibson, Delmar Gillenwater, Harry Hall, Roberta Hantgan, Thomas G. Hull, Phil Junot, Beverly LaHaye, Pierce Lively, Jordan Lorence, Fred McDonald, Archie McMillan, Christy Macy, Brenda Marshall, Gina Marshall, Junior Marshall, Christine Meade, J. F. Meade, Robert B. Mozert, Jr., Wanda Owens, Barbara Parker, Larry Parrish, John Payton, Anthony T. Podesta, Jean Price, Sam Rabinove, Bob Sharp, Harold Silvers, Bill Snodgrass, August W. Steinhilber, Mark Troobnick, Roz Udow, Paul Vitz, Sue Vogelsinger, Jan Whitaker, Steve Whitaker, John Whitehead, Jennie Wilson, Marion Wilson, Judith Wish, Thomas J. Wright, and others who requested anonymity.

I am also grateful to nonparticipants who helped me sort out aspects of the case, its players, or its setting: Jeanette Arakawa, Hugh J. Beard, Lee Boothby, David L. Brand, Mike Carvin, Charles Cooper, David A. Cox, Pam Cox, Dennis Coyle, David W. Dellinger, Mike Dye, Jim Fields, Gary Fowler, John K. Harber, Charles Holland, John Jones, Jr., Margaret Klein, Judith A. Lonnquist, Randy McConnell, John McGough, Beth McLeod, Dorothy Massie, Barbara Mello, Thomas J. Murphy, A. B.

Neil, Jr., Jack Polak, Shirley Roberts, John Roemer, Laurence H. Silberman, Marc D. Stern, Nadine Strossen, Jesse Swanner, John M. Swomley, Oliver S. Thomas, Guy Tilley, Patricia Tucker, Hedy Weinberg, Bernard J. Weiss, Ann Wheeler, and others who requested anonymity.

About education, religion, law, politics, and culture, I benefited from conversations and correspondence with David M. Ackerman, Robert Alley, Tom Atwood, Richard A. Baer, Jr., Jennifer Baggette, Walter Berns, Diane Berreth, Wendell Bird, Robb Boston, James L. Buckley, Robert M. Calica, Angela C. Carmella, Joseph Conn, Kenneth R. Craycraft, Jr., James E. Davis, Millie Davis, Robert Destro, Edd Doerr, James Dunn, Jim Elliott, Barbara Foots, William A. Galston, Pat Graham, Larry Gregory, Erwin N. Griswold, Rosalina Hairston, Donald Harkness, Charles Haynes, A. E. Dick Howard, James Davison Hunter, Bradley Jacob, Barry Karr, Dean M. Kelley, Robert S. Kimball, Irving Kristol, Carolyn Leopold, Patricia Lines, Jack McClanahan, Michael W. McConnell, Dave McQuaid, Robert Maddox, John Mansfield, David R. Melton, Albert J. Menendez, Don Mercer, Robert Michaelsen, James Moffett, Richard John Neuhaus, John Noonan, Warren A. Nord, Robert M. O'Neil, Maryfrances Offermann, Marvin Olasky, John Ottosen, Diane Ravitch, John T. Ridley, Philip Rieff, Kevin Ryan, Joan G. Schine, Eugenie Scott, Gladys Segal, Gilbert T. Sewall, Lou Sheldon, Gerald Skoog, Robert Sperber, Anita Terauds, Glen Thomas, Laurence H. Tribe, Harriet Tyson, Sharon Vaino, Thayer S. Warshaw, John G. West, Jr., John Wheeler, Barbara Bennett Woodhouse, Michael J. Woodruff, Martin Morse Wooster, Elliott Wright, and Kim Yelton.

I acquired documents from several sources. People for the American Way gave me a copy of the trial transcript and let me rummage through some of its files on the case, with the proviso that I get permission before quoting internal documents. I requested permission for about twenty documents, and PAW agreed to let me use nearly all. For their help, I thank David Crane and Carol Keys. Concerned Women for America allowed me to spend a week reviewing twenty-nine cartons of files on the case, also with the understanding that I would not quote any nonpublic materials without permission. I asked to use roughly thirty tapes, memos, letters, notes, and other internal documents, and CWA consented to all of them. For their cooperation, I thank Lee LaHaye, Jordan Lorence, and Lisa King. For allowing me to spend a week reviewing court documents at the law firm Wilmer, Cutler & Pickering, I'm grateful to John Payton. I also studied court documents on loan at the clerk's office in the United States Court of Appeals for the District of Columbia Circuit; my thanks to Marilyn Sargent, Valerie Williams, and Jonathan Boggs. The ACLU gave me copies of memos and board minutes related to *Mozert;* I am grateful to Nadine Strossen and Thomas Hilbink. I thank Mel and Norma Gabler for their publications, articles about them, and copies of Vicki Frost's letters to them (with her permission). Finally, for giving me access to personal documents related to the case, I'm grateful to David Brand, Vicki Frost, Phyllis Gibson, Barbara Parker, and Thomas J. Wright.

Several organizations helped me complete this project. My expenses were underwritten by the Twentieth Century Fund, the Woodrow Wilson Center for Scholars, and a foundation that, as a matter of policy, asks to go unnamed. I was given office space at Harvard Law School, the American Enterprise Institute, the Wilson Center, and the Annenberg Washington Program in Communications Policy Studies. I thank John Samples at the Twentieth Century Fund; Susan DiNapoli at Harvard; Christopher C. DeMuth and Karlyn Bowman at AEI; Charles Blitzer, Dean Anderson, Zed David, Moira Egan, James Morris, Michael Lacey, and Ann Sheffield at the Wilson Center; and Newton N. Minow, Yvonne Zecca, and Fred H. Cate at the Annenberg Washington Program. My thanks also to my researchers, Juliana Gaetano, Gregory Leaming, Timothy J. Lynch, and Felicia Stubblefield.

For helping me locate and acquire photos, I'm grateful to Stan Whitlock of the *Kingsport Times-News*, Frank Trexler of the *Knoxville Journal*, Gene Bryant of *TEA News*, David E. Goodrum of *The Harbinger* magazine, John Jones, Jr., of the *Greeneville Sun*, Tom Woods II of the *Lexington Herald-Leader*, Keri Harrison of Concerned Women for America, and Carol Blum of People for the American Way, as well as Vicki Frost, Phyllis Gibson, Thomas Hull, Tony Podesta, and Bernard Van Leer.

For sage advice and unflagging support throughout the writing and publishing processes, I'm deeply indebted to my agents, Glen Hartley and Lynn Chu; and to my editor at Poseidon Press, Elaine Pfefferblit.

Finally, I am exceedingly grateful to the people who took the time to read and comment on portions of the manuscript in draft: Edwin Diamond, Monroe Engel, Ronald B. Flowers, Douglas Gropp, Robin Gropp, Brian J. Gross, Charles C. Haynes, Jonathan B. Imber, Cheryl Keller, Martin A. Linsky, Ira C. Lupu, Stephen Macedo, Alice Mayhew, James T. Patterson, Arnon Siegel, Donald A. Smith, David A. Stephens, Abigail Thernstrom, Stephan Thernstrom, Christina T. Uhlrich, Terri Wagener, and, most of all, my wife, Polly.

·· INDEX ··

· · ABOUT THE AUTHOR · ·

Stephen Bates is a senior fellow at the Annenberg Washington Program. A graduate of Harvard College and Harvard Law School, he is author of *If No News, Send Rumors* and co-author, with Edwin Diamond, of *The Spot*. His work has appeared in leading periodicals, among them *The New Republic* and *Washington Monthly*. He was born in San Luis Obispo, California, in 1958 and lives with his wife and young daughter in Silver Spring, Maryland.